WINNING WORDS FOR DAILY LIVING

CHARLES U. WAGNER

FOREWORD BY
WARREN W. WIERSBE

KREGEL PUBLICATIONS
Grand Rapids, Michigan 49501

Winning Words for Daily Living: Reaching New Heights for a Satisfying Life, by Charles U. Wagner. Foreword by Warren W. Wiersbe. © 1989 by Kregel Publications, a division of Kregel, Inc. P. O. Box 2607, Grand Rapids, MI 49501.

Cover Design: Brian Fowler
Photo Credits: Front cover and "Truth for Soaring" section opener—Art Wolfe, Inc.; "Strength for Growing" opener—COMSTOCK INC./Comstock, Inc.; "Training for Running" opener—COMSTOCK INC./Comstock, Inc.; "Light for Walking" opener— COMSTOCK INC./Michael Stuckey.

Library of Congress Cataloging-in-Publication Data

Wagner, Charles. U., (1929-   ).
  Winning words for daily living: reaching new heights for a satisfying life / by Charles U. Wagner; foreword by Warren W. Wiersbe.
        p.   cm.
  1. Meditations. I. Title.
BV4832.2.W3   1989   242—dc20   89-11120
                                                                         CIP

ISBN   0-8254-3975-2 (hardcover)

1 2 3 4 5 Printing/Year 93 92 91 90 89

Printed in the United States of America

Contents

Contents

Contents

Dedicated to my wife, Ruth, a co-laborer in the ministry and one for whom Isaiah 40:31 was a very special promise in a time of crisis.

Foreword

There is always a place for a new devotional book, especially one like *Winning Words for Daily Living*.

To begin with, Dr. Wagner captures our interest and makes us *want* to read. We find ourselves asking, "Why is he dealing with this subject? What does it have to do with my life today?"

Then he instructs us from the Word of God, and we find ourselves saying, "Oh, so *that's* what it's all about!" There is a good deal of solid spiritual nourishment in these pages, so expect to be fed.

Finally, the author challenges us to live what we have learned. An experienced educator, Dr. Wagner knows the truth we obey is the only truth we really assimilate. He doesn't want us merely to grow in knowledge, as important as that is, but also to grow in grace and become more like the Lord Jesus Christ.

In short, this is one devotional book that is balanced; and if we use it properly, it can help us become balanced believers who will "mount up with wings as eagles" and live in the strength of the Lord.

WARREN W. WIERSBE

Preface

This book is a collection of devotional articles written over several years. Much of the material was born as a weekly column in *Temple Tidings*, a church publication I authored while pastoring Temple Baptist Church in Tacoma, Washington. Other articles are a result of my regular contributions to the Sunday School papers of Regular Baptist Press or my column in *The Biblical Evangelist*, for which I wrote for several years. More recently, a daily broadcast originating from WCSG, the radio ministry of Grand Rapids Baptist College and Seminary, necessitated my writing six scripts a week. This program airs as "Winning Words." Needless to say, a great deal of material herein is designed and written solely for this book. However, I want to thank the above sources for their kind permission to use some of what I had previously written for their publications.

If the reader is helped in any way from these *Winning Words*, I will be the *winner*, blessed by the assurance that the Lord was willing to use these devotionals to His glory and praise.

Strength for Growing

"But they that wait upon the Lord shall renew their strength;" – Isaiah 40:31

Diagnosis—Prognosis

Diagnosis and prognosis are two common words in the language of medicine. Sometimes they are confused, and often their meanings are misunderstood. The first word, *diagnosis,* means "the act of deciding, on the basis of analyzing symptoms, what disease is affecting the patient." *Dia* "between" and *gignoskein* "to know" are the specific Greek words that give us this important medical term. When you go to your doctor, he seeks to make a diagnosis on the basis of your symptoms.

The second word, *prognosis,* has the same root as the first but with a different prefix. *Pro* means "before." So, a prognosis is "knowing before," or more specifically, "predicting what the doctor can expect to happen, taking all the possibilities into consideration." It deals with the course and probably termination of the disease.

Diagnosis

People often come to me and complain of spiritual problems. They seem to be suffering from a spiritual deficiency, a lack of the joy of the Lord, a generally run-down condition. Nothing is going correctly, for their plans have been upset. Frustration has resulted. Worry and anxiety are symptoms of these deep-rooted spiritual problems. The diagnosis? Anxiety and worry resulting from a lack of day-by-day communion with Christ and a close relationship with Him; an over-occupation with "things" and "circumstances:" a lack of occupation with the Lord.

Such a diagnosis calls for a scriptural prescription.

Prescription

"Be careful for nothing, but in everything, by prayer and supplication with thanksgiving, let your request be made known unto God" (Philippians 4:6).

1. "Be careful for nothing." You have to decide that no matter what happens, you are not going to let it get you down. No care will trouble you, because you are in His care. No worry will be entertained; no indulgence in anxiety will be tolerated, for that reveals a lack of trust and faith in the Lord.
2. "In everything, by prayer and supplication." Without this ingredient, the first will be useless. The way to be anxious for nothing is to be prayerful in everything. Prayer lifts you out of frustrating circumstances and takes you into heaven's throne room where you see those circumstances from a divine perspective. Prayer is spiritual therapy that brings positive results. It is the way to change and to be changed.

3. "With thanksgiving, let your requests be made known unto God." To count your blessings and thank the Lord for them is good medicine. Thanksgiving is vital for robust spiritual health.

Prognosis

"And the peace of God, which passeth all understanding, shall keep your hearts and minds through Christ Jesus" (Philippians 4:7). What a promising prognosis! This is the predicted outcome! This spiritual rejuvenation is the outcome for those who will take "everything to God in prayer."

Dear believer, live prayerfully in the Book—the Bible. This is the best preventive medicine for worry-prone people. Keep that communion established with the Lord, pray to Him, thank Him! Live in His presence. Watch your exposure to the philosophy of the world. God's peace, which is deeper than all knowledge, will "be a garrison to guard your hearts and minds in Christ Jesus." Rejoice in the Lord! The prognosis is good!

 Strength for Growing: "For we have not an high priest which cannot be touched with the feeling of our infirmities; but was in all points tempted like as we are, yet without sin. Let us therefore come boldly unto the throne of grace, that we may obtain mercy, and find grace to help in time of need" (Hebrews 4:15, 16).

Prayer lifts you out of frustrating circumstances and takes you into heaven's throne room, where you can see your circumstances from a divine perspective.

All My Springs Are in Thee

As a young lad spending the summer with my relatives in Tennessee, I learned the difference between cisterns and spring houses. Cistern water is water that runs off the roofs of houses into the well. It is used for drinking water. Of course, a natural spring is water that comes out of a mountain and is always fresh. A spring house is built over the spring to keep it clean and to protect it from the elements. As a child, I was most impressed by the springs we would often discover in the dense woods. There was nothing like finding one in the thick of the brush on a hot day and taking a plunge into the icy, crystal-clear pool of water.

When the children of Israel in Jeremiah's day fell into idolatry and turned from the Lord, they found nothing but emptiness and futility of life. God told them, "For my people have committed two evils: they have forsaken me, the fountain of living waters, and hewed out cisterns, broken cisterns, that can hold no water" (Jeremiah 2:13).

To be sure, a cistern isn't the very best source of water. But here we have a picture of a backslidden people turning from the fountain of living waters and making their own cisterns, which broke when the hot weather came—just when they needed them most. The product of their own hands became almost inadequate for their parched souls. All aid and comfort was gone and the intensity of the thirst increased as the dry season continued. What a picture of the Christian who has gone to the world for satisfaction and finds an empty, broken cistern!

How refreshed we are in heart and soul when we turn to Psalm 87 and read, "All my springs are in thee" (v. 7). How applicable this passage is when we think of the full and complete sufficiency of Christ! In a world groping for true satisfaction, in a society where even Christians are seen searching for a bit of moisture from their broken cisterns, what a genuine delight it is to turn to Him and find our springs.

Notice what Arno Gaebelein said about this passage: "All we have is in Christ; all we are is through Him and we shall be in Him, through Him and with Him. Therefore we rejoice and can sing, 'All my springs are in Thee.' In whom? In HIM—'Who loved me and gave Himself for me.' We really do find in Him, and in Him only, all our springs."

Are you still going to broken cisterns? Do you find in Him more and more your joy and delight? Is He all your comfort, your strength, and your hope? Do you realize your complete need of Him? As never before we need to find in Christ the answer for all our needs.

Spurgeon adds, "The springs of my faith and all my graces; the springs of my life and all my pleasures; the springs of activity and all its right doings; the springs of my hope, and all its heavenly anticipations, all lie in Thee my Lord. Without thy Spirit I should be as a dry well, a mocking cistern, destitute of power to bless myself or others. O Lord, I am assured that I belong to the regenerate whose life is in Thee, for I feel that I cannot live without Thee; therefore, with all Thy joyful people will I sing Thy praises."

Who among us has not expressed utter disappointment in the trends of the world today? How disappointed we often become when we see depravity and spiritual deterioration on every hand. Our hearts are filled with pity when we see men frantically trying to piece together their broken cisterns or patch them up, hoping that they will not crumble again. Oh, let us not lament that our self-made cisterns have failed us. Rather, may our failure and disappointment in any other source of help teach us this lesson: Only Christ can satisfy. Only in Him will we be able to say with full assurance that we will not be disappointed. He alone is our sufficiency. Our springs are in Him! Run to Him in your need; drink deep of His full provision, and find in Him lasting satisfaction.

 Strength for Growing: "As well the singers as the players on instruments shall be there; all my springs are in thee" (Psalm 87:7).

"All we have is in Him and with Him. Therefore, we rejoice and can sing, 'All my springs are in thee'—in Him . . . and we really do find in Him, and in Him only, all our springs" (A.C. Gaebelein).

Bubble and Squeak

How well do you know the foods you consume? For example, if you ordered a dish of bubble and squeak, what do you think you would be served? If you answered, "corn beef and cabbage," you were right. It is said that they first bubble when boiled and afterward hiss or squeak in the frying pan.

Here's another. If, while dining in England, you asked for a biscuit, what would you likely be served? Well, the British would say you were served a biscuit, but you would call it a cracker.

Here is one that really stumped me. Would it be proper to serve pinders and goobers at the same time? The answer might be a little embarrassing unless you know they are the same thing—peanuts.

Finally, suppose your doctor told you that you should not have caffeine, and you were offered a choice of four drinks: tea, coffee, cocoa, and Coke. Which of the four would you select? You would be obeying your doctor if you had water or milk, because all four choices have caffeine. And my doctor tells me that the worst offender of all four, strangely enough, is tea.

Just as physical consumption can sometimes be a little bewildering, so can spiritual consumption. And isn't it also true that there are some types of mental and spiritual consumption that could have an aura of innocence and yet be damaging to one's spiritual welfare?

Do we allow our minds to consume certain television programs that could have a deadening effect on our spiritual outlook? Is it possible to be mesmerized by an "innocent" novel or have a spiritual damper put on our outlook with a certain type of "innocent" music? This is also true of songs with a wild tune and semi-religious words. Somehow, it's almost like calling peanuts "pinders and goobers"—they are still peanuts. Giving something a religious name or words doesn't change it from what it really is.

They say that physically you are what you eat (bubble and squeak notwithstanding). You are also what you consume mentally and spiritually. For this reason, it is important to have a good, balanced spiritual diet. Peter said, "As newborn babes, desire the sincere milk of the word, that ye may grow by it" (1 Peter 2:2).

This "perfect food" is especially good for the Christian beginner. However, spiritual consumption ought to gradually include some heavier and stronger foods. "For every one that useth milk is unskillful in the word of righteousness; for he is a babe. But strong meat belongeth to them that are of full age . . ." (Hebrews 5:13, 14).

That's why Paul said to the Corinthians, "I have fed you with milk, and not with meat; for to this time ye were not able to bear it, neither yet now are ye able" (1 Corinthians 3:2).

Assuming that you missed some of our questions on food, I think it would be fitting to ask, How well do you know the spiritual food of the Word? Is this Book—the Bible—familiar to you? Are its pages worn from constant reading and study? Do you live in it for extended periods of time? Is it a living Book to you? Or would the book of Obadiah be just as strange to you as a helping of bubble and squeak?

Oh, Christian, don't neglect your spiritual diet. Don't be guilty of just dabbling in the Word or treating it like a magic book by "stabbing" at certain pages, hoping to come up with a helping verse in an emergency. You can be forgiven for being stumped with certain types of food, but not to know this spiritual food is almost unforgivable. You need it every day, in large portions. Only then can you be sure of being happy and healthy in your Christian experience.

 Strength for Growing: "Thy word have I hidden in mine heart, that I might not sin against thee" (Psalm 119:11).

Your spiritual diet is as important as your physical one. It is vital to growth as well as being preventive. A balanced diet of large portions of God's Word will result in eternal benefits .

Browsing and Grazing

Many bookstores today have signs in the window suggesting that you come in and browse around. According to the word experts, the word *browse* comes from the old French word *brouz,* meaning "the twigs and leaves on which the animals feed." Today the idea is carried over in the English language, meaning "to nibble." To browse through a book means to nibble at the twigs and leaves of learning contained in it.

There is a distinction between *browsing* and *grazing.* A browsing animal might lean over the fence and nibble at a leaf, while a grazing animal eats grass from the ground.

This reminds me of two kinds of treatment the Bible receives by those who read it. The browsing reader of the Word of God is often caught drowsing. And he just "can't get much out of the Bible. It seems so uninteresting." Browsers get a little from the book of John, a leaf from Romans, and a twig or two tasting among the Proverbs. But their feeble nibbles accomplish little. Their spiritual growth is stunted because of their disjointed Bible reading.

On the other hand, there are the grazers. They are found ruminating on God's revelation. Chewing and digesting the Word, they assimilate it into their lives. They delight in the "green pastures" of the Word and graze in them with genuine satisfaction.

Grazers are also systematic in their grazing. Beginning with a book, they follow it verse-by-verse and chapter-by-chapter. The Spirit of God causes the seed of the Word to germinate and spring forth in their Christian experience. For these hearty feeders, to *graze* upon the Word lifts them out of the *maze* of the world into the realm of God's presence.

Then too, they graze regularly. There are special times set apart for study and meditation. Daily, usually early in the morning, they are found partaking of the good things from heaven.

You can tell the difference between the two kinds of Bible readers, just by being in their presence for a few hours. There is a difference in their attitudes and general outlook on life. Both claim to read the Bible. Both may even read it daily. At first, you may wonder what the difference is; but it becomes clear when you discover that one is a "grazer" and the other a "browser." Which are you?

Strength for Growing: "This book of the law shall not depart out of thy mouth, but thou shalt meditate therein day and night, that thou mayest observe to do according to all that is written therein; for then thou shalt make thy way prosperous, and then thou shalt have good success" Joshua 1:8.

"But his delight is in the law of the LORD; and in his law doth he meditate day and night" (Psalm 1:2).

Meditation is thinking with a view of doing.

Meditation is not browsing; it is grazing.

Worry . . . Worry . . . Worry!

Worry is a sin! John Wesley said he would just as soon swear as to worry.

Someone has said, "Worry saddens, blights, destroys, kills. It depletes one's energies, devitalizes the physical man, and enervates the whole spiritual nature. It greatly reduces the spiritual stature and impoverishes the whole spirit."

Christ said, "Take no thought for your life, what ye shall eat, or what ye shall drink; nor yet for your body, what ye shall put on. Is not the life more than meat, and the body than raiment? Behold the fowls of the air; for they sow not, neither do they reap, nor gather into barns, yet your heavenly Father feedeth them. Are ye not much better than they?" (Matthew 6:25, 26).

> Said the robin to the sparrow,
> I should really like to know,
> Why these anxious human beings
> Rush about and worry so.
>
> Said the sparrow to the robin,
> I think that it must be
> They have no heavenly Father
> Such as cares for you and me.
> —Author unkown

Worry is a sin because it says to the world that our heavenly Father is not able to care for us. It shows our lack of trust in Him. It is a sin because it harms our bodies. It diseases the nervous system, the digestive organs, and the heart. To live in worry is to invite death in a hurry. Someone has defined *worry* as "a circle of inefficient thought whirling around a pivot of fear." But when you read that there are at least 365 "fear nots" in the Bible, you are reminded that worry is one of the greatest inconsistences in the Christian life.

What is the answer? It is so simple that it might well be overlooked. "Casting all your care upon him; for he careth for you" (1 Peter 5:7). How the Lord delights in our leaning so hard on Him and turning over our lives to Him so much that worry is strange to us! How delightful to see a Christian living above worry (prayerfully occupied in the throne room of heaven, away from the fears and frustrations of the world). As the eagle that soars in the upper air does not worry itself as to how it is to cross rivers, so the believer who is occupied daily with Christ will not be found worrying about life's seemingly uncrossable rivers.

Strength for Growing: "Humble yourselves, therefore, under the mighty hand of God, that he may exalt you in due time, Casting all your care upon him; for he careth for you" (1 Peter 5:6, 7).

"It is not work but worry that kills, and it is amazing how much wear the human mind and body can stand if it is free from friction and well oiled by the Spirit. A mind at leisure from itself beats all the best cures" (Vance Havner).

Water Everywhere

How long would you think it takes the average American to use 1,800 gallons of water? It might surprise you to learn that each of us, on the average, uses that amount every 24 hours! You may drink only four or five glasses of water a day; but when you consider the use of water to bathe, cook, wash clothes, and the many uses of water in our routine schedule, it doesn't seem so amazing.

You can also add to this the manufacturing of clothes which involves the use of water, and the processing of lumber for the house in which you live. Take even the paper in this book you are reading. It takes 250 tons of water to make one ton of paper. It is no wonder that there is talk about water shortage in the coming generation. Water preservation is necessary if we are going to prepare for future generations. Two-thirds of the human body is composed of water. It is a commodity essential to life.

The Bible uses water as a symbol to illustrate vital Christian truth. It is used to illustrate eternal life (Revelation 22:17). Water is also used as a symbol of the Holy Spirit (John 4:14). Sometimes, water is used as a picture of the Word of God, the Bible.

Paul also speaks of cleansing the church by the "washing of water by the Word" (Ephesians 5:26). We are born again by the "Word of God, which liveth and abideth for ever" (1 Peter 1:23). So this water (God's Word) is certainly a vital factor in our new birth.

The water of the Word is God's cleansing agent from sin for the believer. "Wherewithal shall a young man cleanse his way? By taking heed thereto according to thy Word" (Psalm 119:9).

When Christ washed His disciples' feet with water, it was His way of showing them that they ought to have their walk cleansed daily by the Word of God. When Peter refused, Christ said, "If I wash thee not, thou hast no part with me" (John 13:8). Christ was showing that our fellowship with Him is hindered and a crisis is created when we neglect our daily spiritual cleansing.

Just as we often take for granted the availability of our so-needed H_2O, the water of God's Word can be considered commonplace. To deprive us of it, as experienced so often by believers under persecution in ages past, would be devastating.

Before you go to school or work tomorrow morning, make sure you are washed in the water of God's Word. The cleansing agent of the Word will begin to show in your life.

It takes 10,000 tons of water to grow one ton of cotton—that's an unquestionable fact. And it takes the vital water of God's Holy Word to produce Christian growth.

 Strength for Growing: "Wherewithal shall a young man cleanse his way? By taking heed thereto according to thy word. With my whole heart have I sought thee; Oh, let me not wander from thy commandments" (Psalm 119:9, 10).

While we can't lose our union with Christ, we can lose our daily communion with Him if we don't get our "feet washed" every day. Have you "washed" your feet today?

Gardol, Estron, Lurex

"Yes, this double strength, super-secret ingredient gives added protection. And remember, an international survey shows that nine out of ten doctors prefer it over five other leading brands." What are we talking about? Toothpaste? Deodorant? Or a cure-all medicine for the common cold? It makes little difference, because this "superscientific" language would fit them all. People are apparently impressed by mumbo jumbo names like Gardol, Estron, Lurex, Lumium, Vionate, Boy-Dyne, Liquifix, Pursent, Opaquelon. We seem to have a built-in vulnerability to superscientific cure-alls. We seem prone to accept the easy way, whether we are talking about cure-all health foods, medicines, or the giant-size tablets you can throw into the washer to get whiter whites and bluer blues.

It shouldn't be surprising then that we are equally vulnerable to spiritual shortcuts and religious gimmicks. We can be taken in by anything from a cleverly written book to advice of a leader with "king-sized" charisma. The important thing to remember, though, is that the solutions we need are really very simple, basic principles. If we want a right relationship with the Lord, we don't need some "miracle-working ingredient."

What we need can be summarized in these practical steps:

Stay in the the Bible every day with a consistent plan of devotional reading. There is no substitute for this quiet time with the Lord, letting Him speak to you. Even here we are often led to paraphrases of the Bible to make our reading easier. While I don't object to the use of easier-reading translations, they should not replace a consistent study of a literal translation.

Maintain a closet prayer time shared by just you and the Lord. Do it regularly and habitually, and it will nourish your soul. Just talk to the Lord. Pour out your heart to Him and let Him bear your burdens.

In this area also, there has been an invasion of innovations. Conversational prayer, resulting in a rather loose, irreverent approach to talking with God seems to be the order of the day in many circles. Again, balance is needed. Truly He is our friend, and we have an access with boldness that is precious indeed. Yet there must be an awareness that He is God, and in the intimacy of prayer a reverential awe must be maintained.

Be faithful in your place with God's people. Our shut-in friends would naturally be the exception. But for the rest of us, even with all the outside activities and special seminars (many of which are good) that are available, there is nothing like a steady faithfulness in the house of God, being fed the Word of God from God's messenger.

Before too long, you will be confronted with the temptation to "taste a new product" or try a new method that has done so much for others. It will not be as obvious as Gardol, Estron, or Byo-Dyne, but probably just as impressive.

Remember, there is no special spiritual secret for maintaining a right relationship with the Lord or getting all God has for you. You need to keep close to Him in communion, daily examining your heart through the open Word, and expecting to enjoy all the blessings and benefits of a Spirit-filled life.

Strength for Growing: "Thy testimonies are wonderful; therefore doth my soul keep them. The entrance of thy words giveth light; it giveth understanding unto the simple" (Psalm 119:129, 130).

Both light and understanding are promised to those who are exposed to the Word of God. It is interesting that in this 119th Psalm (and it is a long one, with 176 verses), every verse speaks of the Word of God. The rewards of staying in the Book and maintaining a quiet time with the Lord are great.

... *Slow Me Down, O Lord*

Slow down! That may seem strange advice from a rather busy person; some might respond with "practice what you preach." But this advice does not mean that we can begin to slacken our hand in our rigorous responsibility, nor does it give any allowance to rest and rust. It is possible and desirable to "storm the fort" and put your heart and soul into your work, providing you are also taking time during the day to "be still" before the Lord, and not running in the power and unction of the flesh. A Pennsylvania Dutchman once said, "The hurrieder I go, the behinder I get." We have all experienced that at one time or another.

Someone prayed:

> Slow me down, O Lord, I'se a-going to fast,
> I can't see my brother when he's walkin' past;
> I miss a lot o' good things, day by day,
> I don't know a blessin' when it comes my way.

Isaiah said, "In quietness and confidence shall be your strength" (Isaiah 40:31). We take this to mean that it is only after we have been still before Him that we shall be empowered by Him to do the task before us. We need to be "recharged" and renewed, and this is done by slowing down and being quiet before Him.

Dr. A. W. Tozer once wrote: "Strong emotion has its place in life and in religion, but the mood in which we find God most real to us is often one of quietness. Only in quiet waters are objects mirrored without distortion, and only in a quiet mind is there a clear perception of truth. Those who have not learned to be quiescent before God miss life's profound lessons."

Here are three suggestions for learning to be still before Him:

Start the day waiting on the Lord. Sir William Osler, famed physician said, "What one does the first 20 minutes of the day sets the moral tone for the rest of the day." As the psalmist says, "My voice shalt thou hear in the morning, O Lord; in the morning will I direct my prayer unto thee, and will look up" (Psalm 5:3). And William Wilberforce once gave this advice to his son: "Let me implore you not to neglect, curtail, or hurry over your morning prayer. Of all things, guard against neglecting God in the secret place of prayer. There is nothing more fatal to spirituality. How much better I might serve God if I had cultivated a closer communion with Him."

If possible, set apart certain times during the day to be alone with Him. This will be difficult for some because of occupational responsibilities. However, if you make your own schedule, take a "Bible break" instead of a coffee break during the day. Get alone with Him and let Him be your company.

Practice communing with Him even during your busiest hours. The words of Paul in Colossians 3, "Set your affections on things above, not on things on the earth," are translated by Williams, "Practice occupying your mind with Christ." This can be done all hours of the day. Somehow you will find Him establishing your pace and making your busy moments more significant. Someone has advised, "Be not in such a hurry to do, that you fail to be; so anxious to give out, that you fail to take in." You are most likely to guard such a tendency if you practice the presence of God.

Strength for Growing: "For thus saith the Lord GOD, the Holy One of Israel: In returning and rest shall ye be saved; in quietness and in confidence shall by your strength: and ye would not" (Isaiah 30:15).

It is a precious paradox to say, "Keep up the good work and give it all you have," along with, "Slow down enough to cultivate a closer communion with Him." Such divine/human compatibility is the answer and secret for spiritual success.

The Blessings of Power Through Pressure

When it comes to understanding cars, I wouldn't know the difference between the muffler and the Johnson rod. (To other car-ignorant people like myself, there is no such thing as a Johnson rod!) My father was an expert mechanic, working for almost 30 years for Chrysler in Detroit. Being raised in Detroit, most of us were car-conscious—whether we liked it or not. We were also power-conscious. We were impressed by a 325 horsepower engine beneath the hood. But what gives a car that power? How is the horsepower produced? Through pressure.

The cylinder head is milled, or ground, as much as a twenty-thousandth of an inch to give a smaller cubic inch displacement in the cylinder head of the engine. This results in an increase in the compression ratio and a substantial increase in horsepower. What is the result? Greater pressure, which means greater power.

Pressure can produce power in life too. It can be the force in motivating men to do momentous tasks—the force in moving mountains. On the other hand, pressure can be also a debilitating thing. Our institutions are filled with people who broke beneath the pressures and demands of life. In desperation, some have reverted into worlds of fantasy, giving them release from the painful plaguing pressures. Pressure has left them weak, emasculated, and too often useless.

What is bane to one is blessing to another. Why the difference? Because the pressure of pain and sickness, the pressure of fluctuating circumstances, and the pressure of unexpected peril can cause us to run into the arms of the Lord—casting ourselves in total and complete dependence on Him. Paul said, "We are pressed out of measure, above strength." His human strength was exhausted. His personal ability and mental insights seemed insufficient. Christ said to him, in his weakness—bending beneath the peril and pressure of the thorn, "My grace is sufficient for thee; for my strength is made perfect in weakness" (2 Corinthians 12:9). The irksome pressure of the thorn resulted in the thrust of new power and strength.

Take two men, both about the same age, both subject to the same pressure and harrowing responsibilities, and both bending beneath the same afflictions. One bends and breaks in utter despair, debilitated and discouraged by his being denied life's potential. The other bends too, but becomes dependent upon His Lord. Fully realizing his own weakness, he harnesses the power of God by recognizing his total nothingness. To him pressure means power, not peril; prospect, not pain. It is hitching a tired horse to the rail and accelerating a 350 horsepower engine to its fantastic capacity.

> Pressed out of measure and pressed to all length.
> Pressed so intensely it seems beyond strength;
> Pressed in the body and pressed in the soul,
> Pressed in the mind till the dark surges roll;
> Pressed by foes, and pressured by friends;
> Pressure on pressure, till life nearly ends;
> Pressed into loving the staff and the rod,
> Pressed into knowing no helper but God;
> Pressed into liberty where nothing clings,
> Pressed into faith for impossible things;
> Pressed into living a life in the Lord,
> Pressed into living a Chirst-life outpoured.
> —W. Knight

 Strength for Growing: "For we would not, brethren, have you ignorant of our trouble which came to us in Asia, that we were pressed out of measure, above strength, insomuch that we despaired even of life; but we had the sentence of death in ourselves, that we should not trust in ourselves but in God, which raiseth the dead, who delivered us from so great a death, and doth deliver; in whom we trust that he will yet deliver us" (2 Corinthians 1:8-10).

Pressure is God's way of making us dependent on Him and not ourselves. It is a blessing not a curse.

Get Acquainted With God

Have you ever been in the company of someone for only a short time, but that fleeting moment made you desire to know that person better? It's happened to me in various churches I have pastored. I have worked with people I loved dearly, but with whom I didn't have enough time to get well acquainted. Some died before I got to know them better, and I regretted that. But there is one acquaintance none of us can afford to pass by.

I speak, of course, of the Lord. Job said, "Acquaint now thyself with him, and be at peace; thereby good shall come unto thee" (Job 22:21). Here are some suggestions on how to become better acquainted with the Lord:

Seek out His company. Yes, there must be an intense desire to be with Him. To read about a person in a biography or hear the experiences of someone else is good, but that's secondhand. That is, you might know a spiritual Christian who has known the Lord for some time. While this is wonderful, you can't really get acquainted with the Lord through a secondhand experience. You must seek Him out. Your desire should be, "That I may know him" (Philippians 3:10).

Let Him know that you are interested in Him and that you would like to enjoy His fellowship. Make it obvious in your prayer that it is not just what He has that you want. Rather, you want to know Him. How the Lord delights in that! Oh, to know Him better! Tell Him that you love Him and that you want to know Him better. Remember that He loves you. You can rest assured that He desires your affection, interest, and acquaintance.

Spend as much time with Him as you can. It is not a pen portrait that you want. It isn't a little five minute biography you are looking for. You can get casually acquainted with the Lord, as many Christians do, by just being superficial. But it takes time to acquaint yourself with Him intimately.

Could it be that you are shut in—one of the privileged ones who has time to get acquainted with the Lord Jesus Christ in an special way? Yours is not a plight of grief but a privileged glory. Yours is not reason to regret but rather to rejoice.

Have you ever met someone about whom you have said, "I am much better for having known him. He had a profound effect on my life?" Oh, how much truer with the Lord; how vital to have a meaningful acquaintance with Him!

"Acquaint now thyself with him, and be at peace . . . Then shalt thou have thy delight in the Almighty, and shalt lift up thy face unto God" (Job 22:21, 26).

Acquaint thyself with Him
Not seeking just His power—
His intervening hand,
But knowing Him this hour.

Acquaint thyself with Him,
What privileged glory mine,
What cherished presence this,
What blessedness sublime.

To hear Him speak, to listen when
He whispers words of cheer,
To be at peace amidst a world
Weighted with mounting fear.

Oh cherished days are these,
How tightly do I cling
To quiet times with Him,
Which turns the heart to sing.

But these fair hours are just foretastes
Of times when we shall know
A limitless, eternal day
Where this acquaintance grows.
—Charles U. Wagner

 Strength for Growing: "May Christ through your faith [actually] dwell—settle down, abide, make His permanent home—in your hearts! May you be rooted deep in love *and* founded securely on love" (Ephesians 3:17, Amplified).

Can you invite Christ into the home of your life as an "old acquaintance"? Would He would feel comfortable in every room?

Me and My Squeaky Viola

As a young person just learning to play the viola in the high school orchestra, I grew very impatient with the music I was given. For one thing, there are very few solo parts in viola music—at least in the music I was given. No, the viola part wasn't even "second fiddle." It was a kind of "fill in" for the rest of the orchestra.

But there was something even more aggravating about the viola. It was the "rests" in the musical score. I spent almost as much time counting (1-2-3-4 . . . 1-2-3-4) as I did playing. During a concert, I would wait patiently for the signal to come in with a few measures of "fill in." Then I'd be off counting again, waiting for another measure or two. I learned a real lesson in that.

First, I learned that God doesn't always expect us to be in the limelight. As a matter of fact, there are some "spiritual violas" that will never do anything but play the second and third parts. But there was another lesson. While there is no music in "rests," they are still a part of making music. Well did Mrs. Charles Cowman observe, "In our whole life-melody the music is broken off here and there by 'rests' and we foolishly think we have come to the end of the tune. God sends a time of forced leisure, sickness, disappointed plans, frustrated efforts, and makes a sudden pause in the choral hymn of our lives; and we lament that our voices must be silent, and our part missing in the music which ever goes up to the ear of the Creator."

What really matters is that we are faithful in doing what the score calls for and keeping our eye on the divine Conductor.

Another thing I remember is that sometimes when we had periods of "rests" in our score, we would be tempted to stop counting and involve ourselves in mischief with other viola players. Somehow we lost our appreciation of the music that was being played. We also lost a sense of being a part of it. I can still hear the rap of the conductor's baton on the stand and his stern reproval for not being ready when it was my turn to play my little measure or two. "You weren't ready when you were needed," he would say. Then, he would go into a little lecture about the importance of the viola and its contribution to the total orchestral sound.

How like the Christian life in times of waiting! The rests are planned and designed in our Father's score. But if we get sidetracked, if our attention draws away from the score of the Conductor, and if we stop waiting in our impatience, we might find ourselves the object of His disappointment when He gestures for us to do our part. Indeed, we may well find ourselves listening to Him say, "You weren't ready when I needed you."

Believe me, friend, without your rests, and without the use of your instrument, however insignificant the strokes across the strings of life, something important will be missing. You are a part of His divine musical score. I've heard a great many symphony orchestras and enjoyed a few master violinists, but I must admit that I have never heard a featured viola soloist. I have noticed, however, that when the orchestra finishes a number and a standing ovation is given for the musical rendition, the viola players stand with the members of the orchestra. They had executed with skill and perfection their part of the musical score.

I'm sure too, that when the Lord views our lives and examines the degree of faithfulness of each of us to "life's score," His "well done" will be just as great for the third seat in the "viola section" as for the "first violin." Our reward will depend on faithfulness to His command—even the times He looked our way and signaled for a rest. Obedience to His "Be still," then to His "Do it" will certainly bring a grand and glorious heavenly ovation.

 Strength for Growing: "Rest in the LORD, and wait patiently for him; fret not thyself because of him who prospereth in his way, because of the man who bringeth wicked devices to pass" (Psalm 37:7).

Be content with the "rests" in life. They can be a very important part of "making music." What really matters is that we are faithful in doing what the score calls for and keeping our eyes on the divine Conductor.

"All Things Are Against Me"

"All things are against me." Ever feel that way? Somehow difficulty and trial seem to come all at once, and you are left wondering just what you had done to deserve so many reversals. Jacob must have felt that way when he said, "Me have ye bereaved of my children: Joseph is not, and Simeon is not, and ye will take Benjamin away; all these things are against me" (Genesis 42:36).

Joseph had been sold by his brothers and carried away a slave to Egypt. His brothers lied to their father and said that he had been slain by wild beasts, so Jacob thought he was dead. Then, when famine spread throughout the land and the brothers went to Egypt for help, they saw Joseph but did not recognize him. Joseph demanded that they leave one of the brothers with him to "prove" they weren't spies. Simeon stayed behind. Then later, still unrecognized, he demanded that the youngest brother be brought to him. When the report came to Jacob, it was too much to take. From where he stood, he saw only that one boy had been slain and two others were all but lost. All things were against him.

But Jacob didn't know that what seemed to be an impossible situation causing heartache and distress was really the working of God to bring happiness and the supplying of all their needs. Joseph had not died. He had been promoted to Prime Minister of Egypt. Simeon and Benjamin were not lost but were to live full lives with their father in Egypt. Later, when the family was reunited in Egypt, Joseph said, ". . . God sent me before you to preserve you a posterity in the earth, and to save your lives by a great deliverance. So now it was not you that sent me hither, but God . . . " (Genesis 45:7, 8). Indeed! God had not forgotten him. What seemed against him was for him. The Lord had been working all along to preserve and provide for His own.

Friend, remember that all things are not against you. "All things work together for good to them that love the Lord" (Romans 8:28). God has promised to care for you, and there is not a difficulty or problem He will not turn into a blessing if you will trust Him and be content to know that His way is the best way.

> My life is but a weaving
>   Between my Lord and me:
> I cannot choose the colors;
>   He worketh steadily.

Oft times He weaveth sorrow,
   And I in foolish pride
Forget He sees the upper,
   And I, the underside.

Not till the loom is silent
   And the shuttles cease to fly,
Shall God unroll the canvas
   And explain the reason why.
The dark threads are as needful
   In the Weaver's skillful hand

As the threads of gold and silver
   In the pattern He has planned.

He knows, He loves, He cares;
   Nothing this truth can dim.
He gives His very best to those
   Who leave the choice with Him.

                —Selected

 Strength for Growing: "What shall we then say to these things? If God be for us, who can be against us? He that spared not his own Son, but delivered him up for us all, how shall he not with him also freely give us all things?" (Romans 8:31, 32).

Remember, all things are not against you. God is working all things together for good in His weaving. God is really for us. Keep reminding yourself of this. It is God's promise, and it is true.

Peace in Panic

We are living in a panic-ridden society. Panic can be caused by a riot, by personal catastrophe, a fire, a sudden sickness or a turn in political affairs. But God's Word says to the believer, "Be not afraid of fear, neither of the desolation of the wicked, when it cometh; for the LORD shall be thy confidence, and shall keep thy foot from being taken" (Proverbs 3:25, 26). The word translated *desolation* means "stormy blast" (Berkeley, Amplified). When the blast breaks against society, when panic penetrates, when the unexpected rushes in alarmingly, remember that there is an inward sustaining power that can bear the shock and sustain in the storm.

"The Lord shall be thy confidence." Or according to the Berkeley translation, "The Lord will be in your inward parts." Remember that as a child of God you are indwelt by the Holy Spirit. "Greater is he that is in you, than he that is in the world" (1 John 4:4). The Spirit's power is greater than that of the world or the god of the world— Satan.

In a time of panic, it is typical to see panic-stricken people running aimlessly with no goal or purpose. How different for the believer, "For as many as are led by the Spirit of God, they are the sons of God" (Romans 8:14). Fear is another characteristic of the man who faces the storm. God assures us that "God hath not given us the spirit of fear, but of power, and of love, and of a sound mind" (2 Timothy 1:7). The vocabulary of the panic-stricken and fearful is punctuated with the cry of help. But for the believer we read, "Likewise, the Spirit also helpeth our infirmities . . ."(Romans 8:26).

These are difficult days. Remember that your confidence is in Him. Run to your confidence and find peace. "In the fear of the LORD is strong confidence, and His children shall have a place of refuge" (Proverbs 14:26).

"The name of the LORD is a strong tower; the righteous runneth into it, and is safe" (Proverbs 18:10). It is almost as if the Lord is saying to us, "Come, my people, enter thou into thy chambers, and shut thy doors about thee; hide thyself as it were for a little moment, until the indignation be overpast" (Isaiah 26:20).

It is interesting to note other ways the word "confidence" is translated in the Bible. In Job 8 it is translated "hope." The verse reads, "So are the paths of all that forget God; and the hypocrite's hope shall perish: Whose hope shall be cut off, and whose trust shall be a spider's web" (Job 8:13, 14).

God's Word says that a man whose confidence rests in anything other than the Lord will have that confidence cut off. Specifically He says, "He shall lean upon his house, but it shall not stand; he shall hold it fast, but it shall not endure" (Job 8:15). It is God's way of saying that everything will cave in for the unbeliever and he will be left with perplexity and panic.

What a contrast to the hope of the child of God and the unchanging confidence that we have in the Lord.

Let Christ be your confidence and peace in this day of mounting panic!

 Strength for Growing: "In the fear of the LORD is strong confidence, and his children shall have a place of refuge" (Proverbs 14:26).

"The God of my rock; in him will I trust: he is my shield, and the horn of my salvation, my high tower, and my refuge, my saviour; thou savest me from violence" (2 Samuel 22:3).

We need not worry about caving in when we have a refuge in the Lord and when our full confidence is in Him alone.

Palm Tree Christians

"The righteous shall flourish like the palm tree" (Psalm 92:12).

When the Lord looked for some vegetable life to describe the great mass of lost humanity, He chose grass. It comes for a season and soon withers. But when He looked for something in His beautiful creation to be a picture of the righteous, He chose the palm tree. There are many reasons for this. The palm tree has a beauty all its own, and it is very useful. The Hindus claim that it can be used at least 360 ways. Unlike the grass, it produces even to old age, and the best dates are produced when the tree is from 30 to 100 years old.

One of the most remarkable features about this tree is that it grows in the desert. It grows where wheat, barley, and corn refuse to grow. The blasts of the heat are too much for other types of plant life. Yet, in spite of the desert weather that burns and parches everything else around it, the palm tree grows and flourishes. It is unaffected by its surroundings. If you were to visit an oasis where the palm tree often grows, you would likely find water around this tree. But it is so brackish it is nearly impossible to drink. The Arabs have a saying about the palm tree, "It stands with its feet in salt water and its head in the sun."

Although the thirsty traveler cannot drink the brackish water of the oasis, he can tap the tree and drink its sweet palm wine. The tree changes the unsavory water into a source of life and strength.

You might well be surrounded with circumstances that would cause others to wither. The bitter waters would be too much, and they would adopt the outlook of the afflicted. But that doesn't have to be the case. The Lord has a way of working in our inner life by His indwelling Spirit to draw from the circumstances surrounding us, changing them into something sweet that can minister to our spiritual growth and development.

There are some things, of course, that the palm tree rejects. While it grows from the sand, the sand is not its food. To apply this idea directly, we could say that the believer finds no nourishment from the world it is in. But the tap roots of the tree do find nourishment from some very unpalatable salt water below. By an inner power, the tree turns it into something sweet and desirable. Upward it grows, tall and stately, producing fruit and flourishing.

More amazing still, in all seasons the leaf of the palm is the same. In the winter, unlike other trees, the leaves do not fall. In the summer it has no special clothing of beauty it changes into when the intemperate weather comes. It is evergreen, and it knows no seasonal change. How blessed it is to find Christians who are consistent in their testimony the year 'round—often having their feet in salt water, but their head in the sun!

Strength for Growing: "The righteous shall flourish like the palm tree; he shall grow like a cedar in Lebanon" (Psalm 92:12).

When our head is "in the Sun" and occupied with "the Son," we will not be dominated and influenced by the climate of circumstances.

Men— Not Methods

In making plans for the future it is important to remember that nothing should be planned without considering the Lord. An example is Asa of old, who was a real success when he was young and took a stand for God. Later, however, in all his "wisdom and maturity," he failed. He died in abject submission and defeat. It is important that we walk humbly before the Lord and see things through His eyes.

Just how does the Lord see things? He sees them in terms of *people* and not just plans. He sees people in terms of their yieldedness to Him. To supplant Madison Avenue techniques for Holy Spirit methods, to think that strength can come by numbers and convenient alliances is a dismal mistake that can lead to dismal failure. Asa started off living by faith and trusting God; he ended by working independently of God and making an alliance with the enemy.

It is not better methods we need, but better men. In this day of neo-everythingism, man is willing to "try a new bag of tricks" to get what he calls "success." We need Spirit-filled *servants* ready to let God show His might through their weakness. In Ezekiel we read, "And I sought for a *man among them,* that should make up the hedge, and stand in the gap before me for the land, that I should not destroy it; but I found none" (Ezekiel 22:30).

God is seeking men, better men, yielded men.

Again in 2 Chronicles, the Lord sent Hanani to Asa to rebuke him for his trust in self and his alliance with others. Asa had descended from the lofty heights of faith to the carnal abasement of self-reliance. Hanani said to the king, "Because thou hast relied on the king of Syria, and not relied on the LORD thy God, therefore is the host of the king of Syria escaped out of thine hand. Were not the Ethiopians and the Lubims a huge host, with very many chariots and horsemen? Yet, because thou didst rely on the LORD, he delivered them into thine hand" (16:7, 8). The king was quickly reminded that past reliance was on the Lord and victory was achieved. But now, God was not sought. Then, Hanani spoke words which should speak to each of us. He said, "For the eyes of the LORD run to and fro throughout the whole earth, to shew himself strong in the behalf of them whose heart is perfect toward him. Herein thou hast done foolishly; therefore, from henceforth thou shalt have wars" (v. 9).

Winning Words for Daily Living

GIVE ME A MAN

Our God is looking for a man;
His eyes run to and fro
In patient searching for that one
Through whom His strength to show.

"A man," He said, "Give Me a man
Of faith, perfect in heart;
A man through whom I'll show My hand
And serving—strength impart."

Council and league were offered God,
With power of place and plan;
Machinery large and iron strong,
God said: "Give Me a man!"

His flashing eyes go to and fro
Searching earth's breadth and length;
Our God still seeks a yielded man
Through whom to show His strength.
—Charles U. Wagner

 Strength for Growing: "For the eyes of the LORD run to and fro throughout the whole earth, to shew himself strong in the behalf of them whose heart is perfect toward him. Herein thou hast done foolishly; therefore, from henceforth thou shalt have wars" (2 Chronicles 16:9).

"We are constantly on a stretch, if not on a strain, to devise new methods, new plans, and new organizations to advance the church and secure enlargement and efficiency for the gospel. . . . Men are God's method. The church is looking for better methods; God is looking for better men" (E.M. Bounds).

You and Your Pet Gourd

Sunshine can produce strong and healthy gourds, but do gourds bring sunshine into your life?

Let me explain. Let's start with what we know about gourds. Gourds are vegetables whose relatives are squashes and pumpkins.

There are many varieties, such as the salt-and-pepper gourds, the nest-egg gourds, or the luffa. While some of them are useful (like the luffa, whose insides can be used for a dishcloth or bath sponge), most of them are simply novelties and ornaments. Whether we are talking about the dipper, the calabash, or the Hercules club, there just isn't much you can do with them. Gourds are gourds.

But Jonah didn't think so. He was very partial to one particular gourd. After he had preached to the city of Nineveh, he went to the east side of the city, found a comfortable spot, and waited to see what could become of it. We read, "And the LORD God prepared a gourd, and made it to come up over Jonah, that it might be a shadow over his head, to deliver him from his grief. So Jonah was exceedingly glad of the gourd" (Jonah 4:6).

In four chapters, the first thing even resembling a note of joy was the gourd God had prepared for Jonah's temporary comfort. We shouldn't downplay the legitimacy of the gourd—after all, God did prepare it for him. What is a little disconcerting is that it meant so much to him. Even God's provision can become a sin if we make more of it than we should.

Think of it! A city had been spared from God's judgment as a result of the prophet's preaching, and the high point in the day was the appearing of Jonah's "pet gourd." No wonder God took it away!

But it gets worse! Jonah went into a rage of anger and desired death. It's almost as though he said, "You took my gourd! My pet gourd. And it meant so much to me—let me die!" It would be humorous if it weren't so pitiful—and so typical of us.

Again we ask our original question, which should make more sense now. Sunshine produces strong healthy gourds, but do gourds bring sunshine into your life? Here's another way of asking it. Are you dependent upon the pleasant, ornamental gourds of life for your sunshine? If so, you are likely to be as desolate as the daughter of Zion. Isaiah said she was "left as a cottage in a vineyard, as a lodge in a garden of cucumbers [gourds], as a besieged city" (Isaiah 1:8).

Now, let's be specific. What is your gourd? Is it personal comfort? It could be that or one of a thousand other things.

In Jonah's case we find the Lord, who gave him the gourd, reprimanding him for having more concern for something temporary than for the souls of the city and, in particular, the children. Jonah's problem was pride. He was all wrapped up in himself. To him his sunshine corner was on the side of the hill beneath a "giant cucumber," where he could benefit from the latest "model" gourd.

Often when we get despondent it is because we get wrapped up with ourselves. To forget ourselves and to be lost in concern for others generally brings a new ray of gladness into our hearts. When we can thank God for His mercies in temporary gourds and yet not make that our prime interest, we reflect a happy, balanced Christian life.

> Where is your heart? Your great concern?
>   What interests you—your treasure stored?
> What is your chief concern today?
>   A needy world, or a Jonah's gourd?
> —Charles U. Wagner

Strength for Growing: "But seek ye first the kingdom of God, and his righteousness, and all these things shall be added unto you" (Matthew 6:33).

God does not want to deny you "gourds" to enjoy. After all, He was the giver of the gourds. He is not advocating the establishment of the International Society to Eliminate Gourds. What matters is what has priority in your life. Is the Lord really first and foremost?

The Committee of Constant Renewal

Duane Orton once said, "Every business organization should have a vice-president in charge of constant renewal." That makes good sense—if a business is going to survive and be vibrant and fresh, meeting the challenges of the future.

If this is true of the business world, how much more important it is in the church! Since we generally have committees for almost everything else, perhaps someone would like to form a Committee of Constant Renewal. Committees are usually good if they are active and in harmony with the spirit of the church. Yet, sometimes a committee of one is best. This is true for the Committee of Constant Renewal. It is a personal and individual matter that will be reflected in church life.

That we need renewal is evident. There can be no standstill in the Christian life. We are either being renewed constantly or we are succumbing to spiritual subversion by the enemy of the soul—the devil.

Yes, you need to be renewed. It is easy to grow spiritually dull and stale so that you mouth your spiritual vocabulary while knowing that they are just words. The motions are the same, but the motivation is gone. Suddenly, you discover you are talking about a state that has become unreal and almost make-believe. There is a simulated spirituality you recognize as being empty and hollow. You are the first to recognize it (while often not ready to admit it), but it is soon detected even by your best friends as your whole attitude changes.

It is time for a spiritual revival and a meeting of the Committee of Constant Renewal.

Paul recognized this need for constant renewal when he wrote, ". . . but though our outward man perish, yet the inward man is renewed day by day" (2 Corinthians 4:16). Here he is contrasting the physical (outward) with the spiritual (inward). He also said, "And have put on the new man, that is renewed [continuously] in knowledge after the image of him that created him" (Colossians 3:10). Now how is this done? Five words in the epistle of Titus give the answer. He speaks of the "renewing of the Holy Spirit" (3:5).

Suddenly we encounter another member on the Committee of Constant Renewal, the Holy Spirit. However, the presence of the Holy Spirit does not assure us of renewal. If this were so, there would be no such thing as Christians out of fellowship who are just "going through the motions." There must be unanimity on the committee. There must be agreement between you and the Spirit about what you are willing to have Him do in your life. You must respond! This brings us to Romans 12.

"I beseech you therefore, brethren, by the mercies of God, that ye present your bodies a living sacrifice, holy, acceptable unto God, which is your reasonable service. And be not conformed to this world, but be ye transformed by the renewing of your mind, that ye may prove what is that good, and acceptable, and perfect, will of God" (Romans 12:1, 2). There must be joint agreement by both members of the committee. Then the Holy Spirit will renew our minds and direct our energies Godward.

This will result in a rekindling of the embers of our heart, a revival of our spirit, and a rectifying and regulating in our attitude to the things of the Lord. This is not a patching up of our lives; it is the divine intervention of the Holy Spirit, who revives us and begins to renew us constantly with a fellowship with the Lord and a fulfillment of His will.

 Strength for Growing: "For which cause we faint not; but though our outward man perish, yet the inward man is renewed day by day" (2 Corinthians 4:16).

This daily renewal is in the inward man. "This is not a fresh bestowment of the Spirit, but a revival of His power, developing the Christian life; this passage stresses the continual operation of the indwelling Spirit of God" (W.E. Vine).

We Can't All Be Giraffes

The giraffe is one of the most interesting animals in God's creation. Take that long, lanky neck, for example. It contains only seven vertebrae—about as many as most animals.

If the giraffe wanted to eat directly from the ground, it would have to spread its forelegs apart and lower its entire body. For some reason or other (probably because it is so uncomfortable), it doesn't usually assume that position. Instead, it feeds on tree branches.

The eyes of the giraffe are as strange as its elongated neck. They protrude from the skull and serve as "rear view mirrors." Yes, he can actually see behind without turning his head. With his height and rear vision, he is very aware of what is going on around him.

Zookeepers have special equipment for feeding the giraffe. With its inflexible neck and a head so far removed from the rest of his body, his nourishment has to be elevated. But suppose the keeper of the zoo tried to feed every animal the same way. The food "out of sight" would be of no value to the other hungry animals.

Did you ever read something that seemed to have been written for intellectual giraffes? You may have picked up a magazine or religious journal and involved yourself in material considered by others as sweet spiritual morsels, only to find yourself puzzled by it. If misery loves company, move over—I've been there too. Perhaps you have heard a speaker about whom others raved. However, you went away exclaiming that it sounded impressive, but you didn't get a word of it.

Often people are discouraged because they have problems with English, let alone Greek and Hebrew. Some sermons and conversations sound so scholarly that you are, at times, almost brought to the point of despair. So you decide to let the giraffes do the eating and just hope for a crumb or two to fall your way.

God knows that we are not all intellectual giraffes. The omniscient (all knowing) Holy Spirit who indwells us is able to put the Word of God down on our level so that we can understand and digest it. He knows our needs and is able to give us understanding. The mark of a good teacher is to make the truth both applicable and digestible. As you come to the Word of God with an open heart, the Spirit is faithful to "guide you into all truth" (John 16:13).

So get your Bible out, read it, and ask the Lord to speak through it to your heart. He has something very special for you.

A right relationship to the Spirit will bring the truth to your level. You will gain an insight and understanding that will result in your spiritual growth and development. We can't all be giraffes.

 Strength For Growing: "But as it is written, Eye hath not seen, nor ear heard, neither have entered into the heart of man, the things which God hath prepared for them that love him. But God hath revealed them unto us by his Spirit; for the Spirit searcheth all things, yea, the deep things of God" (1 Corinthians 2:9, 10).

The Bible isn't just for intellectual pursuit. It is for day-by-day living.

"A certain Christian traveler was packing his suitcase and was about to proceed on a journey. He remarked to a friend standing by: 'There is still a little corner left open in which I desire to pack a guidebook, a lamp, a mirror, a telescope, a book of poems, a number of biographies, a bundle of old letters, a hymn book, a sharp sword, a small library containing thirty volumes, and all these articles must occupy a space of about 3-by-2 inches.'

"How are you going to manage that?" asked the friend.

"Easily," said the traveler, "for the Bible contains all of those things."

—Taken from the *Gospel Herald*.

Let Me Introduce You to the Amaryllis Family

I would like to introduce you to few members of the Amaryllis family. First, we should establish that we are talking about a family of flowers. Most members of this family grow outdoors. While there are family traits in each of them, they also have their distinctive, independent features. About half of them grow from bulbs.

Chive belongs to this family. Its leaves are chopped and used to flavor various kinds of food. Chopped chive leaves are used in salads; you are also likely to taste them in your favorite soup or in cheese dishes. The flower is a lavender color and quite attractive.

Garlic with its pungent flavor is from this family, too. You might see bunches of it in the market. It is difficult to hide the fact that you might have used a little of this in your favorite dish. Perhaps the garlic is the "runt" of the Amaryllis clan.

Leeks and onions. These are two members of the Amaryllis family that are mentioned in the Bible. These "twins" resemble each other, although the onion has a much milder flavor.

Daffodil. Now imagine that! Along with the chopped chives, the pungent garlic, and the rather nefarious leeks and onions (that remind us of the taste of Egypt), there is the bright yellow daffodil, so prominent in the spring.

William Wordsworth wrote,

> I wandered lonely as a cloud
>   Floats high o'er vales and hills,
> When all at once I saw a crowd,
>   A host of golden daffodils.

Would he have been more refreshed by the host of daffodils had he known that the daffodil was from the Amaryllis family? Hardly! To state that the flower was first grown in Europe and that it measures about 15 inches long is interesting, but not necessary for its enjoyment. As a matter of fact, you are to be congratulated that you have read this far. After all, the Amaryllis family is hardly something to write home about.

Still, we hope you get the point. You don't have to know a great deal about the flower to appreciate it and enjoy its beauty.

Many people are reluctant to enjoy all the Lord has given them in His Word because they feel that they lack formal biblical training. They become especially upset when someone mentions the Greek or the Hebrew. While I am not denying the value of studies, I do think you ought to be able to just enjoy the "flower of the Word" without always being concerned with all the technicalities. You don't have to know that the sun has a diameter of 865,000 miles and is made of hydrogen and helium in order to be warmed by its rays. Nor do you need to learn that the moon rushes around the earth at the speed of 2300 miles an hour before you can enjoy its beauty on a clear night.

Enjoy your Bible. May its spiritual fragrance, its sublime beauty, and its pure simplicity thrill your soul. Walk through this garden of 66 flowers (all of one family) and let them be your daily delight.

Strength for Growing: "How I love thy law! It is my meditation all the day" (Psalm 119:97).

"My soul hath kept thy testimonies, and I love them exceedingly" (Psalm 119:167).

"But his delight is in the law of the LORD; and in his law doth he meditate day and night" (Psalm 1:2).

"How sweet are thy words unto my taste! Yea, sweeter than honey to my mouth!" (Psalm 119:103).

Warning: This Book is habit-forming. Regular use causes loss of anxiety, and decreased appetite for lying, cheating, stealing, hating. Symptoms: increased sensations of love, peace, joy, and compassion.

Thistles Are Beautiful

I have always had a love for roses, and I enjoyed them so much while living in the Pacific Northwest. What color, what delicate texture, what symmetry they have!

One day my neighbor said, "Follow me. Let me show you something." She led me to a special area near her garage, and with a smile pointed to a plant. For a minute I thought my eyes needed focusing. She must have sensed my slight confusion and answered my puzzlement with, "It's a thistle."

"Oh, yes," I said, "a thistle."

"Of course, it's not in bloom yet."

"What," I said, "does it look like when it is in bloom?"

"Haven't you ever seen a thistle before?" she asked in her Scottish accent.

This was no joke. She proceeded to tell me that it was the national flower of Scotland. My interest was growing, but had a long way to go. To be sure, a thistle was not a rose.

That day I took several pictures of some beautiful roses as well as the "thistle."

Days later when I picked up my pictures, I was surprised to see how good they were. But the most surprising picture was the thistle! It was actually beautiful. A beautiful weed? No, a flower and a Scottish beauty at that.

This experience made me do some thinking. Generally we think of thistles as an undesirable nuisance. Isn't life like a garden, with many different varieties of color and quality? The diversity of color and quality makes it interesting. But we generally take the thistles with patient endurance. We put up with them because we know we can't always have a bed of roses. Thistles are inevitable. But often what God sends our way is not to be endured but enjoyed, not simply accepted but welcomed.

Indeed, if "all things work together for good," are we not to appreciate the beauty of that part of the garden blend? Our "grin and bear it" can be just as mistaken as my preconceived opinion of what I thought to be a garden weed. A closer look at that part of life cultivated in my garden life might result in a thistle-thankfulness. Certainly if it came from His hand, there is a special beauty in it being there. If we look with a greater deliberation, if we examine it through the lens of the Word of God, we might find that without the thorny thistles in life a very special blend of the total life color might be missing. Yes, this garden taught me a vital lesson.

Strength for Growing: "Rejoice evermore. Pray without ceasing. In every thing give thanks; for this is the will of God in Christ Jesus concerning you" (1 Thessalonians 5:16-18).

God never sends accidental seeds of weeds. Even His thistles are sent, not to clutter, but to play an important part in the spiritual blend designed for us in His garden.

The Burden of the Trivial

Most of us are faithful in taking our large burdens to the Lord. We are aware of our own helplessness in accomplishing the large tasks, and we accept our inadequacy when great problems arise. So we "take our burdens to the Lord—and leave them there."

But how often do you find yourself praying about little things? That is, things that might to others seem of little or no importance?

If you will examine the things on your "worry list," you will find that many of them deal with the trivial—the small, slight, inconsequential problems. Yet small as they are, they wear on us and sometimes bring us down spiritually.

Our response to the small things is often, "I never thought of praying about that." But if you are taunted by the trivial, if you are bothered by the little things, why not share them with the Lord.

Our English words, *trivia, trivial,* and *trifles* are interesting ones. An examination of them might help us in our problem.

Wilfred Funk, in his book *Word Origins*, wrote, "The Romans were human and they knew that where their roads crossed would be the spot where the women would meet and gossip on the way back from market. The words for this in Latin would be *tri,* 'three', and *via,* 'way', that is, *trivia,* which in our language means 'trifles.' The word *trivial* comes straight from the Latin *trivialis,* which means 'of the crossroads.' That is crossroads, small talk. Just gossip."

Isn't it true that we share our trivia along the *trivialis* of life with others? Most of our "small talk" involves such trivia. At the crossroads we talk about our aches and pains, our pet peeves, our paltry problems. This is because they bother us and wear on us.

Try praying about them! Take your small talk to our great God. You will find that He is interested in your sharing trivialities with Him. Anything that concerns you concerns Him.

Take your "trivials" to the mercy seat. Bare your heart there about the matters that concern you—large or small. Remember that one measure of the greatness of God is His concern with our every need. He is just as interested in the burden of the trivial at the crossroads of life as He is in any crisis. Unburden your heart at the mercy seat, and you will be delivered from any threatening tragedy of the trivial.

Strength for Growing: "And all things, whatever ye shall ask in prayer, believing, ye shall receive" (Matthew 21:22).

"Give us this day our daily bread" (Matthew 6:11).

"Be careful for nothing, but in every thing, by prayer and supplication with thanksgiving, let your requests be made known unto God" (Philippians 4:6).

"I never prayed sincerely and earnestly for anything but it came at some time — no matter at how distant a day, somehow, in some shape, probably the last I would have devised, it came" (Adoniram Judson).

It was Hugh Stowell who wrote:

> From ev'ry stormy wind that blows,
>   From ev'ry swelling tide of woes,
> There is a calm, a sure retreat;
>   'This found beneath the mercy-seat.
>
> There is a place where Jesus sheds
>   The oil of gladness on our heads,
> A place that all beside more sweet;
>   It is the blood-bo't mercy-seat.
>
> There is a scene where spirits blend,
>   Where friend holds fellowship with friends;
> Tho' sundered far, by faith they meet
>   Around one common mercy-seat.
>
> There, there on eagle's wings we soar,
>   And sin and sense seem all no more,
> And heav'n comes down our souls to greet,
>   And glory crowns the mercy-seat.

Crying Babies . . . Pass the Bottle

Researcher Harold S. Morgan claims that the average 6-week-old baby cries two hours and forty-five minutes a day.

I don't know how Harold came up with that average. Perhaps he used a stopwatch while his wife administered the bottle. Anyway, with all the "funny faces" we have in our stop-crying repertoire, and with all our gentle pats on the baby's back as we lean over the crib, it is inevitable that baby is going to cry. Whether he needs attention, security, a bottle, or a gentle touch—he is going to cry.

In a sense, Christians are like that too. It is characteristic for babes in Christ to do their share of whimpering. Sometimes they have spiritual indigestion and need to be "gently burped" (if you will excuse the expression). Peter said, "As newborn babes, desire the sincere milk of the Word, that ye may grow by it" (1 Peter 2:2). Paul said, however, that this milk is primarily for babes. "For every one that useth milk is unskillful in the word of righteousness; for he is a babe. But strong meat belongeth to them that are of full age . . ." (Hebrews 5:13, 14b). It is obvious that he was "put out" with them. He said, "For when for the time ye ought to be teachers, ye have need that one teach you again the first principles of the oracles of God; and are become such as have need of milk, and not of strong meat" (v. 12).

These Hebrews weren't the exception to the rule. The Corinthians had the same baby propensities. Paul said to them, "And I, brethren, could not speak unto you as unto spiritual, but as unto carnal, even as unto babes in Christ. I have fed you milk, and not with meat; for to this time ye were not able to bear it, neither yet now are ye able" (1 Corinthians 3:1, 2). Then he listed some things that were characteristic of carnal babies. Their walk was one of spiritual infancy. It was spiritually wobbly!

While it may be annoying to have a baby cry for two hours and forty-five minutes a day (especially if it begins at 3:30 in the morning), there is a tender toleration that comes from a parent's heart. But such action would be intolerable for a 16-year-old teenager.

So it is with the believer. God expects us to grow in grace and knowledge (2 Peter 3:15). We are to "grow up in Him" (Ephesians 4:14). We are to graduate from milk to meat, from the need of coddling to a strong, robust Christian life—helping more than we are helped, comforting more than we are comforted.

If we are more interested in being served than in serving, and if we are forever making demands rather than involving ourselves in the service of others, we have failed to grow up. Life will lack the joy and sunshine that God wants us to have. If we are still pining in pediatrics, or whimpering in the church nursery of life, we will know little or nothing of the gladness that comes through growth and the joy of spiritual maturity.

Can we do something about it? Yes! How many of us remember our parents saying, "Start growing up"? Our Bible study, personal involvement in service, *doing for* instead of *being done for* will all reflect itself in a joyful maturity. Not, "What can they do for me?" But "What can I do for them?" Not, "What do they offer?" But "What can I offer?" This could be the turning point from the cry room to the harvest field of life.

Strength for Growing: "But, speaking the truth in love, may grow up into him in all things, who is the head, even Christ" (Ephesians 4:15).

"As newborn babes, desire the sincere milk of the word, that ye may grow thereby" (1 Peter 2:2).

"But grow in grace, and in the knowledge of our Lord and Savior, Jesus Christ. To him be glory both now and for ever. Amen" (2 Peter 3:18).

Being concerned for others and not just for self, being outgoing and not simply self-centered, wanting to serve rather than being served; these are evidences of Christlikeness and signs of both life and growth.

Safety Pins and Razor Blades

We take many of our common household goods for granted. The safety pin is one example. It was invented by Walter Hunt back in 1946. What did mothers use for that little cherub's diapers before then? I confess I don't know. Then, there is the lawnmower. We are indebted to Edwin Budding for that clipping contraption; he thought it up back in 1830. Of course, what would we do without the electric light bulb? Certainly we would survive. Others did who lived before 1879—the date of Thomas Edison's invention of the incandescent light. Just 3 years later, Henry W. Seely made it easier to press skirts and trousers by inventing the electric iron.

Other inventions we take for granted can be identified by the name of the inventor. In 1895, King C. Gillette helped cut short the time it takes for a man to get ready in the morning. And Clarence Birdseye helped reduce the time it takes for a mother to prepare supper. (Gillette invented the safety razor; Birdseye, the frozen food process.)

Some items seem to have been around longer than they really have. I had to look twice when I first read that the tape cassette is only 30 years old. It was invented by J. J. Schoennaker in 1963.

From zippers (1892) to zeppelins (1852) in the 19th century, to the airplane (1903) and atomic power (1945) in the 20th century, we sometimes act as though these things have always existed.

This is also true spiritually. There are some blessings which, because of their plenitude and availability, are taken for granted.

Take your Bible for example. It took the work of 40 men over a period of 1600 years to give us these 66 books. God the Holy Spirit breathed upon them in the selection of each word. Two hundred years before the Reformation, John Wycliffe, a devout student of Scripture, expressed the desire for God's Word to be in the hands of the common man. He said, "The Sacred Scriptures are the property of the people, and one which no one should be allowed to wrest from them . . . Christ and His apostles converted the world by making known the Scriptures to men in a form familiar to them." His teaching was condemned, and he was excommunicated from the church. Those were the days when it was a precious treasure to have a Bible. It was cherished and searched by hungering souls with hearts ready to receive its message.

But the church is in that "it's always there" category. We often find Christians availing themselves of the Bible only when it is convenient. It is often considered merely as one of many "electives."

We could get along without the atom bomb, but the Bible, the source of the gospel, is the "power of God unto salvation" (Romans 1:16). Mankind did get along before Edison gave us the light bulb, but the believer (taking his place in service with the church) is the "light of the world" to a darkened generation (Matthew 5:14).

Thank God for your Bible—brought to us through the sacrifice of martyrs of old. Thank God for the local church. For centuries it has survived the oppression of evil men. Let's not take them for granted.

 Strength for Growing: "I will delight myself in thy statutes; I will not forget thy word. Deal bountifully with thy servant, that I may live, and keep thy word. Open thou mine eyes, that I may behold wondrous things out of thy law" (Psalm 119:16-18).

THE BIBLE

It is a traveler's map,
    The pilgrim's staff,
The pilot's compass,
    The soldier's sword,
And the Christian's charter.
    Read it slowly, frequently, prayerfully.

It is a mine of wealth,
    A paradise of glory,
And a river of pleasure.
    It involves the highest responsibility,
Rewards the greatest labor, and condemns
    all who trifle with its holy contents.
                                —Author unknown

In His Strength

Fall is the time of year when God's people get excited about the programs in the church. Plans are made, areas of service are laid out, and hopes are high—everyone is looking forward to another church year. The problem frequently is that we start out like atom bombs and end up like firecrackers. Our enthusiasm and zeal for the Lord are high in September, then it begins to wane and wobble a few months later.

What is the answer to this dilemma? It certainly isn't to try harder, because we all make that extra effort every year. Nor is it sincerity, because while it is true we frequently fail, it is not a lack of that important substance. Could it be that we have aimed too high? Possibly, but not likely.

There seems to be another reason for our dilemma. I believe the answer lies in our failure to have an absolute and complete reliance upon the Lord and His strength. I am impressed that the Bible is filled with passages that assure us He will give us the power and strength needed to get the job done, if we will trust Him for it.

Let us take three passages in particular and examine them.

Strength from God the Father! It was to Isaiah the Lord said, "Fear thou not; for I am with thee: be not dismayed; for I am thy God: I will strengthen thee; yea I will help thee; yea I will uphold thee with the right hand of my righteousness (Isaiah 41:10). This is the promise of the Lord. He will give us strength in pressure situations by upholding us wioth His "right hand," which assures us of His special care.

Strength from God the Holy Spirit! One of the prayers of the apostle Paul, found in Ephesians 3:16 is, "That he would grant you . . . to be strengthened with might by his Spirit in the inner man." In addition to the promise of the Father, here we have the promise regarding the Spirit, the source of our strength. To be strengthened with might is to be empowered by the Holy Spirit to get the job done. After all, isn't this God's method in the New Testament church today? As men have the fullness of the Spirit's power, they can know real success in their service.

The Spirit is the difference between a failing, faltering Peter in the Gospels, and a mighty man of God thundering forth one of the greatest sermons in all the world at Pentecost. If we trust Him day-by-day for strength, we can be sure He will produce in and through us that same quality of service that was characteristic in New Testament days.

Strength from God the Son! "I can do all things through Christ which strengtheneth me" (Philippians 4:13). There seems to be a philosophy in the world today that says, "If you think you can, you can." If one gets himself psyched up for a particular situation, he can accomplish it regardless of his limitations.

How many times have you proved this false? Unless I have the ability to run a hundred yard dash, thinking I can won't help me. There must be a source from which I can draw physically (in the case of running). The same is true in the Christian life. Simply to say I can, and then determine that I should square my shoulders firmly, set my jaw, and do it, is not acceptable. But with Paul we can respond, "I can do all things through Christ which strengtheneth me." This precious verse can change *I can't* into *I can.*

Frequently when we consider the Trinity, we do so in a doctrinal connotation. But here we have a very practical application of the work of the Trinity. The Father says, "Fear not:" the Holy Spirit's strengthening power is granted to us; and through Christ we can do all things. Praise God, we can be assured of His abiding strength.

 Strength for Growing:

HIS STRENGTH

"Fear thou not, for . . . I will strengthen thee" (Isaiah 41:10).
>   The Father said, "Fear not, for . . . I will strengthen thee,"
>   What comfort is this promise, so that while I cannot see
>   Beyond this present moment, I surely need not fear,
>   My simple faith believes His strength will persevere.

"That He would grant you—to be strengthened with might by His Spirit in the inner man" (Ephesians 3:16).
>   Another promise makes me realize His plan
>   To strengthen by His SPIRIT— in the inner man.
>   What blest assurance that the Spirit doth indwell,
>   Endue, and strengthen me, His temple citadel.

"I can do all things through Christ which strengtheneth me" (Philippians 4:13).
>   "I can't, such negative response is heard
>   From most of us. But note—the promise of His Word
>   That CHRIST will strengthen us; His hand
>   Makes weakness strong, "I can't" is changed: "I CAN."
>   —Charles U. Wagner

The Cockles of the Heart

"When I thought of all that he has done for me, it warmed the cockles of my heart." Perhaps you have heard the phrase "cockles of the heart" many times, but what does it mean?

It is from the Latin phrase *Cochleae cordis* and means the "ventricles of the heart." If you have ever seen a picture of the human heart, you will know that there is an upper part and lower part of this amazing muscle. The ventricles (and there are two—the left and the right) are the lower part of the heart. To say something warmed the cockles of our heart means that it reaches into the innermost depths of our heart and emotions. It means that you really feel it, whether it is a gratifying sensation or a deep emotional stirring.

The Bible is replete with references to the heart signifying the innermost being of man. For example, in referring to the greatest commandment in the law Christ said, "Thou shalt love the Lord, thy God, with all thy heart, and with all thy soul, and with all thy mind" (Matthew 22:37). On that first Christmas morning when Christ was born, the deep feeling of joy reached down into the cockles of Mary's heart. There must have been a deep, lasting satisfaction in the virgin's heart that was beyond explanation. After the shepherds had departed, making known abroad "the saying which was told them concerning this child," we read, "But Mary kept all these things, and pondered them *in her heart*" (Luke 2:19).

When the disciples reviewed their experience on the road to Emmaus, it is said that their heart burned within them as they listened to Christ (Luke 24:32). Paul, in reflecting the burden he had for Israel said, "I have great heaviness and continual sorrow in my heart" (Romans 9:2). He also said, "My heart's desire and prayer to God for Israel is, that they might be saved" (Romans 10:1).

It is important that our "religion" reach down into the cockles of the heart. Too often it is more intellectual than emotional; more a matter of cold facts than it is a deep experience. We are not suggesting that there is no room for the intellectual. Certainly our emotion should be based on fact; God does not put a premium on ignorance. If we aren't careful, it is easy enough to get lost in the ocean of emotion.

We all need to "examine our hearts" and reflect on the depth of love we have for Him and His people.

May the days ahead bring a deep, abiding love for Him that reaches down into the cockles of the heart and, in turn, reaches out in service to a lost and needy world.

Strength for Growing: "Jesus said unto him, Thou shalt love the Lord, thy God, with all thy heart, and with all thy soul, and with all thy mind" (Matthew 22:37).

Superficial Christianity is not enough! Even the world recognizes shallow, hollow, pretense. A "heart love" manifesting itself in "heart service" and heartfelt devotion should characterize our lives as Christians.

The Apple of Your Eye

Most of us are rather careful about our eyes, and with good reason. And, most of us know more about what the eye does than what it is. Each eyeball, for example, has six ocular muscles attached to it that move the eye. We are familiar with the general appearance of the eye. The pupil is the round hole in the iris that looks like a black circle. It also has two sets of muscles that can change its size. We know, also, that light passes through the pupil.

Did you ever wonder where the name *pupil* came from? The word comes from the Latin *pupilla*, which means "little doll."

What do you see when you look into another person's eye? Exactly, you see an image of yourself reflected there, like a miniature person. Thus, when the Romans looked in another's eye and saw a "little person," they called that part of the eye the "pupilla" or "little doll." The Hebrew words for the pupil of the eye were *eshon ayin*, or "little man of the eye."

If you get out a Young's *Concordance* and look up the word "apple," you will find that the first definition given is "little man" and the Hebrew word *ishon* is given. That word is used in Deuteronomy 32:10. Speaking of His own, we read, "He found him in a desert land, and in the waste, howling wilderness; he led him about, he instructed him, he kept him as the apple of his eye." The Psalmist wrote, "Keep me as the apple of the eye; hide me under the shadow of thy wings" (Psalm 17:8).

When we examine the Scriptures, two ideas come forth from the use of these words, "The apple of the eye."

The Hebrew scholar, Delitzsch, writes of the little man as the apple of the eye "inasmuch as the saint knows himself to be so near to God, that, as it were, his image in miniature is mirrored in the great eye of God." In that same commentary (Keil and Delitzsch), we read, "to keep as the apple of the eye is a figurative description of the tenderest care. The apple of the eye is most carefully preserved."

This speaks of nearness. We are near and dear to Him; we are His very image. Should Satan or any other power touch us, it is as if they were touching Him. To touch us is like touching His pupil. He is that sensitive to our care and keeping.

What a blessing it is to know that we are so special to Him, the "Apple of His eye," the object of His special love and care.

Strength for Growing: "He found him in a desert land, and in the waste, howling wilderness; he led him about, he instructed him, he kept him as the apple of his eye" (Deuteronomy 32:10).

We are very special to God. He loves us and exercises the tenderest care. From the *Gospel Herald* comes this story:

"The Reverend R.I. Williams telephoned his sermon topic to the *Norfolk Ledger Dispatch:*

"The Lord is my Shepherd," he said.

"Is that all?" he was asked.

He replied, "That's enough."

And the church page carried Mr. Williams's sermon topic as: "The Lord is my Shepherd—That's Enough." As so it is! The sheep are very special to the Shepherd.

Blizzards

Many of our English words have French, Spanish, or German roots. Others come from Greek. But there is one good, old English word that has its origin in America. It is the word *blizzard*.

No one knows just where the word *blizzard* originated. It occurred in print back in 1829, but some suggest that it may have been known in frontier speech long before that. In one collection of Americanisms, published in 1871, the usual meaning of the word was "a stunning blow—like hitting someone or something, with a blow of a fist." It carried the idea of a punch. A blizzard could be bruising, to say the least. Later it was used to describe a super storm. A storm that occurred on March 14, 1870, was known as "the great blizzard." Ever since then, it has been so designated.

We are all aware of storms, and not just "weather storms." Storms of life have often come our way. Harsh, unexpected troubles can dash one's hopes like a bruising blizzard. Sometimes they are blessings in disguise, as they drive us to our knees in prayer. On the other hand, unless we see the spiritual value of them, they can discourage us and act as spiritual detours. They can stagger us spiritually.

We should remember that "there hath no temptation taken you but such as is common to man" (1 Corinthians 10:13). We should remember that "He [Christ] was in all points tested like as we are, yet without sin" (Hebrews 4:15). We have a high priest who can be touched with the feelings of our infirmities. Remember, He took that "blizzard blow"—the storm of God's wrath—at Calvary. When we suffer, we remember that He has suffered. When we feel the mounting storms, they are nothing compared to what He endured for us. Call it what you will, blizzard, blow, or a storm with all its severity, we have a companion in tribulation, we have a partner in suffering, we have an understanding High Priest. Someone has written:

> Faith looks across the storm;
>   It does not doubt
> Or stop to look at clouds
>   And things without.
>
> Faith does not question why
>   When all His ways
> Are hard to understand,
>   But trusts and prays.

Yes, there are songs in the storms, there are blessings in blizzards, there is a special fellowship with the Lord when the fist of the world strikes hard against us. We "rejoice that we are counted worthy to be partakers of His sufferings" and we "glory in tribulation" and the "fellowship of His suffering."

So when the storms and blizzards come, we lift our hearts and pray, "Stand by me." He does exactly that. Out of the pain, there is gain; out of the cross, a crown; out of the blizzards, choice blessings.

Strength for Growing: "For whatever is born of God overcometh the world; and this is the victory that overcometh the world, even our faith" (1 John 5:4).

"And Jesus said unto them, Because of your unbelief; for verily I say unto you, If ye have faith as a grain of mustard seed, ye shall say unto this mountain, Remove from here to yonder place; and it shall remove; and nothing shall be impossible unto you" (Matthew 17:20).

"Faith sees the invisible, believes the incredible, and receives the impossible" (David Lloyd George).

"A little faith will bring your soul to heaven; a great faith will bring heaven to your soul" (C.H. Spurgeon).

Danger of Birds in the Beard

More than 100 years ago, a poet by the name of Edward Lear came up with what is believed to be the first limerick. He wrote the following:

> There was an old man with a beard,
> Who said, 'It is just as I feared!—
> Two owls and a hen,
> Four larks and a wren,
> Have all built their nests in my beard.

Not too impressive, but then limericks seldom are. However, sometimes there is wisdom even in a few words of foolishness. To be sure, it is hard to stretch one's imagination to picture eight flying creatures in a single beard.

As a youngster, I remember being told that you can't help birds flying over your head; but if they nest in your hair, that is something else. The idea behind it was that everybody is tempted. Satan makes it his chief business to work on us and invade our thought life. But when we allow the sin to "nest" and permit it to permeate our thought life, we can't blame that on Satan.

We need to be careful that we do not "continue in sin" and harbor sinful thoughts in our mind. When Satan seeks to take over and defeat us, we need to be "casting down imaginations, and every high thing that exalteth itself against the knowledge of God, and bringing into captivity every thought to the obedience of Christ" (2 Corinthians 10:5). We are to "gird up the loins of our mind" (1 Peter 1:10). Paul talks about the "renewing of your minds" in Romans 12:2.

When jealousy, envy, or covetousness seem to be a part of your thinking, don't allow it to nest in your head! Confess it! Cast it down! Put it out! Remember the old man with the beard who complained about the owls, hen, larks, and a wren. That was all his own fault. It is no limerick that Satan may be responsible for exposing you to certain thought possibilities, but God has given us power to handle this sin. There is no excuse for allowing such thoughts to "nest" there.

 Strength for Growing: "(For the weapons of our warfare are not carnal, but mighty though God to the pulling down of strongholds), casting down imaginations, and every high thing that exalteth itself against the knowledge of God, and bringing into captivity every thought to the obedience of Christ" (2 Corinthians 10:4, 5).

"I beseech you therefore, brethren, by the mercies of God, that ye present your bodies a living sacrifice, holy, acceptable unto God, which is your reasonable service. And be not conformed to this world; but be ye transformed by the renewing of your mind, that ye may prove what is that good, and acceptable, and perfect, will of God" (Romans 12:1, 2).

Nature abhors a vacuum. It isn't good enough to decide we will not let Satan dominate our thought life. We also need to set our affection (mind) on Christ.

"If ye, then, be risen with Christ, seek those things which are above, where Christ sitteth on the right hand of God. Set your affection on things above, not on things on the earth." "To set our mind on Christ is to 'practice occupying our mind with Him'" (Colossians 3:1, 2, Williams).

Epitaphs

Let's talk about epitaphs. I once read about the line on the grave of a guide who died while climbing. It said simply, "He died climbing." Then there were the words on the tomb of a Christian astronomer: "We have gazed too long at the stars together to be afraid of the night."

One of my favorites is the epitaph on Benjamin Franklin's tombstone:

> The body of B. Franklin printer
>   Like the cover of an old book
> Its contents torn out
>   And stripped of its lettering and gilding
> Lies here food for worms.
>   But the work shall not be wholly lost
> For it will, as he believes, appear once more
>   In a new and more perfect edition
> Corrected and amended
>   By the author.

But the epitaph that I want you to remember most today is of an unknown individual:

> Remember, friend, when passing by,
>   As you are now, so once was I.
> As I am now, soon you will be,
>   Prepare for death and follow me.
> To follow you I'm not content
>   Until I know which way you went.

My question for you is this: Which way are you going? We take for granted that most of our readers know Christ as Savior. The very fact that you are reading this book would indicate that you have some interest in spiritual things.

But it could be that you have not had a "new birth" experience with Christ. You don't know the Lord personally nor can you say for sure that you know you are going to heaven when you die. While you would like to be able to say that, you really don't know for sure that you are ready to meet God.

Let me assure you that you *can* know which way you are going. The Bible says, "There is, therefore, now no condemnation to them who are in Christ Jesus" (Romans 8:1). If you are "in Christ" and know Him as your Savior, you can be sure that you are free from judgment and ready for heaven. If you have not trusted Christ, let me urge you to do so. Realizing that you are a sinner and that Christ died for you, trust Him today as your Savior. Tell Him that you are a sinner, accept Him as the One who died for you. Remember, it is all of grace; you can't save yourself. It is His work and His alone.

It's wonderful to know that you're saved. It isn't important to be sure of some things, but to be sure of your eternal destiny is important indeed. To accept Christ is to be a prepared person for a prepared place in heaven.

 Strength for Growing: "Jesus saith unto him, I am the way, the truth, and the life; no man cometh unto the Father, but by me" (John 14:6).

"Neither is there salvation in any other; for there is none other name under heaven given among men, whereby we must be saved" (Acts 4:12).

While we live in a pluralistic society and respect one's right to believe as he chooses, Bible believers know that there is only one way to heaven, the Lord Jesus Christ. "There is a way which seemeth right unto man, but the end thereof are the ways of death" (Proverbs 14:12).

But the good news is that all may come to him. "All that the Father giveth me shall come to me; and him that cometh to me I will in no wise cast out" (John 6:37).

Parkinson's Law

There are several laws, or principles, that need to be restated and reapplied in our present generation. One such law or principle is Parkinson's Law, a principle that I find myself referring to several times each year. It is an important one in Christian service. The law, simply stated, is: "Work expands to fill the time available for its completion."

I would suggest that every Christian memorize this law! First, I suppose it is important that you know what it really means. Frankly, it is better illustrated than defined. So let me do just that.

Suppose you are preparing a speech for a special occasion. You have been asked to deliver it around Christmas time. You have 5 months to prepare. Question: How long does it take to prepare the message? Answer: 5 months! Now, let's approach it in another way. There is an emergency, and you have been asked to fill in and give a presentation next Saturday morning. You received the desperate invitation on the Monday morning preceding the actual "message day." How long does it take you to prepare? The answer is 5 days.

Parkinson's Law simply says that if you have a 5-month compartment in which to complete a job, the work necessary to get the job done will fit into that time allotment. Haven't you found this to be true in many areas? Whether it is cleaning the house, studying for an examination, or completing a project for the church—the law is rather reliable. Of course, there are some limitations to the law. You couldn't, for example, prepare a speech in 10 minutes—that would be equal to one which required many hours.

Now, what practical application does this law have? First, we should *be aware of the lateness of the hour*. We need to be walking "not as fools, but as wise, redeeming the time because the days are evil" (Ephesians 5:16). Also, Paul said to the Colossians, "Walk in wisdom toward them that are without, redeeming the time. Let your speech be always with grace, seasoned with salt, that ye may know how ye ought to answer every man" (Colossians 4:5, 6).

Second, we need to *plan our time* in our service for the Lord. We need to compartmentalize it carefully and determine that within a specific time allotment we will accomplish what we have set out to do. Nowhere is this more applicable than in evangelism. While we recognize that "salvation is of the Lord" and that the actual saving is in His hands, we can determine that in a given alloted time we are going to witness to a specific number of people. If you give yourself several weeks to cover the few blocks around the church in a house-to-house witnessing ministry, it will take you just that long. If you determine that you will do it in a week, that is how long it will take.

Parkinson's Law can be of real benefit in understanding why some get more done than others. We need to plan our work and work our plan. We need to drive ourselves and set definite goals in the completion of our work. There is no excuse for laziness in the Lord's work. A loose schedule that is vague and general and leaves much time to do a few things is sin in the eyes of the Lord. It is no wonder that when you want something done, you ask a busy person to do it. Parkinson's Law strikes again.

Now, do you have the law memorized? "Work expands to fill the time available for its completion."

 Strength for Growing: "See then that ye walk circumspectly, not a fools, but as wise, redeeming the time, because the days are evil. Wherefore be ye not unwise, but understanding what the will of the Lord is" (Ephesians 5:15-17).

Let's get busy putting Parkinson's Law into action. Let's be up-and-at-it, redeeming the time. How much time have you been given to get the job done? That's *exactly* how long it will take.

The Great Emancipator

In ancient Rome when a slave was set free, there was a ceremony to celebrate his emancipation. The act of liberation of the slave was called *mancipium*, which literally meant "possession by the hand." Our English word "emancipate" has the opposite meaning. It is from the Latin, *emancipatus*. Broken down, it is spelled out like this: *e-*, and means is "away." *Manus* means "hand." Add to this *capio*, which means "take," and you have "take away the hands." When one is truly emancipated, it means that someone (in this case the slave owners), took away their hands.

Come to think of it, that's exactly what happened when we were saved. We were slaves to sin and Satan. Paul wrote, "Know ye not that to whom ye yield yourselves servants to obey, his servants ye are to whom ye obey, whether of sin unto death, or of obedience unto righteousness? But God be thanked, that whereas ye were the servants [slaves] of sin, but ye have obeyed from the heart that form of doctrine which was delivered you. Being then made free from sin, ye became the servants of righteousness" (Romans 6:16-18).

When we trusted Christ as Savior, it was as though God said to Satan, "Hands off, this one is no longer under your control." We are in new hands, and recognize another Lord. "But now being made free from sin, and become servants to God, ye have your fruit unto holiness, and the end everlasting life" (Romans 6:22).

This was all made possible through Christ. "If the Son, therefore, shall make you free, ye shall be free indeed" (John 8:36). On the cross, Christ stripped Satan of his power over us. "And, having spoiled principalities and powers, he made a shew of them openly, triumphing over them" (Colossians 2:15). We were in the grasp of Satan. We read that, ". . . through death he might destroy [put out of business] him who had the power of death, that is, the devil, and deliver them who, through fear of death, were all their lifetime subject to bondage" (Hebrews 2:14, 15). The great Emancipator has taken away the hands of Satan.

Today, those who have trusted Christ are that company about whom Christ said, "My sheep hear my voice, and I know them, and they follow me. And I give unto them eternal life; and they shall never perish, neither shall any man pluck them out of my hand" (John 10:27-28). What a transfer! What a transformation! All because of Calvary and our great Savior-emancipator.

Strength for Growing: "The Spirit of the Lord is upon me, because he hath anointed me to preach the gospel to the poor; he hath sent me to heal the brokenhearted, to preach deliverance to the captives, and recovering of sight to the blind, to set at liberty them that are bruised" (Luke 4:18).

"Now the Lord is that Spirit; and where the Spirit of the Lord is, there is liberty. But we all, with open face beholding as in a glass the glory of the Lord, are changed into the same image from glory to glory, even as by the Spirit of the LORD" (2 Corinthians 3:17, 18).

Not only has the Lord "delivered us" from the penalty of sin, but He is, by His Holy Spirit, delivering us from its power through His Word. The Spirit of God takes the Word of God and stamps the image of the Son of God on the child of God. As a result we enjoy freedom.

Handicaps

Have you ever heard of *Fanny Farmer's Cookbook?* Even if you have, you probably don't know that the person who was responsible for the culinary secrets of that famous cookbook was handicapped.

We owe a debt to the work and labor of the handicapped. Many famous people have had to overcome some handicap or affliction in their lives. John Milton, the great poet, was blind. About Beethoven, who was deaf, someone observed, "Though so deaf he could not hear the thunder for a token, he made music of his soul, the grandest ever spoken." The eighteenth century English poet Alexander Pope was a hunchback and very weak. Franklin D. Roosevelt, who was crippled by infantile paralysis, became victorious over his handicap. When Thomas Edison invented the phonograph at age 30, he was almost totally deaf and could hear only the loudest of noises.

Blessed is the man who is handicapped, if he learns to be thankful to God for the blessings he has been given and doesn't become bitter, sour and, resentful to God.

Let me interject a word about a man I have already mentioned— John Milton, the blind genius. Have you read his poetry? Julius C. Hare has written a piece that I think is worth quoting: "Blind men seldom quote books, but it is not so with Milton. The prodigious power, readiness, and accuracy of his memory, as well as the confidence he felt in it, were proved when he composed his *Treatise on Christian Doctrine*. This writing was made up of scriptural texts and seemed to require perpetual reference to the Sacred Volume. A still more extraordinary enterprise was the Latin dictionary, a work that one would imagine might easily wear out a sound pair of eyes. After 5 years of blindness, he undertook these two vast works, along with *Paradise Lost*."

This touching poem, written by Hellen Keller, will bless your hearts.

> They took away what should have been my eyes,
> (But I remembered Milton's Paradise.)
> They took away what should have been my ears,
> (Beethoven came and wiped away my tears.)
> They took away what should have been my tongue,
> (But I had talked with God, when I was young.)
> He would not let them take away my soul,
> (Possessing that I still possess the whole.)

Strength for Growing: "And he said unto me, My grace is sufficient for thee; for my strength is made perfect in weakness. Most gladly, therefore, will I rather glory in my infirmities, that the power of Christ may rest upon me. Therefore, I take pleasure in infirmities, in reproaches, in necessities, in persecutions, in distresses for Christ's sake; for when I am weak, then am I strong" (2 Corinthians 12:9, 10).

"I can do all things through Christ, who strengtheneth me" (Philippians 4:13.)

While God is pleased to use man, He is not dependent upon man and his natural ability. A God who is seen guiding is One who is also providing. He delights in taking our weakness and showing His strength. Then the glory goes to Him and not to us. Ours is not to complain in areas where we feel we have been shortchanged, but to delight in God's taking the little that we have and showing the greatness of His power and person through us.

Hunger Can Tell on You

Hunger can tell you something about yourself. At least, that's what nutritionists tell us. When you have cravings for certain kinds of food, this is nature's way of saying you are not getting enough of some vitamins and minerals.

For example, peanut butter is on the "top ten" cravings list. It's not surprising, say nutritionists, because it is a rich source of vitamin B. A craving for peanut butter may indicate that your body is under stress and needs more "B" to cope. The banana is another example. When your body craves potassium, an appetite for this tasty fruit could appear. The same is true, they say, when it comes to cravings for cheese (high in calcium and phosphorus) and chocolate (high in caffeine and sugar). And the list goes on with butter, nuts, pickles, bacon, and even onions.

What is true of the physical is also true of the spiritual. Have you ever had an inner appetite for spiritual food?

If so, that's good news! First, it says that a certain kind of spiritual life wants to be satisfied, and no substitute, however sanctimonious and appealing, can meet the need. Christ once said, "Blessed are they which do hunger and thirst after righteousness; for they shall be filled" (Matthew 5:6).

This is something an unsaved person cannot understand. Not only is righteousness characteristic of the believer, but it is natural for him to hunger and thirst after it. It is his spiritual self crying out for real satisfaction. Earlier, Christ said, "Blessed are the poor in spirit; for theirs is the kingdom of heaven" (Matthew 5:3). A person "poor in spirit" realizes his own deficiencies and needs, and comes to the Lord to have those needs met. Then Christ said, "Blessed are they that mourn; for they shall be comforted" (v. 4). What a natural sequence! Realizing our poverty in our own selves, we react to it with mourning and meekness (v. 5). Then, having a hunger and thirst for the reality of His person and provision, we long for God.

In John 6, Christ said, "I am the bread of life; he that cometh to me shall never hunger, and he that believeth on me shall never thirst" (v. 35). The hunger is satisfied in Christ. As we partake of Him daily by faith, and as we look to Him for satisfaction, the deficiency is met; the spiritual craving is satisfied. No wonder Christ said, "Blessed [happy] is the man who has a hunger and thirst after righteousness." There is a special satisfaction in the Savior; a special contentment in Christ.

Strength for Growing: "Then Jesus said unto them, Verily, verily, I say unto you, Moses gave you not that bread from heaven; but my Father giveth you the true bread from heaven. For the bread of God is he who cometh down from heaven, and giveth life unto the world. Then said they unto him, Lord, evermore give us this bread. And Jesus said unto them, I am the bread of life; he that cometh to me shall never hunger, and he that believeth on me shall never thirst" (John 6:32-35).

Just as the children of Israel took manna daily for sustenance, we are to partake of the heavenly manna daily. We cannot depend on yesterday's time with Him to meet today's needs. Every day we need a taking and feasting on the Lord through His Word. This is the kind of strength that is supplied as we wait Him.

Beginning and Ending the Day

The way you begin your day and the way you bring it to a close could make the difference between living in sunshine or living in shadows.

George Washington Carver won international fame for his agricultural research, revolutionizing the agriculture of the South. But the greatest accomplishment of his life was not in making the 300 products from peanuts (for which he became famous) or his 118 products from the sweet potato and pecan. In the eyes of God, the greatest fruit from his life was the fruit of the Spirit seen in his Christian character. He trusted the Lord in all circumstances, and he knew the meaning of real victory in his life.

What was his secret?

He said, "There is no need for anyone to be without direction in the midst of the perplexities of this life. Are we not plainly told, 'In all thy ways acknowledge him, and he shall direct thy paths'?" Carver would arise every morning at 4 o'clock and seek God's guidance for his life by spending time in prayer and Bible study.

Speaking of those early hours, he said, "At no other time have I had so sharp an understanding of what God means to do with me as in those hours when other folks are still asleep. Then I hear God best and learn His plan!"

Like George Washington Carver, start the day with the Lord. Begin the day with Him and learn "His plan" for your life that day. This includes meditation in the Word, drawing from the sweetness of the blessed honeycomb of the Word, and then letting the Lord share with you some of His sacred secrets. Start the day with Christ, let Him be the first One with whom you commune.

The climax of the day ought also to be with Him! Let Christ be the last One with whom you commune each night.

Donald Grey Barnhouse once wrote, "I frequently noticed that I awoke in the morning thinking the same thoughts that had been in my mind when I closed my eyes in sleep the night before. Many people know from sad experience that the mind frequently drifts to thoughts that are utterly of self and its interests and desires in those half-awake moments that end our day and begin our night. I discovered, therefore, that it was of great importance to capture this half-world of the mind for our Lord Jesus Christ. One morning when I awoke trying to solve a chess problem that had filled my mind as I put my head upon my pillow, I became conscious of this law and determined that, henceforth, I would go to sleep thinking of Christ. As the months passed, I discovered that there was much more than a habit involved in this.

"Here was a proof of the presence of the Lord Jesus Christ in my heart and mind, controlling even the subconscious element of my life. Then I learned that I must not merely go to sleep thinking about Christ, but that I must go to sleep in communion with Him. I began memorizing verses of Scripture at night and reciting them as I fell asleep. Soon He became more real than the inside of my eyelids. I could not see them though they were close to my eyes; Him I learned to know in everything but the touch. And closing one's eyes with Christ takes away all fear of sleepless nights. Let others count sheep jumping over a wall; I shall talk with the Shepherd. 'He giveth his beloved sleep' (Psalm 127:2). 'I laid me down and slept,' says David. 'I awaked; for the Lord sustained me' (Psalm 3:5)."

Yes, it is important that we begin and end the day with God. Then, with the awareness of His presence, we can have sunshine from morning until night. We'll have sunshine in our hearts—no matter what the weather might be outside.

 Strength for Growing: "With my whole heart have I sought thee; O, let me not wander from thy commandments" (Psalm 119:10).

"I will meditate in thy precepts, and have respect unto thy ways. I will delight myself in thy statutes; I will not forget thy word" (Psalm 119:15, 16).

Have you noticed that we often put the heroes of the faith in a category beyond our reach? They are almost like supernatural people different from us. Actually, their secret of power and success can be ours. They met the Lord regularly. It was often early in the day, but it was a constant and regular relationship with Him. He is our God too, and He will help us as He helped them.

Sweeter Than Honey

Every young person looks forward to the time when he can get a part-time job and earn a little extra spending money. As a young boy, I remember looking for a job one summer and finding that a number of boys my age were working in the sugar beet fields. I was hired along with a carload of other "city slickers," and there I received one of my first tastes of farm life.

On this job, I was introduced to the different kinds of sugar. It was explained to me that the two major sources of sugar are sugar cane and sugar beets, and that beet sugar is the sweeter. My problem was that I learned this from farmers growing beets. Growers of sugar cane insist than theirs is much sweeter that beet sugar.

Experts, however, tell us (unbiased experts, that is) that when both are completely refined, they are chemically identical. There is no evidence that one is sweeter that the other. The ordinary granulated sugar of commerce, regardless of whether it is made from beets or cane, consists of sucrose, the better grades running as high as 99.8 percent.

To my surprise, I have discovered that there are hundreds of different kinds of sugar known to science. In addition to sucrose, there is dextrose (grape) and lactose (milk) sugar. But, say the experts again, the levulose found in honey is the sweetest of all common sugars.

That probably isn't very startling news, but I wonder if that is the reason God used honey to show the sweetness of His Word. "More to be desired . . . than gold, yea, than much fine gold; sweeter also than honey and the honeycomb" (Psalm 19:10).

When God the Holy Spirit wanted to describe His Word, He said it was more desired than the most precious metal and sweeter than the sweetest substance.

Why is the Word of God so valuable, and why is it so sweet? The three verses preceding Psalm 19:10 explain it well: The Word of God is precious and sweet because it (1) converts the soul, (2) makes wise the simple, (3) rejoices the heart, (4) enlightens the eyes, (5) endures forever; and because God's judgments are (6) true and (7) righteous altogether.

No wonder the psalmist said, "How sweet are thy words unto my taste! Yea, sweeter than honey to my mouth" (Psalm 119:103). That honey is good for the health is undisputed, even by people who normally have little respect for health foods.

Winning Words for Daily Living

Anyone who tastes the sweetness of God's Word knows by experience that this miracle book can have a miraculous effect on our lives. One thing that makes it so sweet is that in it we meet the Lord. Surely it is the "savor of his [Christ's] knowledge" that makes this book so sweet and precious to our souls (2 Corinthians 2:14).

It is delightful to see someone who is disappointed with the world and its saccharin sweetness turn to the Christ of the Bible and find in Him satisfying salvation.

Yet when we get occupied with the world—when we get distracted from God's sweet Word and the precious Christ of it, and get filled with ourselves—we find that even the honeycomb of the Word loses its taste. "The full soul loatheth an honeycomb" (Proverbs 27:7).

When you are out of fellowship with the Lord, your taste for the sweetness of the Word is soon lost. You might even find yourself using the doubletalk of the world and begining to "put bitter for sweet, and sweet for bitter" (Isaiah 5:20).

When sin is confessed; when our eyes are turned from self to Him; when we lay aside the artificial sweeteners of the world, we will say with the psalmist, "How sweet are thy words unto my taste!" (Psalm 119:103). If you are discouraged, bitter, or dissatisfied, the problem might not be with those around you or even your circumstances. The problem could well be with you and your failure to come to God's Word, which is sweeter than honey.

 Strength for Growing: "More to be desired are they than gold, yea, than much fine gold; sweeter also than honey and the honeycomb" (Psalm 19:10).

Occasionally a good cook will forget an important ingredient when trying to follow a recipe. It doesn't take long to discover that something is wrong. That's the way it is spiritually. A message preached, while impressive in selection of words, lacks something without the Word. This is true when we neglect this ingredient in our daily schedule. Before the day is over, it becomes apparent that some sweetness was omitted from our daily recipe of life.

Your Daily Diet of Wood

Alaska is an intriguing place to visit, especially when you are with a group of missionaries. I had been invited to speak to some missionaries in Ketchikan, Alaska—the salmon capital of the world. In addition to speaking, I had an opportunity to do some fishing. My haul for only a few hours in two days was seven salmon.

One afternoon I joined the missionaries in touring a pulp mill, one of the main industries of this frontier town. It was not surprising to find a mill where the forests abounded like a storybook wonderland. But this was not an ordinary "run of the mill" pulp mill. Here the crude, rugged logs are ground up, and the pulp is moved through an intricate refining process, resulting in the production of cellulose. If you are wearing a rayon shirt or blouse, it may have originated in Ketchikan, Alaska. Other things made from this product are your chewing gum wrappers and even some of the foods you may be eating this weekend, especially if you are are on a strict diet. Incredible? Yes, but true.

A great many diet foods have cellulose in them. If you are in doubt, go to the diet food section of the neighborhood market and note how many of them have some percentage of cellulose. The most common diet food is diet cookies. The reason for the use of this product is obvious. It has plenty of bulk, giving you that full feeling, but absolutely no nutritional value—therefore, no calories. When you eat the food, you think you have something; but in truth you have nothing but pleasant, palatable pulp. While only a few animals, such as kangaroos, can assimilate cellulose, it cannot be assimilated by humans, nor can it harm you. It just doesn't do you any good. It is neutral in nourishment—neither plus nor minus.

How true this is spiritually in a great many areas of our lives. Take some books and magazines on which you feed your mind. No, you can't put your finger on anything that is noticeably bad, neither can you find anything of any spiritual value. It is spiritually "blah" with a total value of zilch. Unfortunately, many so-called religious books are like this too. They give you a temporary full feeling, but having read them, you find it hard to sum up what was really said or how it helped. There were a lot of words—pulp—but no nutritional value.

When Paul wrote that we "may approve things that are excellent" (Philippians 1:10), he was talking about the daily choices we make with regard to spiritual excellence. He urges us not to be satisfied in life with things of no value, even those that are not wrong themselves. Rather, he would have us choose that which will add to our spiritual stature and help build up moral muscle.

Just as you are what you eat physically, so you are what you read mentally and what you believe spiritually. In those last two areas there are a great many attractive "cellulose" food parcels that could divert you and hinder your growth.

Be choosy about what you read. One thing is sure, you can never go wrong on a steady diet of the Word of God. "As newborn babes, desire the sincere milk of the Word, that ye may grow by it" (1 Peter 2:2).

Then we are to go from milk to meat—and all the spiritual nutritional value God's Word can bring. Unlike the foreign pulp matter, the Word of God can be assimilated into every fibre of your being and make you a stronger and better Christian. So shun the trite, trivial bulk and get into the timeless, trustworthy Book. It will do you good.

 Strength for Growing: "And I went unto the angel, and said unto him, Give me the little book. And he said unto me, Take it, and eat it up; and it shall make thy belly bitter, but it shall be in thy mouth sweet as honey" (Revelation 10:9).

Are you a reader? There are so many people who sit in front of a television set every day when they could be gaining spiritual strength from good Christian books, and, of course, most of all, THE Book. Someone has written: "Reading makes a man full." Of course, just "filling up" is not what really counts. What counts is the spiritual strength that comes with the right kind of food. Be a Bible reader.

Too Busy?

*H*urry, hurry up, hustle, rush, accelerate, prod, push, press, drive. These are some of the verbs I recently ran across in the thesaurus under the word *haste*. They are all familiar to us for we are a nation of rushers. *Immediate, urgent, step lively, on the double*, are others. Open the kitchen cupboard and we find instant rice, instant coffee, instant tea, and instant potatoes. Open the freezer and we see instant TV dinners neatly stacked for that special breakneck day when speed is vital. Feverishly, we reach for instant quick-shave lather, slip the blade out of our handy quick-loading dispenser, shave, dress, and sit down to a quickly prepared snap, crackle, and pop breakfast. Then we speed off in our latest model car powered by gasoline specially prepared for quick starts.

Phillips Brooks, talking about the hurry of the world, related an interesting story. "A friend says to me, 'I have not time nor room in my life for Christianity. You don't know how hard I work from morning till night. When have I room for Christianity in such a life as mine?'"

Commented Mr. Brooks, "It is as if the engine had said it had no room for the steam. It is as if the tree had said it had no room for the sap. It is as if the ocean had said it had no room for the tide. It is as if the man had said he had no room for his soul. It is as if life had said it had no time to live. It is not something added to life; it is life. A man is not living without it. And for a man to say, 'I am so full in life that I have no room for life,' you see immediately to what absurdity it reduces itself."

Does it impress you that we have more time-saving devices than ever before in this computer world, yet we seem to have less time? Not only did our fathers not have all the available means of transportation, but neither did they have microwave ovens. The word *computer* spoke of someone who computed with a paper and pencil—certainly not the 640 K, 50 megabyte hard disk that I use on my computer. (Believe it or not, I have the whole Bible at my fingertips and can call up any verse or verses in the Bible in about 2 seconds.) But we are still in a hurry! We seem to have less time for spiritual things. We are so very busy.

It is not wrong to be busy; you are to be commended for your diligence. But it is wrong if you are too busy for the Lord. Do you have a daily quiet time with the Lord? When you take time to pray, read the Bible, and wait on the Lord—giving Him His rightful place—

hours are never lost. They are gained. It is essential in this fast-moving life to take the time to examine our relationship with the Lord.

"But seek ye first the kingdom of God, and his righteousness, and all these things shall be added unto you" (Matthew 6:33).

Strength for Growing: "Let the words of my mouth, and the meditation of my heart, be acceptable in thy sight, O LORD, my strength, and my redeemer" (Psalm 19:14).

Remember that you cannot meditate in a hurry. Meditation involves reflection. It demands time for the patient inspection of the Word and the equally patient application of it. The "words" and "meditation" in Psalm 19 do not indicate 3-minute distant conversations. It is "taking time to be holy" and giving quality time to our Savior, our Lord, and our Friend.

Give Your Face a Rest

"A whisper of a laugh" is the way someone has described a smile. No one would doubt that a genuine smile is of great value, but just how valuable is it? As a result of an automobile accident, a boy lost the power to smile. He was awarded $5,000 in damages. In another case, Judge Harold Canavan in Municipal Court in Boston awarded $10,000 to Mary Shafter, age 6, for "an injury that impaired her ability to smile." Monetary consideration aside, a smile has worth.

A smile is valuable to your well-being. Years ago as children we sang, "Smile awhile and give your face a rest." There's no doubt about it, a happy heart and a smiling face will do you a host of good physically. Someone humorously suggested that it also conserves energy. It takes 65 muscles to produce a frown, but 5 to bring a good healthy smile. The smile belongs exclusively to mankind. Gems can reflect light, but this can't be compared to the charm of a smile. Someone has written, "It is the prerogative of man. It is the color which love wears; it is the light in the windows of the face by which the heart signifies it is at home and waiting. A face that cannot smile is like a bud that cannot blossom and dries up on the stalk."

A smile enhances your appearance. It is superior to any cosmetic money can buy. Mark Twain said, "Wrinkles should merely indicate where the smiles have been. The best dressed man and woman are wearing a genuine smile."

A smile is valuable in helping others. Smiling is contagious. A friendly attitude and a hearty smile usually invite a smile from another. Scripture says, "A merry heart doeth good like a medicine" (Proverbs 17:22). A smile might come in the flash of a second and yet be permanently stored in one's memory forever. Even your enemies are on their way to defeat when you greet them with a good attitude and a smile. It is no mystery, either, that a man who is happy, optimistic, and smiling has more friends.

> The man whose face is long and grim,
> Will have few friends to cling to him;
> While he whose face is wreathed in smiles,
> Will have friends tagging him for miles.

A smile, when it is genuine, can help in your witness. We are reminded of a person doing visitation work for his church. He approached the door with his Bible, tracts, and a ready word of invitation. But he lacked a friendly smile. It is no wonder that the person answering the door took one look at him and said, "Thanks, but I have enough troubles of my own." You can let your light shine before men with your smile.

So when you get dressed in the morning, put on a smile. It will be beneficial to you, encouraging to your fellow Christians, a witness to your unsaved friends, and glorifying to God.

"Smile awhile and give your face a rest."

 Strength for Growing: "I will bless the LORD at all times; his praise shall continually be in my mouth. My soul shall make her boast in the LORD; the humble shall hear of it, and be glad. Oh, magnify the LORD with me, and let us exalt his name together" (Psalm 34:1-3).

We must be careful that we do not equate a holy life with a person who has a "sound-proof head," refuses to listen to anybody and who, if the truth were known, just doesn't like people. Isolation and a sour disposition are not signs of holiness. They are frequently signs of pride and arrogance. A holy Christian is a happy Christian who shows it in many ways.

Dickering

When the Romans bartered with the barbarians, one of the most desired commodities was fur. Ten pelts were a *decuria; decem* is the Latin for ten. From the ancient days, the *decuria* was recognized as the unit of fur trade. In 1526 a writer spoke of a *dyker* of hides tanned. Three hundred years later, the word was used for the action of bargaining or dickering—probably a haggling between traders and Indians over a *dicker* of skins.

Now that we know the background of the word *dickering,* let's get a little more personal; moving from furs to bicycles and cars. Is it wrong to dicker and bargain? It seems to be the American way of life to dicker and outdo the other fellow. In some countries it is expected. Not to dicker, they say, is an insult to the merchant. I'm not sure about the source of this idea.

To dicker or not to dicker, that is the question. Nobody wants to get the reputation of being a tightwad, making an issue over every sale. We've all heard about the man who is so closefisted that he only gives you one finger when he shakes your hand. Or the one who keeps $10 bills folded so long that Hamilton gets ingrown whiskers. But how far do you go in this enterprising spirit?

A good question to ask is this: Is bargaining a hindrance to my testimony? While it seems right and proper to get a good value, and to speak up if we think an item is overpriced, it is also possible to be obnoxious in our dickering dealings. Should the person with whom you are bargaining suddenly discover you are a Christian—and it might be difficult at times—would it prove embarrassing?

Does God's Word speak on this subject? Yes, Scripture speaks of the man who bargains: "It is naught, it is naught, saith the buyer; but when he is gone his way, then he boasteth" (Proverbs 20:14). Translated in our modern language the verse is speaking of a man who dares to dicker, claiming that the asking price is too much. But when the bargain is consummated he leaves, stating, "Boy, did I get him!"

While we should try to use our money wisely, a good policy would be to bargain honestly. And be careful that even here you don't find yourself marring your testimony. You can be sincere and honest, yet not be tactful.

So don't "get your fur up" when I suggest that you ask the Lord to give you wisdom and discernment in your dickering. Otherwise in your bargaining, you might be the loser.

 **Strength for Growing:** "Let your light so shine before men, that they may see your good works, and glorify your Father, who is in heaven" (Matthew 5:16).

"For ye were sometimes darkness, but now are ye light in the Lord; walk as children of light" (Ephesians 5:8).

The idea that "no man is an island" is certainly true with believers. We do not live unto ourselves. We will reflect favorably or unfavorably on our Lord. He is "the light of the world" (John 8:12), and we are to reflect Him in everything. While "dickering" can be fun, and is expected, especially in other countries, we need to be careful that every act and action reflects Christ in a becoming way.

A Bar o' Soap

Even since we were small children, our parents (usually our mothers) told us, "Be sure to wash your hands!"

It is no wonder that the annual per capita consumption of soap in the United States is about 40 pounds. Of course, that includes washing clothes and shampooing hair—among other things. But still, that's quite a lot of soap compared to Russia, where 14 pounds of soap per person is used each year. Cleanliness is pretty important in the U.S.A.

While soap has been known for 2300 years, the first English soapmakers appeared at the end of the twelfth century in Bristol. Soap was highly taxed, and at one time in the history of England, tax collectors locked lids on the pans every night to prevent "under cover" production. Apparently they felt that the clean up people were going to clean up financially with some dirty doings!

In the nineteenth century, a German chemist by the name of Justus von Liebig said that the quantity of soap consumed by a nation was an accurate measure of its wealth and civilization.

Soap is mentioned only twice in the Bible. When God warned backslidden Judah of her sins, He said, "For though thou wash thee with nitre, and take thee much soap, yet thine iniquity is marked before me, saith the Lord God" (Jeremiah 2:22). The Lord seems to be saying that they were so willful in their sins that it would take more than soap and water to cleanse what was wrong with them.

Soap is mentioned the second time in the last book of the Old Testament, Malachi. "But who may abide the day of his coming? And who shall stand when he appeareth? For he is like a refiner's fire, and like a fuller's soap" (Malachi 3:2). This is an obvious reference to judgment in a coming day. The word *fuller* means "to trample." The only washing machine that women of the East knew in Bible times was their hands and feet. The cycles were rather different then—human agitators took their turns in the laundry work. But don't miss the point! God is saying in Malachi that there is going to be a trampling work of the Lord in judgment. God has a final remedy for the soil of sin. A day of reckoning is coming!

How wonderful it is to know that the Lord has a cleansing remedy today for any who will come to Him. There is a condition among us that cannot be cured by the finest detergent; it is the condition of sin. The only hope for cleansing is in the work of Christ. "The blood of Jesus Christ, his Son, cleanseth us from all sin" (1 John 1:7).

The average junior-higher has about 3,500 square inches of skin (and a billion pores or openings). But we are talking about a cleansing far beneath the skin—a heart cleansing. (Read Mark 7:21-23.) David prayed, "Wash me thoroughly from mine iniquity, and cleanse me from my sin" (Psalm 51:2). Again, "Purge me with hyssop, and I shall be clean; wash me, and I shall be whiter than snow" (Psalm 51:7).

After we come to Christ as Savior, having been cleansed by His blood, we still need a daily cleansing. "Wherewithal shall a young man cleanse his way? By taking heed thereto according to thy word" (Psalm 119:9). Christ talked about this cleansing when He washed His disciples' feet. When He came to Peter, Peter said, "Thou shalt never wash my feet." Christ answered, "If I wash thee not, thou hast no part with me." (See John 13:8.) Christ was saying, in effect, "It is important that you get your feet washed in the Word. If you don't, you lose fellowship with Me."

God's remedy for sin in a believer's life is the Word of God. Whether or not Liebig was right when he measured wealth by the quantity of soap, one thing is sure—the measure of our fellowship and usefulness depends on a washing of our spiritual lives before we begin our daily walk. So in the morning, when you reach for your favorite soap, don't forget to reach for your Bible. Clean Christians are the most useful Christians.

 Strength for Growing: "Wherewithal shall a young man cleanse his way? By taking heed thereto according to thy word" (Psalm 119:9).

"That he might sanctify and cleanse it with the washing of water by the word" (Ephesians 5:26).

While we are not of the world, we are in the world and are liable to get our feet soiled. We need to get them washed in the "water of the Word." It is impossible to "walk worthy of the vocation wherewith we are called" (Ephesians 4:1) without this daily cleansing. To "walk as He walked" (1 John 2:6) demands our being "in touch" with the Father as He was. God's means of doing this is through His Word.

The Lion in Your Room

You were looking for a nice place to rent, and the way it looked you were going to have it. You had found it hard to believe, but you ran across this 20-room place. The rent was only $100 a month. Incredible! Each bedroom had a full bath. There was a recreation room and everything else your heart desired. Imagine, 20 rooms for only $100!

But the deal fell through. You knew something like this would happen. In making the final arrangements and signing the papers, the real estate man casually stated that there were actually 21 rooms in the house. "Actually," he said, "you are getting 20 rooms for a song. I didn't think you would mind if one room was reserved and used by the owner of the house."

Even that didn't seem too bad until he said the owner wanted to keep his pet lion in that room. Obviously, the deal was off.

A preposterous story? Perhaps, but it does have a point. If you can understand why you wouldn't accept such a "good bargain," you might have some idea why the Lord is not interested in being Lord of just part of your life.

The Bible says, "But sanctify the Lord God in your hearts, and be ready always to give an answer to every man that asketh you a reason of the hope that is in you, with meekness and fear" (1 Peter 3:15).

Literally, the passage says, "Sanctify Christ in your heart as Lord ..." To recognize the lordship of Christ is to let Him have every room of your heart-house, every room of your life. Sometimes we are willing to give Him all except a closet or two, or a room where we keep our "pet lion." If any area of our lives is off limits to the Lord, or if any part of our time schedule fails to include Him, we are failing to let Him be "Lord of all." It may sound trite, but it's still true that He will be Lord of all, or He will not be Lord at all.

Only when we are willing to let Him be "Lord of every room" will we be ready to give an answer to everyone who asks us a reason for our hope. As a matter of fact, it will not even be necessary for us to tell people where we stand. Once we let Him be Lord of all, people will be asking about it. They will recognize that there is something different, even without our volunteering to tell them.

Full surrender is what He wants! So deal with that lion in your house—whatever it is. Then surrender the "whole place" to Him, letting Him have freedom, access, and the last word in every area of your life. This is full surrender. Only then will you be supremely happy.

 Strength for Growing: "Neither yield ye your members as instruments of unrighteousness unto sin, but yield yourselves unto God, as those that are alive from the dead, and your members as instruments of righteousness unto God" (Romans 6:13).

Is there any area in your life that is not yielded to Him? Can you really say that as far as you can tell in your own heart, He is really Lord, and Lord of ALL? It is still true, "He will be Lord of all, or He will not be Lord at all."

Your Quickness of Scent

Someone has suggested that the one feature of the body everybody "overlooks" is the nose.

I suppose there is no part of the body that draws as much attention and is used more in jest than the part that snoops, snubs, and sneezes. Humorous puns about the nose abound. Like, "The nose is in the middle of the face because it is the scenter."

Beyond the joke and jest about the nose is its more serious function—the sense of smell. In his book, *The Wonders of the Human Body*, Dr. R. I. Brown points out some of the intricate wonders of this God-given sense. He says, "In your nose, high up at the top where the smell machine resides, there are many small cells from which wires or nerves pass right through the bony ceiling, which is the floor of the skull. These wires bear hairs of extreme thinness."

He continues, "The particles thrown off from the odorous material bang into the hairs, causing them to vibrate like the prongs of a tuning fork."

He then explains that the moisture in the nasal cavity dissolves the chemical which comes with the odor. The smell is made on the records of the central office, which we call memory. When you once smell violets, you never forget the smell because its records are permanent. This sense is so acute we can detect one eighty-millionth of a grain of musk, and one four-hundred-sixty-billionth of a grain of mercaptan, which smells like garlic. Truly, this is a wonderful part of the human body!

God often uses the senses to declare spiritual truth. The Bible refers to hearing with our spiritual ears and seeing with our eyes of understanding.

The nose might be considered a picture of the spiritual discernment that God gives his own. This organ tells the difference between that which is alive or dead, spoiled or good.

It is interesting to note in the Old Testament that a son of Aaron whose nose was broken could not serve as a priest (Leviticus 21:18). While it didn't affect his sonship, it did affect his service as a priest of God. Failure to be able to sense and discern between the spoiled and the good made him ineligible to serve in divine matters.

God wants us to be able to "discern between the righteous and the wicked, between him that serveth God and him that serveth him not" (Malachi 3:18). This discerning power comes through right relationship to the Spirit of God. Spiritual things are "spiritually discerned" (1 Corinthians 2:14).

The indwelling Spirit, when given complete control of our lives, will sharpen that sense of discernment. He reveals to us the true difference and values of life through the Word. The Bible "is a discerner of the thoughts and intents of the heart" (Hebrews 4:12).

This does not mean that a spiritual Christian is entitled to set himself up as a judge of evil for others. Nor does it give him the right to snoop and involve himself in others' business. It does mean that he is able to make right choices that relate to his everyday Christian living.

In the epistle to the Philippians, Paul prayed that their lives might abound ". . . yet more and more in knowledge and in all judgment [or quickness of scent]" (Philippians 1:9). He refers to that sensitive perception that would prevent love from doing, saying and thinking the wrong thing.

Often in the guise of "showing our love," we are urged by the world to compromise our stand. A keen spiritual sense of discernment will help gear and direct our love.

Well does Guy King say, "A spiritual sense of smell is of greater importance, and is both beneficial to love and endowed by love."

One who possesses this "quickness of scent" will be able not only to distinguish between the good and the bad, but the good and the best. He can then "approve things that are excellent" (Philippians 1:10).

With this divine discernment he puts to the test "things which differ" and makes right and proper judgments. A daily exposure to the Word of God and a constant subjection to the Holy Spirit will assure this keenness of scent and discernment in this present world!

 Strength for Growing: "For the word of God is quick, and powerful, and sharper than any two-edged sword, piercing even to the dividing asunder of soul and spirit, and of the joints and marrow, and is a discerner of the thoughts and intents of the heart" (Hebrews 4:12).

Of course, I do have scriptural warrant for speaking of a spiritual nose. In 1 Corinthians 12:1, Paul writes of those who are, as it were, spiritual feet, spiritual hands, spiritual ears, and spiritual eyes. Though he shrinks from naming some as nasal men, he does imply their existence in his phrase, "If the whole were hearing, where were the smelling?" (v. 17). Let it be freely acknowledged that, in the course of the centuries, the church has had reason to be grateful for her spiritual noses (like Athanasius and Luther).

Take Time

I would like to get more involved in my church, but I just don't have the time. Familiar words? Of course. Let's think about taking time for the things that are really important. We all have the same amount of time. Someone has said, "Footprints in the sands of time were not made sitting down?" So, if you are going to do what is really important and have no regrets in the days to come, you should take time.

> Take time to work—it is the price of
> success.
> Take time to think—it is the source of
> power.
> Take time to play—it is the secret of
> perpetual youth.
> Take time to read—it is the foundation of
> wisdom.
> Take time to worship—it is the highway to
> reverence.
> Take time to be friendly—it is the road to
> happiness.
> Take time to dream— it is hitching one's
> wagon to a star.
> Take time to love and be loved— it is the
> privilege of the gods.
> Take time to live—it is one secret of
> success.
> Take time for friendship—it is a source of
> happiness.
> Take time to laugh—it helps lift life's load.
> Take time to pray—it helps to bring Christ
> near, and washes the dust of earth from
> our eyes.
> Take time to be holy—for without holiness
> no man shall see the Lord.
> Take time for God—it is life's only lasting
> investment.

I think that item from the *Hawkinsville Dispatch News* is worth remembering. Take time!

You know, there is a familiar hymn that says it in an even lovelier way. You know it well.

> Take time to be holy, speak oft with thy Lord;
> Abide in Him always, and feed on His Word.

Make friends of God's children; help those who are weak;
　Forgetting in nothing His blessing to seek.
Take time to be holy, let Him be thy Guide,
　And run not before Him, whatever betide;
In joy or in sorrow, still follow thy Lord,
　And, looking to Jesus, still trust in His Word.
　　　　　　　　　　　—William Longstaff

 Strength for Growing: "Wherefore, he saith, Awake thou that sleepest, and arise from the dead, and Christ shall give thee light. See, then, that ye walk circumspectly, not as fools but as wise, Redeeming the time, because the days are evil. Wherefore, be ye not unwise but understanding what the will of the Lord is" (Ephesians 5:14-17).

It was Edward H. Griggs who said that 15 minutes a day devoted to one definite study will make one a master in a dozen years. Such a consistent application to any given subject would make you an expert on that subject. Think that one through. Is it not also true spiritually? Fifteen minutes a day *with the Master* would give us a deepened and broadened spiritual life *for the Master*.

Think on These Things

"As a man thinketh in his heart, so is he" (Proverbs 23:7).

As unsaved people, our thought life was controlled by sin (Mark 7:21, 22). When Christ died, we died, and the power of Satan over us was broken (Hebrews 2:14). Therefore, we are to gird up our mind (1 Peter 1:13) and bring our thoughts into captivity (2 Corinthians 10:4, 5). Our minds are renewed (Romans 12:1-3), and we are to set our minds on heavenly things (Colossians 3:1, 2). We can do this through daily meditation on the Word of God.

Psychiatrist Paul Meier said, "Daily meditation on the principles of life passed on from man's loving Creator is more important for his health than food, sex, or any other factor. Many of my anxious, depressed, and even suicidal patients are born-again believers who have not yet been taught how to appropriate personally God's thought patterns and behavioral principles as outlined in the Bible. They have learned to think negative, self-critical, and destructive thoughts. They have become accustomed to behavior patterns that result in increased guilt, insecurity, and feeling of insignificance."

In a study of seminary students, psychologists tested three groups:

Group A - Those with exceptionally good mental health and high level of maturity.

Group B - Those with apparently normal mental health and maturity.

Group C - Those with statistically significant psychological conflict and emotional pain.

Commenting on the findings of that research, Dr. Meier said, "Those seminary students who had been Christians for many years were only slightly healthier and happier than those who had accepted Christ in the past one or two years. My disappointment turned to joy when I learned one of the most valuable lessons of my life. I found the factor that made the difference—meditation on Scripture. Students who practiced almost daily Scripture meditation for three years or longer were significantly healthier and happier than students who did not meditate on Scripture daily.

"Renewing of the mind comes from various sources: confrontation by loving friends, therapy with a Christian professional counselor, conviction from the Holy Spirit, confrontation with scriptural principles in sermons or seminars, and daily meditation on Scripture.

"Renewing of the mind is the continual process, a progressive sanctification requiring continual, preferably daily, input from God's Word.

"Daily meditation on Scripture, with personal application, is the most effective means of obtaining personal joy, peace, and emotional maturity.

"On the average, it takes about three years of daily Scripture meditation to bring about change in a person's thought patterns.

"None of the students in Group C were presently meditating on Scripture daily, although some were reading their Bible regularly as a textbook for their classes."

The solution is simple: Get into the Word every day! Meditate on it and pray for guidance. Be in church where you can hear the Word and think on it. Dr. Meier concludes, "If Christians meditate in such a manner for 30 minutes morning and evening, they would probably experience a greater knowledge of Scripture, greater personal application of scriptural principles, greater understanding of who God is, lower blood pressure and other beneficial physiological responses, longer life of usefulness for the Lord, greater ability to passively resist anxieties of the day, and greater awareness of unconscious truths about their blindspots as they become less afraid of the truth."

 Strength for Growing: "My soul shall be satisfied as with marrow and fatness, and my mouth shall praise thee with joyful lips, when I remember thee upon my bed, and meditate on thee in the night watches" (Psalm 63:5, 6).

Meditation is not something that is simply done at specific, appointed times. While habitual, regular seasons set aside for meditation are good, even in the "night seasons" when we can't sleep, or in long stretches of driving in the car or waiting at the airport, we can be occupied with the Lord. Instead of being frustrated, we can gain great spiritual blessings and strength.

Forty Winks

I feel so much better if sometimes in the mid-afternoon I can have 40 winks. How about you? I don't apologize for feeling that way; I have some pretty impressive company who felt the same way. Winston Churchill, for instance, was a napper.

But that little phrase, *40 winks*. Ever wonder where it came from? Of course, it means a little snooze—a short nap. Let me give you background about when it first showed up in print.

Ever hear of the *Thirty-nine Articles?* Well, it refers to 39 articles of faith that make up the doctrine of the Church of England. It is a document the clergy were required to accept. Parliament took the action back in 1571 during the reign of Elizabeth I. It was 100 years later, on November 16, 1872, that a writer in the magazine *Punch* wrote, "If a . . . man, after reading through the *Thirty-nine Articles,* were to take 40 winks . . ." That is the first record of that many winks. Thirty-nine articles and 40 winks—rather clever.

Now, this leads me to ask whether or not you are ready for 40 winks after sitting through 60 minutes of a church service or 30 minutes of a sermon. If so, what do you think it means? Well, some would suggest that if a person takes 40 winks in the middle of a sermon, the usher ought to get a long pole and poke the preacher. After all, he put the person to sleep. Maybe he should be prodded with a polite poke.

Okay, I'll go along with that—at least sometimes. I don't belong to the Society for the Protection of the Preacher. But let me suggest that a drowsy, languid, listless response, or 40 winks, could show a heart that is less than excited about the things of the Lord. Here are some suggestions to help you avoid 40 winks.

1. When you pray in the morning (Sunday morning- or any other time you are going to a service), ask the Lord to show you some special truth by which to live.
2. Go to church or Sunday school expecting such a blessing.
3. Carry your Bible with you. Look up the passages the pastor refers to and take part in the process. Be an active learner, not a passive one.
4. Look for personal nuggets for your own life. Accentuate the positive, not the negative. Don't pay attention to the response of others; get into the message.
5. Take notes as the pastor preaches. Then plan to transcribe them more clearly when you get home.

6. Try and find ways to use the information you have received. Teach it to others. By claiming this ownership, you will become a better listener.

Thirty-nine Articles or Forty Winks? Just be sure that when the Word of God is opened you remember it is the Word of God to you.

 Strength for Growing: "For the time will come when they will not endure sound doctrine but, after their own lusts, shall they heap to themselves teachers, having itching ears; and they shall turn away their ears from the truth, and shall be turned unto fables. But watch thou in all things, endure afflictions, do the work of an evangelist, make full proof of thy ministry" (2 Timothy 4:3-5).

How can it be that what is a spiritual treat to one is boring to the other? How can some get so excited about something spiritual while others find it banal and uninteresting? The answer is obvious. The speaker is the same, but there are different listeners. If we are not in tune spiritually, or if we are more interested in what is pleasant to the ears (as the carnal world would define pleasantness), it will have a significant effect on our attitude. Let's have an attitude check and read ourselves correctly.

Prayer: the Greater Work

One of the most talked-about subjects in the world, and yet one of the most neglected in practice, is prayer. Even though that is true, I still want to talk about it because it is so very important.

Prayer is talking to God. It is conversing with Him. It is a conversation with our heavenly Father as we approach Him in Jesus' name. It was practiced by Christ Himself—the greatest example of prayer. It was the secret of the moving, dynamic New Testament church as they boldly proclaimed the gospel.

I like this statement about prayer, made by an unknown writer, "The doorway into the secret place of the Most High is always open to the hand of need, and at the knocking of that hand only."

Recently, I wrote a letter to a very special group of friends of Grand Rapids Baptist College and Seminary. They are prayer partners of the college—people who pray for us. What a great congregation! What a blessed group! I give them requests about which to pray and tell them about students for whom they can pray. I share needs, and they pray. We knock together on heaven's door, and we pray together. Does it surprise you that a college and seminary asks people to pray for it? We have friends all over America who are praying for these precious students, for our faculty and administration. Maybe you will join them and pray for us—or for a Christian work in your community. We certainly need it. You know, "You cannot stumble if you are on your knees."

As much as I respect preaching, I find it interesting that the Bible doesn't say "preach all the time," but it says, "pray all the time" (1 Thessalonians 5:17). Oswald Chambers has written something special on prayer: "Prayer does not fit us for greater works; prayer is the greater work. We think of prayer as a common sense exercise of our higher powers in order to prepare us for God's work. In the teaching of Jesus Christ, prayer is the working of the miracle of redemption in others by the power of God."

Say, how are you on prayer? Or should I ask, Do you spend time with Him, every day in prayer? Or do you pray quick, one-line, formal prayers? Someone had said, "Life gets scorched and lumpy when we forget to stir it with prayer."

> Is your anemic, powerless prayer
> A prayer with no concern or care.
> Impatient prayer ending too soon
> Which never learns to importune?

Or, is yours academic prayer?
A "know how" prayer, the phrases there
Are choice and excellent in form,
Refusing heart and soul to warm.

Anemic, academic, each
Falls short of Heaven's reach.
One farce and quick to end,
The other form, quick to pretend.

Oh, give us, Lord, this needy hour,
A taste of active prayer, a power
That knocks at Heaven's doors, demands
And then receives from Your blest Hand.
—Charles U. Wagner

Strength for Growing: "I cried with my whole heart. Hear me, O LORD; I will keep thy statutes. I cried unto thee. Save me, and I shall keep thy testimonies. I prevented the dawning of the morning, and cried; I hoped in thy word. Mine eyes prevent the night watches, that I might meditate in thy word" (Psalm 119:145-148).

"When we rely on organization, we get what organization can do; when we rely on education, we get what education can do; when we rely upon eloquence, we get what eloquence can do; and so on. Nor am I disposed to undervalue any of these things in their proper place; but when we rely upon prayer, we get what God can do" (A.C. Dixon).

Your Sense of Humor

When I am visiting a church to fill the pulpit, I enjoy standing at the door after the message to shake hands with people as they leave. They often comment, "I appreciate your sense of humor." I'm sure they mean it, and I appreciate their saying so. I don't believe it is spiritual to be dull. Laughing is good for you and I enjoy it.

Believe it or not, J. Oswald Sanders lists humor as one of the qualities that is essential to spiritual leadership. I believe he's right. Here is what Sanders said, "Since man is in the image of God, his sense of humor is a gift of God and is found in His divine nature. But it is a gift which is to be controlled as well as cultivated. Clean, wholesome humor will relax tension and relieve a difficult situation more than anything else. It can be of untold value to a leader, both for what it does for him and for the use it can be in his work." Frankly, I enjoy hearing a speaker who has a twinkle in his eye. It is evident that he enjoys himself and others when he speaks and enjoys making people laugh.

Samuel Johnson once said, "A man should spend part of his time with the laughers." Agnes Strickland said, "Next to virtue, the fun of this world is what we can least spare."

Did you ever hear of anyone refer to "holy fun"? I have. This does not mean having fun at someone else's expense or delighting in putting others down. It is not shady or soiled fun in any way, but fun that is set apart and is wholesome and refreshing. The great Baptist preacher, Charles Spurgeon, was once scolded by someone for introducing humor in his preaching. With a twinkle in his eye he replied, "If only you knew how much I hold back, you would commend me." Should a person have a humorous touch in the pulpit? Spurgeon thought so. He wrote, "There are things in these sermons that may produce smiles, but what of them? The preacher is not quite sure about a smile being a sin, but at any rate he thinks it less a crime to cause momentary laughter than a half-hour of profound slumber."

So, dear friend, don't be hesitant to have a sense of humor. A. E. Norrish, missionary to India, said, "I have never met leadership without a sense of humor; this is the ability to stand outside oneself and one's circumstances, to see things in perspective and laugh. It is a great safety valve! You will never lead others far without the joy of the Lord and a sense of humor."

Strength for Growing: "To every thing there is a season, and a time to every purpose under the heaven: a time to weep, and a time to laugh; a time to mourn, and a time to dance" (Ecclesiastes 3:1, 4).

Take time to laugh and begin laughing with yourself. When we take ourselves too seriously, we become brittle and hard. Take time to laugh with children, for they develop the art very early. In your laughing, laugh *with* someone and not *at* someone. Laughter is good medicine because it is conducive to relaxation. One of the great differences between man and animals is that man has a God-given sense of humor. Cultivate it.

Open Wide Your Mouth

The name George Müller immediately brings to mind a childlike, implicit faith in the Lord, trusting Him for everything. On December 2, 1835, the first formal step was taken to open an orphan house. A. T. Pierson writes about those first days of trusting and looking to the Lord for guidance:

"Three days later, in reading the Psalms, he was struck with these nine words:

"Open thy mouth wide, and I will fill it" (Psalm 81:10). From that moment this text formed one of his great life-mottoes, and this promise became a power in molding all his work. Before this, he had not prayed for the supply of money or of helpers. But now he was led to apply this Scripture confidently to this new plan and at once boldly to ask for premises, for one thousand pounds in money, and for suitable helpers to take charge of the children. Two days after, he received, in furtherance of his work, the first gift of money—one shilling—and within two days more the first donation in furniture—a large wardrobe.

"The day came for the memorable public meeting—December 9. During the interval, Satan had been busy hurling at Mr. Müller his fiery darts, and he was very low in spirit. He was taking a step not to be retraced without both much humiliation to himself and reproach to his Master: and what if it were a misstep and he were moving without real guidance from above! But as soon as he began to speak, help was given him. He was borne up on the Everlasting Arms, and had the assurance that the work was of the Lord."

The rest of George Müller's life is living proof of this text. By 1898, seven day schools with 354 pupils had been established. The number of children in attendance from the beginning was 8,501. The number of orphans on Ashley Down during that period was 10,024. Almost two million Bibles and Scripture portions had been distributed.

God was good to His Word. Today, as in George Müller's day, the Lord delights in our childlike faith. He wants us to trust Him for our every need. God can meet your needs; He has promised to do so: "Open your mouth."

OPEN YOUR MOUTH

The hungry child whimpered in mother's arms,
Expressing that he wanted to be fed.
Her mother love was quick to sense his need:
It was prepared, "Open your mouth," she said.

The child of God in desperation prayed,
The need was great, He looked to God alone:
Remembering His words: "If a small child
Will ask for bread, would you then give a stone?"

And so, the Christian with a child-like faith,
Expressing each and every need, was led
Into a place of bountiful supply.
All was prepared, "Open your mouth," He said.
                                    —Charles U. Wagner

 Strength for Growing: "I am the Lord thy God, who brought thee out of the land of Egypt; open thy mouth wide, and I will fill it" (Psalm 81:10).

"Who satisfieth thy mouth with good things, so that thy youth is renewed like the eagle's" (Psalm 103:5.)

Two blessed things are accomplished here: 1) We are satisfied with His provision. The Lord satisfies! 2) Our youth is renewed. There is a special source of strength that comes from the Lord. Satisfaction is inward and involves that spiritual appetite. The renewal is a manifestation of that satisfaction and a practical outworking of it in obedient service.

Jehovah-jireh

Jehovah-jireh means "The Lord will provide" or "The Lord will see." The word *Jireh* is translated both ways, "to see" and "to provide." At first reflection, it might seem that the two English words used to translate *Jireh* are not very similar. Another English word for "see" is *vision* (from the Latin, *video*). Actually, what we have in this passage is both the vision and the provision of God. God looks upon us, sees our need, and then divinely intervenes. God's pre-vision is an assurance of God's pro-vision. It is inconceivable that God would view our problem without showing His power on our behalf.

Paul said it this way, "He that spared not his own Son, but delivered him up for us all, how shall he not with him also freely give us all things?" (Romans 8:32).

Now, what is included in these "all things" that He will provide? To be sure, it includes spiritual strength. "That he would grant you, according to the riches of his glory, to be strengthened with might by his Spirit in the inner man" (Ephesians 3:16). It also includes material things, whether it is the next meal or next month's payment coming due. "But my God shall supply all your need according to his riches in glory by Christ Jesus" (Philippians 4:19). Jehovah Jireh!

The best proof is the very Scripture from which we received our text. Abraham, who at long last had been blessed by a "miracle son," Isaac, was now commanded to do a most staggering thing. God had said, "Take now thy son, thine only son Isaac, whom thou lovest, and get thee into the land of Moriah; and offer him there for a burnt offering upon one of the mountains which I will tell thee of" (Genesis 22:2). In complete obedience, Abraham obeyed. After three days he said to his servants, "Abide ye here with the ass; and I and the lad will go yonder and worship, and come again to you" (v. 5). In those two verses we have the twin truths of trusting and obeying. He obeyed implicitly and trusted in the wisdom of the Lord, "accounting that God was able to raise him up, even from the dead" (Hebrews 11:19).

After arriving at the mountain, Abraham built an altar, laid the wood in order, and bound his son. As the blade of the knife flashed in the noonday sun, God intervened, saying, "Lay not thine hand upon the lad, neither do thou anything unto him; for now I know that thou fearest God, seeing thou hast not withheld thy son, thine only son from me" (Genesis 22:12). It was then that Abraham called the place *Jehovah-jireh*—the Lord will provide.

Winning Words for Daily Living

There are many lessons to be learned from this passage. If we obey God, trust Him, fear and love Him as we should—He will always show His hand, sometimes just in the "nick of time" and be *Jehovah-jireh* to us. This doesn't mean we will always be given detailed explanations as to what He plans to do tomorrow. The vision of the future is His, the provision is ours.

F.E. Marsh has written the following acrostic on Jehovah-jireh.

THE BELIEVER IS:

J - Justified by His grace (Romans 3:24)
E - Equipped by His armor (Ephesians 6:13)
H - Harbored by His presence (Proverbs 18:10)
O - Observed by His eyes (Psalm 34:15)
V - Vitalized by His life (Ephesians 2:5)
A - Assisted by His strength (Isaiah 41:10)
H - Honored by His Name (1 John 3:1)

J - Joined to Himself by His Spirit (1 Corinthians 12:13)
I - Inspired by His love (2 Corinthians 5:14)
R - Raised by His power (Ephesians 2:6)
E - Encouraged by His Word (Deuteronomy 31:6, 7)
H - Helped by His Spirit (Romans 8:26)

God's provisions are always available to those who trust Him.

> My feeble hope in miracles had waned,
> My faith that He would soon provide was strained;
> Then, prompted by His Spirit, my heart cried:
> Jehovah-jireh! My Savior will provide.
>
> My needs were great, but greater than my need
> Was He—Jehovah-jireh, so quick to heed
> And help, to hold, to hide me from the storm,
> And shelter through the darkest night till morn.
> —Charles U. Wagner

 Strength for Growing: "And I beheld, and I heard the voice of many angels round about the throne and the beasts and the elders, and the number of them was ten thousand times ten thousand, and thousands of thousands, saying with a loud voice, Worthy is the Lamb that was slain to receive power, and riches, and wisdom, and strength, and honour, and glory, and blessing" (Revelation 5:11, 12).

It Shall Be Done

The children of Israel had reached a crucial point in their wilderness journey. At Kadesh-barnea Moses sent spies into the land of Canaan to search out the land. The best from every tribe was sent, one man representing each tribe. After four days they returned and gave their report. The majority report was that the situation was hopeless.

They said, "And there we saw the giants, the sons of Anak, who come of the giants; and we were in our own sight as grasshoppers, and so we were in their sight" (Numbers 13:33). Caleb, however, representing the minority of two (Joshua and Caleb), said, "Let us go up at once, and possess it; for we are well able to overcome it" (Numbers 13:30). It was in that context that the Lord gave the above promise, "But my servant, Caleb, because he had another spirit with him, and hath followed me fully, him will I bring into the land whereinto he went; and his seed shall possess it" (Numbers 14:24).

The whole history of Israel wandering in the wilderness for 38 years is a history of unbelief. They were a backslidden nation. It is interesting and enlightening that in Hebrews 11, when God gives the "Honor Roll of Faith," He mentions Moses forsaking Egypt, then refers to the victory at Jericho. The whole thirty-eight years of wandering were passed over as though it did not take place. They were wasted, fruitless, abortive years.

Forty-five years later we find Caleb (now a man of 85) possessing his possessions. In Joshua 14, we hear him say, "Forty years old was I when Moses, the servant of the Lord, sent me from Kadesh-barnea to spy out the land; and I brought him word again as it was in my heart. Nevertheless my brethren who went up with me made the heart of the people melt; but I wholly followed the Lord my God" (Joshua 14:7, 8).

What a blessing Caleb is to our hearts! Now still a strong, robust man physically, he is also robust in his faith. He said, "As yet I am as strong this day as I was in the day that Moses sent me; as my strength was then, even so is my strength now, for war, both to go out, and to come in. Now, therefore, give me this mountain . . ." (Joshua 14:11, 12). Then the "old man" took the mountain where the giants were (see 15:14, 15).

God had promised Caleb and his seed the land. Caleb believed God and took it, enjoying the fruits of his victory. How gracious the Lord is and how true to His word. Let us "possess our possessions"

by faith. Let us dare to believe Him, take Him at His Word day-by-day. In faith we need to cry, "Give me this mountain!" Whether we are talking about the salvation of souls, the building of the church, the day-to-day necessities of life, or the understanding of spiritual truth, He will supply if we look to Him in faith.

Too many Christians are wandering in the wilderness of unbelief. They have come to Kadesh-barnea and faltered. They have eyes only for the giants and are defeated. They may even allow the sedative of the "majority report" to soothe their guilty conscience.

How much better to dare to be in the minority, yet still stand against the threatening giants, through the power of the Lord.

"Give me this mountain!" This is the language of faith that looks to the promise and cries, "It shall be done."

Strength for Growing: "Now faith is the substance of things hoped for, the evidence of things not seen. For by it the elders obtained a good report. Through faith we understand that the worlds were framed by the Word of God, so that things which are seen were not made of things which do appear" (Hebrews 11:1-3).

> Faith, mighty Faith the promise sees
> And looks to God alone;
> Laughs at impossibilities and cries,
> "It shall be done."
>
> And cries and cries, "It shall be done!"
> And cries and cries, "It shall be done!"
> Laughs at impossibilities, and cries:
> "It shall be done!"
> —Author unknown

Truth for Soaring

"...they shall mount up with wings as eagles;"
Isaiah 40:31

Wyrgan ... Wyrgan ... Wyrgan

Our English word *worry* comes from the old Anglo-Saxon word *wyrgan*. The word originally meant "to strangle or to choke." That was the way it was used back in 1606. Later (1779) it was used specifically for choking a person or an animal with a mouthful of food. Then, nearly a hundred years later it meant "to seize by the throat with the teeth and tear or lacerate; to kill or injure by biting or shaking." Charlotte Bronte wrote, "She bit me. . . . She worried me like a tigress."

This information about the background of the word gains new significance when we remember what worry does to us today. It "strangles and chokes." Nobody would look kindly on someone who would deliberately grab him by the neck and cut off his air supply. But we think nothing of choking ourselves spiritually and physically by allowing ourselves to worry. Worry seizes us, shakes us, and even devours us, yet we keep coming back for more.

What's worse, we tend to worry more about little things than about major concerns. Josh Billings said, "It is the little bits of things that fret and worry us; we dodge an elephant, but we can't a fly." Yes, it's the little things that give us trouble. Here's one way to prove that. Try and remember what you were worrying about one year ago today!

If worry is the problem, what is the solution? First, *we must recognize it for what it is: sin*. It is easier for us to deal with it if we can see it in this light.

It is a sin against the Lord because it means we are not willing to leave everything with Him. It is unbelief in disguise. Christ said, "Take no thought for your life, what ye shall eat, or what ye shall drink; nor yet for your body, what ye shall put on. Is not the life more than meat and the body than raiment?" (Matthew 6:25). Paul said, "Be careful [anxious] for nothing" (Philippians 4:6). People were no different in those days than they are today. They, like us, were prone to worry.

Then too, it is a sin against ourselves. There is no question about it, it will do us bodily harm. Ken Anderson writes, "Modern medical research has proved that worry breaks down resistance to disease. More than that, it actually diseases the nervous system—particularly that of the digestive organs and of the heart. Add to this the toll in unhappiness of sleepless nights and days void of internal sunshine, and you have a glimpse of the work this monster does in destroying the effectiveness of the human body."

The second part of the solution is *to confess all past worry to the Lord*. Tell Him you're sorry you failed to trust Him and look to Him instead of your circumstances. Then, in that prayer, commit your whole future to the Lord; turn your life over to Him. Here's how Hudson Taylor put it, "Let us give up our work, our plans, ourselves, our lives, our loved ones, our influence, our all, right into His hands. Then, when we have given all over to Him, there will be nothing left for us to be troubled about, or to make trouble about."

Paul has a formula too. It is, of course, God's formula. Try this: "Be careful for nothing, but in everything, by prayer and supplication with thanksgiving, let your requests be made known unto God. And the peace of God, which passeth all understanding, shall keep your hearts and minds through Christ Jesus" (Philippians 4:6, 7).

Once we are enveloped with the person of Jesus, empowered by His presence, and strengthened by His provision, we cannot be moved by external circumstances, large or small.

 Truth for Soaring: "Therefore, I say unto you, Take no thought for your life, what ye shall eat, or what ye shall drink; not yet for your body, what ye shall put on. Is not the life more than meat and the body than raiment? Behold the fowls of the air; for they sow not, neither do they reap, nor gather into barns, yet your heavenly Father feedeth them. Are ye not much better than they?" (Matthew 6:25, 26).

From Peter Marshall, former Chaplain of the United States Senate, comes this powerful prayer:

"Help us to do our very best this day and be content with today's troubles, so that we shall not borrow the troubles of tomorrow. Save us from the sin of worrying, lest stomach ulcers be the badge of our lack of faith. Amen."

His Eminent Domain

As citizens of the United States, we are subject to its laws and regulations. One of those laws deals with *eminent domain*. This is the sovereign right of a government to take private property for public use without asking permission of the owner. For example, this law would come into force if part of your property was needed for a post office, a military camp, a freeway, or some other public necessity. Of course, the Constitution provides that adequate compensation be made to the owner of property taken under eminent domain.

According to one authority, "Eminent domain is based on the principle that an individual's private interest should not be permitted to stand in the way of the interest of the entire community in which he lives."

There is a similar principle that works in the Christian life. We are citizens of heaven, subject to the regulations and principles of God's laws. Paul said, "For our conversation [citizenship] is in heaven, from which also we look for the Savior, the Lord Jesus Christ" (Philippians 3:20). As a result, God has the right to eminent domain in our lives. He has the right to do with us what He pleases without even asking.

It could be that we have some very strong ideas about what we want to do with our lives. But suddenly our designs are interrupted by His plans, which are quite different from ours. Perhaps something we had decided to use for personal comfort was designed by Him as a training ground for the development of a Christian soldier. Or our plans may have called for extended areas of rest and leisure, only to find that these areas of our lives had been confiscated by Him for purposes of trial and testing. We are quick to complain, until the Holy Spirit directs our minds to the constituted authority of the Scripture. We read, "That in all things He might have the pre-eminence" (Colossians. 1:18). That means He has eminent domain!

Human government, subject as it is to error, has probably taken advantage of its constitutional provision of eminent domain. But we can rest assured that our sovereign Lord will never take advantage of us. And He compensates us grandly when He overrules our wills and plans. He turns the backyards of our lives with its patches of weeds into the lovely landscaping of His will and purpose. And He takes our strong bodies and sometimes allows them to be weak, so we might learn the meaning of real strength. We learn what Paul meant when he said, "For when I am weak, then am I strong" (2 Corinthians 12:10).

How rewarding to see the Lord take the backroads of our plot of cherished "ground of life" and by His skillful divine engineering, design a freeway which, when finished, will add to the effectiveness of our lives. Only when we stop holding out and protesting His sovereign prerogative in every area of our lives do we begin to appreciate the fact that His way and plan is best.

> I give, O Lord, this life of mine,
>   With all its self-made goals and plans,
> Relinquishing my 'private rights,'
>   Submissive, now to your commands.
>
> Take now, that portion of my life,
>   So long, in selfish greed, I claimed,
> All things of mine, I count but loss—
>   Subject to His eminent domain.
> —Charles U. Wagner

 Truth for Soaring: "For by him were all things created, that are in heaven, and that are in earth, visible and invisible, whether they be thrones, or dominions, or principalities, or powers—all things were created by him, and for him; and he is before all things, and by him all things consist. And he is the head of the body, the church; who is the beginning, the firstborn from the dead, that in all things he might have the preeminence" (Colossians 1:16-18).

Are we willing for Him to be sovereign in every area of our life today, with no reservations? To be "Lord of all" is what He demands. Blessings always follow a yielded life.

Where Are Your Sins?

Twelve of the world's twenty highest mountains can be found between the Indian peninsula and the land mass of China and Russia. It's often called the rooftop of the world. The highest of these mountains is Mt. Everest, the top of which was not reached until Sir Edmund Hillary and Tenzing Norgay scaled it in 1953. To think of a mountain more than five miles high staggers the imagination!

It's even more staggering to contemplate the depths of the oceans! If you could drop Mt. Everest into a certain place in the ocean called the Marianas Trench, the 29,028-foot summit of Everest would be covered by more than a mile of ocean water! No wonder the Lord used the depth of the sea to describe His forgiveness of the believer's sins: ". . . Thou wilt cast all their sins into the depths of the sea" (Micah 7:19).

Not only does the Lord use a vertical dimension to describe the banishment of our sins, but He also gives a horizontal one. "As far as the east is from the west, so far hath he removed our transgressions from us" (Psalm 103:12).

It was Rudyard Kipling who said, "Oh, East is East, and West is West, and never the twain shall meet." While there are certain points called North and South at the poles, there is no such geographical designation for the East or West. That's how far the Lord has removed our transgression!

While provision of forgiveness has been made for all men, only those who trust Christ as Savior have the actual assurance of sins forgiven. The next time you see the sun rising in the East and setting in the West, or when you consider the depths of the seas, remember that God has used both dimensions to assure you of the absolute banishment of your sin.

WAY—TRUTH—LIFE

Oh, wandering soul so prone to search
    And in bewildered searching stray
To darker mazes of confusion;
    Turn thou now to Christ, the Way.

Oh, searching soul, who sought in vain
    Philosophers from days of youth;
From disappointments' depths now turn
    In sweet relief to Christ, the Truth.

Winning Words for Daily Living

Soul, physically alive and yet
  So dead in sin and bent on strife;
Know now the quickening power of Him
  Who through His conquering death is Life.
The Way—Be reconciled to God;
  The Truth—Illuminations given;
The Life—regenerating power;
  These three, in Christ from Heaven.
                              —Charles U. Wagner

 Truth for Soaring: "For as the heavens are high above the earth, so great is his mercy toward them that fear him. As far as the east is from the west, so far hath he removed our transgressions from us" (Psalm 103:11,12).

In God's eyes, a sin forgiven is a sin forgotten—forever!

Whiter Than Snow

Looking out the window of my study in the winter, I often see everything blanketed with snow. Because this "white, fluffy stuff" could possibly interfere with my daily plans, I may begin to wonder about the purpose of it all. Why is the Lord so pleased to send it?

Heavy snow is not unusual in Michigan, but it is still often unexpected. Isn't that the way it is with a great many things in life? Surprises come and we are not always prepared for them. "It really isn't supposed to do this!" we exclaim. Sometimes everything is either slowed up or closed down because of the snow.

Such language isn't new for some. They know about the unexpected—the storm that comes when things looked so bright. Some of our shut-in friends could give the rest of us a lesson or two on the value and importance of not questioning His will and power but rather yielding to it.

There are real lessons to be learned as we view the snow falling. Here are some:

1. *The Lesson of the Power of God Over the Elements.* " . . . Great things doeth he, which we cannot comprehend. For he saith to the snow, Be thou on the earth . . ." (Job 37:5, 6). The snow that falls shows the greatness and power of our Lord. His purposes and plans are different from ours. He controls the elements, and we ought to learn this lesson. Without questioning, we should submit to His will or power.

2. *The Lesson of the Hidden Treasures in Common Things.* When the Lord answered Job out of the whirlwind, He said, "Hast thou entered into the treasures of the snow?" (Job 38:22).

   People who study these things tell us that each snowflake has its own perfect design and that there are no two alike. Such is the beauty and uniqueness of design from the Lord's hand. To see it in its abundance as we Northerners see it makes it rather common and dreaded. But in the very commonest and sometimes most dreaded of matters the Lord is able to show His hand of design. How we ought to be careful not to overlook the little treasures in the experiences God sends. Not to be moved by the storm but to be quick to see the beauty of God's gifts to us is an important lesson.

3. *The Lesson of God's Forgiving Grace.* Twice the word *snow* is used in the Scripture to denote the work of the Lord for us in forgiving sins. Both times it is used in a symbolic sense. After his ter-

rible sin, David prayed, "Purge me with hyssop, and I shall be clean; wash me, and I shall be whiter than snow" (Psalm 51:7). David must have remembered the familiar snow on the tops of the mountains of Lebanon or the banks of snow in the valleys of the northern slopes even in the summer. He was a man of the fields and might have remembered earlier days when he saw the pure white snow near the mountain caves during the winter time. When thinking of the power of the Lord to cleanse Him of sin, he becomes aware that the Lord's cleansing hand can make Him whiter than the brightest snow.

And we hear the prophet Isaiah plead with a message from the Lord: "Come now, and let us reason together, saith the Lord: though your sins be as scarlet, they shall be as white as snow; though they be red like crimson, they shall be as wool" (Isaiah 1:18). How great is our God to take sinners and save us by His grace and cleanse us by His blood. Whiter than snow! So rejoice with us. What relief to know that we are right with God. As we look out from our homes and see the snow piled high in our driveways, let it be God's object lesson to us today. Thank Him for His power and His design in common things, but most of all for that power and design demonstrated in providing for us this "so great salvation."

Truth for Soaring: "Purge me with hyssop, and I shall be clean; wash me, and I shall be whiter than snow" (Psalm 51:7).

Psalm 51 describes the lowest day in David's life. Although he had committed the awful sin of adultery and was guilty of murder, he found forgiveness. The joy of his salvation was restored (Psalm 51:12). What a great and forgiving God we have!

Go Fly a Kite

There was a time when I didn't mind someone telling me to "go fly a kite." I remember well some of those March days in Michigan, where I lived when I was young. The gang would all get together to fly kites. The corner store sold them for just a few cents, and Dad would often help me put it together. There was a certain secret in getting just the right tension on the cross string. Also, the loop in the front had to be just so, as did the tail of the kite. Mother would give me old rags to tie on my masterpiece. They couldn't be too heavy; not just any old rag would do. And, of course, the twine had to be new and fresh. It was always a disappointment to find that the twine was so old that it would break after getting my dream kite in the sky.

However, there was one more ingredient that was absolutely necessary. You could have the most artistic touch in the construction of the kite and the finest of material, as well as a huge vacant lot from which to operate, and still not be a successful "kite pilot." The one ingredient that was most important was the wind. Without a good blustery wind, kite construction skills are worthless.

There was something else I noticed. A kite doesn't rise with the wind, but against it. The greater the opposing wind, the greater the possibility for a soaring kite in the tall blue sky.

Isn't life like that? Sometimes we have what we feel to be all the ingredients for a successful Christian life. Having been saved, we know from the blessed Word of God all the privileges of the believer. We have a good church, friends who care about us, and a place where we can be actively engaged in Christian service. Then the Lord sends some opposition and difficulty which, at the time, seems so unnecessary. What we don't realize is that the Lord, in order to make us all that He wants us to be, sends an opposing wind our way. He wants us to soar to heights beyond the mediocre.

Like the string, the kite, and the tail, everything is there. The vacant lot and the know-how are all available. But the winds—blustery, contrary, and unpredictable—make the difference between victory and defeat.

Something else I learned when kite flying. Always have enough string. The opposing winds would come to carry my kite so high I could hardly see it. Then, to my dismay, I would run out of string. With my child's imagination I had thought there was no limit to how high I could have climbed. But I had limited myself.

The degree of success we have in letting the winds of our difficulties take us to new spiritual heights depends on our readiness to trust God by faith. How often we limit ourselves. Like a great many kite flyers, we get just a few feet off the ground, wildly careen back and forth, and come crashing to the ground.

Yes, the winds of adversity plus our readiness to receive them adds up to success—with kites and with Christians.

Truth for Soaring: "And it came to pass, when the sun did rise, that God prepared a vehement east wind; and the sun beat upon the head of Jonah, that he fainted, and wished in himself to die, and said, It is better for me to die than to live" (Jonah 4:8).

A whale, a gourd, and an east wind—all prepared by God to teach Jonah about Himself. The prophet needed to realize—and so do we—that God sends stormy winds to lift us up, not drag us down.

A Sweet Mirage?

It was William Wetmore Story who wrote:

> Give me the old enthusiasm back,
>   Give me the ardent longings that I lack,
> The glorious dreams that fooled me in my youth,
>   The sweet mirage that lured me on it track,
> And take away the bitter, barren truth.
>   Ah, yes! Success, I fear, has come too late!

Story expresses what many feel. They would prefer the "sweet mirage" that lures, over the "bitter barren truth."

What is a mirage? Well, have you ever driven on a paved road in the summer and, while looking ahead, noticed what looked like a distant pool of water? You were probably seeing a mirage.

What gave you a smile of amusement on a highway could well be an awful disappointment in the desert for some desperate, thirsty person whose mirage looked like an oasis. In either case the cause is the same. Warm air refracts light rays from the sky toward the viewers eyes, resulting in a mirage.

Life is full of mirages. Something in the distance may seem so promising and alluring, only to be disappointingly unreal. While some may prefer to be fooled because of the joy that comes in thinking something is there, the price one pays when reality shows its ugly head hardly makes the sweet mirage worthwhile.

Once in a while we hear well-meaning Christians say, "I know that the Lord is real and that heaven is certain; however, if I were to find that it is not true after all, it was still worth it, because I found real happiness in this life."

This is absolutely unsatisfactory! Our faith is not built on "I hope so" or "I'm willing to take the chance."

Paul said, "If Christ be not raised, your faith is vain, ye are yet in your sins. Then they also who are fallen asleep in Christ are perished. If in this life only we have hope in Christ, we are of all men most miserable" (1 Corinthians 15:17-19). Then, with a delightful fixed finality, he said, "But now is Christ risen from the dead and become the firstfruits of them that slept" (v. 20).

Our choice is not between the "bitter truth" and the "sweet mirage." Our faith is built on Christ, who is the Truth. The people of the world grasp their fanciful melancholy dreams as they look to the future from their barren present, only to find them unreal. But our faith has found a resting place in the reality of a living Christ.

Christ is alive! Christ is alive and aware of our needs! He will come again to receive us unto Himself. This is not a vapory mirage. It's a living reality.

 Truth for Soaring: "For I am persuaded that neither death, nor life, nor angels, nor principalities, nor powers, nor things present, nor things to come, nor height, nor depth, nor any other creature, shall be able to separate us from the love of God, which is in Christ Jesus, our Lord" (Romans 8:38, 39).

"For the which cause I also suffer these things; nevertheless, I am not ashamed; for I know whom I have believed and am presuaded that he is able to keep that which I have committed unto him against that day" (2 Timothy 1:12).

Christians are not dreamers who find sweetness in a misty, foggy unknown. We don't trust the promise of a reality rather than reality itself. We are anchored in Christ, our living Savior and Lord. We have a "know so" salvation.

You and Your Depth of Field

Every amateur photographer knows the meaning of depth of field. It means that if you are taking a picture of a person, good depth of field would show not only the person in the foreground in focus but also the background.

Good depth of field provides a clear picture of not only the person, but the trees a hundred yards away and the mountains in the distant background. A picture that has no depth of field would be one where the person is in focus and everything else is vague and fuzzy. While good depth of field is often desired in pictures in which you want to emphasize the background, you might want the person to be emphasized and the background de-emphasized, so as not to detract from your subject.

If you have a camera with different lenses you can do this very simply. When the aperture is closed (let us say to f 16 or f 8), the depth of field will be greater in the picture. On the other hand, to open the lens (let us say to f 1.8 or f 2) will reduce the background and accentuate the subject.

So far, this has been a little technical, but if you can understand this simple concept of photography, you are on your way to understanding an important spiritual lesson.

Let us liken the Christian to a camera body and the lens to the Word of God. We are in the hands of the Holy Spirit, who is doing the focusing and bringing everything into its right perspective. We are the instrument. He is the divine photographer. We will react according to His choices and desires; the lens setting is up to Him.

For example, sometimes it is His desire to give us an overall view of what is going on in the world, making both the background and the foreground important. Through the Word (the lens of the camera), He lets us see the many vistas of the future. Prophetic landscapes are made clear in their full dimension. This does not surprise us; Christ said, "Howbeit, when he, the Spirit of truth, is come, he will guide you into all truth; for he shall not speak of himself, but whatever he shall hear, that shall he speak; and he will show you things to come" (John 16:13).

Here, depth of field is important. Everything is in focus and we are exploring the events of the future and examining them as they relate to each other. The depth of perspective is more than informing; it has a profound effect on our lives. This is a must in prophecy!

On the other hand, there are times when the Lord wants the aperture to be opened, decreasing the depth of field. Then everything in the background fades and nothing is seen except the Lord Himself. He, and He alone, is in focus. Undistracted by surrounding circumstances, we are made to see Jesus only. Again, this is the ministry of the Holy Spirit.

In the John 16 passage, Christ said, ". . . when he, the Spirit of truth, is come, he will guide you into all truth; for he shall not speak of himself, but whatever he shall hear, that shall he speak; and he will show you things to come. He shall glorify me; for he shall receive of mine, and shall shew it unto you" (vv. 13-14). And in John 15 we read, "But when the Comforter is come, whom I will send unto you from the Father, even the Spirit of truth, who proceedeth from the Father, he shall testify of me" (v. 26).

We need yield ourselves daily into the hands of the Holy Spirit. We must let Him so direct our lives that He will bring into focus just what we need. He may point us to heaven and remind us that "in my Father's house are many mansions" (John 14:2). In our disappointment with events and circumstances, He may be pleased to make them all out of focus and bring into clear view the Lord alone. Nuances of His person are more clearly seen when there is no background distraction.

One thing more. Assuming the camera is versatile, with the full range of aperture stops, the quality of picture now depends on the quality of lens and the ability of the photographer. With the perfect lens of the Word of God in the hands of the Spirit of God, life can be a masterpiece for the believer.

 Truth for Soaring: "But as it is written, Eye hath not seen, nor ear heard, neither have entered into the heart of man, the things which God hath prepared for them that love him. But God hath revealed them unto us by his Spirit; for the Spirit searcheth all things, yea, the deep things of God" (1 Corinthians 2:9, 10).

When the Word of God is opened to us by the Spirit of God, our perspective and depth of field will make of us a bountiful picture of Christlikeness.

The Song of the Singing Bird

Did you know that most song birds sing their song either while in flight or while perched on a high limb? Although there are some exceptions to this—the turnstone, a shore bird, for instance, sings only while high above the ground.

In a sense, this is so with Christians too. When we are grounded and gravitated to the things of the world, we usually lose our song. We may gain in popularity and esteem of men, and we may climb the social ladder with some success; but a Christian who is disobedient, out of the will of God, and grounded to the world soon loses his song.

But the Lord is able to lift us up like the singing birds soaring in the sky—if we allow Him to. In Exodus 19 the Lord, speaking to Moses, said, "Ye have seen what I did unto the Egyptians and how *I bare you on eagles' wings,* and brought you unto myself" (v. 4). The Lord lifted up the people who for so long were in bondage, and He brought them to Himself. In Philippians, Paul said, "For our conversation is in heaven, from which also we look for the Savior, the Lord Jesus Christ" (Philippians 3:20). That word *conversation* means "citizenship."

Those who are born-again are citizens of heaven. We aren't there yet in body, but our heart, mind, and affections should be there. As a matter of fact, we read this in the Word, "If ye then be *risen with Christ*, seek those things which are above, where Christ sitteth on the right hand of God. Set your affections [or mind] on things *above*, not on things on the earth" (Colossians 3:1, 2). The Lord, then, has lifted us above this world and all its affairs.

Guy King, in his work, *Crossing the Border*, suggests that we are to accumulate *possessions in heaven* (Matthew 6:20), we are to value the *popularity of heaven*, (Psalm 16:11), and to rejoice in the *position in heaven* (Luke 10:20). He says, "We are to endure and energize for the *prize of heaven*, "forgetting those things which are behind, and reaching forth unto those things which are before, I press toward the mark for the prize of the high ("upward," Gk.) calling of GOD in CHRIST JESUS, (Philippians 9:25). So different from the 'corruptible crown' (1 Corinthians 9:25), which is the best that earth's striving can attain. We are to covet the *power of heaven*— 'tarry ye . . . until ye be ended with power from on high" (Luke 24:49).

We are a heavenly people. We should be heavenly minded and occupied with our heavenly Father. This doesn't mean that we become no earthly good or neglect mundane responsibilities. Rather, it means that our heart's affections find their object in a risen, ascended Christ. And that will influence our earthly walk. When we are above circumstances, above the cloud of difficulties and problems, like a soaring, singing bird, there is a melody in our hearts.

 Truth for Soaring: "He brought me up also out of an horrible pit, out of the miry clay, and set my feet upon a rock, and established my going. And he hath put a new song in my mouth, even praise unto our God; many shall see it, and fear, and shall trust in the LORD." (Psalm 40:2, 3).

Different hearts sing different songs. What a difference between the song of the world and the song of the believer! Ours is the song of heaven, the song of the soaring bird—rising above the mundane affairs of the world.

My Stars!!!

Hundreds of years ago when a person wanted to make fun of the Bible, he simply had to turn to a passage or two that referred to the immensity of the heaven, particularly a passage like the one in Jeremiah that says, "As the host of heaven cannot be numbered . . ." Why, everybody who was anybody knew that there were only 1,025 stars. The Greek astronomer Hipparchus said so, and he was an authority on such subjects. That is until Ptolemy, an Egyptian scholar, came along and added four more stars to the list.

Then in 1602, Tycho Brahe catalogued 777 stars. No, insisted Johannes Kepler 25 years later: There are 1,005. That settled the matter, despite what the Bible said! That is, until Galileo saw the heavens for the first time with a telescope. My stars! Unbelievable! John Flamsteed, the first Astronomer Royal of England, was able to catalogue 3,310 stars. We could go on and on and cite the 300,000 designated in the Bonn Durchmusterung, or the great International Photographic Chart of the Heavens prepared in the last century on which fifty million stars was the latest count.

But after a while, it gets a little long and laborious to hear of the way man is slowly reaching the same conclusions found in the Bible. According to my 1972 encyclopedia, there are more than 200 billion billion (2,000,000,000,000,000,000,000) stars. If this is difficult to comprehend, you might remember that each person on earth could count more than fifty billion stars without the same star being counted twice. That's another way of saying there are at least 50 billion stars for each person in the world. Enough to keep Hipparchus eating crow for a number of years.

Sir James Jeans once wrote, "All the nebulae (universes) between them must contain about as many stars as there are grains of sand on all the sea shores of the world." Thank you, Sir James, but did you ever read Genesis 22:17? "I will multiply thy seed as the stars of heaven, and as the sand which is upon the sea shore" (Genesis 22:17).

Besides showing the accuracy of the Bible in the universe, such vast numbers of stars gives us an appreciation of the power of the Lord. But there is something else that we must not overlook. The Bible says, "He calleth them all by their names" (Psalm 147:4). "Lift up your eyes on high, and behold who hath created these things, that bringeth out their host by number; he calleth them all by names by the greatness of his might" (Isaiah 40:26). Yes, God has a name for each star. From the largest (large enough to fill the space between the earth and the sun) to the smallest (smaller than the earth),

He not only created them but knows them by name. But how precious that constantly He links up the number and vastness of the stars with His promises to believers (Jeremiah 33:22).

God pointed to the stars and said to Abraham "So shall thy seed be" (Genesis 15:5). And in Deuteronomy 1:10 we read, ". . . behold ye are this day as the stars of heaven for multitude." To bring it down to the personal level, this Creator is even more interested in His new creation (2 Corinthians 5:17). "We are His workmanship, created in Christ Jesus unto good works" (Ephesians 2:10). He knows us by name, moreover, "even the very hairs of your head are all numbered" (Luke 12:7).

This great God of the universe is our personal God. Not only is He all-powerful and all-knowing, but He has a personal concern and interest in your needs and is ready to intervene for you as you look to Him. His never-failing hand in the universe is the same hand in your life. Great is His faithfulness, whether it is stars . . . or saints!

Truth for Soaring: "And he had in his right hand seven stars; and out of his mouth went a sharp two-edged sword; and his countenance was as the sun shineth in his strength" (Revelation 1:16).

". . . The mystery of the seven stars which thou sawest in my right hand, and the seven golden candlesticks. The seven stars are the angels of the seven churches; and the seven candlesticks which thou sawest are the seven churches" (Revelation 1:20).

The stars are not just in His hand, they are in his right hand, a place of special care and keeping. The "angels" (literally "messengers") are apparently church leaders. What a blessing to know that we are assured of this kind of care and interest from God.

Occupied With Christ

This Seat is Occupied.

The sign was conspicuously placed over the back of the airplane seat. The message was brief but clear. The plane had stopped for a brief layover, and I was told in four short words not to occupy that particular seat. It was a nice way of saying, "keep out."

And this message also made me think of some verses in Colossians 3 that have always been a very special blessing to me. They read, "If ye, then, be risen with Christ, seek those things which are above, where Chirst sitteth on the right hand of God. Set your affections on things above, not on things on the earth. For ye are dead, and your life is hidden with Christ in God" (Colossians 3:1-3).

The Williams translation renders the words, ". . . set your affection on things above," as "Practice occupying your minds with heavenly things." What Paul is saying is that since you are risen with Christ, it is just natural that you will want to lift your heart and thoughts to the very realms of Heaven where the Lord is.

One way of doing that is to be occupied daily with the Lord. Sometimes we get too occupied with other things, ". . . what ye shall eat, or what ye shall drink . . . what ye shall put on" (Matthew 6:25). So many things are on our minds in the business world, the political world, and the social world. Our involvement in these realms is so great that we fail to be occupied with the most important Person in our lives—our precious Lord. How the Lord would have us be daily, yes hourly, occupied with Him! Not just what belongs to Him, or what concerns Him, but *Him*. We need to have our quiet time when we put our sign out and tell the world, "This heart and soul and mind is occupied. It is taken up with the Lord! No trespassing! Keep out!"

It occurs to me that sometimes our being ill is a blessing. This should not be considered a time of treading water or marking time. It ought not be looked upon as a time of standing still. Rather, it ought to be an opportunity to more fully be occupied with Christ. How natural this becomes in the quietness of your home. "You have been saved; risen with Christ! You are seated in the heavenlies!" (Ephesians 1:3). Now is your chance to lay hold on the blessings of His presence and appropriate experimentally what is yours by virtue of your position. Practice occupying yourself with heavenly things. You are risen there, your Savior is there, you are seated there with Him; what could be more natural than to be occupied with Him in secret meditation in the sleepless hours of the night and the long days isolated from the world. Praise God you do not have to be in a sanctuary to be occupied with Him. As blessed as that place is where God's people congregate, you must remember that your body is His and He desires to walk with you, talk with you, and share your burdens and needs, communing with you as your friend.

This is surely more than just Bible reading or an occasional prayer. It is to be occupied hourly with Him. Let Him be the object of your affection there in your confinement; let Him be the main subject of your thoughts and meditation. Just bow your heart and thank the Lord for this opportunity of putting out your sign for the world to see in all the hustle and bustle; "This heart, soul and mind is occupied . . . ."

> Lord, to be occupied with Thee
> Amidst the clamor of the day,
> How can I shut this old world out—
> So pressing in demands—and pray.
>
> Such days' demands so heavily bear
> Upon the mind; trivial affairs
> Crowd out the things that count,
> The soul's cast down heavy with care.
>
> Oh, to be occupied with Thee—
> Not in rare moments which remain—
> But hourly, daily occupied
> In quiet Heavenly refrain.
>
> To know, dear Lord, your perfect peace
> Again to know your tender love,
> But most of all to occupy
> My heart and soul with Thee above.
> —Charles U. Wagner

Truth for Soaring: "Delight thyself also in the Lord, and he shall give thee the desires of thine heart. Commit thy way unto the Lord; trust also in him, and he shall bring it to pass" (Psalm 37:4, 5).

Our delight with God is not simply to depend on what He brings or the benefits that come from His giving hand. Our delight is to be in Him! It is not His giving of presents that is important, but our living in His presence.

You and the Waves

Almost everybody enjoys watching the waves on a seashore. Many enjoy playing in them and even riding on them. Waves can get rather high, but generally they don't get higher than 60 or 70 feet from trough to crest. However, waves estimated to have heights of 110 to 112 feet were observed from a ship in the North Pacific about 40 years ago. In actual measurement the highest wave observed by the United States Navy Department was about 80 feet. This was measured on board the British *S.S. Majestic*. But, even with all our modern technology, we find it rather "rough" to measure waves. They just don't seem to be measurable.

How wide do they get? From the bottom of one trough to the bottom of the next is estimated to be about 15 times its height. So, a wave 50 high feet would have a base width of 750 feet. A 100 foot wave would have a 1500-foot base. Imagine being caught in a wave 50 feet high (that's over eight times the height of a 6 foot man) with a width of 750 feet (that's over two times longer than a football field)!

It is no wonder that waves are often used in the Bible to depict an overwhelming situation. For example, David wrote, "Thy wrath lieth hard upon me, and thou hast afflicted me with all thy waves" (Psalm 88:7). And he said, "Deep calleth unto deep at the noise of thy waterspouts; all thy waves and thy billows are gone over me" (Psalm 42:7). In both cases he was ready to acknowledge that the waves were from the Lord, but also in both cases he seemed overwhelmed by them. However high they were, and however wide, he was confident that the Lord would intervene for him. In the latter passage he cries, "Yet the Lord will command His loving-kindness in the daytime, and in the night his song shall be with me, and my prayer unto the God of my life" (v. 8).

Jonah was also overwhelmed when God sent him to Sea Bottom Seminary to learn a lesson in obedience. He cried, "For thou hadst cast me into the deep, in the midst of the seas, and the floods compassed me about; all thy billows and thy waves passed over me" (Jonah 2:3). Doubtless you have had circumstances in which you felt overwhelmed.

When I took a minute to look up the subject of waves in my encyclopedia, I found it very interesting. I discovered that there were many different kinds of waves. There are transverse waves and longitudinal waves. There are traveling waves and standing waves. I discovered also that there is a great deal written on wave theory. Somehow, however, I found very little in the article that would help me here. The reason is obvious. When a man is in the midst of a wave, like David or Jonah, there is very little comfort in knowing that he is involved in a transverse wave as opposed to a longitudinal one. Likewise, the wave theory isn't on the mind of one who is striving to keep alive.

The same is true, to some degree, of theology. As important and interesting as it is, its detail seems less essential when in desperation we are overwhelmed. What is important is that the Lord can still the storm and cause the waves to be abated. Said the psalmist, "Thou rulest the raging of the sea; when the waves thereof arise, thou stillest them" (Psalm 89:9).

Our help is in Him from trough to crest.

 Truth for Soaring: "Thy wrath lieth hard upon me, and thou hast afflicted me with all thy waves. Selah. Thou hast put away mine acquaintance far from me; thou hast made me an abomination unto them. I am shut up, and I cannot come forth. Mine eye mourneth by reason of affliction. LORD, I have called daily upon thee, I have stretched out my hands unto thee" (Psalm 88:7-9).

When we feel the overwhelming surge of worry that flows from the depths of our trials, how wonderful to know that we can be led to a rock of safety: The Rock that is "higher than I" (Psalm 61:2).

Eternity—How Long?

How long is eternity? Even a child knows that *eternity* means "forever." But what is "forever?" How can we understand it? You can't measure it in time. The hymn writer wrote it this way:

> When we've been there ten thousand years,
> Bright shining as the sun
> We've no less days to sing God's praise
> Then when we've first begun.
> —John Newton

As we look at eternity, let us see it—in its outset—in terms of time. Will we be in heaven a thousand years? Yes! A million? Yes! A billion? Yes, but here again we are working ourselves out of the area of human understanding. For example, let us suppose that someone started counting some 6,000 years ago. If he started to count at the rate of 200 per minute, day and night, he would have reached the number 599,742,720,000 by September, 1931. To reach one billion in the British numbering system, he would continue to count until the year A.D. 5757. And a billion is hardly a speck in eternity.

Suffice it to say that life for the believer is everlasting. It is beyond any concept or dimension of time that we know or measure in our finite world. Those who trust Christ as Savior "shall not perish, but have everlasting life" (John 3:16). Christ speaks of the water "springing up into everlasting life" (John 4:14). Three times in John 6 the Lord uses the word "everlasting" (*aionios*). "Labor not for meat which perisheth, but for meat which endureth unto everlasting life, which the Son of man shall give unto you; for him hath God the Father sealed" (John 6:27). "And this is the will of him that sent me, that everyone who seeth the Son, and believeth on him, may have everlasting life; and I will raise him up at the last day" (John 6:40). Finally, "He that believeth on me hath everlasting life. I am the bread of life" (John 6:47, 48).

In Isaiah we read, "For thus saith the high and lofty One that inhabiteth eternity . . ." (Isaiah 57:15). The God of eternity made us for eternity. Someone has suggested that the soul is made for eternity (Genesis 2:7). Life is the seek-time of eternity (Galatians 6:7, 8). Time is given to prepare for eternity (2 Corinthians 6:2). Death is the gate of eternity (Luke 16:22). Then the question is asked: Where will you spend eternity? The same *everlasting* used for the saved is also used for the unsaved.

Every believer should be living in time with eternity's values in view. Shakespeare speaks of one who "sells eternity to get a toy." Earthly "toys" ought to seem so insignificant in the light of eternity and eternal values. Each of us should learn to have a loose hold on anything and everything that does not have eternal value. Today's pains and strains are insignificant in the light of eternity. Today's fears and tears will, in eternity, fade away into oblivion. For the believer, time flees and moments pass, fading into that eternal day where there is no night.

> There they need no sunshine bright,
> In that "city four square,"
> For the Lamp is all the light,
> And there is "no night there."
> God shall "wipe away all tears;"
> There's no death, no pain, no fears;
> And they count not time by years,
> For there is "no night there."
> —John R. Clements

 Truth for Soaring: "For thus saith the high and lofty One that inhabiteth eternity, whose name is Holy: I dwell in the high and holy place, with him also who is of a contrite and humble spirit, to revive the spirit of the humble, and to revive the heart of the contrite ones" (Isaiah 57:15).

Our God is the eternal God, but He is not remote or distant from us. While He inhabits eternity, He promises to dwell with us. How wonderful to know that He will dwell with us forever. His plan for eternity is an encouragement to run the race with patience today and share an eternal crown tomorrow.

You and Your Family Tree

Some people get really excited about their family tree. They can bore you for hours about their claim of a connection with some aristocratic background. Others are interested in the subject but often get stopped suddenly in their investigation. One wonders why!

Then there are certain sects that make their ancestral background a vital part of their beliefs, such as the Mormons or the followers of Armstrongism. It was the English poet of the seventeenth century Sir Thomas Overbury who wrote, "The man who has not anything to boast of but his illustrious ancestors is like a potato—the only good belonging to him is underground."

It is humorous to listen to two parents talk about their child—his liabilities and assets. Strange that he always gets his little quirks from the other side of the family—depending on who's speaking at the time.

Actually, a little reflection will bring us to the conclusion that none of us have much to be proud of if we trace our family tree back far enough. An ancient Scottish epitaph reads as follows:

> John Carnegie lies here,
> Descended from Adam and Eve.
> If any can boast of a pedigree higher,
> He will willingly give them leave.

As much as one might want to boast of such a pedigree as the first parents, we should remember that we got into our present condition because of them. None of us, therefore, have too much to boast about. Our sinful Adamic nature produces nothing good.

While some continue to boast about their family trees, we ought to be thinking about our new family. Having been born again, we are to take on the characteristics of this new relationship. Traits of the Lord should become obvious to everyone we meet.

Should you desire to read in two verses a succinct, condensed version of the life of Christ, you can find it in the fifth chapter of Galatians: "But the fruit of the Spirit is love, joy, peace, longsuffering, gentleness, goodness, faith, meekness, temperance . . ." (vv. 22, 23). This is what Christ is like; it is a thumbnail portrait of our Lord. When we are born again, it becomes the business of the Holy Spirit to produce in us these family traits. God the Holy Spirit is interested in making us more like Him.

When you come right down to it, the world is not as interested in what you claim to be as what you are and what you produce. Do they see family traits of our Father in your life? Emily Dickinson wrote:

> The pedigree of honey
> Does not concern the bee;
> A clover, any time, to him
> Is aristocracy.

May Christ be seen in us. Yes, may the blessed traits of the Godhead be clearly noted in our lives. Our human family tree might be interesting and deserving of passing note, but our new family relationship is more important. It should not only be told in lip but in life. Oh, that others would recognize these divine family traits in our lives. May the sweetness of Christ be seen in us and recognized as "divine aristocracy."

 Truth for Soaring: "Abide in me, and I in you. As the branch cannot bear fruit of itself, except it abide in the vine, no more can ye, except ye abide in me. I am the vine, ye are the branches. He that abideth in me, and I in him, the same bringeth forth much fruit; for without me ye can do nothing" (John 15:4, 5).

There is a relationship between Christ and His own. To abide in Him is to enjoy a communion that is the result of that relationship union.

The Sledgehammer Syndrome

E ver feel like you have been hit by a sledgehammer?
Something came into your life unexpectedly, and the impact of the "hammer blow" was swift and sudden. The thick thud of the sledge left you weakened and wondering why God had allowed it.

Back in Paul's day, a sledge that was used for pounding corn into powder was called a *tribulum*. From that unusual looking word we get our English word, *tribulation*. Tribulation, when it comes, is like the pounding of the sledgehammer-*tribulum*, in its pounding, grinding effect.

In the first century, when the price for being a Christian was the crushing blow of the Roman sledge, this word, from the Latin, was often used in reference to the suffering of the Christian martyrs.

It is no wonder that the word *tribulation* is used so often in the New Testament. In New Testament Greek it is the word *thlipsis*, which means "pressure, or the pressure of affliction." Christ said, "In the world ye shall have tribulation: but be of good cheer; I have overcome the world" (John 16:33). Think of it, Christ speaks of "good cheer" even in times of the hammering pressure of life. Adding to that, Paul said, ". . . we glory in tribulations also, knowing that tribulation worketh patience; and patience, experience; and experience, hope . . ."(Romams 5:3, 4).

While nobody actually enjoys tribulation, we can enjoy what it brings; we can appreciate the result of a "hammer blow" when it comes, if this is a way the Lord uses to teach us patience and endurance. Later, Paul said we are to be "patient in tribulation" (Romans 12:12). Even John, on the Isle of Patmos, referred to himself as a "companion in tribulation" (Revelation 1:9).

Perhaps you have endured some unexpected persecution because of your attempt to live a godly life. Maybe you have been the object of disparaging remarks and harsh criticism. Your immediate reaction was that you couldn't believe someone could treat you that way, when you were actually doing the right thing. The sledge was as baffling as it was bruising.

Actually, when the sledgehammer comes, its pounding pressure speaks volumes. It really tells us something about ourselves. Paul wrote, "Yea, and all that will live godly in Christ Jesus shall suffer persecution. But evil men and seducers shall wax worse and worse, deceiving, and being deceived" (2 Timothy 3:12, 13).

So when the hurting hammer strikes hard and heavy, remember the words of our Lord who said, "If the world hate you, ye know that it hated me before it hated you" (John 15:18). We are in good company when the blows of the sledge come our way. To be "partakers of his sufferings" (1 Peter 4:13) and to be a partner in the "order of the *tribulum*" is an honor indeed.

 Truth for Soaring: "And not only so, but we glory in tribulations also, knowing that tribulation worketh patience; and patience, experience; and experience, hope; and hope maketh not ashamed, because the love of God is shed abroad in our hearts by the Holy Ghost who is given unto us" (Romans 5:3-5).

Do you see how a believer begins to "soar" spiritually in this passage? Starting at the ground level of tribulation we move upward to patience, then experience, and even higher, to hope! Upward and onward, from tribulation to hope!

Let Me Tell You About
Your Grandchildren

"Cast thy bread upon the waters; for thou shalt find it after many days" (Ecclesiastes 11:1).

When we plant seed today, we certainly don't cast it on the water. But they did in Bible times, especially when the rivers overflowed. They would fling it into the water knowing that some fruit could be expected when the water receded and the seed took root near the river. Translated into daily living, this verse means that you could be delightfully surprised to find your deeds bearing fruit, fruit that could come back to you many days after the seed is sown.

One day my secretary informed me that a couple was in the lobby and wanted to see me. Frankly, I didn't recognize their name. When they came in, the man came over by my desk and gave me a big bear hug.

"Am I ever glad to see you," he said.

"Well," I replied, "I'm glad to see you too. . . . whoever you are. . . ."

It was almost amusing. A man was happy to see me, and I wasn't sure who he was!

Soon though, I got the rest of the story. More than 30 years ago, George Miller and his wife came into a service where I was preaching through the book of Ephesians. It was his first visit to a Baptist church, probably his first to a Protestant church. He was a butcher. When he and his wife heard the gospel, they both responded. I dealt with him and my wife talked with his wife. They were both saved. Due to a number of different circumstances, we lost contact with them. Because we soon moved to another state, there was no opportunity for follow-up.

God began to work in their lives, and George Miller left the meat-cutting business to go to college. Over the years he has pastored churches and has been very much involved in the Lord's work. More recently he was director of alumni and church relations in a well-known Bible college. His son is the director of student affairs in that institution. What a delight it was to see him and to know that he had been so used of the Lord. What a blessing to hear him say, "Let me tell you about all your grandchildren." He was speaking of the people he and his wife had led to the Lord since his conversion.

Certainly, when we get to Glory, we are going to meet scores of people who were touched by our witness and our testimony, people who have been forgotten by us but not by the Lord. Don't be surprised if someone comes up to you someday in eternity and says, "Remember me?" Then, after learning that you were his spiritual father, you might hear him say, to your delight, "Let me tell you about your grandchildren."

 Truth for Soaring: "For the Lord himself shall descend from heaven with a shout, with the voice of the archangel, and with the trump of God; and the dead in Christ shall rise first; then we who are alive and remain shall be caught up together with them in the clouds, to meet the Lord in the air; and so shall we ever be with the Lord" (1 Thessalonians 4:16, 17).

What a reunion that will be when we go "soaring" to Glory at the return of Christ! It will also be a time of meeting one another again to rehearse, reminisce, and rejoice at the workings of the Lord in our lives. "Remember me?" will certainly be a delightful question for us all.

Good Job, God!

The little boy is looking up into the heavens, obviously enjoying what he sees. What does that little guy think as he studies the starry heaven with his inquisitive eye and unique childlike imagination? His dad was quietly observing the youngster's delightful look of wonderment and was very interested in his son's reaction. He was happy to see that he was beginning to notice the world around him.

"Daddy," the little boy asked, "Did God make all that Himself? Dad, did He make all that?" Of course the "all that" was everything the little guy could drink in plus what his imagination added to it.

"Yes, He sure did," answered his father, sensing that this would be a great opportunity to witness to his boy and talk to him about the Creator, who is also our Savior. "He made all that, all by Himself."

"Wow," said the young boy. That said it all. A "wow" explained his feeling very well.

"Now let me tell you all about our God and what He did for us," Dad began. (Yes, this was a good time for a gentle witness.) But the little guy wasn't ready for all that yet. He interrupted his father and said, "Just a minute, Dad." Then he stepped back, took a deep breath and said, "Good job, God!"

No, he wasn't being deliberately irreverent. He wouldn't have known what the word *sacrilegious* even meant. He was awestruck; but more than that, he was impressed with the work God had done. He expressed it in a way that would have seemed irreverent if anyone else had said it in that way.

"Good job, God!" That does express it very well, doesn't it? Yes, God had done a good job—one that was in keeping with His divine handiwork. "The heavens declare the glory of God, and the firmament sheweth His handiwork" (Psalm 19:1). Someone has translated it: "They are a marvelous display of His craftsmanship." The heavens say something about God.

As a matter of fact, everything God does is good. Don't forget that. He is good, and His handiwork is good. One of the best jobs God has ever done is His making man. On the sixth day when He made man, He said it was "very good." We were made in His image.

However, the image was marred when man disobeyed God and fell. So He made the "new creation." "For we are His workmanship, created in Christ Jesus unto good works" (Ephesians 2:10). God has created us and made us new spiritually. Every born-again person is the product of His divine creative power. "If any man be in Christ, he is a new creation" (2 Corinthians 5:17).

Let's thank Him for what He has done. We might even find ourselves agreeing with a little boy and exclaiming to our Father-Creator—"Good job, God!"

Truth for Soaring: "And we know that all things work together for good to them that love God, to them who are the called according to his purpose. For whom he did foreknow, he also did predestinate to be conformed to the image of his Son, that he might be the firstborn among many brethren. Moreover, whom he did predestinate, them he also called; and whom he called, them he also justified; and whom he justified, them he also glorified. What shall we then say to these things? If God be for us, who can be against us?" (Romans 8:28-31).

God, who knows the end from the beginning, has an eternity of good things in store for us. Let's rest in the assurance that He is working out His plan for our good.

Guitar or Violin?

Most of us know the difference between the guitar and the violin. While both are stringed instruments, they are very different. A guitar has six strings that are tuned in fourths, while a violin has four strings that are tuned in fifths. Guitars are made of light wood and have arched or flat tops and backs. Violin makers usually use soft pine or spruce for the front of the instrument and maple or sycamore for the back and sides. The head and neck are made of maple. Many people try to play the guitar a little. (Mine is tucked away in my closet, for which most people are grateful.) There are 90,000 classical guitarists, and another 9,000,000 who just make noise. Well, I'm in good company.

But there is an intriguing difference in the two musical instruments. Their longevity. According to experts, the life expectancy of a fine guitar is about 15 years. Then it starts to deteriorate. However, violins mellow with the years and get better with age. If properly cared for, a violin that is 100 years old is better than a new one. That's why there is no such thing as a Stradivarius-quality guitar. Most of us know that violins made by Antonio Stradivari in the late 1600's and early 1700's have never been surpassed. Most every other thing we have that is over 300 years old really looks like it.

Just as there are differences between the violin and guitar, there are different kinds of Christians. Some reach a peak in their lives and then begin to decline. Their effectiveness wanes and the best part about them is their past. Then there are others who mellow and mature with age. Their years of service are but first steps to a greater potential and capacity. I'm not speaking only in terms of what we call "senior citizens" who are still effective. Rather, I'm talking of this matter of Christian constancy to "higher ground" that should be characteristic of each of us. What a shame to "peak out" when we have just begun to become effective for God in our lives. While we all admit to reaching a plateau occasionally so we can regroup, it should be "onward and upward and forward" for us all. The hymn writer put it beautifully:

> I'm pressing on the upward way;
> New heights I'm gaining every day
> Still praying as I'm onward bound,
> Lord lead on to higher ground.

> My heart has no desire to stay
> Where doubts arise and fears dismay;
> Tho some may dwell where these abound,
> My prayer, my aim, is higher ground.

Lord, Lift me up and let me stand
By faith on heaven's table land;
A higher plane that I have found—
Lord plant my feet on higher ground.
—Johnson Oatman, Jr.

Yes, it should be "higher ground" for us as we look to new challenges and new opportunities to serve the Lord. The passing years ought to result in new peaks not new lows. Let's be "striving for the summit" with our vision focused upward.

 Truth for Soaring: "Brethren, I count not myself to have apprehended; but this one thing I do, forgetting those things which are behind, and reaching forth unto those things which are before, I press toward the mark for the prize of the high calling of God in Christ Jesus" (Philippians 3:13, 14).

Which will you be? A guitar that declines and deteriorates? Or a violin that matures and mellows. It's up to you.

Calling Upon the Lord

Calling upon the Lord is simply talking to Him. Sometimes it means we implore Him; other times it means we make a gentle request like a child to the Father. The idea is not only that we are to ask and call, but that we are to call upon Him.

Prayer is not a last resort. It is ludicrous for a committee to meet, and after failing to get anything done, resort to prayer. Prayer is not a stop-gap measure. Nor is prayer a tool to use in emergency situations after all other attempts fail.

The advantages of prayer are not only that the Lord will meet our need and give us an adequate answer to our problems, but also that He will go beyond what we ask and show us great and mighty things we know not—things that reach beyond our expectation.

The word *mighty* in the Hebrew carries the idea of "hidden things." It is used of the walls or cities (Numbers 13:28; Deuteromony 1:28; Joshua 14:12). The idea seems to be that the things the Lord will give are those that are inaccessible by any means other than prayer. In New Testament language, it means He "is able to do exceedingly abundantly above all that we ask or think" (Ephesians 3:20). How we need to pray, and then believe and see the great and mighty things from His hand.

As a college and seminary president, I have been doing some serious thinking about the needs of the school, both for the present and for the future. I have been thinking in terms of the direction we should go. Serious questions come up as we look at the educational world and the great need we will face monetarily.

How far should Christian institutions go with the "Madison Avenue" approach? Is it really right to put our dependence on professional advertisers who know how to project the correct image and who flood the public with multi-media methods and garish gimmicks? While concluding that there is a legitimate place for tasteful advertising that properly conveys a need and keeps people informed, I also concluded that the most proper and, indeed, the greatest resource for help is in using the divine provision of prayer.

Surely, to employ even legitimate efforts in fund raising without turning to the Lord and the simple but scriptural method, is both foolish and in insult to God. The God of George Müller is also our God. The resources of the Lord are not drained by time; they are both inexhaustible and accessible. Did not He say, "The cattle on a thousand hills are mine"? Harry Ironside tells of some who took that literally. They turned to the Lord and actually asked for the cattle! Their prayers were answered. Is not our only real limitation our lack of faith that He will do what He says He will do?

Great and mighty things are ours, whether we are talking about the supply of God for our churches, our colleges and seminaries, or our families. The secret is so simple we stumble over it as we reach for the most recent marketing tool. "Call upon Me!" This is a promise that will result in miracles from His mighty hand. Let us believe it and be the recipients of His "great and mighty things."

 Truth for Soaring: "Call unto me, and I will answer thee, and shew thee great and mighty things, which thou knowest not" (Jeremiah 33:3).

PRAYER AND PROMISES

I will not therefore minimize my prayer,
    But make it large as are the promises.
Since God is willing thus to bless,
    No less an answer would I share.
Alas, for my small faith,
    Compared with what He saith.

Therefore, henceforth, shall prayer be heard
    From me according to God's Word.
I will request, as long as I shall live,
    All God has shown His willingness to give.
As are the love and power His truth declares,
    So shall faith make the measure of my prayers.
                          —William Olney

The Gypsy

They called him "Gypsy." "Gypsy Smith." His real name was Rodney Smith, a remarkable person who was born in a gypsy tent in the parish of Wanstead, near Epping Forest, England. He turned out to be one of the world's most remarkable evangelists. Interestingly enough, he received no education. His mother died of smallpox when he was a small boy. When Rodney was in his teens, his father was converted. Later, at the age of 15, Rodney trusted Christ as his Savior. Shortly after he was married, he preached to 1,500 people. He wrote these words:

> Let the beauty of Jesus be seen in me,
> All His wonderful passion and purity;
> O Thou Spirit divine,
> All my nature refine,
> Till the beauty of Jesus be seen in me.

That was Gypsy Smith's desire—that Christ might be seen in him. In his book, *The Beauty of Jesus*, he talked about revival. He said, "You may tell me a revival cannot be organized. I agree. I defy anyone to organize a revival. You can no more do it than you can organize the spring. You can plant the seeds. You can dig the soil. You can plow. That's the order. That is common sense. You cannot do more. You cannot make the things grow. You cannot work up a revival. You must leave it to the Holy Spirit."

Continuing that analogy to spring, he later wrote, "Who objects to spring—to spring music and spring flowers with their promise of harvest and of plenty? Would any sane person lift his voice and definitely proclaim, 'I don't believe in spring and I refuse to have spring?' Can you conceive what it would mean if spring failed to come? A year without spring! What havoc! What ruin! What a waste! A bare world—everything dry. No sap, no germination, no life, no new creation; not a bird nor a blossom. All nature stagnant, fields without grain, orchards without fruit, fountains and rivers dry, birds without young, flocks without lambs, herds without kine, meadows without grass, gardens without flowers, birds without song. But let spring smile, the seeds burst, the trees break into beauty. And what spring is in the world of nature, grace is in the world of Spirit. What the church needs is a quickening, renewal, reclothing, and putting on of her beautiful garments. Oh, for a breath of the Holy Spirit everywhere. . . ." Yes, Gypsy Smith was interested in revival. Shouldn't we be also? A work of God in our city, state, and country is badly needed: a work of the Holy Spirit among us. It can't be manufactured or scheduled.

In the last chapter of his book, Gypsy Smith wrote, "A friend of mine, who was a great preacher, told me a story. He was staying with a friend and while dressing, out of his bedroom window he saw a seagull in the backyard with his wings clipped. That poor seagull was trying to take a bath in a pie dish filled with rain water. Fancy a seagull, born to free-wheel over an ocean and born to circle the moon and stars. A gull, the child of empires and worlds, trying to feed and satisfy itself in a pie dish. There are thousands of people who are doing the same thing today. We are made out of the material from which God builds the stars and moon. When they go out like sparks from a blacksmith's anvil, our hunger continues if we fail to keep in contact with the living God. We need Him, for only in Him do we find the source of light, peace and joy."

Truth for Soaring: "Give unto the LORD the glory due unto his name; bring an offering, and come before him; worship the LORD in the beauty of holiness" (1 Chronicles 16:29).

"One thing have I desired of the LORD, that will I seek after: that I may dwell in the house of the LORD all the days of my life, to behold the beauty of the LORD, and to inquire in his temple" (Psalm 27:4).

> Earthly pleasures vainly call me
> I would be like Jesus.
> Nothing worldly shall enthrall me
> I would be like Jesus.
>
> Be like Jesus this my song
> In the home and in the throng;
> Be like Jesus all day long!
> I would be like Jesus.
> —James Rowe

Doors . . . Doors . . . Doors

As a child I can remember being reprimanded by my mother for getting "trapped" in a revolving door at Hudson's Department Store in Detroit. My brother and I enjoyed getting involved in that inexpensive "merry-go-round" two or three times, only to come out where we started — outside!

Then it was electric doors. Remember when they first appeared? How intrigued we were to find as we approached the door that it would swing open just in time to make the entrance clear. Sometimes, at first, we wondered if if could be trusted; but the electric eye was gauged so that a normal walk approaching the store would open the door—just in the nick of time.

As a youngster, I had some rather ridiculous reflections about those electric doors. For example, how fast could a person be going when entering the door and not run into it? Suppose one was in a hurry and forgot that the "eye" was timed for a certain pace. To be sure, he would end up rather bruised if not seriously injured. Of course, if one walked as he should, the door would open properly, and there would be no mishap or accident.

Thinking of those doors—both revolving and electric—make me think of the Christian life. How many of us enter into areas of life and find ourselves in what seems to be an endless circle. Life often consists of restless revolving and meaningless motion. An entrance that was intended to bring us into a place of blessing has turned into a circuitous, confusing maze. And, like the revolving door, the harder we pushed the faster we would go, and the more complicated the task of release and relief became. Of course, the secret for the believer is to walk in the Spirit (Galatians 5:16, 25). A day-by-day reliance on Him and trust in Him will put purpose in our walk and give us an entrance into areas of life that will bring blessing and fulfillment.

Indeed, the Christian life is a life of walking in the Spirit and leaving the future with Him. It is almost like walking through electric doors. Paul, when speaking of going to Troas to preach the gospel, said that "a door was opened unto me of the Lord" (2 Corinthians 2:12). It might be noted that he didn't say that a door was opened unto him, and then he went to Troas. Rather, when he submitted to the Lord's direction in coming to Troas, the door was opened just in the nick of time. This does not mean that the Lord's opened doors make us immune from all difficulty. Later he said, " . . . a great door, and effectual, is opened unto me, and there are many adversaries"

(1 Corinthians 16:9). However, if the Lord opens the door, He will certainly care for the difficulties we encounter in the coming days. To cross the threshold into new areas of Christian experiences is to find Him there, ready to continue the walk with us.

What is important is that we don't rush ahead of His will as we cross such thresholds. Sometimes in periods of pressure and crisis we are found rushing in our walk. To go ahead of God's plan and will for our life—like hurrying through electric doors—might well result in a bruise or two of the inner man. It means that in fleshly haste we have gone ahead of the pace or walk that He has designated and designed for our lives. If we walk properly, the doors of the will of God will open properly.

Are you facing sickness, financial reverses, or unexpected news of necessary surgery? Keep walking in faith and leave the rest to Him. You can be sure that the door of His leading will open just in time. "God is faithful who will not suffer us to be tempted above that which we are able, but will with the temptation make a way of escape that ye may be able to bear it" (1 Corinthians 10:13). He is never unaware of our need and never unresponsive to our walk of faith.

 Truth for Soaring: "And to the angel of the church in Philadelphia write: These things saith he that is holy, he that is true, and he that hath the key of David, he that openeth, and no man shutteth; and shutteth, and no man openeth. I know thy works; behold, I have set before thee an open door, and no man can shut it; for thou hast a little strength, and hast kept my word, and hast not denied my name" (Revelation 3:7-8).

Reflect on this: Our God is a sovereign God who is in full control of all things. The God who controls the universe is also the "door keeper." He opens and closes it according to His will. Rest in that! Believe it! Keep moving ahead, and leave the opening and closing to Him.

Quite Suddenly

"And if I go and prepare a place for you, I will come again, and receive you unto myself, that where I am, there ye may be also" (John 14:3).

Jesus is coming! The Bible is unequivocally clear on that subject. From the lips of the Lord Himself comes this precious promise: "I will come again." He was speaking to troubled hearts. They had hoped He would have overthrown the heavy Roman yoke; instead, He tells them that He is going away. He says, "Let not your heart be troubled. . . . I will come again." He spoke of heaven—a real place. Then He gave His promise—He would come and take His prepared people to His prepared place.

Like other promises, this one should have a profound effect on our lives. It is a comforting hope (1 Thessalonians 4:13-18). It is a purifying hope (1 John 3:2). It prompts godly living in a warped, perverted world (Titus 2:11-13). It is an incentive to right relationship with our Lord. "And now, little children, abide in him, that, when he shall appear, we may have confidence and not be ashamed before him at his coming" (1 John 2:28).

Included in this promise is the fact that He can come at any moment. Paul expected to be alive when His Lord returned for His saints. "Then, we who are alive and remain shall be caught up together with them in the clouds, to meet the Lord in the air . . ." (1 Thessalonians 4:17).

How sad is to see a person not believing the precious promise that He may come at any time—and that we should look for Him and wait for Him (1 Thessalonians 1:9, 10). Simply stated, the proof of this promise is the Word of God itself. Let us broaden on this point by saying that just as He came the first time and kept His promise in a literal way, He will also come the second time. The Old Testament told of His coming: the place (Micah 5:2); the Person— virgin born (Isaiah 7:14); and even the time (Daniel 9). Just as He had promised, the Lord Jesus Christ came, fulfilling the Scripture with minute accuracy.

The condition is very simple: The literal fulfillment of His second coming is as valid and sure as His first coming. While the time of His return cannot be pinpointed, just as His first coming, the sure reality of His coming is both fixed and final.

Truth for Soaring: "Behold, I shew you a mystery: We shall not all sleep, but we shall all be changed, in a moment, in the twinkling of an eye, at the last trump; for the trumpet shall sound, and the dead shall be raised incorruptible, and we shall be changed" (1 Corinthians 15:51, 52).

QUITE SUDDENLY

QUITE SUDDENLY—it may be of the
   turning of a lane,
Where I stand to watch a skylark from out
   the swelling grain,
That the trump of God shall thrill me, with
   its call so loud and clear,
And I'm called away to meet Him, whom
   of all I hold most dear.

QUITE SUDDENLY—it may be as I tread
   the busy street,
Strong to endure life's stress and strain, its
   every call to meet,
That through the roar of traffic, a trumpet,
   silvery clear,
Shall stir my startled senses and proclaim
   His coming near.

QUITE SUDDENLY—it may be in His
   house I bend my knee,
When the kindly voice, long hoped for,
   comes at last to summon me;
And the fellowship of earth-life that has
   seemed so passing sweet,
Proves nothing but the shadow of our
   meeting 'round His feet.

QUTIE SUDDENLY—it may be as I live in
   dreamless sleep,
God's gift to many a sorrowing heart, with
   no more tears to weep,
That a call shall break my slumber and a
   Voice sound in my ear;
"Rise up, my love, and come away! Behold
   the Bridegroom's here!"
               —Author Unknown

The Just Shall Live by Faith

To be justified is to be declared righteous. Scripture says that justification comes by faith. "Therefore, being justified by faith, we have peace with God" (Romans 5:1). Faith in Him results in knowing peace with God and the subsequent peace of God (Philippians 4:6, 7). What a promise! All of our sin was laid on Him (1 Peter 2:24), and all His righteousness is laid on us. We read, "He hath made him, who knew no sin, to be sin for us, that we might be made the righteousness of God in him" (2 Corinthians 5:21). All of this is a result of His work and our acceptance of Christ by faith.

Someone has suggested that to be justified means that we are "just as if we'd never sinned." While this is true, the promise includes more than that. It does more than cause all past sins to be forgiven and blotted out. It also deals with the future. It means that we are once-for-all declared righteous and that from now and throughout all eternity God sees us in Christ—perfect and righteous.

Of course, this promise deals with our position rather than our condition. It challenges us to strive to bring our condition up to our position. But it is no less real. We are as near and righteous to the Father as the Son is because we are in Him. What a blessing comes when this promise is understood and claimed. "The just shall live by faith!"

The greatest proof of the clarity of Scripture and the reality of the phrase, "the just shall live by faith," is found in Habakkuk 2:4. It is interesting that these six words epitomize three whole epistles of Paul, namely, Romans, Galatians, and Hebrews (assuming his authorship). "The just" is covered in Romans, which shows how a man can be just with God. "Shall live" is covered in Galatians, which emphasizes that portion of truth. "By faith" is covered amply in Hebrews. It is a proof of the promise in Habakkuk that it is quoted in all three of these books.

Another proof of this promise is in the life transformation of men and women in history. Indeed, the great Reformation was built on the Scripture promise: "The just shall live by faith." We might consider Luther's own words:

"I greatly longed to understand Paul's epistle to the Romans and nothing stood in the way but that one expression, 'the justice of God,' because I took it to mean that justice whereby God is just and deals justly in punishing the unjust. My situation was that, although an impeccable monk, I stood before God as a sinner troubled in conscience, and I had no confidence that my merit would assuage time. Therefore, I did not love a just and angry God, but rather hated and murmured against Him. Yet I clung to the dear Paul and had a great yearning to know what he meant.

"Night and day I pondered until I saw the connection between the justice of God and the statement that 'the just shall live by faith.' Then I grasped that the justice of God is that righteousness by which through grace and sheer mercy God justifies us through faith. Thereupon I felt myself to be reborn and to have gone through open doors into paradise. The whole of Scripture took on a new meaning, and whereas before the 'justice of God' had filled me with hate, now it became to me inexpressibly sweet in greater love. This passage of Paul became to me a gate to heaven. . . .

"If you have a true faith that Christ is your Savior, then at once you have a gracious God, for faith leads you in and opens up God's heart and will, that you should see pure grace and overflowing love. This it is to behold God in faith that you should look upon his fatherly, friendly heart, in which there is no anger nor ungraciousness. He who sees God as angry does not see Him rightly but looks only on a curtain, as if a dark cloud had been drawn across His face." (Taken from the book, *Here I Stand*, by Roland H. Bainton, Abingdon-Cokesbury Press).

 Truth for Soaring: "Therefore, being justified by faith, we have peace with God through our Lord Jesus Christ, By whom also we have access by faith into this grace wherein we stand, and rejoice in hope of the glory of God" (Romans 5:1, 2).

"For in it is the righteousness of God revealed from faith to faith; as it is written, The just shall live by faith" (Romans 1:17).

> I hear the words of love,
>   I gaze upon the blood;
> I see the mighty Sacrifice,
>   And I have peace with God.
>
> 'Tis everlasting peace,
>   Sure as Jehovah's name;
> 'Tis stable as His steadfast throne,
>   Forever more the same.
>   —Horatius Bonar

Mirror, Mirror on the Wall, Who's the Fairest of Them All?

"Mirror, mirror, on the wall, who's the fairest of them all?" If mirrors could speak, we would like them to be as complimentary as possible. Some mirrors are. I have looked into some that seem a little less than honest (specially tinted-type ones that distort your image). On the other hand, if your mirror is honest, it will surely tell you if you have the kind of charm that rubs off.

If you admit to admiring your face in a mirror, you are using two words that have a single Latin source. The Latin word for *mirror, mirari*, means "admire." Mirrors are made for self-admiration. But if you have a winning smile and a losing face, I would admire you for your honesty in "facing up to it." We can't all be beautiful. On the other hand, few of us are like the proverbial person whose face looked like it had worn out six bodies.

On the more serious side, there is a mirror that can do miracles for you. (Incidentally, that word *miracle* is from the same Latin family as *mirror*.) Paul talked about it when he wrote, "But we all, with open face beholding as in a glass the glory of the Lord, are changed into the same image from glory to glory, even as by the Spirit of the Lord" (2 Corinthians 3:18). Note the reflection is from glory (what we see in Christ) to glory (when we become like Christ). The word translated *changed* is the same word translated *transfigured* in Mark 9:2, when it speaks of Christ on the mount.

When Paul said, "And be not conformed to this world: but be ye transformed," he was using the same word (Romans 12:2). It speaks of a miraculous mirroring of the beauties and moral excellencies of Christ in our lives day-by-day. The mirrors in our bedroom or bathroom show us what we are, but the mirror of the Word of God shows us what we can be. One is telling; the other is transfiguring. The first is fixed; the second shows how a condition can be changed, leading to the radiation of an inner beauty.

Now, how is this done? Look again at Romans 12:2, which says, "but be ye transformed by the renewing of your mind." How is the mind renewed? Our Corinthian's passage says, we are "changed into the same image from glory to glory, even as by the Spirit of the Lord." Now put it all together. The Holy Spirit takes the Holy Bible and reflects the Holy Son of God, and the believer experiences a renewed mind and holy life. Thus, the mirror brings about a miracle and people will begin to admire Christ as they see Him in us.

Winning Words for Daily Living

You may or may not be endowed with a becoming face. But with this "miracle mirror," God the Holy Spirit is able to bring out an inner beauty—a Christlikeness that will transcend all our natural features.

Mirrors are made to be used. Much more so is God's mirror, the Word of the Lord. The more we are exposed to Him in His Word, the more Christlike we will become. The answer to the prayer, "Let the beauty of Jesus be seen in me" is answered by the Spirit's use of the Word to transform and transfigure the believer's life.

 Truth for Soaring: "But we all, with open face beholding as in a glass the glory of the Lord, are changed into the same image from glory to glory, even as by the Spirit of the LORD" (2 Corinthians 3:18).

> Let the beauty of Jesus be seen in me
> All His wonderful passion and purity.
> O thou Spirit divine,
> All my nature refine,
> Till the beauty of Jesus be seen in me.
> —Albert W. T. Orsborn

Gaggle and Gangs

How do you describe a group of cattle? The answer, of course, is a *herd*. And the word for a bunch of sheep is easy too—a *flock*. But what about geese or foxes or monkeys? Now the going is a bit more difficult. Geese groups are known as *gaggles*, and a hunter would be proper if he hunted for a *skulk* of foxes. If you think these are difficult, did you know it is a *sloth* of bears that can be dangerous or a *troop* of monkeys that can send you into convulsive laughter?

Now honestly, did you know any of those categories? Well, move over, I would have flunked that test too. Stranger still are the designations of a *sord* of mallards or a *cete* of badgers or a *down* of hares. Some of these labels are almost obsolete. But in the days when hunting was a matter of survival rather than a sport, they were very serious designations.

One thing is certain, you are identified by the group or gang with whom you associate. Sheep are not comfortable with a *rout* of wolves. A *gaggle* of geese would be out of place with a *cast* of hawks .

Similarly, you are out of your group when you find yourself walking "in the counsel of the ungodly" or standing "in the way of sinners" or sitting "in the seat of the scornful" (Psalm 1:1). The Bible says we are to "have no fellowship with the unfruitful works of darkness but, rather, reprove them" (Ephesians 5:11).

Does it surprise you to hear God say, "Be ye not unequally yoked together with unbelievers; for what fellowship hath righteousness with unrighteousness? And what communion hath light with darkness? And what concord hath Christ with Belial? Or what part hath he that believeth with an infidel?" (2 Corinthians 6:14, 15). For light and darkness to walk together is just as inconsistent as it is for a flock of sheep to mix with a pride of lions, or a cast of hawks to mix with a watch of nightingales.

It is time to be worried when you feel conformable with a gang that was once quite foreign to your way of life. Taking the habits and appearances of another gang means you are finding it more comfortable to conform and compromise. Actually, you are losing your identity.

Sometimes a Christian feels he can stay in a group and change it, but what inevitably happens is that he finds himself changing. It is just plain sense to assume a down of hares will always be just that. They are not likely to change their hops any more than a gaggle of geese would change their waddles.

So take your stand with the called out assembly of God's people—the group designation is called a church—and openly identify with the body of Christ. Remember, you are known not only by your fruit but by your group.

Check up on your gaggle or gang:

1. Does being with them make you want to read your Bible more?
2. Can you talk before them about some good things the Lord has done?
3. Do your gang activities take you places that honor the Lord?
4. Does the language of your gang reflect a love for the Lord?
5. Has your gang ever tried to lead a sinner to Christ?
6. Has your gang actively taken part in the church prayer service?
7. Can you comfortably pray that God will bless your gang's plans?

 Truth for Soaring: "For ye are the temple of the living God; as God hath said, I will dwell in them, and walk in them; and I will be their God, and they shall be my people. Wherefore, come out from among them, and be ye separate, saith the Lord, and touch not the unclean thing; and I will receive you" (2 Corinthians 6:16-17).

God has high expectations for His children. Because we are a "heavenly people," we are not expected to be attracted to the earthly. Walking in the council of the ungodly leads to standing in the way of sinners and sitting in the seat of the scornful (Psalm 1). The happy Christian is the one who is separated *from* the world and *unto* the Lord.

Lo, I Am With You Always

The name John Gibson Paton is a familiar one to anyone interested in the history of missions.

J.G. Paton was a missionary to the New Hebrides. His exploits done there for God in both evangelism and teaching were great indeed. After laboring as a city missionary in Glasgow, Scotland, he felt called of the Lord to take the gospel to the many in the New Hebrides who had never heard the name of Christ. After his ordination in March, 1858, he and his wife sailed to that yet uncivilized land.

Reflecting on those days, Paton wrote, "My first impression drove me to the verge of utter dismay. On beholding the natives in their paint and nakedness and misery, my heart was as full of horror as of pity."

Historian F. W. Boreham wrote, "If ever a man seemed lonely, J. G. Paton seemed lonely when 3 months later he had to dig with his own hands a grave for his young wife and his baby boy."

How could one man endure such awful loneliness? Consider Paton's favorite text, and you'll gain some understanding. "Lo, I am with you always" (Matthew 28:20).

Paton said, "I was never altogether forsaken. The ever-merciful Lord sustained me to lay the precious dust of my loved ones in the same quiet grave. But for Jesus and the fellowship He vouchsafed me there, I might have gone mad and died beside that lonely grave."

For years this text followed this great man of God. He once stated that he knew of 50 times when his life was in imminent danger and his escape was due solely to the grace of God. He faced death in a hundred forms.

In another of these crises he wrote, "During the crisis I felt generally calm and firm of soul, standing erect and with my whole weight on the promise, 'Lo, I am with you always.' Precious promise! How often I adore Jesus for it and rejoice in it! Blessed be His name!"

Another great missionary in a different part of the world but committed to the same gospel was David Livingstone. In his journal he speaks of his absolute reliance upon the Lord. He referred to the same text when he wrote, "It is the word of the gentleman of the strictest and most sacred honor, and there's an end of it."

Livingstone believed the promise of God; he took God at His word and great works were done by God through him in the darkened continent of Africa.

It's one thing to think of John Paton kneeling at his wife's grave and claiming the promise of God or to remember the faith of Livingstone who leaned hard on this promise. But it's quite another thing for you and me to sense His presence for our needs.

Paton's trust in the Lord followed his obedience to the Word, as did Livingstone's. When you obey the Lord and trust Him, you are walking in the footsteps of great men of God. If you are lonely, remember that they also knew the meaning of the word. If you are disappointed in circumstances, remember that they too suffered disappointments. But if you are God's child, their God is your God. You can look to Him just as they did.

As a result of the ministry of Paton, it is said that the whole area in which he labored turned to God. Livingstone's impact on Africa is known to the world.

Christian, trust Him, obey Him, and hold on to His promises. He is with you! He is with you NOW! He has promised, "Lo, I am with you always."

 Truth for Soaring: "And Jesus came and spake unto them, saying, All power is given unto me in heaven and in earth. Go ye, therefore, and teach all nations, baptizing them in the name of the Father, and of the Son, and of the Holy Ghost, teaching them to observe all things whatsoever I have commanded you; and, lo, I am with you always, even unto the end of the world. Amen" (Matthew 28:18-20).

The Lord made a promise and He will keep it. He said that along with His power and authority comes His presence. To lay hold of that power and to be aware that He is with us enables us to do His bidding.

How to Be Handsome and Enjoy It!

When we use the word *handsome* today, we generally use it in terms of a person's face or figure. Some would say it means good-looking, but most word experts insist it is more of a beauty that is combined with dignity and stateliness. But while we understand the dictionary use of the word, most of us, no matter how we try, will never be handsome.

When the word first came to our language, it meant "easy to handle or manipulate or to wield, deal with or use in any way." So, *handsome* meant "easy to handle and use," just as *toothsome* used to mean "pleasant to bite." It does not surprise us to read of a knight who, unarmed, picked up a few cobblestones that were good and handsome to throw at the enemy. By no stretch of the imagination could you consider a rock handsome in our present understanding of that word—not even the "pet rock" that someone gave me for Christmas one year. Later the word took on another facet, meaning to be "ready at hand, convenient, suitable."

If we combine these earlier definitions, it isn't difficult to apply them to our lives. We turn to the Word that instructs us how to be handsome—easy to handle and be used.

First, to be spiritually handsome we must be surrendered to His will. That is, if we are egocentric and self-oriented, we will find ourselves trying to handle rather than be handled. We are to present our bodies "a living sacrifice" (Romans 12:1). Today when we speak of someone who is hard to handle, we mean he is self-willed, stubborn, inflexible, and intractable. This is an apt description of an unyielding Christian. His unyielding, adamant attitude makes him difficult to handle and be used of the Lord. A truly handsome Christian is responsive to God's will and is as pliable as clay in the hands of the Potter who forms us and makes us after His own will.

Another facet of meaning in this word, as it was once used, is "ready at hand and suitable." We are reminded of Peter's injunction, "But sanctify the Lord God in your hearts, and be ready always to give an answer to every man that asketh you a reason of the hope that is in you, with meekness and fear" (1 Peter 3:15). If there ever was a man who was hard to handle, it was Peter. But the apostle was filled with the Spirit and greatly used of God. He was God's divine penman to tell us that to be handsome we must recognize His lordship in our lives. (This is the meaning of "sanctify the Lord God in your hearts.") We are to recognize His sovereignty over our lives and be constantly available and responsive to His will.

But we must not forget our present use of the word. Today's usage is not without some connection with its history. Don't you think those who surrender their lives to God are easy to handle, and who make themselves constantly available to God have a special beauty about them? Those who try to be like the Lord, however unendowed they may be with natural beauty of form and face, have a special dignity that comes with fellowship with the King of Kings and Lord of Lords. To be "changed into the same image"—to be like Him—is to become handsome in the holy sense of the word (2 Corinthians 3:18). This reflected holiness develops into a handsomeness and a happiness that are always the result of doing the will of God.

 Truth for Soaring: "Neither yield ye your members as instruments of unrighteousness unto sin, but yield yourselves unto God, as those that are alive from the dead, and your members as instruments of righteousness unto God" (Romans 6:13).

How hard are you to handle? Does the Lord have difficulty using you—His tool—in His desire to get the job done here on earth? Are we yielded and pliable? Are we available? Are we responsive to His work in our lives? Are we more willing to be handled than to handle?

"Gold in Them Thar Hills!"

A few years ago I visited the historic northern California Mother Lode country that is famous for its gold. Almost in the center of the gold chain extending from Oakhurst to Loyalton along Highway 49 is Sutter's Mill, where gold was first discovered by James Wilson Marshall on January 24, 1848.

This precipitated the California gold rush that brought men and women to the area by boat, horseback, and even on foot. It lasted for 10 years (1848-1859) and resulted in the discovery of almost $600 million worth of gold. So many people caught the fever that San Francisco became a boomtown overnight, growing from a small town to a sizable city of 25,000 in one year. Frantically, people swarmed into California to seek their fortune. They willingly paid up to $100 a week for a room and up to $15 a day for a night's rest. Gold! Gold!

"There's gold in them thar hills!" Those words set hearts beating with fanciful dreams of an affluent life. Today people are still talking about gold—not only finding it but investing in it. Gold coins and gold stocks are the subject of many conversations throughout the land.

Job talked about the quest for gold when he wrote, "Surely there is a vein for the silver, and a place for gold where they fine it. . . . As for the earth, out of it cometh bread: and under it is turned up as it were fire. The stones of it are the place of sapphires; and it hath dust of gold. . . . He putteth forth his hand upon the rock; he overturneth the mountains by the roots. He cutteth out rivers among the rocks; and his eye seeth every precious thing. . . . But where shall wisdom be found? And where is the place of understanding?" (Job 28:1, 5, 6, 9, 10, 12). Job was saying that there are riches sought by men and there are true riches that are not mined from the earth. Of course, the greatest source of the true riches of wisdom and understanding is the Bible, the Word of God.

David, one of the more wealthy kings in the Bible, said of God's words, "More to be desired are they than gold, yea, than much fine gold; sweeter also than honey and the honeycomb" (Psalm 19:10). In a later Psalm he wrote, "The law of thy mouth is better unto me than thousands of gold and silver" (Psalm 119:72).

Take a trip to the Mother Lode country, and you will find hundreds of mounds and hills that were left desolate from the diggings of excited men looking for their fortune. Many of them left the mounds, frustrated and disillusioned. Others panned and scanned only to leave with their dreams shattered. Their searching was in vain. But such is never the case for the young person who comes to the mine of the Word of God. He digs and delights in his discovery, exclaiming, "Therefore, I love thy commandments above gold; yea, above fine gold" (Psalm 119:127).

Are you making daily discoveries in the Bible? Are you willing to dig deep to get your share of this treasure? Did you find some special "fine gold" that met your need this past week? As a spiritual prospector, the prospects that you will become more wealthy every day are not only good but sure. Happy prospecting, partner!

Truth for Soaring: "More to be desired are they than gold, yea, than much fine gold; sweeter also than honey and the honeycomb" (Psalm 19:10).

How wonderful to come to this "gold mine" and find new treasures each day! Although you have read a chapter before, there is always some rich, new nugget of truth that can help you in today's situation. Going deep in the mine is an investment in eternal riches.

WORTH OF THE BIBLE

This Holy Book I'd rather own,
Than all the gold and gems
That e'er on monarch's coiffure shone,
And all their diadems.

Nay! were the sea one chrysolite,
The earth one golden ball,
And diamonds all the stars of night,
This Book is worth them all!
—Tom M. Olsen

Goals

An expert marksman who was passing through a small town was surprised at what seemed to be evidence of some of the most amazing shooting he had ever seen. On trees, fences, and barns he found countless targets with a bullet hole in the center of the bullseye. He had never seen such shooting, such accuracy, before. There were no misses, not even a close-to-center shot. The bullet hole was always in the center.

Finding the man responsible for such marksmanship, he remarked, "This is the most wonderful shooting I have ever seen. How in the world did you do it?"

"Easy as pie," he answered. "I shot first and drew the circles afterwards."

Some serious reflection on this story could result in some positive results in the matter of setting goals. The "marksman" simply shot his gun without thought of a target. His aim didn't matter. The goal was determined after the trigger was pulled.

What is your goal? What is your aim in life? It's important to know. Paul wrote of pressing "toward the mark for the prize of the high calling of God in Christ Jesus" (Philippians 3:14).

Someone has written that the difference between a pilgrim and a vagrant is clear. A pilgrim is one who is traveling to a certain place. A vagrant is a mere stroller with no settled purpose or goal. Here are some goal-setting tips that will keep you on target.

1. *Determine your goal.* Churches are full of people who don't know what they want to do or what their goals are. It may be that God hasn't revealed exactly what He wants you to do. But you should be sure that your problem isn't a simple matter of failure to seek His will or your failure to get down to business and give goals some real consideration. A person in the will of God should at least know the general direction and plan for the future. The Lord will give details as to how to get there. But you must take the initiative.

   Goal planning is important. A number of options ought to be considered. Expose yourself in prayer to the will of God and determine whether or not He would have you in full-time Christian service. This should always be considered as a possibility. Then leave yourself open to His leading.

2. *Plan with your goal in mind.* Once you have determined either generally or specifically what God's will for you is, plan your life accordingly.

3. *Stick with your goal.* Don't be distracted from your goal. A fox hound that settles for a rabbit along the way is a disgrace to his owner. Don't let a rabbit by the wayside—she could have blue eyes and be very attractive—turn your head from your goal. Charles C. Noble said, "You must have long-range goals to keep you from being frustrated by short-range failures."

4. *Stay in the right direction.* Personal, periodical evaluation is important. People, like tacks, are useful if they have good heads and are pointed in the right direction.

5. *Plan your work and work your plan.* Goals are important, but you must do something about them. Direction without action will result in failure. Remember, the first two letters in "goal" are "go."

So determine your goal, plan accordingly, stick with it, go in the right direction, and don't give up. Then, on a distant day you won't find yourself drawing circles around bullet holes. What's more, you will have the satisfaction of knowing that your aim for your life was the same as the Lord's goal for you.

Truth for Soaring: "For God is my witness, whom I serve with my spirit in the gospel of his Son, that without ceasing I make mention of you always in my prayers, making request, if by any means now at length I might have a prosperous journey by the will of God to come unto you. For I long to see you, that I may impart unto you some spiritual gift, to the end ye may be established; that is, that I may be comforted together with you by the mutual faith both of you and me" (Romans 1:9-12).

Paul had goals. He set out to serve the Lord with all His heart. Occasionally the Lord closed the door, and he was directed another way. But his attitude was "this one thing I do" (Philippians 3:13). When Paul set a goal, he followed through faithfully. The result was up to God.

Only a Second

"One thousand one. One thousand two. One thousand three." Three seconds have gone by. The measurement of one second is about as long as it takes to say, "One thousand one." On the surface it doesn't seem very long; yet, a great deal can take place in that little second. Lightning, for example, travels about 28,000 miles per second. One of the fastest animals, the cheetah, can be moving 45 miles an hour in 2 seconds from a standing start, and then travel 103 feet in a second, or 70 miles an hour. At the end of a 100-yard dash, an excellent sprinter can cover 3 feet in one-tenth of a second.

Translating this into practical, spiritual truth isn't difficult. The Bible says, "God is our refuge and strength, a very present help in trouble" (Psalm 46:1). That is, just "in the nick of time" He's ready to help us in times of difficulty. With split-second response, new strength and grace are made available to the child of God who is in desperate need. David knew that when he prayed, "and hide not thy face from thy servant; for I am in trouble. Hear me speedily" (Psalm 69:17). Again, the psalmist says, "Hear my prayer, O Lord, and let my cry come unto thee. Hide not thy face from me in the day when I am in trouble; incline thine ear unto me; in the day when I call, answer me speedily" (Psalm 102:1, 2). It is significant that in one psalm we hear the cry, "hear me speedily" and in the other, "answer me speedily." God does both, quicker than any measurement of speed understandable to us!

While we can find comfort and blessing in the knowledge that He hears us speedily, we can rejoice in the knowledge that someday there will be a split-second change of environment for every redeemed child of God. Four times in the book of Revelation we hear Christ say, "I come quickly." The meaning isn't that He is coming soon; although, praise God, He may come soon—at any moment. It means, rather, that when He comes, it will be quickly or speedily! Three of these occurrences are in the last chapter of the Bible (Revelation 22). Indeed, the last recorded words of the Lord are these: "Surely I come quickly" (Revelation 22:20).

The apostle Paul also talked about that sudden, swift return of the Lord. In 1 Corinthians he addressed the believer when he said, "Behold, I shew you a mystery: We shall not all sleep, but we shall all be changed, in a moment, in the twinkling of an eye, at the last trump; for the trumpet shall sound, and the dead shall be raised incorruptible, and we shall be changed" (15:51, 52).

With Christ's instant coming there will be an instant change. We will be transformed as fast as the "twinkle of an eye." When you consider that the human eye blinks in one-fortieth of a second, you might get some idea of the speed of that change. Yet our word translated *twinkling* means a "sudden motion of the eye." Some consider it to mean "the quiver of the eye." Without straining the thought, it is delightfully sufficient to say that this day of victory will be swift and sudden! Our imaginations stagger when we think of such an instant change into His wonderful likeness.

Yes, He is with us now, just when we need Him most. And someday (perhaps soon) He will speedily rapture us out of this present world scene. The long, hard hours of service will be climaxed in sure and swift victory though our Lord Jesus Christ. "Therefore, my beloved brethren, be ye steadfast, unmovable, always abounding in the work of the Lord, forasmuch as ye know that your labor is not in vain in the Lord" (1 Corinthians 15:58).

 Truth for Soaring: "God is our refuge and strength, a very present help in trouble. Therefore will not we fear, though the earth be removed, and though the mountains be carried into the midst of the sea" (Psalm 46:1, 2).

Praise the Lord that His presence is not limited to time! There is not an hour of the day that He is not actually "with us." Not only is He a present help, but His presence helps us unceasingly.

First, Count Nine

How's your temper? Ever get angry? Someone has described the temper as the banana skin of intelligence. It is the only thing you can lose and still have! How do you handle yours? (Or do you fly off the handle?) Life is filled with things that irritate us and people who rub us the wrong way, so we need to get a grip on our temper.

One rather well-known way of handling your temper is to hold your breath and count to ten. The theory is that this helps you cool down slightly below the boiling point and gives you time to recover your senses.

Let's imagine that someone has upset you almost beyond your power of self-control. It is supposed to work something like this: "I feel like giving him a piece of my mind . . . 1 . . . 2 . . . 3 . . . How could anyone be so cruel? . . . 4 . . . 5 . . . 6 . . . Really, anybody with an ounce of intelligence wouldn't . . . 7 . . . 8 . . . 9 . . . If he does it again, I'll . . . 10 . . . Oh, well, consider the source." Of course, it doesn't usually work that way. More often than not, the offense results in brooding, if not outright retaliation!

I have a much better idea! Count to nine instead! It works much better for Christians. No, it isn't the decrease in the numerical figure that counts; rather, it's the substitution of words (and their accompanying ideas) for numbers.

These words are found in Galatians 5:22, 23: "But the fruit of the Spirit is 1) love, 2) joy, 3) peace, 4) longsuffering, 5) gentleness, 6) goodness, 7) faith (or faithfulness), 8) meekness, 9) temperance . . . "

It should first be noted that here is the fruit of the Spirit. Indwelling each child of God, the Spirit makes it His business to produce in us what we are incapable of producing ourselves.

For example, Jane Whittle has just said some very unkind things about you. You know that she is accusing you of the very things that are in her own life, and you are about to tell her so! The verse giving the ninefold fruit of the Spirit comes to your mind. Counting to the ninth you come to "temperance" or "self-control." You pray, "Lord, help me to control myself and be the kind of testimony that will most please You." It is marvelous the way the Spirit takes over and honors your faith in Him.

Or you have just discovered that Frank Star, a leader in the Sunday evening youth fellowship, hasn't shown up to discharge his duties. You also learn that he went with a gang of young people to another church where a certain Christian film was being shown. You would like to have seen the film too, but you knew your duty was to your own church. Discouragement mixed with anger wells up in your heart. Then you remember the verse, "Love, joy, peace, longsuffering, gentleness, goodness, *faithfulness* . . ." Yes, that's what matters—my faithfulness to the Lord in spite of the actions of others! "Lord, help me to keep my eyes on You, and to be faithful." Again the Spirit produces His fruit in your life.

Danny Frolik has an ugly disposition. There was something about his attitude that bothered everybody. He was one of those "know-it-all" people you seldom feel comfortable around. He has just finished imparting some "words of advice" to the guys and gals at the church. A whisper is overheard from a friend: "What a phoney! I just can't stand that guy." You're just about to agree until you begin to apply God's Word to your own heart. You don't get beyond fruit number one: "But the fruit of the Spirit is love. . . ." You learn that the Spirit of God can produce a love in your heart even for those who may be unlovely to you. Victory again!

This doesn't mean that there is magic in these words. Nor is it a mechanical recitation of the verses that will produce great results. Rather, it's an awareness that the Spirit has provided a way to meet every difficulty and problem in everyday living. This is how Christ lives His life through us. "I am crucified with Christ: nevertheless I live: yet not I, but Christ liveth in me . . . " (Galatians 2:20).

Reason enough, indeed, to bow our heads and pray, "Thank You, Lord, for supernatural power to meet the pressures and problems in everyday living."

 Truth for Soaring: "And be not drunk with wine, wherein is excess, but be filled with the Spirit, speaking to yourselves in psalms and hymns and spiritual songs, singing and making melody in your heart to the Lord, giving thanks always for all things unto God and the Father in the name of our Lord Jesus Christ, submitting yourselves one to another in the fear of God" (Ephesians 5:18-21).

To be filled with the Spirit is to know the moment-by-moment control of the Holy Spirit in our lives. The evidence of the Spirit-filled life is the "fruit of the Spirit."

Are You Limiting God?

Of all the sins of Israel in the wilderness, one of the most puzzling is their sin of limiting God. Some of their sins are catalogued in Psalm 78. In this chapter we have a clear statement of what the Lord did for them. He "opened the door of heaven" to them (v. 23). He rained down manna upon them to eat, and He had given them the corn of heaven. Man did eat angels' food; he sent them meat to the full (vv. 23-25). "So, they did eat, and were well filled; for He gave them their own desire" (v. 29).

Yet, after all this limitless blessing we read, "Yea, they turned back and tempted God and limited the Holy One of Israel" (v. 41). After God opened heaven's doors, filled them "to the full" and assured them of His forgiving power, they added to their sins. They, the creatures, limited the Creator. They, the recipients of all His bountiful blessings, limited the One who had never failed them.

But before we are quick to say much more about the puzzling nature of Israel's blatant sin, let us examine our own hearts to make sure we are not limiting the Lord. Here's one way we limit Him: While we accept His power to save us, we are less reluctant to accept His power to sustain us. Another limitation is our willingness to commit our spiritual welfare to Him but somehow limit Him concerning our physical and material needs. It is almost like inheriting a million dollars from someone, then worrying about a bill for 10 cents that suddenly confronts us.

Are you needlessly worrying about areas of your life that should be committed to the Lord? When we speak of the power of the Lord, are we unwilling to believe that the power stretches over into other areas of our lives besides salvation?

Years ago, James Smith wrote, "This was Israel's sin, and has it not been ours? Our God is the Holy One and will do what is most for His glory; He is the Holy One 'of Israel,' and will therefore consult His people's welfare. We must not limit His wisdom, for it is infinite; we must not limit His power, for it is omnipotent; we must not limit His mercy, for it is as high as heaven and as deep as hell; we must not limit Him to time, for He will display His sovereignty; He will not be tied to walk by our rules, or be bound to keep our time; but He will perform His word, honor our faith, and reward them that diligently seek Him."

Stop limiting the Lord! Stop hemming Him in by the bounds of your own human understanding. Don't be guilty of dictating to Him the way things should be and insisting that He meet your demands. Rest in His limitless wisdom; His plan for you is better than anything you might devise. Rest in His limitless power and be careful not to relegate to Him areas only connected with the spiritual; He knows no such finely drawn division. Rest in His limitless resources; all things are His to give. Better still, rest on His limitless Person. "He that did not withhold or spare (even) His own Son but gave Him up for us all, will He not also with Him freely and graciously give us all (other) things" (Romans 8:32, Amplified).

 Truth for Soaring: "Yea, they turned back and tempted God, and limited the Holy One of Israel. They remembered not his hand, nor the day when he delivered them from the enemy" (Psalm 78:41-42).

If Israel had only remembered what the Lord had done for them, they would not have limited Him. Likewise, if you will reflect on the Christian race in "past laps," you can forge on and "run that ye may obtain" (1 Corinthians 9:24). Whenever you are prone to limit God, remember where you are and what God has done to get you this far.

Bored or Blasé

What is the difference between being blasé and being just plain bored? Well, everyone knows what it means to be bored. It is better illustrated than defined.

You are sitting in the living room and your father is discussing business with a friend. You are trying to be polite; but actually you are bored to tears. Your interest is "zilch." Or someone is explaining a special knitting stitch to a neighbor and you are waiting for lunch; you are hardly "in stitches." Actually, you are bored and impatient.

But to be blasé is something else. It is boredom with a special effect. It is to be bored with some things that would be delightful to someone else. It implies that you are satiated with this particular thing and no longer find an interest in or desire for it.

Blasé is a French word which means "to be worn out." It is from an older word which means "blown." The idea is that you are exhausted; the breath is out of you. On the other hand, we often speak of a person who is not bored or blasé as being breathless with excitement. Both seem out of breath, but for different reasons and with different effects.

Is it possible to be blasé about the things of the Lord? It surely is! Your pastor is probably a good preacher, maybe the best in town. But having heard such preaching week after week, if you aren't careful, you might develop the blasé syndrome. Or if you are going to a Christian school and hear spiritual truth day after day and then again on Sunday, if you aren't careful, you could become blasé about the things of God.

The world often looks at a blasé person with admiration. While the simple would be delighted in some little pleasure, Mr. and Mrs. Sophistication would look upon it as "simply nothing." It seems to put them in a special class.

For the believer to be blasé is hardly commendable. The things of the Lord should never be "old stuff." Even when we have heard a good preacher many times, we ought to be freshly blessed and daily thankful. Also, there should be gratitude for our Christian schools and the consistency of their stand and teachings.

But how does one guard against a blasé attitude? We need to keep spiritually fresh. Every truth can leave us breathless with excitement if we have a right relationship with the Lord. On the other hand, we can become worn out and exhausted with hearing something more than once when we are out of touch with Him.

So if you are bored or blasé, chances are it is because of an adjustment you must make with the Lord. When you are in tune with Him, divine things are never "old hat."

Truth for Soaring: "So they read in the book in the law of God distinctly, and gave the sense, and caused them to understand the reading. And Nehemiah, who is the Tirshatha, and Ezra, the priest, the scribe, and the Levites who taught the people, said unto all the people, This day is holy unto the LORD, your God; mourn not, nor weep. For all the people wept, when they heard the words of the law. Then he said unto them, Go your way, eat the fat, and drink the sweet, and send portions unto them for whom nothing is prepared; for this day is holy unto our LORD. Neither be ye sorry; for the joy of the LORD is your strength" (Nehemiah 8:8-10).

When Ezra read the Word of God, the people were certainly not blasé. The emotion found in their reception of the Word is a blessing, both the weeping and the joy. The day was a holy day. The two are opposites—holy and blasé. What is holy is always fresh, real, and invigorating. Its uplifting effect rises above the banal and dull.

Bigwig

The stern, august judge entered the courtroom. No one would doubt his distinction as everyone noted his large powdered wig.

The time: The eighteenth century. The place: England. The point: From this scene we get our word *bigwig,* which speaks of "a person who ranks himself higher than the rest of his neighborhood—or church." Sometimes a bigwig is spoken of as a stuffed shirt, someone "high and mighty."

"Someday, I'm going to be a bigwig!" This is the language of a person who aspires to be above others in a place demanding respect by underlings. Carnal? Yes, that is one of a number of appropriate words for it. People who aspire to be bigwigs need big heads. I once heard of a person who was so bigheaded he couldn't get an aspirin to fit him.

There should be no bigwigs in the church. Paul wrote, "For I say, through the grace given unto me, to every man that is among you, not to think of himself more highly than he ought to think, but to think soberly, according as God hath dealt to every man the measure of faith" (Romans 12:3). You will notice that this verse is right next to the verses you know so well regarding the surrendered, yielded life. When Paul said, "And be not conformed to this world," he was also speaking out against the be-a-bigwig-if-you-can philosophy.

Paul's reasoning is clear: "For as we have many members in one body, and all members have not the same office, so we, being many, are one body in Christ, and every one members one of another" (Romans 12:4, 5). We are interdependent members of the same body. One part of the body cannot boast over the other parts, because he didn't become a part of the body by his own choice. That was God's choice. His gift and function is Spirit-imparted. This is why Paul said on another occasion, "If the foot shall say, Because I am not the hand, I am not of the body; is it, therefore, not of the body? And if the ear shall say, Because I am not the eye, I am not of the body; is it, therefore, not of the body? . . . But now hath God set the members, every one of them, in the body, as it hath pleased him" (1 Corinthians 12:15, 16, 18).

Each of us is to function as a member of the body with no thought of one being greater or more important than the other. This means that a person who has a high attitude about himself and his superior function tends to be carnal. Paul said so in a way no one could misunderstand: "Let nothing be done through strife or vainglory, but in lowliness of mind let each esteem other better than themselves. Look not every man on his own things, but every man also on the things of others" (Philippians 2:3, 4).

Our prime example of a humble and lowly person is Christ, as the following verses show: "Let this mind be in you, which was also in Christ Jesus, who, being in the form of God, thought it not robbery to be equal with God, but made himself of no reputation, and took upon him the form of a servant, and was made in the likeness of men; and, being found in fashion as a man, he humbled himself and became obedient unto death, even the death of the cross" (Philippians 2:5-8).

If you're suffering with a serious case of self-infatuation, ask God to forgive you. Then determine that the big wig will be worn by someone else.

 Truth for Soaring: "For thou wilt save the afflicted people; but wilt bring down high looks" (Psalm 18:27).

"For the day of the LORD of hosts shall be upon every one that is proud and lofty, and upon every one who is lifted up, and he shall be brought low" (Isaiah 2:12).

One thing is sure, there is no spiritual soaring when there is pride. But when we humble ourselves, we are made to soar and enjoy the blessings from God's hand. "Humble yourselves in the sight of the Lord, and he shall lift you up" (James 4:10).

Shaking the Tree

Martin Luther once said, "I study my Bible like I gather apples. First, I shake the whole tree so the ripe ones might fall. After I shake each limb, I shake each branch and twig. Then, I look under every leaf."

He continued, "I search the Bible as a whole just like I shook the whole tree. Then I shake every limb—study book after book. I continue by shaking every branch—giving attention to the chapters. Finally, I shake every twig—careful study of the paragraphs and sentences as well as words and their meanings."

I rather like that, don't you? Do you have a systematic approach to your study of the Bible? Have you gathered any ripe fruit from the Word today? Have you shaken a limb or two?

Charles Spurgeon produced 135 books and edited 28 more. Including his shorter writings, he topped the 200 mark. Spurgeon was a lover of the Bible. He said, "The quarry of the Holy Scripture is inexhaustible. I seem hardly to have begun to labor in it; but the selection of the next block and the consideration as to how to work it into form are matters not so easy as some think."

I like that analogy. Digging in the quarry of the Holy Scriptures and laboring in it. Putting blocks together in sermons and Bible study—that's good. By the way, that is what happens in some of our nation's great Bible conferences. The preachers and teachers are masters at their skill. They dig deep into the quarry, and then they work some of the treasure into a form that will bless our hearts.

> There is a Treasure,
> Rich beyond measure,
>   Offered to mortals today;
> Some folk despise it,
> Some folk criticize it,
>   Some would explain it away.
>
> Some never read it,
> Some never heed it,
>   Some say "it's long had its day";
> Some people prize it,
> And he who tries it
>   Finds it his comfort and stay.
>
> God has this Treasure,
> Rich beyond measure,
>   His Word, we call it today.
> Let us believe it,
> Gladly receive it,
>   Read, mark, and learn to obey.
>   —A. M. N.

We can speak of shaking the tree and gathering ripe fruit (as Luther did). Or we can talk of digging into the precious resource of the richest treasure in the world. Either way, the result is the same. We are blessed by the Word of God.

Truth for Soaring: "All Scripture is given by inspiration of God, and is profitable for doctrine, for reproof, for correction, for instruction in righteousness" (2 Timothy 3:16).

When you shake the tree, you are not just getting some exercise. You are being productive. Shaking the tree is profitable in many ways: for doctrine, for reproof, for correction and instruction. So shake it and enjoy the results.

The Sun and Its Creator

The sun is one of God's most remarkable creations. It is so common to us that we often take it for granted. Speaking of God, the psalmist wrote, "the day is thine, and the night also is thine; thou hast prepared the light and the sun" (Psalm 74:16). And he said, "He appointed the moon for seasons; the sun knoweth his going down" (Psalm 104:19).

No wonder we read later, "praise ye him, sun and moon; praise him, all ye stars of light" (Psalm 148:3). It is the created praising the creator.

When God made the sun, He made it just right. It is the largest object in the solar system, with a diameter of about 109 times that of the earth. It is about 91,400,000 miles from the earth (at its shortest distance). It takes sunlight about 8 minutes and 20 seconds to reach the earth, traveling at more than 186,000 miles per second. The temperature of the sun is about 27,000,000 degrees fahrenheit. Amazingly, the earth intercepts only one two-thousand-millionth of the sun's total energy.

Experts say that if the sun's temperature dropped by just 13 per cent, the earth would become imprisoned in a cocoon of ice a mile thick. And, if the heat increased by 30 per cent, every last vestige of life on earth would be fried to extinction.

What a wonderful God we have! He has worked it out just right. We have exactly what we need. Any more or any less would create numerous problems. This great source of energy is available to us all.

I'm not surprised to find that God even used the sun to describe Himself. The psalmist wrote, "For the LORD God is a sun and shield; the LORD will give grace and glory. No good thing will he withhold from them that walk uprightly" (Psalm 84:11).

Notice that he is called a sun and a shield. Spurgeon said it well, "Pilgrims need both as the weather may be, for the cold would smite them were it not for the sun, and foes are apt to waylay the sacred caravan, and would haply destroy it if it were without a shield. Heavenly pilgrims are not left uncomforted or unprotected. The pilgrim nation found both sun and shield in that fiery cloudy pillar which was the symbol of Jehovah's presence, and the Christian still finds both light and shelter in the Lord his God. A sun for happy days and a shield for dangerous ones. A sun above, and a shield around. A sight to show the way and a shield to ward off its perils" (*Treasury of David*). He is our sun. He is our source of energy and light. He is the center of our lives, which revolve around Him.

As you are greeted by the rising sun, warmed by its rays, and delighted by its energy, let the sun remind you of the greatness of our God. Let it remind you of His provision. Or as Daniel Wilcox wrote, "O my soul! look up to the Father of lights: the Lord is a sun, whose steady beams shall direct thy steps. Is there an inward veil to be removed from my mind, as well as obscurity from my path? He is sufficient for both. God who commanded the light to shine out of darkness, can shine into the heart, to give the light of the knowledge of his glory, and lead on to it."

 Truth for Soaring: "The Law of the LORD is perfect, converting the soul; the testimony of the LORD is sure, making wise the simple. The statutes of the LORD are right, rejoicing the heart: the commandment of the LORD is pure, enlightening the eyes" (Psalm 19:7, 8).

"God, who commanded the light to shine out of darkness, can shine into the heart to give the light of the knowledge of His glory, and lead on to it" (Daniel Wilcox).

Via Butter

Two frogs fell into a can of milk,
Or so I've heard it told;
The sides of the can were shiny and steep;
The milk was deep and cold.
"Oh, what's the use?" croaked the Number One,
"Tis fate; no help's around.
Goodbye, my friend! Goodbye, sad world!"
And weeping still, he drowned.

But Number Two, of sterner stuff,
Dog paddles in surprise;
Then, while he wiped his milky face
And dried his milky eyes.
"I'll swim a while, at least," he said—
Or so I've heard it said.
"It really wouldn't help the world
If one more frog were dead."

An hour or two he kicked and swam,
Not once he stopped to mutter,
But kicked and kicked and swam and kicked—
Then hopped out, via butter!
—T. C. Hamlet

Say, how about that? That's more than humor. That just makes good sense. We need to keep alive and kicking—to keep keeping on. That's not just good poetry, but good sense. There is something special about a person who endures and stays by the stuff even when he's against all odds. Real character is shown by the person who "holds on" and never gives up.

Did you know that the honey bee must visit 56,000 clover heads to produce one pound of honey? No wonder we speak of the busy bees. Since each clover head has 60 flower tubes, a total of 3,360,000 visits are necessary to get a pound of honey.

Are you going through some difficult times these days? Let me encourage you to "hang in there." Don't give up, say stop, or throw in the towel. Keep at it.

One step won't take you very far:
You've got to keep on walking;
One word won't tell folks who you are;
You've got to keep on talking;

Winning Words for Daily Living

One inch won't make you very tall;
    You've got to keep on growing;
One deed won't do it all:
    You've got to keep on going.
                    —*Arkansas Baptist*

 Truth for Soaring: "Whatsoever thy hand findeth to do, do it with thy might" (Ecclesiastes 9:10).

Remember the frog and the butter. Remember the bee and the honey. "Stay by the stuff" and keep on keeping on.

Yawns: Silent Shouts

"An involuntary reaction to fatigue or boredom." That's the official definition of *yawn*. Are you a yawner? I once read in a *Farmer's Almanac* that "a yawn is at least an honest opinion." Actually, there are some who suggest that a yawn stimulates the brain.

One Japanese transistor manufacturer has scheduled 30-second "yawn breaks" in the factory schedule. On cue, everyone raises his hands over his head and yawns in unison. And, listen to this! The manufacturer claims production has jumped considerably.

Can't you just see us doing this in church? Right in the middle of the pastor's message? I wish I had a dollar for every yawn I've seen from the pulpit when I've preached. The next time it happens, I'll just think that it is stimulating the people to stay with me for the rest of the sermon. When a person is bored, it is usually because the speaker is boring or because the person is not interested in the subject matter.

I once heard about a person who was so boring that he was as stimulating as a mouthful of sawdust and water. He had a wide circle of nodding acquaintances. When there's nothing more to be said, he continues to talk. On the other hand, it could be a little indication that his heart is not right. G.K. Chesterton once wrote that a yawn is a silent shout.

What does this mean? Maybe it means a person is not interested in spiritual things. Maybe it says, "I want to be entertained. You must give television some competition. I must be piqued, diverted, and amused." What is the answer to this condition? I suppose the answer is found in spending time getting ready for the spiritual. It is to detach ourselves from the secular or mundane, from the demands of the "tell me something new" society with its fast-paced propensity.

The next time you find yourself yawning, check it out. Ask the Lord to help you consecrate your concentration. May your mind's eye be turned to Christ Himself. Don't be embarrassed by a yawn— it is a silent shout, demanding that you make some inward adjustments.

 Truth for Soaring: "But the natural man receiveth not the things of the Spirit of God; for they are foolishness unto him, neither can he know them, because they are spiritually discerned" (1 Corinthians 2:14).

"But he that is spiritual judgeth all things, yet he himself is judged of no man" (1 Corinthians 2:15).

"For who hath known the mind of the Lord, that he may instruct him? But we have the mind of Christ" (1 Corinthians 2:16).

When the transition is made from the carnal to the spiritual, there is also a transition from boredom to excitement; from the secular to the sacred; from the meaningless to the meaningful. It is the difference between gravitating toward the worldly and soaring in the heavenlies.

Keys

I have a terrible time keeping track of things. When I was a boy, my mother used to say, "Son, you would lose your head if it weren't attached to your shoulders." Ever hear that one? Of course you have. You may say it to your own children. But seriously, I have a tough time when it comes to losing things. Ask my wife, my secretary, or my friends. And the number one things I lose are my keys.

Keys are important. Car keys especially. The last things I check before going to bed at night are my wallet, my car keys, and my house keys. Really, I have so many of them I don't know how I lose them. Master keys to the college and seminary. Keys to the car. Keys for special places in the seminary—to lose them would put me out of commission. I've seen a little gismo that causes keys to buzz like an alarm when you clap your hands. This is encouraging to me because it confirms that I am not alone.

On a more serious note, whoever keeps the keys is important. Not everyone has a master key to the college and seminary. And only a few people have keys to our house and car. Keys show ownership and responsibility, and they denote a special relationship. The Bible has a great deal to say about keys. Christ, for example, has the keys of death and hell. That is, He is sovereign over those areas. The Bible refers to the keys to the kingdom. But let me talk about the keys to your life. Who has authority there? Are you willing to let the Lord be Lord to the extent that He is the One who governs, controls, rules, and keeps the keys?

> Is there some problem in your life to solve?
>   Some passage seemingly full of mystery?
> God knows who brings the hidden thing to light;
>   He keeps the key.
>
> Is there some door closed by the Father's Hand
>   Which widely opened you had hoped to see?
> Trust God and wait—for when He shuts the door
>   He keeps the key.
>
> Is there some earnest prayer unanswered yet?
>   Or answered not as you had thought would be?
> God will make clear His purpose by and by;
>   He keeps the key.

Have patience with your God, your patient God,
    All wise, all knowing, no long tarrier is He.
And to the door of all thy future life
    He keeps the key.

Unfailing comfort, sweet and blessed rest,
    To know of every door He keeps the Key
That at last when He sees tis best
    Will give it to thee.

                           —Author unknown

 Truth for Soaring: "Behold, I stand at the door, and knock; if any man hear my voice, and open the door, I will come in to him, and will sup with him, and he with me. To him that overcometh will I grant to sit with me in my throne, even as I also overcame, and am set down with my Father in his throne" (Revelation 3:20, 21).

This verse refers to sanctification, not salvation. It's is not Christ's desiring to save, but rather to "come in" for fellowship. It is the communion that He wants with you: personal communion. Will you open the door?

Lord of Pots and Pans

When you ask a woman where she works, she may answer with tongue planted firmly in cheek, "Oh I don't work, I'm a homemaker." Unfortunately, some people really think that is true. But I'm not one of them.

I say hats off to the mother or wife who keeps house and home together and works hard at being a homemaker. If you are one of them, I will not "preach" to you about the problems that occur when mother or wife work outside the home. But I will "reach" to you who stay at home and do the will of God at home. I think a special accolade is to be given to you, homemaker—for your faithfulness. Believe me, it is certainly not a put-down to be at home.

I remember a mother—my mother—who faithfully kept the house and home and raised my brother and me in the admonition of the Lord. Today my wife Ruth is a homemaker, a homekeeper. And while she is a qualified Registered Nurse, she finds being at home very special. She enjoys it, and I enjoy her doing it.

I think we are going to be very surprised when we get to heaven and see the rewards given by our Lord. I think we will find a special place for a mother, a wife, who honored the Lord in keeping the home. Most men would agree that without our wives, our home would be just a house—a place in which to live overnight until work the next day. But what a difference a woman's touch makes to every part of the home. So, for your faithfulness we pay tribute to you:

THANKS

Thanks for the special touch you give the home.
Thanks for the thoughtfulness in little details that make
 our home special.
Thanks for the good balanced meals that you think
 about and prepare.
Thanks for the atmosphere that pervades this place.
Thanks for the spirit and tone of the home which is
 almost sacred because God's will is being done here.
Thanks for the sacrifice and service that are performed
 with a willing heart and willing hands.

An unknown author has written this little prayer:

THE KITCHEN PRAYER

Lord of all pots and pans and things,
 since I've not time to be

Winning Words for Daily Living

A saint by doing lovely things or
    Watching lake with Thee,
Or dreaming in the dawn light or
    storming heaven's gates,
Make me a saint by getting meals
    and washing up the plates.
Although I must have Martha's hands,
    I have a Mary mind,
And when I black the boots and
    shoes, thy sandals, Lord, I find.
I think of how they trod the earth,
    what time I scrub the floor
Accept this meditation Lord, I haven't
    time for more.
Warm all the kitchen with Thy love,
    and light it with Thy peace,
Forgive me all my worrying and
    make my grumbling cease.
Thou who dids't love to give men food,
    in room or by the sea,
Accept this service that I do, I do it
    unto Thee.

Truth for Soaring: "And whatever ye do in word or deed, do all in the name of the Lord Jesus, giving thanks to God and the Father by him" (Colossians 3:17).

Is it possible to "soar" in the kitchen? Can one soar spiritually and mount up with wings as eagles in a place like that? Of course, there and everywhere, when we do all in the name of the Lord Jesus.

Praise the Lord

Someone has written that the hardest thing any man can do is to fall down on the ice and still get up and praise the Lord. I think that is one of Josh Billing's observations.

Praising the Lord is something that we all need to be reminded to do. Of course, when things go right, it is easy enough. But David wrote, "I will bless the Lord at all times; his praises shall continually be in my mouth" (Psalm 34:1). Then he said (note how closely connected this thought is to praising), "My soul shall make her boast in the LORD; the humble shall hear thereof, and be glad. Oh, magnify the LORD with me, and let us exalt his name together" (vv. 2, 3). One way to magnify the Lord is to praise Him. Later in the Psalm we have the same idea, "Whoso offereth praise glorifieth me" (Psalm 50:23). Do you want to glorify God? Most of us do. That is one of our prime objectives—to glorify God in our bodies and spirits which are God's (1 Corinthians 6:20). Well, praise Him under all circumstances.

I think the classic passage on praise is in the last Psalm. Perhaps you will enjoy reading it out loud: "Praise ye the LORD. Praise God in his sanctuary; praise him in the firmament of his power. Praise him for his mighty acts; praise him according to his excellent greatness. Praise him with the sound of the trumpet; praise him with the psaltery and harp. Praise him with the timbrel and dance; praise him with stringed instruments and organs. Praise him upon the loud cymbals; praise him upon the high sounding cymbals. Let every things that hath breath praise the Lord. Praise ye the Lord" (Psalm 150:1-6).

In this day when we are so health-conscious, we should remember that praise, especially praising the Lord, is healthful. It is good for you. In his book, *None of These Diseases*, Dr. S.I. McMillen points out that three things must be practiced if one is to adapt successfully to life's disease-producing stress factors:

1. Diversify the stressful agent. Continued exposure to any one stress factor isn't good.
2. Avoid long exposure to such agents by resting.
3. Take the proper attitude of mind.

A little quotation at the beginning of the chapter says it well: "Two men look out through the same bars: one sees the mud, and one the stars." Your attitude and frame of mind are very important in life. I once wrote a poem entitled "A Healthy Dose of Praise." Let me share it with you:

Winning Words for Daily Living

If you get down in the doldrums
  In the basement of despair,
Count your blessings, count your mercies,
  Then, add a little praise to prayer.

Aggravated by your problems,
  Plain "fed up" with others' ways?
Give yourself a spiritual tonic
  Try a healthy dose of praise.

Pinching pennies, stretching dollars,
  Coupons, green stamps are the ways,
Still the budget isn't budging.
  Stop and try a little praise!

Meat is higher in your shopping,
  Coffee's up—and mayonnaise,
Still, your table's never empty,
  Stop and try a little praise.

Miffed at something said unkind,
  Maybe, slightly hurt or dazed.
Here's the sure way to recover
  Try a healthy dose of praise.

Praise Him for your many blessings.
  Praise for daily strength to raise
Sweet and lovely little children
  Watch their spiritual growth and praise.

Praise Him for a faithful spouse,
  For your friends, faithful and true,
Praise Him for His faithful meeting
  All your needs, and all life through.

Problems? Yes, but you'll agree
  That His blessings sure outweighs
The light afflictions that are yours.
  So, thank Him with a word of praise.

Truth for Soaring: "I will call on the LORD, who is worthy to be praised; so shall I be saved from mine enemies" (2 Samuel 22:4).

While praise helps us, this is not the only reason for it. God, the Father and Giver, is worthy of praise. Lift up your heart in gratitude to God, and soar to a new spiritual dimension of praise.

The Taming of the Shrew

We are all somewhat aware of Shakespeare's work, *The Taming of the Shrew*. The word *shrew* is often used to describe "a brawling, scolding woman." But, to be honest, there are some male shrews strewed around in the stew of life as well.

The word is a very descriptive one, because the shrew, while it is the world's smallest mammal, is one of the most ferocious. This little mammal guy is only 2 inches long and weighs about as much as a nickel. Experts say that his appetite and aggressiveness makes a lion seem tame by comparison. He has a bite like a cobra, eats twice his own weight in meat every day, and can whip an animal three times his size. His teeth are needlelike and he has a mouth full of poison to help bring other animals down to his size. Believe it or not, the shrew's saliva contains a strange, virulent poison that can kill a mouse within 3 minutes—and he has enough of it (poison that is) to kill 200 mice. This mini-mammal is a tough customer indeed.

But to be compared to a shrew is hardly complimentary.

Have you met people who were shrew-like? The Bible speaks of people like this: "Their throat is an open sepulcher; with their tongues they have used deceit; the poison of asps is under their lips; whose mouth is full of cursing and bitterness. Their feet are swift to shed blood; destruction and misery are in their ways" (Romans 3:13-16). Mankind is that depraved. Way back in 1589, Puttenham wrote of "a shrew in the kitchen, a saint in the church." He was commenting on a woman named Jane Shore.

Well, male or female, young or old, God can tame the shrew—don't forget it. Sure there are hypocrites—shrews in the kitchen, but saints in the church—and they are dangerous. But don't forget that when Paul described that wicked person in Romans 1 through 3 and then concluded that "all have sinned and come short of the glory of God," he told us that we are all sinners and that the sinners' Savior can make the difference. Whether a person is a shrew trying to imitate a saint, or a wolf in sheep's clothing, or someone who is sinful and just admits it—it doesn't do any good to cover it up. For all kinds of sinners, dyed or double-dyed, religious or non-religious, conservative or liberal sinners, He makes the difference. Yes, he can tame the shrew.

Well, He doesn't really tame us—he makes us new. We are new creations, "created in Christ Jesus" as Paul says, "unto good works."

So, better than taming the shrew, like all of us, He makes us new—all new creatures in Christ.

 Truth for Soaring: "Therefore, if any man be in Christ, he is a new creature; old things are passed away; behold, all things are become new" (2 Corinthians 5:17).

What the world needs is not reformation, but regeneration. Not a new leaf, but a new life. Do you know Him as your Savior? Has He changed the shrew in you to something new?

Honor the Lord

God will not share His glory and honor with sinful man. To the church of Corinth, Paul said, "But God hath chosen the foolish things of the world to confound the wise; and God hath chosen the weak things of the world to confound the things which are mighty; and base things of the world, and things which are despised, hath God chosen, yea, and things which are not, to bring to nought things that are, that no flesh should glory in his presence" (1 Corinthians 1:27-29). When we are willing to lose ourselves in the Lord's will and give Him all the glory and credit for any advancement or blessing that comes, He will give us honor.

However great in intellectual capacity a man may be, however skilled in eloquence and endowed with charisma, if he seeks to bring glory to his own name, he will not be honored of God. Any service that brings self-glory will result in "wood, hay, and stubble" in the day of the believer's accounting. However, when we come to Him with a heart willing to give Him the glory in our lives, He will smile upon us and bless us in spite of any lack we may have.

In C. H. Spurgeon's *Autobiography*, we read:

> The greatness of our work compels us to confess that it must be of God, and of God alone. And, dear friends, we see that it must be so if we consider the little with which we began . . . Glory be to God, this cannot be man's work! What effort, made by the unaided strength of man, will equal this which has been accomplished by God? Let the name of the Lord, therefore, be inscribed upon the pillar of our memorial. I am always very jealous about this matter: if we do not, as a church and congregation or as individuals, always give God the glory, it is utterly impossible that He should continue to work by us. Many wonders have I seen, but I never yet saw a man who arrogated the honor of his work to himself, whom God did not leave sooner or later."

The same note of humble and hearty gratitude to God was very prominent in the discourse delivered in the Tabernacle on the Lord's Day morning, May 3, 1863, after the Pastor had returned from a preaching tour in Holland: "Praise be to God for the acceptance which He gave me among all ranks of the people in that country! I speak to His praise, and not to my own; for this has been a vow with me, that, if God will give me a harvest, I will not keep even an ear of it myself, but He shall have it all. . . . While going from town to town, I felt the Master helping me continually to preach. I never knew such elasticity of spirit, such bounding of heart in my life before; and I came back, not wearied and tired, though preaching twice every day, but fuller of strength and vigor than when I set out. I give God the glory for the many souls I have heard of who have been converted through the reading of the printed sermons, and for the loving blessings of those who followed us to the water's edge with many tears, saying, 'Do thy diligence to come again before winter,' and urging me once more to preach the Word in that land. There may be mingled with this some touch of egotism; the Lord knoweth whether it be so or not, but I am not conscious of it. I do praise and bless His name that, in a land where there is so much philosophy, He has helped me to preach the truth so simply that I never uttered a word as a mere doctrinalist, but I preached Christ, and nothing but Christ. Rejoice with me, my dear brethren; my loaf of praise is too great for me to eat it all."

 Truth for Soaring: "Wherefore the Lord God of Israel saith, I said indeed that thy house, and the house of thy father should walk before me forever; but now the Lord saith, Be it for from me; for them who honor me I will honor, and they who despise me shall be lightly esteemed" (1 Samuel 2:30).

I YIELD, OH LORD, MY HEART

Oh Lord, when I apart from Thee
    Attempt to serve, I find within
My heart increasing tendency
    To seek approval from all men.

Then, in my vain attempts to do
    His will, I strangely realize
That I've remembered my will too,
    While pressing toward the highest prize.

What shame then floods my heart;
    To think I'd dare attempt to share
His glory, and to then depart
    From His command—His cross to bear.

I yield, O Lord, my life to thee
    With full rejection of the goals
My flesh has made, and pray to be
    Lost in Thy will of reaching souls.
                  —Charles U. Wagner

Train Up a Child

"Train up a child in the way he should go and, when he is old, he will not depart from it" (Proverbs 22:6).

This promise has been claimed as much as any other verse in the Bible. How many parents have quoted it through a veil of tears after hearing some saddening news of a wayward son or daughter. God's Word is clear. When a child is trained properly, while there may be a time of "sowing wild oats," he will not soon forget what he has learned, and more often than not he will come back to the "old-time religion."

However, there seems to be so many exceptions to this promise. While God's Word does not need defense, it is important to state that some who claim this promise shouldn't. What is described as "the way he should go" is not simply a matter of occasional church attendance or general adherence to a few moral principles.

To train up a child includes a full-time devotion to the training of the child, including life at home, school, and church. It involves praying with the child and disciplining the child (with a hard, firm hand when necessary). It includes an insistence that he be in the Lord's house, worshiping with other believers. It includes restrictions that are made in love as to where he can go and what company he keeps. It involves explaining clearly, and with a burdened heart, the way of salvation and praying through until the child does become a Christian. It involves consistency on the part of Mom and Dad as they live their lives before the child as an example of obedience to the Word. It includes helping the child with his priorities and impressing on him that the true values of life and the most important investments are not in materialism, but in spirituality.

A young boy and his brother had been saved the same night in an evangelistic service. From that time on, the oldest of the two boys felt that God had called him to be a preacher. His parents lived a humble, consistent Christian life and saw that he was in church every time the doors of the church opened. The family would often gather together and sing the old hymns before they would bow before the Lord in prayer. The young man and his brother were bathed in prayer and enveloped in love. Yet, in spite of the love and affection, coupled with the godly example of their parents, both boys "fell away" and were out of fellowship with the Lord. Years passed, and the praying parents never gave up on their boys. Finally, after seasons of intercession with the Lord and an unwavering godly example from their parents, both sons returned to the Lord.

Praise the Lord, both are in Christian service. One plays the organ in one of the largest Baptist churches in Detroit while the other serves as president of a Christian college—yes, he is the writer of this book! God is good to His Word!

 Truths for Soaring: "And when she had weaned him, she took him up with her, with three bullocks, and one ephah of flour, and a bottle of wine, and brought him unto the house of the LORD in Shiloh; and the child was young. And they slew a bullock, and brought the child to Eli. And she said, Oh my lord, as they soul liveth, my lord, I am the woman that stood by thee here, praying unto the LORD. For this child I prayed; and the LORD hath given me my petition which I asked of him. Therefore also I have lent him to the LORD; as long as he liveth he shall be lent to the LORD. And he worshipped the LORD there" (1 Samuel 1:24-28).

What is the significance of parents bringing their children to a dedication service? Simply this: The parents are dedicating themselves, indeed, laying their own lives on the altar and in solemn resolution pledging to raise their child in the admonition of the Lord.

A PARENT'S PRAYER

We thank Thee; Lord, that Thou has given
This sweet and precious gift from Heaven,
A blessed heritage from Thee
Is this sweet child; help us to be
Examples in the years to come.
Then, may this child of ours be won
To Thee, saved by Thy matchless grace
And in Thine own dear family placed.

We are aware that nothing here
Can save his soul or make him fear
The Lord. We fully understand;
We place OURSELVES in Your dear hands.
We dedicate ourselves to do Your will
And pray for wisdom to instill
Your Word within his mind, and strive
To LIVE that Word in our own lives.
—Charles U. Wagner

God's Supply

"But my God shall supply all your need according to his riches in glory by Christ Jesus" (Philippians 4:19).

This promise, which is one of the most familiar in the Bible, has been claimed by hundreds of thousands of Christians in every generation. It shows a personal relationship with the Lord. Note that it says, "My God shall supply." It is not an optional thing with God to meet the needs of His own. He will do it. He is as good as His Word.

This promise is also unlimited: ". . . shall supply all your need." Every need, all needs, in every situation and circumstance! His promise is explicit. The resource of His abundant supply is precious indeed: "According to his riches in glory by Christ Jesus." It isn't simply "out of" His riches, but "according to" His riches. All the wealth of heaven is at our disposal.

Finally, it doesn't say, "all your wants," but "all your needs." Only in this is it limited. However, if our delight is in Him, our desires and needs will be the same. "Delight thyself also in the Lord, and he shall give thee the desires of thine heart" (Psalm 37:4).

Years ago when I was president of the Northwest Baptist Seminary in Tacoma, Washington, I observed many miracles from the hand of the Lord as students arrived. Because most of them were married, it became a serious matter when they pulled up in front of the seminary without a place to live and with no assurance of a job. One young couple with two children were on their way to Canada to involve themselves in a business venture when the Lord made it very clear, just before they were to cross over into Canada, that his place was in seminary. So he turned his trailer around and headed for Tacoma.

He had turned down a promising job, and now he needed one. He began looking for a house because the rented trailer was costing him money every day. No house was to be found. Would the Lord supply his need? He finally went to the trailer dealership and told them he would have to go to Seattle to find housing. The dealer ended up directing him to a house that met their needs perfectly. And what about the job? Only minutes after the young seminarian left my office, a man walked in and told me he needed a manager to take over his service station. I had never seen the man before, but he had heard about the seminary. The young seminarian now had both a job and a house.

Was it a miracle? Well, not on a par with parting of the Red Sea or the Jordan, but a miracle of God's leading and supply just the same.

I still see events such as this one duplicated over and over. Yes, He is our wonderful Lord! He is good to His Word.

 Truth for Soaring: "Ask, and it shall be given you; seek, and ye shall find; knock, and it shall be opened unto you; for every one that asketh receiveth; and he that seeketh findeth; and to him that knocketh it shall be opened. Or what man is there of you whom, if his son ask bread, will he give him a stone? Or if he ask a fish, will he give him a serpent? If ye then, being evil, know how to give good gifts unto your children, how much more shall your Father, who is in heaven, give good things to them that ask him?" (Matthew 7:7-11).

Just as a father delights in giving his son what he asks for, so the Lord takes great delight in exercising His omnipotent hand on our behalf.

OMNIPOTENT IS THIS MY LORD

Omnipotent this mighty Lord!
　"Let there be light," He spoke, 'twas done;
The worlds were framed at His command,
　All planets whirling round the sun.

Omnipotent this precious Lord!
　"Be still," He said, and all the sea
Respected the Creator's word,
　And stopped its wild, tempestuous spree.

He holds the keys of hell and death,
　Alive forevermore is He;
Alive to word to act, to save,
　And set the captive sinner free.

Omnipotent this saving Lord!
　I ponder this best Lord today,
Who condescended in His choice
　Of this frail, faltering house of clay.

At His Divine disposal there
　In Heaven's royal and regal room,
Triunal Counsel met and planned
　His birth, the cross, the empty tomb.

Omnipotent this keeping Lord!
　How dare I question the great power
Who saved me from my sin and shame;
　Shall He not meet my need this hour?
　　　　　　　　—Charles U. Wagner

Jehovah-shalom

"Thou wilt keep him in perfect peace, whose mind is stayed on thee, because he trusteth in thee" (Isaiah 26:3,4).

It has been pointed out that the phrase "perfect peace" is most significant in the Hebrew. It means literally, "peace peace." There is a double peace that belongs to the believer. One might be considered at peace *with* God, which happens when we trust Christ as our Savior (Romans 5:1). Then there is the peace *of* God, which is our constant help "keeping our hearts and minds through Christ Jesus" (Philippians 4:7). Double peace is referred to by the Lord when He said, "Peace I leave with you, my peace I give unto you; not as the world giveth, give I unto you. Let not your heart be troubled, neither let it be afraid" (John 14:27).

What a difference between what the world calls peace and what the Lord gives! Someone has insightfully observed that our text does not simply say, "God will keep us in perfect peace whose mind is stayed." A mind could be stayed and motionless without being rested. One's mind could be numb with disappointment and grief, paralyzed by problems. The point is that our minds should be stayed on Him. The difference in our peace and the world's is that our peace rests on a Person. Christ said it was "My peace." Paul says, "the peace of God;" Isaiah says, "stayed on thee." Indeed, the Lord is the procurer of peace (Isaiah 53:5), the personification of peace (Isaiah 9:6), the publisher of peace (Isaiah 52:7), the perfection of peace (Isaiah 26:3), the power of peace (Isaiah 26:12), the promise of peace (Isaiah 32:17), and the perpetuator of peace (Isaiah 9:6).

This peace comes through our trusting Him. Our minds are stayed on Him. J. Stuart Holden said, "It is significant that these words do not identify the experience of peace with the absence of loss and sorrow, but rather with the *Presence of God*. It is not that we are to be withdrawn from the reach of the influence of these things, but that we are to be drawn into close unison with Himself" (*The Pre-eminent Lord*, p. 71).

Perhaps the time that was most similar to our contemporary day was the awful times of the Judges. It was in this fourth apostasy of Israel that they cried unto the Lord in repentance and God sent the sixth judge, Gideon. The angel of the Lord appeared to him and said, "The Lord is with thee, thou mighty man of valour." On the surface, Gideon was anything but mighty. God, however, saw what he would be when he trusted Him. Gideon responded, "Oh my Lord, if the Lord be with us, why then is all this befallen us? and where be all his miracles which our fathers told us of . . . ?" (Judges 6:12, 13).

Like our present day, Gideon was filled with fear and doubt. He was both hysterical and historical. He had heard about the great history of God's help, but it was hardly more than a myth to him. Again, the Lord assured Gideon that He would be with him and then manifested His power to him (vv. 16-21). A change came over Gideon and his restless heart. He began to "stay his mind" on the Lord and enjoy a measure of His peace (v. 23).

Gideon then built an altar unto the Lord and called it *Jehovah-shalom*—The Lord our Peace. Sensing the presence of the Lord, he threw down the altars of Baal and cut down the groves. Later, when the odds were 400 to 1, he led 300 men against 135,000 of the enemy. The Midianites hadn't changed; the change was in Gideon! The Lord was with him, he was staying his mind on God instead of the enemy; he was going forth in the strength of the Lord—not his own. He had met Jehovah-shalom and was enjoying the peace and presence of God.

 Truth for Soaring: "Peace I leave with you, my peace I give unto you; not as the world giveth, give I unto you. Let not your heart be troubled, neither let it be afraid" (John 14:27).

JEHOVAH-SHALOM

When burdens build and cares increase
    And wear upon the soul and mind,
JEHOVAH-SHALOM is my peace
    The help is sure—the source Divine.

When unexpected testing comes
    Threatening this peace—promising pain,
I flee to this all-faithful One,
    JEHOVAH-SHALOM is His Name.

Worry and fear insult His power,
    What shame His Name is to persist
In handling one's own trying hour
    As though this Lord did not exist.

Oh, fearsome soul, cast all your cares
    And troubles on this God-sent Son.
His death made peace, His life declares
    JEHOVAH-SHALOM'S victory's won.
                    —Charles U. Wagner

Good Medicine

"A merry heat doeth good like a medicine; but a broken spirit drieth the bones" (Proverbs 17:22).

A man was doing door-to-door visitation; he shouldn't have been, because he was anything but a happy Christian. He knocked at one door and the person answering took one look at him and said, "No thanks; I have troubles of my own."

It was a good lesson. An unhappy person simply adds to another's troubles. On the other hand, there is something healing and helpful about a genuine smile resulting from the joy of the Lord. Nothing is worse than the poor advertisment that comes from a Christian who is irascible as a sick monkey. They are as helpful and stimulating as a squeezed lemon. But a merry heart . . . ! Ah, the Bible says it is good like medicine.

This verse is both a promise and a prescription. The prescription is praise; the promise is that such praise will help and heal the troubled soul. This is true both of the giver of the praise, and those who are around to listen and share.

"Praise ye the Lord; for it is good to sing praises unto our God; for it is pleasant; and praise is comely." (Psalm 147:1). In Nehemiah's day, when he saw and heard the people weep, he said, "Go your way, eat the fat, and drink the sweet, and send portions unto them for whom nothing is prepared; for this day is holy unto our Lord. Neither be ye sorry; for the joy of the Lord is your strength" (Nehemiah 8:10). "Dr. Nehemiah" was prescribing a spiritual vitamin that would result in moral muscle and fortitude for future days—a healthy dose of praise. And they took his advice, for we read, "And there was great gladness" (Nehemiah 8:17).

When you begin to praise the Lord for everything, you will find that your whole perspective will change and life will take on new meaning. Praise the Lord!

Of course, the joy of the Lord can't be turned on like a water faucet. God doesn't want us to go around with a smile like a slit in a pumpkin—pretending to be happy and hoping that we will be. Such psychology is ridiculous. His joy comes from a right relationship with Him. It is the fruit of the Spirit: "But the fruit of the Spirit is love, joy, peace . . ." (Galatians 5:22). Incidentally, joy is a sheltered fruit. It is sheltered by love on one side and peace on the other. And, if we are not loving as we should be, and have not the peace of God "keeping our hearts and minds," we will not have the "joy of the Lord."

The proof that the merry heart results in a helping effect is found throughout the Scriptures. "Heaviness in the heart of man maketh it stoop, but a good word maketh it glad" (Proverbs 12:25). "A merry heart maketh a cheerful countenance" (Proverbs 15:13). A happy heart and joyful disposition is a cosmetic that cannot be duplicated by Revlon. A happy smile is the prerogative of man. Gems can reflect, flowers are beautiful, but neither can smile. The happy smile belongs to man, and more specifically, to the Christian.

Proof also comes from the medical world. In his book, *None of These Diseases*, Dr. S.I. McMillen quotes another doctor, Dr. William A. Sadler: "No one can appreciate so fully as a doctor the amazingly large percentage of human diseases and suffering which is directly traceable to worry, fear, conflict, immorality, dissipation, and in ignorance—to unwholesome thinking and unclean living. The sincere acceptance of the principles and teachings of Christ with respect to the life of mental peace and joy, the life of unselfish thought and clean living, would at once wipe out more than half the difficulties, diseases, and sorrows of the human race" (pp. 64, 65).

 **Truth for Soaring:** I will praise the name of God with a song, and will magnify him with thanksgiving. This also shall please the LORD better than an ox or bullock that hath horns and hoofs. The humble shall see this, and be glad; and your heart shall live that seek God (Psalm 69:30-32).

"You cannot change the order of patience, person, praise. When God's people repent and give themselves to God they will have a song. It will be spontaneous, for what is down in the well will come up in the bucket" (Vance Havner).

Meek But Not Weak

It should be noted that we are not to pray for humility. We are rather to humble ourselves. Nor must we misconstrue this to be a groveling self-effacement, a constant putting down of ourselves, a feigned humility that is spineless and invertebrate. James said, "Humble yourselves in the sight of the Lord . . ." (4:10). This is a humbleness of mind that is directed God-ward.

A good example of this is the meekest man of his day, Moses. "Now the man Moses was very meek, above all the men who were upon the face of the earth" (Numbers 12:3). However, you would not detect this humility as you viewed his strong, robust, and courageous leadership. He was forthright in his dealing with sin and compromise. He was deliberate in his decisions and was perhaps the greatest leader Israel ever had. Yet, he was meek.

Perhaps he was not all that meek when he grew up in Egypt. Someone has suggested that the first 40 years of his life convinced him that he was "something" because he received all the advantages of his education as the son of Pharaoh's daughter. Then God put him on the backside of the desert to show him that he was "nothing." Finally, the last 40 years of his life God showed him what He can do with a man who is nothing. God lifted him up (Deuteronomy 34:10-12).

The greatest example of this principle is the Lord Jesus Christ. Paul enjoined the Philippians to be humble, to be meek. He said, "Let this mind [the humble—meek mind] be in you, which was also in Christ Jesus." Then he describes the self-humbling work of the Lord: "Who, being in the form of God, thought it not robbery to be equal with God, but made himself of no reputation, and took upon him the form of a servant, and was made in the likeness of men; and, being found in fashion as a man, he humbled himself and became obedient unto death, even the death of the cross" (Philippians 2:5-8).

"Humble yourselves therefore under the mighty hand of God," Peter writes—knowing well the prime example of Christ—"that he may exalt you in due time" (1 Peter 5:6). How beautifully this is also illustrated in Paul's letter to the Philippians: "Wherefore, God also hath highly exalted him, and given him a name which is above every name, That at the name of Jesus every knee should bow, of things in heaven, and things in earth, and things under the earth, and that every tongue should confess that Jesus Christ is Lord, to the glory of God, the Father" (Philippians 2:9-11).

Christ humbled Himself; He was also exalted. While we do not humble ourselves that we might be exalted (for such would not be true humility), the spiritual equation is still true. Nor do we know how that exaltation will come to be, nor when it will be. We are content to know that the way up spiritually is down, and the way down is to put ourselves up (see Proverbs 16:18, 19).

In a day when man is concerned about his image, his personal advancement, and his own aggrandizement, it is a real testimony for a Christian to humble himself before the Lord and to know that with this genuine humility is a precious promise of blessing.

 Truth for Soaring: "I therefore, the prisoner of the Lord, beseech you that ye walk worthy of the vocation wherewith ye are called, with all lowliness and meekness, with longsuffering, forbearing one another in love" (Ephesians 4:1, 2).

"To speak evil of no man, to be no brawlers, but gentle, shewing all meekness unto all men" (Titus 3:2).

MEEK BUT NOT WEAK

Lord, to be meek yet not be weak,
  Gentle in deed, in spirit strong;
To bow in meekness at HIS feet,
  In boldness stand before the throng.

Lowly in heart, just like my Lord,
  In humble action meekly serve,
Conmtending strongly with the Sword
  Never to falter, faint or swerve.

Lord, to be meek but never weak;
  When self's involved to meekly kneel,
But when His Name's at stake to speak
  Giving no ground, never to yield.

Lord, for a lowly, humble mind,
  So gentle, mild and Christ-like meek,
But never once in me to find
  A wayward soul not weak, but meek.
                    —Charles U. Wagner

The Full Dimension of His Love

There are five promises that can all be considered one. Combined, they give us an understanding of the full dimension of God's love.

THE FULL DIMENSION OF HIS LOVE

Am I alone? Have I a friend who cares?
Is there a "present help" in desperate need?
In which direction should I look? Who shares
My heart's concern? Who will my crying heed?

"The Angel of the Lord encampeth round about them that fear him" (Psalm 34:7).

I look *around*, the enemy surrounds
And then attacks, but greater than the foes
Are His encamping hosts–whose power abounds,
Preserving from evil, Satanic thrones.

"Underneath are the everlasting arms" (Deuteronomy 33:27).

I look *beneath*, the miry clay invites
Me to that place from whence I came:
I do not fear, the strength, the might
Of everlasting arms bring sweet refrain!

"He openeth the doors of heaven" (Psalm 78:23).

I look *above*, I'm suddenly aware
Of open doors from which His blessings flow.
Sufficient is *His* grace, ample *His* care,
The trusting heart will *His* provision know.

"And when He putteth forth his own sheep, he goeth before them . . ." (John 10:4).

But look *ahead*, what does the *future* hold?
Tomorrow brings problems unknown today!
The answer comes! Am I not of *His* fold?
The Shepherd goes before . . . prepares the Way.

"Surely goodness and mercy shall follow me" (Psalm 23:6).

Finally, I look *behind*, and now I see
The *full dimension* of His love and care,
The *full extension* of His grace for me,
Look back! Goodness and mercy . . . *follow* there.

Wherever we look, and from whatever perspective we stand, we are impressed that the Lord is caring for us in His love.

The arrangement of these verses (or verses like them) is not original. Somewhere, years ago, I read a message showing the complete adequacy of God's provision. To the weary, lonely, discouraged saint, there is no better set of promises. They are like five precious facets of a perfect diamond, gleaming against a black velvet background.

Looking around, we are sometimes unaware of the great host of God's provision in the unseen angels. How precious that He delegates hosts of heavenly emissaries to care for us and to surround us.

Looking beneath, we are impressed that we are held up, safely and securely by His everlasting arms. Once we were in miry clay. David said, "He brought me up also out of an horrible pit, out of the miry clay . . ." (Psalm 40:2). We never need to fear that we might fall.

Having seen beneath us His full protection, we naturally look up to be impressed with his full provision. How precious it is, knowing that "my God shall supply all your need according to his riches in glory by Christ Jesus" (Philippians 4:19).

Now, having seen His work for us in these other dimensions, what can we say of the future? What does it hold? More important than the questions about what the future holds is the assurance that God holds it.

The final facet of this "diamond promise" is not anticlimactic. What could be more fitting than to ponder the fact that both the full dimension of His love and care, and the full extension of His grace are seen in the little "twins" that bring up the rear: "Surely goodness and mercy shall follow me all the days of my life . . ." (Psalm 23:6). God is good; God is merciful. Both His goodness and mercy, already displayed in His saving grace, will follow us until faith shall be sight and until we see goodness and mercy personified in the person of His dear Son.

The proof of these verses is in the poetry of your own life, in the way the Lord has shown you Himself over the years, including His mercy and goodness. Be assured that what He has done, He will continue to do. Praise God for the full dimension of His love!

 Truth for Soaring: "That Christ may dwell in your hearts by faith; that ye being rooted and grounded in love, may be able to comprehend, with all saints, what is the breadth, and length, and depth, and height, and to know the love of Christ, which passeth knowledge, that ye might be filled with all the fullness of God" (Ephesians 3:17-19).

It passeth knowledge, that dear love of Thine,
My Jesus, Saviour; yet this soul mine
Would of Thy love, in all its breadth and length,
Its height and depth, its everlasting strength
Known more and more.
—Mary Shekleton

The Victory Is Won

Jesus Christ is coming back! Praise the Lord for this precious prospect! When He comes, faith will be sight and the blessed hope of the believer will be a reality. Jesus' return will be a time of a multitude of changes across the face of the earth.

It will also be a time of change for the believer: "We shall all be changed" (1 Corinthians 15:51). In another place Paul expressed it vividly, "For our conversation is in heaven, from which also we look for the Savior, the Lord Jesus Christ, who shall change our vile body, that it may be fashioned like his glorious body, according to the working whereby he is able even to subdue all things unto himself" (Philippians 3:20, 21). John said it similarly, "We shall be like him; for we shall see him as he is" (1 John 3:2). And, in another epistle Paul said, "Then we who are alive and remain shall be caught up together with them in the clouds, to meet the Lord in the air; and so shall we ever be with the Lord" (1 Thessalonians 4:17).

What is the greatest proof that all this will be a reality? The answer of Scripture is loud and clear in Paul's first epistle to the Corinthians. Our resurrection—the reality of this promise—is based on the resurrection of Christ! Paul said, ". . . if Christ be not risen, then is our preaching vain, and your faith is also vain." (15:14, 15). Later in the chapter he wrote, "If in this life only we have hope in Christ, we are of all men most miserable" (v. 19). The idea that if we are wrong we are still a happy people and it was worth it all anyway—is not an acceptable one. If Christ be not risen, we are deluded fools! Paul, however, seems to be saying, "Away with such a thought!" He writes, "But now is Christ risen from the dead and become the firstfruits of them that slept" (v. 20). How precious! Paul is saying that just as the firstfruits are ample proof that there will be a harvest, so the firstfruits of Christ's resurrection are proof that we will also be raised (v. 23).

 Truth for Soaring: "Who was delivered for our offenses, and was raised again for our justification. Therefore, being justified by faith, we have peace with God through our Lord Jesus Christ, by whom also we have access by faith into this grace wherein we stand, and rejoice in hope of the glory of God" (Romans 4:25—5:2).

A few years ago, while in the Holy Land, I stood near the empty tomb and preached a message on the death and resurrection of Christ. I was impressed that the assurance of our justification and ultimate glorification was before us. Full sufficiency of the cross and receipt of victory was attested to by the emptiness of the tomb. There I wrote the poem "Behold the Hill-Behold the Tomb." It expresses the victory that is assured to every believer.

BEHOLD THE HILL—BEHOLD THE TOMB

Behold, the hill, grotesquely shaped;
    The skull, the brow, in bold relief
Against the sky a testimony to
    His anguish, agony, and grief.

How different now the open sky
    So bright and blue, how darkened then
When God forsook His precious Son
    Bearing my guilt, my awful sin.

Behold, the hill, Golgotha's hill,
    And now, look back—review that day,
See Him, outstretched, bridging the gap,
    What access here through Christ—the Way

Behold and see the empty tomb,
    What victory in its vacancy,
What triumph in its emptiness
    And sure receipt of victory.

No towering shrine erected here,
    No gaudy work of men, to spoil
Its sweet and plain simplicity,
    No worship of its stone and soil.

EMPTY! One word makes it unique;
EMPTY! One word explains our joy;
EMPTY! One word rings loud and clear;
EMPTY! One word our tongues employ.

Annulled are all Satanic powers
    By Son of God and God the Son,
Behold the tomb! Hear now this word:
    EMPTY! PRAISE GOD, THE VICTORY'S WON!
                    —Charles U. Wagner

Acceptance in the Beloved

People who put their trust in Christ have the promise that they have been placed in Christ. Notice how Paul makes that clear in these two verses, "Therefore, if any man be in Christ, he is a new creature; old things are passed away; behold, all things are become new" (2 Corinthians 5:17). "But of him are ye in Christ Jesus, who of God is made unto us wisdom, and righteousness, and sanctification, and redemption" (1 Corinthians 1:30).

"In Christ!" How precious a promise! What a blessed assurance! Someone has written:

> Near, so very near to God,
> Nearer I cannot be,
> For in the person of His dear Son
> I am as near as He.

How assuring it is that when God looks at us, He sees us "in Christ" and accepts us on that basis alone. We are made "accepted in the beloved." All that Christ is, we are. No wonder the Bible says, "There is, therefore, now no condemnation to them who are in Christ Jesus . . ." (Romans 8:1).

There are several ways of illustrating this great truth. From H.A. Ironside's biography by E. Schuyler English comes this illustration, which makes clear the truth:

"Some years ago H.A. Ironside was holding some meetings in the state of Washington. He was a guest in the home of a rancher who raised sheep. It was the season of the year when the little lambs that had just been born played about in the green pastures, and Ironside remarked that one morning he was amazed and shocked to see a most awkward and rather gruesome little lamb following a ewe. It seemed as though it had six legs, the last two, however useless and dragging along on the ground behind the little creature. The skin of the lamb seemed to be torn. In all, it was a pitiful sight.

"Ironside asked the herder about his lamb and what had happened to it. He was told that it did not actually belong to the ewe that it was following. This lamb's mother had been killed, and the ewe that it was following had lost her lamb some way. The rancher tried to get the bereft ewe to mother the motherless lamb, but she recognized it as not her own and would have nothing to do with it. Then the herder struck upon an ingenious thought. He stripped the skin from the little lamb that had been killed and drew it over the orphan lamb, resulting in this strange-looking creature that Ironside beheld. When this seeming monstrosity was brought to the old ewe, she recognized in its scent the family odor, and happily adopted the baby as her own."

What a beautiful picture this is of the sinner saved by grace! Dr. Ironside reminds us that we were "forever without hope, outcasts who have no merit in ourselves and no claim upon God! But He sent His Son, the Lamb of God who takes away the sin of the world, who died in our place and in our stead. God the Father has happily adopted us as His children because we are clothed in His righteousness through Christ—we are accepted in His beloved Son!"

Truth for Soaring: "To the praise of the glory of his grace, through which he hath made us accepted in the beloved; in whom we have redemption through his blood, the forgiveness of sins, according to the riches of his grace" (Ephesians 1:6, 7).

ACCEPTED IN THE BELOVED

"In the Beloved" accepted am I,
Risen, ascended, and seated on high;
Saved from all sin thro' His infinite grace,
With the redeemed ones accorded a place.

"In the Beloved"—how safe my retreat,
In the Beloved accounted complete;
"Who can condemn me?" In Him I am free,
Savior and Keeper forever is He.

"In the Beloved" I went to the tree,
There, in His Person, by faith I may see
Infinite wrath rolling over His head,
Infinite grace, for He died in my stead.

"In the Beloved," God's marvelous grace
Calls me to dwell in this wonderful place;
God sees my Savior and then He sees me
"In the Beloved," accepted and free.
                              —Mrs. C. D. Martin

Training for Running

"...they shall run, and not be weary;"
Isaiah 40:31

On the Mark

Running is fun! Most of us, at one time or another, have participated in games or sports that require some amount of running. A church picnic or weekend retreat often involves us in some running activity. But some people take this business of running seriously; like Jim Ryun, for example. He once owned the world record for the mile run. He was clocked in 3 minutes, 41.3 seconds at Berkeley, California.

Sports Illustrated gave a rather detailed description of Jim's training program. It showed a rigorous schedule of training and body discipline. To Jim Ryun, running was more than fun. He became a track champion through sacrifice and hard work.

The apostle Paul must have been a sports enthusiast! He often made reference in the Bible to racing. The Christian life is a race! While it is enjoyable, it is more than that. It requires a full-fledged effort of service, sacrifice, and surrender. "And every man that striveth for the mastery is temperate in all things. . . ." (1 Corinthians 9:25). The Beck translation renders it: "Anyone who enters a contest goes into strict training." The thrust of Paul's exhortation is that the believer has a greater incentive to go "all out" for Christ in the racecourse of life because the crown is eternal.

In his book, *Track and Field*, track expert Ray M. Conger outlines for aspiring champions some racing tactics for the mile run. The spiritual application isn't hard to make. Here are a few of them:
1. "Get down on the marks."
2. "Go out with a fast sprint for 40 yards for position." It is obvious from these first two suggestions that in the Christian race too, it is important to begin with real zeal. Don't wait to become an expert in the things of the Lord. Our churches are filled with people who would serve the Lord but they "just aren't ready yet." They are found limping along the track in later life regretting they didn't start sooner.
3. "Think of others, their position, their condition; and not of personal fatigue." The idea here is to get your mind off yourself. Paul said, ". . . let us run with patience the race that is set before us, looking unto Jesus . . ." (Hebrews 12:1, 2). That "I just can't go on" feeling will leave us when we forget ourselves and get lost in the race—looking daily unto the Lord!
4. "Never trail a novice; he is bound to interfere." More than one Christian has become mediocre in life because he has fallen into the relaxed jog of the world when the Lord expected a fast, brisk sprint. While we are not to be the judge of the novices, neither are we obligated to follow behind them. To follow in their steps

rather than the Lord's is to ignore the pace the Lord Himself has set.

5. "Stay with the leaders on the third quarter no matter what the condition." The Bible shows how Mark (who later authored the Gospel of Mark) made the mistake of not staying with the leaders. When the going got hard, Mark returned to his home. His example has been followed by many who started off keeping pace with dedicated pastors and laymen and ended up being a spectator. Of course, God gave Mark another chance and he proved successful in the final lap of life. So take courage if you failed at the outset in your Christian life. Start again!

6. "Never look back." Paul said, ". . . forgetting those things which are behind, and reaching forth unto those things which are before, I press toward the mark for the prize of the high calling of God in Christ Jesus" (Philippians 3:13, 14). It is imperative to keep our eyes fixed on the goal. To glance—even for a moment—around or behind will often bring discouragement and delay.

7. "Aim to finish 3 yards beyond the tape. Many races are lost in the last 2 yards." To run successfully for the first three quarters and fizzle out in the last few yards is to be disappointed with failure. Aware of life's obstacles, Paul wrote, "But none of these things move me, neither count I my life dear unto myself, so that I might finish my course with joy . . ." (Acts 20:24). Indeed, this intense desire was fulfilled. Just before Paul laid down his life in Rome, he said, "I have fought a good fight, I have finished my course, I have kept the faith; henceforth there is laid up for me a crown of righteousness, which the Lord, the righteous judge, shall give me at that day; and not to me only, but unto all them also that love his appearing" (2 Timothy 4:7, 8).

Our thanks to Mr. Conger for his advice for prospective champions on the track. But a greater thanks of appreciation goes to God for His simple instructions for Christian champions in the race of life for Christ!

Training for Running: "Know ye not that they who run in a race run all, but one receiveth the prize? So run, that ye may obtain. And every man that striveth for the mastery is temperate in all things. Now they do it to obtain a corruptible crown, but we, an incorruptible. I, therefore, so run, not as uncertainly; so fight I, not as one that beateth the air" (1 Corinthians 9:24-26).

It is not enough to run, we must run "reaching for the prize" and "pressing toward the mark." So, "On the Mark"—let's make our life count for Christ!

Laugh a Little—It's Good for You

I like to laugh. Have you noticed that as you read through these devotionals? When a person gets so serious that he cannot indulge in a good hearty laugh, I become very uncomfortable. Laughing is good for you; I'm convinced of it. You've met people, haven't you, who are super critical, are very "quick on the flaw" and would rather die than smile? For them, laughing is confined to laughing *at* people, not *with* them.

Here is an anonymous poem about laughter that I like:

> Build for yourself a strong box,
>   Fashion each part with care;
> Fit it with hasp and padlock,
>   Put all your troubles there.
> Hide therein all your failures,
>   And each bitter cup you quaff,
> Lock all your heartaches within it
>   Then sit on the lid and laugh!
>
> Tell no one of its contents;
>   Never its secrets share;
> Drop in your cares and worries,
>   Keep them forever there,
> Hide them from sight so completely,
>   The world will never dream half.
> Fasten the top down securely,
>   Then sit on the lid and laugh!

Not the best poetry in the world, I'll admit, but true just the same. Someone has said that we never stop laughing because we are old. We grow old because we stop laughing. Josh Billings said, "Laughing is the sensation of feeling good all over and showing it principally in one spot."

You can tell a lot about a person by whether or not he laughs. Also, you can tell a lot about him when he laughs. If there is scorn in his laugh, that is telling. If the laugh is forced, that is telling. If a laugh is at someone else's failure, that is certainly telling. But when laughter comes from a pure heart, shows a care-free spirit, and is real, sincere, and spontaneous, it is actually contagious.

From the *Executive's Digest* come these facts:

"Scientists have been studying the effect of laughter on human beings and have found, among other things, that laughter has a profound and instantaneous effect on virtually every important organ in the human body. Laughter reduces health-sapping tensions and relaxes the tissues as well as exercising the most vital organs. It is said that laughter, even when forced, results in beneficial effect upon us, both mentally and physically. Next time you feel nervous and jittery, indulge in a good laugh." That's good advice.

Sterne has written, "I am persuaded that every time a man smiles, but much more when he laughs, it adds something to this fragment of life." "Laughter is wholesome," said one wise man. "God is not so dull as some people make out. Did He not make the kitten to chase its tail?"

 Training for Running: "A merry heart maketh a cheerful countenance, but by sorrow of the heart the spirit is broken" (Proverbs 15:13).

"A merry heart doeth good like a medicine, but a broken spirit drieth the bones" (Proverbs 17:22).

Our attitude is important in the race we are running. When we are "down on everything we are not up on," and when we are "crossed, crusty, and crabbed," it will have an effect on the spiritual progress we make. The right kind of laughter is not just good—it is healthy.

Baseball

I am a baseball fan! I can't help it; it is something inherited from my father. To show you how avid a fan he was, I was named after a baseball player. So when the World Series comes around, I take a few hours off and join the millions of Americans who view those exciting contests.

Those of you who share this interest will understand the baseball jargon you hear at a World Series game. The platter, of course, is home plate; while the mound, the rubber, or the hill describe the pitcher's area in the center of the diamond. Bases loaded means there are runners on first, second, and third bases. And a grand slam is a home run with the bases loaded. It's always a thrill to see that happen, especially if it's your team that does it!

Are there spiritual lessons from baseball terminology? You be the judge:

The clutch hitter. A clutch hitter is one who comes through when he is most needed. For example, it is the last half of the ninth inning with two out and a man on third base. The score is tied—3 to 3. A hit from the clutch hitter would bring in the man on third and win the game.

Some Christians are like this. In times of pressure and real need, they come through to help do the job. They may not be as skillful as another person who may be batting a remarkable .350, but they can be counted on when the going is rough and they're most needed.

Flustered by a change of pace. For those of you who are not up on such language, I hasten to explain that a change of pace or a change-up is a slow ball that is pitched after a fastball or two. More often than not, it comes as a surprise, because the motion of delivery by the pitcher hasn't changed.

In the spiritual realm, this is what separates the ordinary Christian from the spiritually keen Christian. A spiritual Christian is not flustered or thrown off balance when an unexpected turn of events comes his way. A device of Satan is to create a situation that will throw us off balance. In the life of a person who is not ignorant of such devices, the change up or slow ball that was delivered to deceive is often turned into a delightful reversal—sometimes even a grand slam. Ask the Lord to help you take each pitch in stride.

The reprehensible rhubarb. A rhubarb, simply stated, is an argument on the field; generally a noisy argument, often involving the umpire and various players. For some reason, some players seem to be more inclined to such altercations than others. It seems strange that they always get the "bad end of things."

Isn't this so among Christians? Don't be a chronic complainer. Don't see yourself as the one who always gets the bean ball—the ball deliberately pitched at the batter, usually his head. Such paranoia could ruin your effectiveness in Christian service. Everybody is not picking on you.

Here comes the payoff pitch. Finally, a payoff pitch is delivered when the count is 3 balls and 2 strikes. Barring a foul ball, the payoff pitch must result in something happening. In other words, it is a minor crisis and options are at a minimum. Life is full of these situations. Blessed (happy) is the Christian who can come through these situations without discouragement.

Success or failure. Speaking of discouragement, a good, dependable hitter (one who bats .300) generally gets a hit only three times out of ten. It's been almost 50 years since a player hit .400 (just four hits out of ten times at bat). What is important is that he is in there—ready for the curve, the change-up, or the fastball—with his eyes faithfully "on the ball."

Whether we are talking about baseball or the Christian life, the major leagues or the minors, it is dependable faithfulness and consistency that really count.

The bases are loaded and you're up. More power to you!

 Training for Running: "Wherefore seeing we also are compassed about with so great a cloud of witnesses, let us lay aside every weight, and the sin which doth so easily beset us, and let us run with patience the race that is set before us, looking unto Jesus the author and finisher of our faith; who for the joy that was set before him endured the cross, despising the shame, and is set down at the right hand of the throne of God" (Hebrews 12:1-2).

There are many people who could play professional baseball better than the men on the field. The problem is getting them to put down their hot-dogs and popcorn long enough to come out of the bleachers to get the job done. How true with believers! We need more than observers in this game of life for Christ. Not just advice, but action. Not just speculation, but participation!

Bringing in the Sheaves

"He that goeth forth and weepeth, bearing precious seed, shall doubtless come again with rejoicing, bringing his sheaves with him" (Psalm 126:6).

I f souls are going to be reached with the gospel, it is up to us to take the gospel to them and to bring them where they can hear the gospel preached with power.

There is first, then, the *going forth*. Christ said, "The harvest truly is great, but the laborers are few; pray ye, therefore the Lord of the harvest, that he would send forth laborers into his harvest" (Luke 10:2).

We should start *in prayer*. But to stop at that point proves the insincerity and shallowness of our prayer. In the very next verse, Christ said, "Go your ways; behold, I send you forth as lambs among wolves" (Luke 10:3). "Pray ye." "Go ye." That is the substance of the Lord's command. To pray and not go proves we are lazy; to go and not pray proves we are fools. I'm not sure which is worse, to be lazy or a fool. But the very worst is to be a *lazy fool!*

It is God's will that we involve ourselves in evangelism. This includes a day-by-day involvement in soul winning, as well as concerted efforts with the church to reach the lost through evangelistic campaigns. I have noticed that a church that is not interested in special evangelistic campaigns also lacks interest in a weekly evangelistic outreach through visitation. The truth is, where there is no work there are no results. No sweat, no sweet; no labor, no harvest; no going forth with precious seed, no coming again rejoicing.

Perhaps the greatest evangelist in his time (and certainly one of the greatest of all times) was D.L. Moody. We remember him for his great but simple evangelistic preaching. In his day, the whole world knew of him. Even today many enterprises carry on because of his faithful evangelistic ministry.

Moody's work in bringing boys and girls to Sunday school was known to men far and wide. On his way to enter his first term of office as United States President, Abraham Lincoln visited Moody's Sunday school. There, 600 teachers were involved with Moody, taking in hoodlums from the area and inculcating the gospel in their hearts. Yes, North Market Hall was the place in Chicago where the Lord was working through believers who were going forth and scattering the precious seed.

The very beginning of this man's monumental work started in reaching boys and girls for Christ. From that time on, everything he did was motivated by a compassion to share the gospel.

How involved are we in reaching the lost? Are we engaged in evangelistic efforts? Are we praying for souls daily? Are we disseminating good gospel literature? Are we supporting worthy evangelistic projects in our prayers, our perspiration, and our pocket books? Are we seized by a passion to reach the lost? Or are we making excuses for our indifference? Oh, that we might catch the vision that Moody had, and share his passion. Oh, to be lost in winning souls to Christ.

 Training for Running: "He that goeth forth and weepeth, bearing precious seed, shall doubtless come again with rejoicing, bringing his sheaves with him" (Psalm 126:6).

THE BACKSLIDER'S PRAYER

Dear Lord, I'm tired, so much to do
　This time of year; the work I've planned
Keeps mounting up, can't get involved
　Too much; I hope you understand.

The Pastor urged us all to come,
　Support the special meetings, so
He'll be most disappointed hearing
　I'm occupied and just can't go.

To work those meetings in my plans
　Is losing time I can't afford,
And that included a handsome sum
　I've planned to give to you, dear Lord.

And then, I bowl a night or two,
　The rest I need when pressures grow
Releases tension, helps increase
　Capacity for work, you know.

They have these meetings every year—
　I have my doubts they merit such
Investment of our time and funds;
　What we get back just isn't much.

Now, I'll be criticized I know,
　But Lord, I'll bear my cross
And do my part next year
　And sacrificially take my loss.
　　　　　　　　　　—Charles U. Wagner

Building or Tearing Down

Are you basically a builder or a wrecker? Are you a help or a hindrance? Are you down on everything you are not up on, or are you a rather positive person with clear goals and a purpose in life? These are important questions.

Every born-again Christian is in the body of Christ. The Bible says, "There is one body, and one Spirit, even as ye are called in one hope of your calling; one Lord, one faith, one baptism, one God and Father of all, who is above all, and through all, and in you all" (Ephesians 4:4-6). This is true unity. It is not merely an organization, but a living organism.

Just before Paul's strong word on the unity in the body, he urges us to "walk worthy of the vocation to which ye are called, with all lowliness and meekness, with longsuffering, forbearing one another in love, Endeavoring to keep the unity of the Spirit in the body of peace" (Ephesians 4:1, 2). These two verses contain all the elements for unity that we need. If we are humble, meek, longsuffering, and loving, and if we make an effort to keep the unity of the Spirit, we will find ourselves in a building mode. Rather than hurting one another, we will be helping one another; instead of pulling down, we will build up. How we need this attitude in our churches!

On the Lord's Day you make your way to church to meet with God's people and to be ministered to by the pastor or Sunday school teacher. How are you looked upon in your church? A trouble-maker, or a trouble-breaker? An optimistic plodder, or a pessimistic complainer? Do you have a "let's do it" attitude, or "it won't work here" attitude. Is there a bond of peace, or a bag of pieces? Will you hurt or help?

Walking worthy of our high calling means recognizing the unity of the body—even the local body of the church. And it means fitting into that church, exercising the gift that has been given to you as a member of that body. A little honest, serious introspection here would be good. Are you are builder or a wrecker? Gilbert Keith Chesterton put it this way:

> I watched them tearing a building down-
> A gang of men in a busy town -
> With a yo-heave-ho and a lusty yell,
> They swung a beam and the side wall fell.

I asked the foreman: "Are these men skilled
    The kind you would hire if you wanted to build?"
He laughed and said: "Why, no indeed,
    Just common labor is all I need:
They can easily wreck in a day or two
    What builders have taken years to do."

I asked myself, as I went my way,
    "Which of these roles have I tried today?
Am I a builder, who works with care,
    Measuring life by the rule and square,
Shaping my deeds by the well-made plan,
    Patiently doing the best I can?
Or am I a wrecker who walks the town,
    Content with the labour of tearing down?"

 Training for Running: "Therefore, my brethren dearly beloved and longed for, my joy and crown, so stand fast in the Lord, my dearly beloved. I beseech Euodia, and beseech Syntyche, that they be of the same mind in the Lord. And I intrest thee also, true yokefellow, help those women who labored with me in the gospel, with Clement also, and with other my fellowlaborers, whose names are in the book of life" (Philippians 4:1-3).

Personal evaluation is important, whether we are training to run or planning to build. Are we a help, or a hindrance? Are we a plus, or a minus? Are we pleasing the Lord, or displeasing? Are we a loner, or one who cooperates with others? Not only are we to be of the same mind, but we are also to help others who labor in the gospel.

Carte Blanche

O nly the most consecrated and surrendered Christian young person is willing to give the Lord *carte blanche* over his life.

Carte blanche means giving blanket permission to someone to do what he thinks best. This was first a military phrase meaning "unconditional surrender." It is from the French, and it literally means "white paper." To let someone have *carte blanche* is to give a blank paper with your name signed at the bottom, letting the recipient fill in anything he wants to.

Webster's New International Dictionary defines it as: "A blank paper with a person's signature, etc., at the bottom, given to another person with permission to superscribe what conditions he pleases. Hence: Unconditional terms; unlimited authority; full discretionary power."

When applied to our relationship with the Lord it is saying, "I will" to His will before we know what it is. It is surrendering our lives to any dealing on His part before we know what that action may be. It is saying "yes" to His design for us, signing our names at the bottom of the white sheet of His providential plans, fully aware that the conditions and specifics on that sheet might not be what we, in the flesh, would choose. It is singing the song, "Only to be what He wants me to be," and meaning it. It is saying, "Have Thine own way, Lord . . . Thou are the Potter; I am the clay. . . . "

Abraham gave the Lord *carte blanche* over his life. "Now the LORD had said unto Abram, Get thee out of thy country, and from thy kindred, and from thy father's house, unto a land that I will shew thee; . . . So Abram departed, as the LORD had spoken unto him . . ." (Genesis 12:1, 4).

The New Testament commentary on this Old Testament passage makes this *carte blanche* surrender of Abraham clear. "By faith Abraham, when he was called to go out into a place which he should after receive for an inheritance, obeyed; and he went out, not knowing where he went" (Hebrews 11:8).

Generally, young people want to know the whys and wherefores for every area of life. They want to know what is going on in the world and how it will affect them. Being worldly-wise, they carefully calculate their future and program their life on the basis of what will bring maximum benefit to them personally. They know where they are going and how they will get there. More often then not, they have a don't-stand-in-my-way attitude. Their plans, their future, and the aggrandizement of their cause are most important in their thinking.

Even after a person is saved and given new life in Christ with attending new desires and aspirations, this pull and demand of the flesh for self-elevation often remains. Real victory is his when he comes to the place where only God's will really matters.

Probably the greatest difference between the surrendered child of God and the ego-directed unregenerate son of Adam is the striking contrast in their attitude toward their future plans. The unregenerate young person lists his plans and dreams and signs his name, vowing to spare no energy until they become a reality. The surrendered child of God signs his name at the bottom of the blank sheet of paper, praying for God's energy in and through Him to effect *His* plans and *His* programs according to *His* time schedule.

Happy is the Christian who is content to let his will be lost in God's will, praying, "Lord, I surrender my life *carte blanche* to Thee. Do with it as *You* please."

 Training for Running: "By faith Noah, warned of God of things not seen as yet, moved with fear, prepared an ark to the saving of his house, by which he condemned the world, and became heir of the righteousness which is by faith" (Hebrews 11:7).

Noah had certainly given the Lord *carte blanche*. He must have been the ridicule of the world. But He continued to have faith in the Lord, to trust Him implicitly, and to obey even though he may not have fully understood.

Cliché

Let's talk about clichés. You know what they are, don't you? The word *cliché* is from the French, where it means "a stereotype plate." A *cliché* is a word that is used to describe an expression that is repeated in the same form over and over.

Some sermons contain many clichés. You can feel one coming, and you can almost fill in the rest of the sentence when you hear it started. Sometimes quotations are clichés, such as: "To be or not to be." Some are allusions to myth or history: "The Gordian knot, Achilles' heel." Others are alliterative: "first and foremost," "fast and furious." Some are legalisms: "null and void," "each and every." Others are euphemisms: "a fate worse than death," "better half." Also, there are figurative phrases: "hit the nail on the head." And some are meaningless, like "in the last analysis" or "by the same token."

Now, if we aren't careful we will find ourselves using religious clichés, repeating them without meaning them. "All things work together" can become one, as well as other words that sound churchy and appropriately religious.

Let me say something in defense of the cliché. The reason some phrases, such as "Trust and Obey" or "Keep Looking up" or "We'll pray about it" seem like clichés, is that they are important ideas or words in the first place. They express a thought concisely and clearly—one that really has some power. Some speakers who try to avoid clichés wind up using many more words than they need and, sometimes at least, missing the point of what they want to say.

We need to avoid mere repetition of empty phrases. And we must avoid them when they are just a substitute for precise thinking. But we shouldn't be put-down for using some of the old and precious phrases—especially biblical ones—when the words, however familiar, are verbalized from a sincere heart. In our attempt to be modern, let's not overdo it. I'm a little saddened when good biblical expressions are set aside as trite and overused. I think it was Mark Twain who said (and here is another cliché), "The difference between the right word and the almost right word is the difference between lightning and the lightning bug."

So, be careful that you don't just "mouth words" and fall into a rut of clichés. But at the same time, with deliberate thought, don't be afraid of the powerful words in the Old Book—words that express our true faith.

Training for Running: "Forasmuch as ye are manifestly declared to be the epistle of Christ ministered by us, written not with ink but with the Spirit of the living God; not in tables of stone but in fleshy tables of the heart" (2 Corinthians 3:3).

Paul was stressing that his service was more than the engagement of words (clichés). He said, "Ye are our epistle, written in our hearts, known and read of all men" (2 Corinthians 3:2).

Paul's living epistles were the evidence of his labor. He was not just talking or "beating the wind." Let's ask God to help us be just as effective and fresh for Him in His work. May He help us have new things to say about our Lord—not just repeated phrases that have long since lost their meaning.

Crossed Wires

Years ago I was the proud owner of a volkswagen Beetle—a "Bug." It was very special to our family and very dependable transportation. One day I jumped into my VW, turned on my windshield wipers, and found to my surprise that my turn signals began to operate. We had laughed about many of the bugs in my Bug, but never before had this happened. I checked the turn signal levers and found them in the off position. Then I turned off the windshield wipers. Off went the turn signals too. I touched the brake pedal and the signals began to blink again. I was completely bewildered. I then tried my horn—what else was left?—and you guessed it, the turn signals flashed on again.

How could I drive my car this way? It wouldn't work unless I decided to turn every time I applied the brakes. It would be no better when it rained! With the help of some friends, we began to probe the car's electrical system, but to no avail.

After some reflection as to the reason for this strange "directional turning" of events, we decided to take it to the service station. I told them that when I "told" the car to "Stop," my Beetle said, "Turn." The mechanic lifted the hood and immediately began to do some testing. I could have told him that we had tried that before and had no success. But to our surprise, in a matter of minutes he straightened out the wires on the electrical panel and everything was back to normal.

When I expressed my surprise at the obvious simplicity of the problem, he smiled and said, "Pastor, you take care of the church and leave your car to us."

I learned an important lesson in that bewildering experience. How often in life we get our wires crossed up. Our "stops" and "turns" conflict, and we are brought to a place of frustration and confusion. Then we do a little probing on our own to solve our problem, and it only adds to our consternation. We discuss it with others and they give us some advice which, more often than not, leaves us confused and still crossed up. When we pray, we tell the Lord that we are helpless, and we assure Him that there is little hope for solving our problem. Finally, we reluctantly turn it over to Him and find that He begins to work. He solves our difficulty with divine simplicity.

How foolish that we didn't take it to God to begin with. It would be almost humorous, if it weren't so pitiful, to see ourselves dabbling in our difficulties when His masterful hand could lift the burden and set us on the normal path again. God knows the way to uncross our wires and get our stops and turns back where they will have meaning and purpose.

Somehow, I can hear God say, after He has corrected the problem that was so great to us, "My son, you obey the Word. And when these difficulties come, leave the problems to Me."

 Training for Running: "The steps of a good man are ordered by the LORD, and he delighteth in his way. Though he fall, he shall not be utterly cast down; for the LORD upholdeth him with his hand" (Psalm 37:23-24).

"Order my steps in word, and let not any iniquity have dominion over me" (Psalm 119:133).

Our steps and stops are all ordered from Him—even the turns. Whether there is a spiritual adjustment to be made, or whether He is allowing something to come our way as an important ingredient of His plan for us, one thing is sure: We need to consult Him first.

The Divine Umpire

"And let the peace of God rule in your hearts . . ." (Colossians 3:15).

It might surprise you to know that every believer has a divine umpire. The Rotherham translation of the above verse is the most literal of all renderings: "And let the peace of Christ act as umpire in your hearts. . . ." This is not just a clever way of stating a thought, and it isn't taking liberty with the text as is the case with many modern translations. Scholars agree (Nicholson, Vincent, Vine, etc.) that the word *rule* means "to preside as umpire in the games; to decide and award the prizes."

No one would doubt that there are constant conflicts in our hearts. Whether we are removed from the outside world or surrounded by the busy world, there are still inner conflicts and impulses; there are inner emotional disputes that need to be settled. An arbitrator is needed, an umpire to decide all doubts and settle all questions for the believer. This umpire is the peace of Christ. It is the same peace referred to when Christ said, "Peace I leave with you, my peace I give unto you; not as the world giveth, give I unto you. Let not your heart be troubled, neither let it be afraid" (John 14:27). It is His presiding peace.

How is this applied in a practical way and what does it actually mean? How easy it is to be ruffled by circumstances, to be involved in an inner dispute with one's self about an immediate problem, or engulfed in worry about the uncertain future. Our hearts become like seething pots of turmoil. Then we do what we should have done in the first place—we surrender to the will of the indwelling Umpire. This is the meaning of "let the peace of Christ act as Umpire. . . ." There must be that abandoning of our personal insistence to decide the matter ourselves.

There is first a need to let our wills get lost in His, to agree to the precious arrangement of letting His will and way be final. While we sometimes hesitate to use the word "feelings" because it is often misused, I know of no other more appropriate word. It isn't simply a judicial or positional peace (as in Romans 5:1). To be specific, it is putting various thoughts to the test, weighing various courses of action prayerfully, and then knowing His ruling peace as the divine Umpire is selecting the right course.

Often when these conflicts arise and decisions are to be made, we are heard to say, "I don't have real peace in my heart about this particular decision." Or we may say, "I have prayed about this matter of the future, and the Lord has given me real peace of heart in the matter. As far as I'm concerned, it is settled." This is the composure that comes after the Peace of God has ruled as umpire in our hearts. Suddenly the anxiety is gone, the conflict has vanished, the doubts are banished, and the game of life continues—pressing toward the prize.

Praise the Lord—we qualified in this race by His grace. Not only do we see Him as the divine *Terminus*—the object and goal of the race—but we have His peace as the ruling, presiding *Umpire* all along the way.

 Training for Running: "And above all these things put on charity, which is the bond of perfectness. And let the peace of God rule in your hearts, to the which also ye are called in one body; and be ye thankful. Let the word of Christ dwell in you richly, in all wisdom teaching and admonishing one another, in psalms and hymns and spiritual songs singing with grace in your hearts to the Lord. And whatsoever ye do in word or deed, do all in the name of the Lord Jesus, giving thanks to God and the Father by him" (Colossians 3:14-17).

"If the peace of Jesus Christ is the umpire in any man's heart, then, when feelings clash and we are pulled in two directions at the same time, the decision of Christ will keep us in the way of love and the Church will remain the one body it is meant to be" (William Barclay).

Don't Quit

Ever feel like quitting? I guess we all have. As a young man working in Detroit factories, I can remember people getting sick of their job and just quitting. In school, I can remember fellow students deciding that they had had it, and they quit. They felt they could do better than just study. They quit. It is as simple as that. We have people who quit in college and seminary. Someone has written:

> On the plains of hesitation
> Lie the bleached bones of thousands
> Who on the very threshold of victory
> Sat down to rest, and while resting died.

They were so close to victory, they were almost there, and they decided just to quit, to rest, to get back at it later. And their quitting, even that hesitation, was their end. They died.

I can remember when I was young that if someone didn't get his way in a game of baseball or touch football, he would quit. People who get into the habit of quitting generally go through life that way—they don't finish.

How many churches have you quit? How many times have you taught a class in Sunday school and felt like throwing in the towel? Demus quit. Paul said, "Demus hath forsaken me, having loved this present world" (2 Timothy 4:10). Mark was a quitter, but he started again. We must give him credit for that.

Pastors sometimes feel like quitting. Especially on Monday mornings. Even when they have had a good day, there is something about the day after Sunday. It's a letdown that causes them to wonder if their work is through in that Church. Let me encourage you, don't quit!

> When things go wrong as they sometimes will,
> When the road you're trudging seems all uphill,
> When funds are low and debts are high,
> And you want to smile, but have to sigh,
> When care is pressing you down a bit—
> Rest if you must, but don't quit.
>
> Life is strange with its twists and turns,
> As every one of us sometimes learns;
> And many a fellow turns about
> When he might have won, had he stuck it out,

Winning Words for Daily Living

Don't give up though the pace seems slow
　　You may succeed with another blow.

Often the goal is nearer than
　　It seems to a faint and faltering man;
Often the struggler has given up
　　When he might have captured the victor's cup;
And he learned too late when the night came down,
　　How close he was to winning the crown.

Success is failure turned inside out
　　The silver tint of the clouds of doubt,
You never can tell how close you are,
　　It may be near, when it seems afar:
So stick to the fight when you're hardest hit
　　It's when things seem worst that you mustn't quit.
　　　　　　　　　　　　　　　—Author unknown

 Training for Running: "And Barnabas and Saul returned from Jerusalem, when they had fulfilled their ministry, and took with them John, whose surname was Mark" (Acts 12:25).

"And Barnabas determined to take with them John, whose surname was Mark. But Paul thought it not good to take him with them, who departed from them from Pamphylia, and went not with them to the work. And the contention was so sharp between them that they departed asunder one from the other; and so Barnabas took Mark, and sailed unto Cyprus" (Acts 15:37-39).

"Only Luke is with me. Take Mark, and bring him with thee; for he is profitable to me for the ministry" (2 Timothy 4:11).

Mark is an example of a man who quit. Paul had very little sympathy for quitters and as a result broke with Barnabas when Barnabas insisted on giving him a second chance. Paul was wrong. In his last letter, he asks for Mark to come. God does give second chances. If you have quit, start again!

Enthusiasm

"Kill the Umpire!" Well, people don't usually really mean that—although we do get a little upset with the umpire once in a while when we feel he has missed a close call. You just know he was wrong, and you almost put down your bag of popcorn and go out there to tell him so. While we never really wish umpires any harm, there seems to be an unwritten law that it is okay to get excited at a baseball game.

Whether it's extra baseball innings or a drive on a football field with just 5 yards to a touchdown, some of us get rather excited and not the least bit interested in maintaining our composure. We're even a little suspicious of anyone sitting next to us who doesn't get warmed up to what's going on.

But one thing has me puzzled. While we seem justified in getting excited about sports, why don't we get as excited about spiritual things? Why are we so puzzled when someone does get excited about the things of the Lord?

When the apostle Paul spoke of his desire to serve the Lord he said, "For the love of Christ constraineth us" (2 Corinthians 5:14). The word *constrain* means to "pour all your energies into one channel." It is a compelling love. Paul said, "For whether we be beside ourselves, it is to God" (2 Corinthians 5:13). Do you suppose some people thought Paul was "beside himself" in his eagerness and enthusiasm for the things of the Lord? Probably so! Remember, while Paul was a scholar, he was also enthusiastic about the things of the Lord and his obedience to the command of the Lord to evangelize the world.

No, we must not limit the idea of enthusiasm to sports. In reality, the words were originally borrowed from a spiritual connotation. Our word *enthusiast* comes from the Greek word *enthusiasts*. Broken down, the *en* means "in the power of." *Theos* is the word for God. So we have a right to be enthusiastic for true spiritual enthusiasm is "God in us" or "in the power of God."

This does not mean we are to be wild and uncontrollable. To the very same Corinthians Paul said, "Let all things be done decently and in order" (1 Corinthians 14:40). There should be an excitement, a God-given enthusiasm about our work for the Lord.

With a zeal that forgets self and an excitement about the Lord and His work, we need to share the good news of the gospel with those around us. When they know the power of the gospel, they too will want to pass it on.

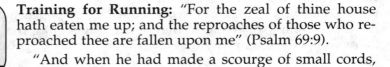

Training for Running: "For the zeal of thine house hath eaten me up; and the reproaches of those who reproached thee are fallen upon me" (Psalm 69:9).

"And when he had made a scourge of small cords, he drove them all out of the temple, and the sheep, and the oxen; and poured out the changer's money, and overthrew the tables; and said unto them that sold doves, Take these things here; make not my Father's house an house of merchandise. And his disciples remembered that it was written, The zeal of thine house hath eaten me up" (John 2:15-17).

Christians ought to be eager and enthusiastic about the things of the Lord. We need men and women with a clear vision of the goal and a fortitude and tenacity to reach the goal. Someone has written:

> I hate the guys
> Who criticize
> And minimize
> The other guys
> Whose enterprise
> Has made them rise
> Above the guys
> Who criticize.

Enterprise! Enthusiasm! Spirit and spunk! That's what is needed in this race.

F.B. Meyer

"I wish I had known him personally." Ever find yourself saying that? I say or think it often when I am in my library reading and being blessed by the clear message written by a saint of yesteryear. Somehow the author's very personality leaps out from the page, and I find myself wondering what he was like in person. I get those feelings about F. B. Meyer, who was born April 8, 1847. I have literally scores of Meyer's books in my library, and I have read most of them. If you are a pastor or Bible teacher, you understand what I mean. His material was more of a devotional nature, but certainly we need that kind of material—the kind that feeds the soul.

Once when I was in Northfield, Massachusetts, I visited an old cabin where A. T. Pierson studied. It was located near the birthplace of D. L. Moody, and it is noted for its conferences where many great men have ministered the Word. I stuck my head in that old cabin in the woods and saw on the old fireplace signatures of C. I. Scofield, W. H. Griffith Thomas, D. L. Moody, and . . . F. B. Meyer. It was quite an experience.

In his book, *Listening to the Giants*, Warren Wiersbe writes about this man of God:

> He may have been a mystic, but Meyer worked hard and never wasted time. His ability to concentrate on one task at a time enabled him to work his way through a long agenda without being distracted. Constantly on the go, he learned to use his hours of railway travel productively. "If he had a long journey before him," one friend wrote, "he would settle himself in his corner of the raiway carriage with a sigh of relief, open his dispatch case (which was fitted up as a sort of stationary cabinent), and set to work in supreme contentment on some abstruse article" (p. 96).

Others attested to Meyer's godliness. Spurgeon said of him, "Meyer preaches as a man who has seen God face to face." Wilbur Chapman spoke of a sermon by Meyer which changed his life and ministry. He said, "I owe more to this man than anyone in the world." The great preacher Joseph Parker wrote of him, "He brings a benediction with him, a better air than earth's poor murky climate, and he never leaves me without the impression that I have been face to face with a man of God." Adds Alexander Gammie, "and it is because of this that he was able to throw such a vision on the drab canvas of our common life, and became one of the preachers who could lead the souls of men out of the shadow into the sunlight of eternal love."

What was the secret of his success? Without a doubt, it is expressed in these words from someone who knew him, "His words, his looks, his very presence helps others because they reveal that he is one of the King's illumined servants. He lives so constantly in the sunshine of the Unseen that to come in contact with him is to get a glimpse of Heaven's own brightness." Yes, he lived with the abiding assurance that the Lord was with him. You cannot read his books without being aware that here is a man who walked with God.

Training for Running: "That I may know him, and the power of his resurrection, and the fellowship of his sufferings, being made conformable unto his death" (Philippians 3:10).

"This is the prerogative of all holy souls. They are permitted not simply to know about Christ, but to know Him; not only to read of His excellency and beauty in the Book that is fragrant with the myrrh, aloes, and, cassia of His presence, but to have fellowship with the apostles, who saw, heard, beheld, and handled the Word of Life" (F. B. Meyer).

The Breastplate of Saint Patrick

When one thinks of Saint Patrick, he may think of a man claimed by Catholicism as a patron saint. But history shows that in all the writings of Patrick, there is no hint of the trappings of the Roman church. He traveled throughout Ireland preaching the simple gospel of Jesus Christ, a message that proclaimed that faith in Christ was the only way to heaven. A translation from *The Tri-partite Life of Saint Patrick, with other Documents Relating to that Saint*, edited and translated by Whitley Stokes, (London, 1887), gives us one of the most powerful pieces of Christian poetry ever written. Entitled *The Breastplate*, it is a rhythmic declaration of that faith in which Patrick calls upon the Triune God to protect him in his hour of need. It was written in the first year of his missionary life when he kindled a spiritual fire, "contrary to the king's orders and the pagan priests of Tara."

I bind myself today,

> To the power of God to guide me,
> The might of God to uphold me,
> The wisdom of God to teach me,
> The eyes of God to watch over me,
> The ear of God to hear me,
> The Word of God to speak for me,
> The hand of God to protect me,
> The way of God to lie before me,
> The shield of God to shelter me,
> The host of God to defend me . . .

> Christ with me, Christ before me,
> Christ behind me, Christ within me,
> Christ beneath me, Christ above me,
> Christ at my right, Christ at my left,
> Christ in breadth, Christ in length, Christ in height . . .

> Christ in the heart of every man who thinks of me,
> Christ in the mouth of every man who speaks to me,
> Christ in the eye of every man that sees me,
> Christ in the ear of every man who hears me . . .

> Salvation is the Lord's,
> Salvation is the Lord's,
> Salvation is the Lord's,
> Let thy salvation, O Lord, be ever with us.

Training for Running: "According to my earnest expectation and my hope, that in nothing I shall be ashamed, but that with all boldness, as always, so now also Christ shall be magnified in my body, whether it be by life, or by death" (Philippians 1:20).

Every runner must have a goal. Goals are important in the Christian race too. Patrick's goal was Christ. It is as simple as that! We begin our race by accepting Him; we run it in His power; and He is the goal. To be accepted of Him, at the Bema Seat, is our greatest prize.

Go South to Canada?

When Americans think of the geographic location of Canada, we naturally think north. Canada is north of the United States. This is certainly no new and startling discovery, but when we make that familiar statement we ought to remember that there is one exception to this. Yes, there is a city in Canada that is south of a city in the mainland United States. It is a geographical believe-it-or-not worth considering.

The American city is Detroit, Michigan. The Canadian city is Windsor, Ontario. A map will verify this fact. There are two ways to cross the Detroit River from Detroit to Windsor. One is the Ambassador Bridge; the other is actually under the river by way of a tunnel. Either way you will be going almost due south.

Normally, however, the way to Canada is north. In Washington State you would go north into Vancouver, British Columbia. In Montana it might be north to Cardston, Alberta. In North Dakota it would be north to Estevan, Saskatchewan, or farther east into Winnipeg. Of course, you could journey north to get to Ontario from Port Huron, Michigan.

What a lesson we learn about spiritual geography from this! How often we plan our course of life in minute detail. Every mile is pre-planned and every major milestone anticipated. It may be "up all the way" with our sights steady and our objectives clear and plain. Then suddenly we suffer unexpected reverses. Detour signs stare us in the face and we suffer disappointment and regret. Others have traveled this way before and have enjoyed ease commensurate to cruising north across the border from Blaine to Vancouver. Why, you may think, has the Lord made the way so difficult and so unreasonable for me? Surely if His will for me in my Christian life is north, He wouldn't send me south.

Believe it or not, He may find if necessary to send you south to get you north. Sounds just plain unreasonable and illogical, doesn't it? It does unless you see things as God sees them! This shouldn't really surprise us since God often takes His children in the opposite direction in order to get them to the place of His will just in time. To use our illustration of Canada again, the slowest way to Canada from Detroit is north via Port Huron. The quickest is south to Windsor.

Peter found it hard to realize this truth of blessing through the opposite direction. When Christ told the disciples He was to die, Peter said, "Be it far from thee, Lord; this shall not be unto thee."

Christ answered, "Get thee behind me, Satan. Thou art an offense unto me; for thou savorest not the things that be of God, but those that of men" (Matthew 16:22, 23).

Peter was looking at suffering and death from the normal perspective. He did not understand that through death comes victory and through the Cross would come ultimate triumph. A few verses later, the Lord again referred to the blessing of going into an apparent opposite direction when He said, "For whosoever will save his life shall lose it; and whosoever will lose his life for my sake shall find it" (Matthew 16:25). Years later Peter remembered this principle when he said, "Humble yourselves, therefore, under the mighty hand of God, that he may exalt you in due time" (1 Peter 5:6).

Christian friend, the Lord makes His direction clear. When reverses and apparent contradictions come, just remember His compass is never inaccurate. While He might lead you south, it may be the only way to get you north again. Leave that decision with Him.

 Training for Running: "By faith Jacob, when he was dying, blessed both the sons of Joseph, and worshipped, leaning upon the top of his staff. By faith Joseph, when he died, made mention of the departing of the children of Israel, and gave commandment concerning his bones" (Hebrews 11:21, 22).

Jacob and Joseph are prime examples of "going north to get south." They left the land God gave them to go to Egypt in order that, true to His promise, they might go to Israel—the land promised them. (Technically, they went south to go north.) To obey the Lord at all costs—even when it doesn't sound reasonable to us—is the test of an obedient servant of the Lord.

Gossip

Morgan Blake, sportswriter for the *Atlanta Journal*, wrote, "I am more deadly than the screaming shell from a howitzer. I run without killing. I tear down homes, break hearts, and wreck lives. I travel on the wings of the wind. No innocence is strong enough to intimidate me, no purity pure enough to daunt me. I have no regard for truth, no respect for justice, no mercy for the defenseless. My victims are as the sands of the sea and often as innocent. I never forget and seldom forgive. My name is Gossip."

There are times when silence is golden, "In the multitude of words there wanteth not sin, but he that refraineth his lips is wise" (Proverbs 10:19). Have you heard of the names of the seven misses who cause trouble? Let me introduce you to them. They are mischievous misses, to be sure. They are *mis*information, *mis*quotation, *mis*representation, *mis*interpretation, *mis*construction, *mis*conception, and *mis*understanding.

Someone has said it with poetry, using various Bible verses:

Guard with thy lips; none can know (Proverbs 13:3)
What evils from the tongue may flow (James 3:5, 6)

What guilt, what grief may be incurred (Jude 11:35)
By one incautious word (Mark 6:22, 25, 26)

Be "slow to speak," look well within (Proverbs 4:5)
To check what there may lead to sin (James 1:25)

And pray unceasingly for aid (Colossians 4:2)
Lest unawares thou be betrayed (Luke 21:34)

Condemn not, judge not, for man (1 Corinthians 4:3)
Is not given his brother's faults to scan (Matthew 7:3)

The task is God's and His alone (Malachi 7:5)
To search out and subdue His own (1 Corinthians 9:27)

Indulge no murmurings, oh, restrain (Philippians 2:14, 15)
Those lips so ready to complain (Job 27:4)
And if they can be numbered, count (Psalms 103:2,3)
Of one day's mercies the amount (Lamentations 3:23)

Shun vain discussions, trifling themes (Titus 3:9)
Dwell not on earthly hopes and schemes (Deuteronomy 6:4, 7)

Let words of wisdom, meekness, love (James 3:13)
Thy heart's true renovation prove (Luke 6:45)

Set God before thee; every word (Genesis 17:1)
Thy lips pronounce by His is heard (Psalm 139:4)

Oh, couldst thou realize this thought (Luke 12:2)
What care, what caution would be taught (Luke 12:3)

Training for Running: "He that keepeth his mouth keepeth his life, but he that openeth wide his lips shall have destruction" (Proverbs 13:3).

"Even so the tongue is a little member and boasteth great things. Behold, how great a matter a little fire kindleth! And the tongue is a fire, a world of iniquity; so is the tongue among our members that it defileth the whole body, and setteth on fire the course of nature, and it is set on fire of hell" (James 3:5-6).

Take the time to look up the verses given in this scriptural poem. It could have a meaningful impact on your life. Determine that you are going to glorify God with your speech. Remember, you're seldom sorry for what you don't say!

The Hated Hedge

"Hast not thou made an hedge about him, and about his house, and about all that he hath on every side?" (Job 1:10).

This is the language of Satan as he approached the Lord with the angels, the sons of God. It was part of an answer to the Lord who had said, "Hast thou considered My servant Job . . ." (Job 1:8). This passage teaches us a number of things about the Lord and His enemy, Satan. It also gives us some insight into the ways of the Lord on behalf of His people.

First, we learn that *a great many of our trials are not simple contests between ourselves and Satan, but between Satan and God.* Certainly it was not Job who was on trial in the book of Job, but the Lord. Satan had accused God of buying Job's allegiance with the protection he gave. According to Satan man was a mercenary, and God was a fool to believe that man was faithful for any other reason but that he gave allegiance to the one who buttered his bread. Satan was proved wrong when Job, having had almost everything of human value snatched from him, said, "Though He slay me, yet will I trust Him" (Job 13:15). Satan simply doesn't understand that kind of language. He and his kingdom of darkness fail to understand the Christian's simple trust in God in spite of all that comes His way. Saints down through the ages have been nothing short of a puzzle to him.

Second, the passage in Job assures us *that we are hedged in by the Lord with a guarding and protecting hand.* There were three hedges around this tried saint, Job. First, a personal hedge; then, a family hedge; and finally, a property hedge. The Lord accepted the challenge of Satan who sought to cast reflection on the claims of the Lord and the character of Job. He lifted two of the protecting hedges. But emphatically he said, "Upon Himself put not forth thy hand" (Job 1:12). How Satan hates that protective hedge! While he could not touch Job himself, he did try to get to Job through the loss of his possessions, friends, and even bodily health. But he couldn't touch Job!

Dear friend, if you know Christ, you can rest assured that while trials may come, He is keeping you. He may for a moment allow the forces of darkness to touch what you have, but they can never act without His permission, and they will never touch you and your security on the other side of that divine protective hedge.

Indeed we know a hedge of protection of which even Job knew nothing. It is the surrounding, enveloping person of Christ. We are "in Christ" (2 Corinthians 5:17). Scripture tells us that we are "faithful in Him" (Ephesians 1:1); "chosen in Him" (Ephesians 1:4); and

Winning Words for Daily Living

"accepted in Him" (Ephesians 1:6). What a hedge! What an assurance! And, like Job, who after the trial of his faith, received "twice as much as he had before" (Job 42:10), so the "sufferings of this present time are not worthy to be compared with the glory which shall be revealed in us" (Romans 8:18). The Lord put an inner hedge around Job to preserve him to enjoy the good things after his trial. Christ is our hedge; we are kept in Him to share in a "far more exceeding and eternal weight of glory" (2 Corinthians 4:17).

 Training for Running: "And the LORD said unto Satan, Hast thou considered my servant, Job, that there is none like him in the earth, a perfect and an upright man, one that feareth God, and eschewed evil? Then Satan answered the LORD, and said, Doth Job fear God for nought? Hast not thou made an hedge about him, and about his house, and about all that he hath on every side? Thou hast blessed the work of his hands, and his substance is increased in the land" (Job 1:8-10).

THE HATED HEDGE

How hideous is this hedge to him, in subtle guile
    The Devil walks about, his simple air-defile.
This trusting child of God, he sees doth humbly seek
    God's perfect will—he orders quick and sure defeat.

Though strong is he, with power exceeding human flesh,
    Much stronger is the towering hedge which doth
    suppress.
And in abeyance holds his devilish design.
    This never-failing hedge, is to the child, divine.

Attacked by Lucifer, and all his hellish fiends,
    Like Job, he loses all those finally-fulfilled dreams.
With body weak, and then exposed to family scorn
    Soon joined by friends accusing, the child is sad, forlorn.

But in the realm invisible to human sight,
    The evil forces view a hedge, surrounded tight
Around the inner soul. The fainting child has won,
    The hedge around this trusting soul—is GOD THE SON.
                    —Charles U. Wagner

Let's Face It

Have you ever noticed how many phrases we have with the word *face* in them. If you "face someone down," you withstand them boldly. If you "face it out" you are said to persist. Or to "face the music" means to stand up in a crisis. How about the phrase "to lose face," which means to be lowered in the esteem of others.

Do you ever try to "save face" in a situation? One of the most uncomplimentary things that could be said about you is that you were "two faced," which might suggest that you are pretending to be religious while actually not being religious at all.

So, these phrases have a variety of meanings and a variety of applications. Let me share one or two more. When a person says, "on the face of it" he means "to all appearances" or "in the literal sense of the words." To "draw a long face" is to look dissatisfied.

But there is another use of the word *face* which is beautiful. It is "face to face." It means in the immediate presence of another. Speaking to the Thessalonians, Paul said, "But we, brethren, being taken from you for a short time in presence, not in heart, endeavored the more abundantly to see your face with great desire" (1 Thessalonians 2:17). Later Paul said that he was "night and day praying exceedingly that we might see your face, and might perfect that which is lacking in your faith" (1 Thessalonians 3:10).

In the love chapter, 1 Corinthians 13, Paul wrote, "For now we see through a glass, darkly; but then face to face" (v. 12). Think of it:

> Face to face with Christ my Savior,
> Face to face what will it be,
> When with rapture I behold Him
> Jesus Christ, who died for me?

In the last book of the Bible, Revelation 22, we are taken in to Paradise, and to the throne of God and of the Lamb. We read, "And there shall be no more curse, but the throne of God and the Lamb shall be in it, and his servants shall serve him; and they shall see his face . . ." (Revelation 22:3, 4).

> Face to face - Oh, blissful moment.
> Face to face to see and know
> Face to face with my redeemer,
> Jesus Christ who loves me so.
> —Carrie E. Breck

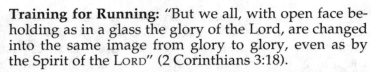

Training for Running: "But we all, with open face beholding as in a glass the glory of the Lord, are changed into the same image from glory to glory, even as by the Spirit of the LORD" (2 Corinthians 3:18).

The words *open face* literally means "unveiled face." There is a face to face relationship today with the Lord as the Spirit of God takes the Word of God and stamps the image of the Son of God on the child of God. Face to face with His image in Scripture makes us like Him. Let's face it! The Christian life is wonderful!

Heaven

What do you think of when you hear someone speak of crowns in heaven? I once heard of a Sunday school teacher say, "If you are a good boy, Tommy, you will go to heaven and have a crown of gold on your head." Tommy answered, "Not me! I had one of those things put on a tooth once."

Tommy wasn't being sacrilegious. He just didn't know what his teacher was talking about. He took the words and gave them the meaning that was consistent with the way he heard them used. By the way, the teacher was not right when she stated that he would get to heaven by being good. Salvation is all of grace, not of works.

But crowns are another thing. They *are* a result of our good works. They represent commendation and reward. And, of course, their use is figurative. In Scripture, crowns are called incorruptible. "And every man that striveth for the mastery is temperate in all things. Now they do it to obtain a corruptible crown, but we, an incorruptible" (1 Corinthains 9:25).

In Paul's day, the only accolade received by a winning runner was a crown that faded. But this heavenly crown for faithfulness in running is one that does not fade. Paul speaks of "the crown of righteousness, which the Lord, the righteous judge, shall give me at that day. It will not come to me only, but to everyone who loves his appearing" (2 Timothy 4:8). This crown is for those who are eagerly waiting for Him.

The man who endures temptation, says James, will be given a crown of life. "Blessed is the man that endureth temptation; for when he is tried, he shall receive the crown of life, which the Lord hath promised to them that love him" (James 1:12). Peter adds, "And when the chief Shepherd shall appear, ye shall receive a crown of glory that fadeth not away" (1 Peter 5:4).

You see, salvation is by faith, but crowns are by works. Salvation comes by Christ's faithfulness at Calvary. He paid the price for our sins. Rewards, though, come as a result of our faithfulness. John wrote, "Behold, I come quickly; hold that which thou hast, that no man take thy crown" (Revelation 3:11).

But, what would I do with a crown anyway? That's a good question. It isn't a matter of pride. In Revelation 4, we read about the 24 elders who are symbolic of the church, "I saw four and twenty elders sitting, clothed with white raiment; and they had on their heads crowns of gold" (Revelation 4:4). Then we read in verse 10, "The four and twenty elders fall down before him that sat on the throne, and worship him that liveth for ever and ever, and cast their crowns before the throne, saying, Thou art worthy, O Lord . . ." (Revelation 4:10, 11). So the crowns are going to be a means of glorifying Him. We will cast them at this feet. What a day that will be! Will you have a crown to lay there, at the feet of Jesus? Pretty important question. A crown—commendation from Him—that you can give back to Him in love and adoration. Appropriate indeed! What a great day that will be!

Training for Running: "For I am now ready to be offered, and the time of my departure is at hand. I have fought a good fight, I have finished my course, I have kept the faith; henceforth there is laid up for me a crown of righteousness, which the Lord, the righteous judge, shall give me at that day; and not to me only, but unto all them also that love his appearing" (2 Timothy 4:6-8).

Heaven will be full of surprises when the crowns are passed out and we cast them at His feet. The faithful servants who may not have received a great deal of publicity from this world (even the evangelical world) will certainly be honored by the Lord in that great day. It is faithfulness that matters!

His Constraining Love

What did Paul mean in 2 Corinthains 5:14 when he said, "For the love of Christ constraineth us"? I don't believe he was indicating that our love for Him is a constraining force, although that may be true. He was speaking, I'm sure, of the Lord's love for us. "For God *so loved* the world" (John 3:16). "Herein *is love*, not that we loved God, but that He loved us" (1 John 4:10). What love Jesus manifested when He ". . . loved me and gave himself for me" (Galatians 2:20).

This word, *constraineth*, is an interesting one. At first glance you would almost think that it means "urging or driving," but this is not the principal meaning of the word. It is used 12 times in Scripture, 9 of them by Luke. Paul uses the word when he says, "For I am *in a strait betwixt two*, having a desire to depart and to be with Christ, which is far better" (Philippians 1:23). The word means "to be held together, confined." Of Paul, Luke said he was "pressed in the Spirit," more properly translated "constrained by the Word" (Acts 18:5). It is used by Luke describing Peter's mother-in-law as she was suffering from a fever (Luke 4:38).

In our present passage you might say that an awareness of the Lord's love for us constrains us or compresses our energies in one channel. His love shuts us up and confines us to one purpose. We are held by it, taken by it, pressed by it, encompassed by it. How blessed is this truth! Whatever your situation today, however heavy the burden, however great the care, just continue to be aware that the Lord understands your needs and loves you with a love that knows no description. Knowing that He loves us so much enables us to be willing to endure the trial that is ours. We realize that it is simply one more step He has planned for us, since we are committed to the single purpose of doing His will.

Paul was so zealous that men thought he was "beside himself" (2 Corinthians 5:13). They couldn't understand a man being so filled with ambition that he would act with that kind of urgency. Now it could be that you are not in the place where you can serve the Lord with such vigor. But wouldn't it be a wonderful thing if others would observe about you that you certainly must be a fanatic, you must indeed be beside yourself to go on through life with all your affliction and difficulty without complaining. You might hear others say, "Why, that just isn't normal. After all she's been through and to take it as though she is totally unaffected by it." You might answer, "Beside myself? Ah, no. I'm just basking in the sunshine of His love. While my bodily condition is not the most desirable, my heart is warmed by His presence, my mind is fixed on His person, and I am day-by-day made aware of His abiding love for me in saving me and in keeping me."

Scripture says that Christ, "having loved His own which were in the world, He loved them unto the end" (John 13:1). This love, real and effective, constrains me—compresses all my energies (however weak and faltering) into one channel and focuses me, even if in confinement, on one purpose—that of pleasing Him.

 Training for Running: "Herein is love, not that we loved God, but that he loved us, and sent his Son to be the propitiation for our sins" (1 John 4:10).

"But God commendeth his love toward us in that, while we were yet sinners, Christ died for us" (Romans 5:8).

"But God, who is rich in mercy, for his great love wherewith he loved us" (Ephesians 2:4).

> Oh, the bitter pain and sorrow,
>   That a time could ever be
> When I proudly said to Jesus
>   All of self and none of thee
>
> But He found, me—I beheld Him
>   hanged upon the cursed Tree
> And my foolish heart said faintly
>   Some of self and more of thee.
>
> Day by day His tender mercies
>   Healing, helping, full and free,
> Brought me closer, while I whispered
>   Less of self and more of thee.
>
> Higher that the highest mountain
>   Deeper than the deepest sea,
> Lord, at last thy love hath conquered
>   None of self, and all of thee.
>   —Author unknown

Holding Lightly

Many of the words we commonly use in the church are taken for granted. We use some of them so often that they no longer have an impact on us. We use them glibly, and they flow from our lips as part of the "religious vocabulary" we've always used. Words like *faith* and *hope* and *love* have a nice sound, and they look good in poetry.

Another word that can be in this same category of words we use is *surrender*. What does *surrender* mean? It can have awful, shameful connotations in many arenas. *Surrender* then becomes a word synonymous with *fear* and *defeat* because it means "to lose, to give up, to concede, to throw in the towel." As a matter of fact, in the secular vocabulary there is hardly a good or pleasant application of the word *surrender* to life. Today the idea is win, conquer, and assert yourself. We are more interested in success than surrender.

But surrender can be a beautiful word. Think of what it means to surrender to God's will. Most of us have heard the words of this song: "All to Jesus I surrender, all to him I freely give." Sometimes at the end of a church service, we sing "I surrender all, I surrender all. . . ." Ah, it becomes a touching idea. But, again, as beautiful as it is, let's not let it become so regular that it belongs to our glib vocabulary.

I think the best brief definition of surrender is to "hold lightly" to things. That is, we are so given over to doing God's will, and we have so surrendered our lives to Him, that anything of material value that comes our way is of only passing importance. It is a none-of-self-and-all-of-Thee philosophy. It is a "for me to live in Christ" attitude (Philippians 1:21). It is "presenting our bodies a living sacrifice." Careful here—we are treading on what has become common ground again. We all know Romans 12:1, 2—but are we practicing it? Yes, surrender is abandonment of self. It is a total yielding, it is relinquishing my rights, it is giving God *carte blanche*. It is holding everything lightly, and being occupied with Christ.

Martha Snell Nicholson, in her beautiful poem "Surrender" wrote:

> Let me hold lightly
> Things of this earth;
> Transient treasures,
> What are they worth?
>
> Moths can corrupt them,
> Rust can decay;
> All their bright beauty
> Fades in a day.

Winning Words for Daily Living

Let me hold lightly
  Temporal things,
I who am deathless,
  I, who wear wings!

Let me hold fast, Lord,
  Things of the skies,
Quicken my vision,
  Open my eyes!

Show me Thy riches,
  Glory and grace,
Boundless as time is,
  Endless as space!

Let me hold lightly
  Things that are mine -
Lord, Thou hast given me
  All that is thine!

 Training for Running: "But what things were gain to me, those I counted loss for Christ. Yea doubtless, and I count all things but loss for the excellency of the knowledge of Christ Jesus, my Lord; for whom I have suffered the loss of all things, and do count them but dung, that I may win Christ" (Philippians 3:7-8).

The greatest test of our willingness to surrender all is what we do when we have to give up a little. If we can't hold the little things lightly, we'll never give God the big things in our life.

Is There a Genius in the House?

Although I have met some very intelligent people, I'm not sure I have ever met a genius. Did you ever feel "put down" by being around someone who seemed so very smart?

There have been some people in history who would give any of us a complex. Take Mozart, for example. It is said that he composed minuets at the age of 3. Beethoven played the piano in public when he was 8 years old and composed works that were published when he was 10. Hummel was giving concerts at 9, and Chopin was 9 when he gave his first public concert.

I was playing the piano when I was 9, too, but I think it was "The Big Bass Singer" or some other little ditty. But think of William H. W. Betty of England. He performed the heaviest Shakespearean role at age 11. He was such a prodigy that Parliament adjourned one day in 1802 so its members could see his portrayal of Hamlet.

Most of us haven't reached such intellectual heights, nor are we categorized as being brilliant. Now, what does this mean? First, let us understand that these geniuses were born that way. What natural talents they had are just that—natural. Isn't it wonderful to know that we aren't judged by how intelligent we are but by the extent we use that which God gave us. Let's be thankful for who we are and for what endowments we have received. We need to use them to the fullest for God's glory and praise. There is no need for jealousy when we see another who is more gifted. Nor is there room for pride if we are gifted. There is no reason for a "high and mighty" attitude, because we had nothing to do with our natural aptitude or intelligence.

No, we will not be a Mozart or a Beethoven, but we can be ourselves and God can use us. He is not looking for better brains, but yielded brains. He is not looking for impressive talent, but surrendered talent; not geniuses, but ordinary people who can be used to do extraordinary exploits in the name of a mighty God.

Lord, take what little we have and multiply it to Your glory. Help us be willing to understand that "little is much when You are in it." Challenge us to include our brain, talents, and natural endowments when we sing "I Surrender All."

Training for Running: "For we are laborers together with God; ye are God's husbandry, ye are God's building. According to the grace of God which is given unto me, as a wise master builder, I have laid the foundation, and another buildeth on it. But let every man take heed how he buildeth upon it" (1 Corinthians 3:9-10).

In *Life-Power or Character, Culture and Conduct* by A.T. Pierson, there is one chapter devoted to "The Genius of Industry." He writes, "Where there is found patience that can wait slowly to gather, a perseverance that can hold fast an end yet unreached, a method that can store up results, there is all that is essential to a man thoroughly furnished for his work; give him time and health, and the wealth of success is his."

The Nose

Of all parts of the body, I think the part that gets the most ridicule is that part that snoops, snubs, and sneezes. Yes, I mean the nose.

Have you ever noticed how many times the nose is used figuratively? We speak of a person being "led by the nose," meaning he has no will of his own. Or a person being in church "on the nose," meaning right on time. (That is one of the good uses of the word.) Sunday morning we "count noses"—we want to know how many people are there. When we "pay through the nose," we pay too much, don't we? (even if they say it was on sale). Or if someone gets on our case, we often get our "nose out of joint." That is, we are humiliated. How many times have you lost something yet it was really "right under your nose." Well, so it goes—with the nose.

The one that interests me most is the phrase, "To put one's nose to the grindstone." Now there's an apt phrase for you. It means, of course, to really get with it, to stay hard at work. Years ago, tools such as scythes and chisels were repeatedly sharpened on a stone. So the expression relates to the quality of our work—it means to give it all you have. And, for the most part, we believe that makes good sense.

Hard work, my mother used to say, never hurt anybody. But there is such a thing as all work and no play: work for work's sake, with never a time of joyous reflection or innocent amusement. That will make you old very fast. I'm not putting down work; it's good for us. But it is equally important that we step back and reflect, even on our work. To stop and smell the flowers, to enjoy one another's company, to laugh (what would I do if I couldn't laugh?). Listen, if you keep your nose to the grindstone too much, you are likely to find yourself "paying through the nose." And that's too high a cost.

A good friend of mine, Gene Sickler, sent this to me in the mail—about that very thing. Maybe friend Sickler thought I needed it, and maybe I do. Listen, you may need it too.

> If you put your nose to the grindstone rough
> And hold it there just long enough
> You'll never see clear mountain springs
> Or jump for joy when the robin sings
> But soon enough your world will compose
> Just you
> Your stone
> And your ground-down nose.
> —Author unknown

Training for Running: "Oh taste and see that that LORD is good; blessed is the man who trusteth in him" (Psalm 34:8).

Sometimes we get a better understanding of our relationship with the Lord when we get off the frantic merry-go-round of our day-to-day responsibilities and take time to think and pray. This is the reason for retreats (some say we ought to call them "advances"). Not everything we do has to be hard work and "climbing the ladder". To stop, rest, and do some serious reflection is good for us. It helps redirect and renew us. It helps us slow down and "taste the Lord."

Rivals

While everybody around us seems to be keyed in on good healthy rivalry—we see it in sports every day—this good old "rugged individualism" spirit is not necessarily the best thing when it comes to the work of the Lord. We shouldn't think of our churches as being competing rivals. This matter of the things of the Lord is more than a game to be won—indeed, rivalry can be carnal.

The word *rival* comes from the Latin *rivalis*. The word originally meant "one who lives on the same river or stream." It comes to us from *rivus*—a brook. So, the idea is that there are two people, on opposite sides of the brook sharing the same water source, the same stream. They are at odds. One wants to use the water one way, and the other insists on using it another way. Yes, there is contention over the water; there is rivalry over the river, or the *rivus*. There is a difference, a contention, a rivalry.

In the John 7, Christ said, "If any man thirst, let him come unto me, and drink. He that believeth on me, as the scripture hath said, out of his belly [innermost being] shall flow rivers of living water" (vv. 37, 38). The next verse makes it clear that he is talking about the Holy Spirit. "But this spake he of the Spirit . . ." (v. 39). Christ says that the believer is one the Spirit uses. Indeed he flows through us— and when unimpeded, is a flowing through of rivers to a lost and thirsty world.

Would you think that there could be a rivalry in spiritual outflow among God's people? What an awful thought—competition in spiritual things; a rivalry with the Spirit's work. Yet this river is one that is inexhaustible. It knows no limit to the believer who is Spirit controlled. Often we sing:

> Channels only, blessed Master,
> But with all Thy wondrous power
> Flowing through us, Thou canst use us
> Every day and every hour.
> —Mary E. Maxwell

The next time you see another person blessed of God and used of God, don't look on him as a rival, but as one whom the Spirit has been pleased to use. For he is a person who depends on the same river, the same source, the same stream.

> . . . flowing through us
> Thou canst use us. . . .

A river without rivalry!

Training for Running: "At the same time came the disciples unto Jesus, saying, Who is the greatest in the kingdom of heaven? And Jesus called a little child unto him, and set him in the midst of them, and said, Verily I say unto you, except ye be converted, and become as little children, ye shall not enter into the kingdom of heaven" (Matthew 18:1-3).

> What poet would not grieve to see
> His brother write as well as he?
> —Jonathan Swift: *On the Death of Dr. Swift*

While we do not like to admit it, we often have a rival spirit in the work of the Lord. To see others excel is hard on us. But with the Spirit of Christ—a servant's spirit—all this will change. Let us pray for a service that does not have rivalry. We are all drinking from the same river!

"Less Than Ten" Club

When you pray, do you belong to the "Less Than Ten" club? I know that is a foreign phrase, so let me explain.

In Genesis 18 we have the record of Abraham going before the Lord and praying for Sodom and Gomorrah's escape from destruction. God had said that because of the awful sin of this city He would destroy it by fire. Abraham said, "Lord, peradventure there be fifty righteous within the city: wilt thou also destroy and not spare the place for the fifty righteous that are therein?" (v. 24). "If," prayed Abraham, "there are just fifty will you spare it?" The answer was affirmative. Then he asked if 45 would be enough. The Lord answered that even for 45 he would spare the city.

Abraham went one step further and in verse 29, he asked about 40. God said, "I will not do it for forty's sake." The figure of 20 then were brought before the Lord. God said, "I will not destroy it for ten's sake . . ." (v. 32). Imagine in that whole city—there were not 10 righteous. The disappointing thing, however, is that Abraham stopped right there. I believe most assuredly that if he had asked God to spare the city for 5 or less, He would have done it. We have here a typical picture of incomplete intercession, of going so far and yet falling short of praying on for real victory. He got down to 10 and quit! He stopped asking and left the scene. Then God brought fire down upon the wicked cities. He was down to 10 and stopped.

Now do you know what I mean when I say the "Less Than Ten" club? We need prayer warriors today—Christians who will keep on interceding, keep on importuning God in fervent prayer—praying through impossible things. Too many of us go just so far in our prayers, and then fall short of what might have been done.

Roger Bagson said, "Prayer is the greatest unused power in the world, and faith is the greatest undiscovered resource." But this power will not avail unless we persist in it—and do not stop with 10.

It is said that Alexander the Great was asked by a courtier for some financial aid. Alexander told him to go to his treasurer and ask for whatever amount he wanted. Later the treasurer appeared, according to the story, and told Alexander that the man had asked for so much money that he was very hesitant to give it to him. "Give him what he asks for," said the conqueror, "he has treated me like a king in his asking, and I shall be like a king in my giving!"

How God must be grieved when we go only so far with Him and ask so little when He wants to answer the most impossible of our prayers.

> Thou art coming to a King,
> Large petitions with thee bring
> For His grace and power are such,
> None can ever ask too much!
> —John Newton

Training for Running: "But I have prayed for thee, that thy faith fail not. And when thou art converted, strengthen thy brethren" (Luke 22:32).

"Praying always with all prayer and supplication in the Spirit, and watching thereunto with all perseverance and supplication for all saints" (Ephesians 6:18).

"I exhort, therefore, that first of all, supplications, prayers, intercession, and giving of thanks, be made for all men, for kings, and for all that are in authority, that we may lead a quiet and peaceable life in all godliness and honesty. For this is good and acceptable in the sight of God our Savior" (1 Timothy 2:1-3).

Christ is our great example in intercessory prayer. He prayed for others; so should we. Also, we need to pray in the Spirit, and pray for all saints. But it goes beyond that to all men. The circle enlarges, as so does our vision.

Little Lips

Remember when we were little children and sang that chorus, "Oh, Be Careful Little Lips What You Say"? I guess it is cute; at least we seem to think so when we hear small children sing it. But it's more than cute; it is correct and it makes good sense. We have all been around people who are a constant source of irritation. Or should I spell it "earitation?"

Frankly, there are some people whose chief delight is giving others the lowdown on the higher-ups. They are never happier than when they deride others.

It was the godly Jeremy Taylor who wrote the following:

"Every man hath in his own life, sins enough; in his own mind, trouble enough; in his own fortune, evils enough; and in performance of his offices, failings more than enough to entertain his own inquiry. So that curiosity after the affairs of others cannot be without envy and any evil mind" (taken from his book *Holy Living*). What he is saying is that there are enough shortcomings in our own lives, so why should we be occupied with other's mistakes and problems?

I read about a person who made this statement about another: "It is too much to hope that one day he may come forth with a few brilliant flashes of silence." A preacher once told me that we are seldom sorry for what we don't say.

Be careful that you don't hurt another by a careless remark or by passing on something that you heard and are not sure of. Don't be like the person who said, "And I can tell you all this without the slightest fear of verification."

THE TONGUE

The boneless tongue, so small and weak,
"Can crush and kill," declared the Greek

"The tongue destroyes a greater horde,"
The Turk asserts, "than does the sword."

The Persian proverb wisely saith,
"A lengthy tongue—an early death."

Or sometimes takes this form instead:
"Don't let your tongue cut off your head."

"The tongue can speak a word whose speed,"
Says the Chinese, "outstrips the steed."

While Arab sage doth this impart:
"The tongue's great storehouse is the heart."

From Hebrew wit the maxim sprung,
"Though feet should slip, ne'er let the tongue."

The sacred writer crowns the whole,
"Who keeps his tongue doth keep his soul."
—Philip Burrows Strong

Training for Running: "Let my prayer be set forth before thee as incense; and the lifting up of my hands as the evening sacrifice. Set a watch, O LORD, before my mouth; keep the door of my lips" (Psalm 141:2-3).

Someone has said that "electricity is something that starts the Lord knows where and ends in the same place. It is 1/36th of a second faster than its nearest competitor—backyard gossip. And consider this: "Great minds discuss ideas, average minds discuss events, small minds discuss people." Let's be careful with our lips. At the Judgment Seat of Christ we must give an account of how we used our lips.

Little Things Do Count

Sometimes little things are mighty things. Ralph Waldo Emerson said, "The creation of a thousand forests is one acorn."

Orison Swett Marden penned this provocative parable:

"Two drops of rain falling side by side are separated by a few inches with a gentle breeze. Striking on opposite sides of the roof of a courthouse in Wisconsin, one rolled southward through the Rock River and the Mississippi to the Gulf of Mexico while the other entered successively the Fox River, Green Bay, Lake Michigan, the Straits of Mackinaw, Lake Huron, St. Clair River, Lake St. Clair, Detroit River, Lake Erie, Niagara River, Lake Ontario, the St. Lawrence River, and finally reached the Gulf of St. Lawrence." Thus two drops of rain, falling side by side, ended up at opposite ends of the nation, one in the Southeast and the other in the Northeast. The difference was a gentle breeze."

Small things! Small things make the difference!

They say that among the lofty Alps, guides often demand absolute silence, fearing that the smallest vibration from the voice might bring down an avalanche. Writing about small things, someone has said, "Big moments seldom come. Great deeds are rare. Most of the elements that go into the making of a human life are in themselves infinitesimal and of small consequence. The unmeditated word, the spontaneous action, the glance and smile that we think nothing of, are the strands of which a life is woven. Our character is determined by the sum total effect of all these small things upon us."

Sometimes there are little things to offer, like five loaves and two small fish. And often there are little tasks to be done with little credit resulting. But little is much when God is in it; His "well done" should be all sufficient. Yes, little things matter, whether it is a work or a word, an action or an attitude.

Do you know that an unkind word or harsh voice in answer to a question might also result in a devastating blow to a friend? Someone has said, "The bad thing about a little sin is that it won't stay little." While reflecting on this subject some time ago, I wrote these words:

> A garment tears from one weak thread,
> A heart is torn by one word said;
> A gossiped word passed on can grow
> For little things do count, you know.

Winning Words for Daily Living

A pleasant smile, a heartening word
　Can set a saddened heart astir;
In spite of bane and bitter blows
　For little things do count, you know

A mighty minute in our prayer
　For loved ones low in deep despair
Could mean a victory o'er the foe
　For little things do count, you know.
　　　　　　　—Charles U. Wagner

 Training for Running: "There is a lad here, who hath five barley loaves and two small fishes; but what are they among so many? And Jesus said, Make the men sit down. Now there was much grass in the place. So the men sat down, in number about five thousand. And Jesus took the loaves; and when he had given thanks, he distributed to the disciples, and the disciples to them that were set down; and likewise of the fishes as much as they would. When they were filled, he said unto his disciples, Gather up the fragments that remain, that nothing be lost" (John 6:9-12).

If we believe that "the steps of a good man are ordered of the Lord" (Psalm 37:23), then the small steps of a small boy with five small loaves and two small fishes were ordered by the Lord that day. But God took the small and used it to His glory. He can and will do the same in our lives as we trust Him.

Your Gratitude Is Telling

The degree of thanksgiving you have in your heart tells a great deal about you. A proud person is seldom thankful. Henry Ward Beecher once said, "Pride slays thanksgiving, but a humble mind is the soil out of which thanksgiving naturally grows. A proud man is seldom a grateful man, for he never thinks he gets as much as he deserves."

If you are a chronic faultfinder, chances are you are not a thankful person. Another great preacher, John Henry Jowett, wrote, "Gratitude is a vaccine, an antitoxin and an antiseptic." This vaccine has a deadening effect on the grumbler, and faultfinder. If you have gratitude in your veins you will find if difficult, if not impossible, to mumble and grumble. To quote Jowett again: "Life without thankfulness is devoid of love and passion. Hope without thankfulness is lacking in fine perception. Faith without thankfulness lacks strength and fortitude. Every virtue divorced from thankfulness is maimed and limps along the spiritual road."

Thanksgiving also reveals our jealousy and envy. Have you ever met a jealous person that was truely thankful? They spend their time enviously observing the grass on the other side of the fence, and rationalizing away the reasons why their grass is not as green. Envy and thanksgiving never go together.

One of the remedies of worry is to be thankful. It is no wonder that after Paul speaks of thanksgiving he notes "the peace of God, which passeth all understanding, shall keep your hearts and minds through Christ Jesus" (Philippians 4:7). Are you a worry wart? Try thanksgiving!

True thanksgiving begins in the heart, not at the table. True thanksgiving has a single purpose—to express gratitude. It is never a down payment on the next favor.

> Of all the many, many gifts
> We long so to possess,
> The one that is the best is this,
> The gift of thankfulness.
> Of all the blessings we receive,
> Which happiness impart,
> The one that brings real joy is this—
> Thanksgiving in the heart.
> —*Rocky Mountain Churchman*

Examine your own heart. Are you thankful? Then you will find pride, faultfinding, jealousy, and envy strangers to you. Conversely, if there are evidences of those sins in your life, a good cure for them is confession and thanksgiving.

 Training for Running: "Be careful for nothing; but in every think by prayer and supplication with thanksgiving let your requests be made known unto God" (Philippians 4:6).

Gratitude of heart—a thankful spirit—is essential for the race of life. It is a barometer of your spiritual condition. Ask God's forgiveness for allowing any poison of ingratitude to find its way into your life. Then, with a grateful heart, press toward the mark!

God's Presence, God's Promises

"Go ye, therefore, and teach all nations, baptizing them in the name of the Father, and of the Son, and of the Holy Ghost, teaching them to observe all things whatsoever I have commanded you; and, lo, I am with you always, even unto the end of the world. Amen" (Matthew 28:19, 20).

Usually when this verse is read, it is done to emphasize our responsibility to get out the message of the gospel—and with real justification. However, there is more than a challenge and a command here. There is also a promise! God the Son says, "You obey me, and do my bidding, assured that I will be with you."

How many missionaries have held tenaciously to that promise as they moved into virgin territory? How many pastors and laymen have trusted God that He would be good to His word and give them a sense of His presence and a portion of His power? Have any of them been disappointed? Never! When the believer responds in obedience, the Lord will be good to His promises.

In a letter to his father, William Carey wrote: "To be devoted like a sacrifice to holy uses, is the great business of a Christian. . . . I consider myself as devoted to the service of God alone, and now I am to realize my profession. I am appointed to go to Bengal in the East Indies, a missionary to the Hindus. . . . I hope, dear father, you may be enable to surrender me up to the Lord for the most arduous, honorable, and important work that ever any of the sons of men were called to engage in. I have sacrifices to make, I must part with a beloved family and a number of most affectionate friends. . . . But I have set my hand to the plough."

History shows that this young enthusiast was successful as he pioneered the movement of modern missions. "Lo, I am with you always!" How precious was this promise to a missionary who left family and friends to obey the Lord. (His immediate family joined him later.) After his work was over and he had proved that Christ was good to His promise, he slipped into the presence of the Lord. In accordance with the directions of his will, his gravestone had the following inscription: "William Carey, Born August 17, 1761—Died June 9, 1834. A wretched, poor and helpless worm, on Thy kind arms I fall." His life can be summed up in the words he made famous: "Expect great things from God; attempt great things for God." This was his motto. It was the driving force of a man who obeyed God and held to that great promise:

"Lo, I am with you alway . . ."

"A Thousand Tongues—Or One"

"Oh for a thousand tongues to sing,"
  The moving hymn was sung so
  clear;
The blend of voices spread throughout
  The village square for all to hear.

A thousand tongues to sing HIS
  praise?
  "That's mighty strange," a listener
  said,
I know a member of the church
  Who talks of other things instead.

The weather's fine—you're looking
  good,
  The market's up—this is the sum,
But of the Great Redeemer's praise,
  A saddening fact—a silent tongue!

Again, the choir-like blend resounds
  Into a home of deep despair.
If only ONE had cared enough
  To sing, to speak the Gospel there.

"The glory of their God and King"
"The triumphs of His grace" must
  be,

One thought, for just a few
  But surely, it included me.
For in that song, I hear them sing,
  "Ye BLIND, behold your Savior
  come:
"And leap, ye LAME, for joy," so will
  One help this blind and halting one?

"Oh, for a thousand tongues" the
  words
  Articulated crisp and bold
From strong and able souls resound.
  The words were warm, the hearts
  were cold.

A thousand tongues would multiply
  My trivia, my foolishness,
A thousand tongues for idle words,
  Would merely entertain at best.

Oh, Lord, ONE TONGUE anointed
  from
  Oh high to speak of Thee,
  empowered
To tell in no uncertain sound
  The triumphs of His grace this hour.

—Charles U. Wagner

 Training for Running: "Let your moderation be known unto all men. The Lord is at hand. Be careful for nothing, but in everything, by prayer and supplication with thanksgiving, let your requests be made known unto God" (Philippians 4:5-6).

"The Lord is at hand" means that He is "near," and that He is with us. What a promise! Carey did not run alone. And he was goal-oriented as he ran the race. He expected to win, and He did. He had that great promise: "Lo I am with you always."

Remember When?

"Listen to those crickets," I said. "There is absolutely no sound like a cricket symphony in the heart of Tennessee." Childhood memories deluged my mind as I visited some old familiar places during a recent trip south. While there, this city boy learned the joys of catching bullfrogs by the old pond near my Uncle Gilbert's place. There too, I got my first ride on the plow mules and explored the verdant fields for Indian arrowheads. And, more important, there as a boy of about 10, I preached my first sermon in an old church on "chigger hill." Strong feelings of nostalgia welled up in my heart as we sat around the old home place. Almost every other phase was punctuated with "Remember when?"

Memory is a wonderful thing. The daily jaunts to the old swimming hole at Yellow Creek; the laughter that came from understanding relatives when as a child we expressed dismay at the hogs, which were "barking" at us; the unforgettable experience of finding wild honey in the woods and fighting the bees for their treasure; the adventure of treeing a possum on the way home from church; and the never-to-be-forgotten howls of the fox hounds as they chased their prey into the wee hours of the morning.

Precious and cherished memories are these, yet the greatest memory is the way the Lord has sustained and guided this child of His over the years since those youthful days. There was not a doubt in my mind then that God had called me to the ministry. And now, several decades later, a heart bows before the Lord in thanksgiving that He had led all the way.

Have you also found this true in your life? Has not the Lord down through the years been faithful to you and intervened for you in countless ways? Remember the day you were saved? Then, remember the crisis that came in your life as a child—that incident that seems quite insignificant now, but was very real and serious then. How thrilling to know that there was an understanding heavenly Father who saw you though every situation. With David we exclaim, "I remember the days of old" (Psalm 143:5).

It is good for us to remember. To reminisce is to be reminded that God has never failed us and that the trials and vicissitudes of today will be precious recollections of tomorrow. And in a coming day, a visit to a familiar place, perhaps the touch of an old fence post where you stopped to breathe a special prayer in a desperate hour, will be a sweet little reminder of God's faithfulness and goodness. Every victory, every crisis that takes place today will increase in preciousness in the coming years as we remember His unfailing companionship through it all.

> "Remember when?" those words now introduce
> A score or two of precious recollections;
> Blest thoughts of earlier days now flood the soul
> Of His choicest of plans—Divine directions.
>
> "Remember when?" the trying days and crisis hours
> Reviewed, invoke those unexpected tears.
> Reminding hearts again of His unfailing
> Love and care through countless yester-years.
>
> The days with strange vicissitudes now pass,
> Mixtures of joy, then, sadder days which rend
> And flail the heart, driving us to our knees—
> Strength comes again from heaven's precious Friend.
>
> These present joys and sorrows take their place
> In precious memory's books, for which we'll send
> In future days, rehearsing His blest grace,
> And in a thankful heart, exclaim, "Remember when?"
> —Charles U. Wagner

 Training for Running: "And I said, This is my infirmity; but I will remember the years of the right hand of the Most High. I will remember the works of the LORD; surely I will remember thy wonders of old. I will meditate also of all thy work, and talk of thy doings" (Psalm 77:10-12).

The psalmist had it right! He remembered the years of the Lord's workings, and he remembered the works of the Lord and the wonders of old. Then, from memory he moved into meditation. Deep reflection followed historical review. When we remember what He has done, it isn't hard to trust Him for the future, is it?

My Gift

I am amused when I hear people say that tithing is not for today. The fact that it was practiced before the giving of the law makes no difference to them. They are just dead set against it. "It's legalistic," they say. "It's under the law." It is true that many commands covering the tithe are Mosaic, but there are many moral principles which, while also in the Law, have always existed as principles.

Take capital punishment, for instance. While capital punishment is stated in the law, the moral principle of this command is as old as Noah. It never ceases to amaze me to see how we are so willing to turn to the Old Testament and its blessings and be refreshed by them, while, at the same time, we reject many of the moral principles by writing them off as not for our age. I suppose it depends on whether or not we are on the giving or the receiving end.

If there is any argument against giving the tithe, I would think that it is not enough to give. We are under grace, so a tithe should only be a good place to start. Many great blessings are missed by God's people because of their refusal to face this vital principle of giving. As we prove the Lord and give by faith, He will bless us accordingly. As we act in obedience, He opens the windows of heaven.

One of the first lessons I ever learned from my pastor when I was just "knee high to a piano stool" was the lesson of proportionate giving. I can hear him today as if it were just yesterday, "You can't outgive God. If you give God a spoon full, He will give you a shovel full." These words came when none of us had too much. The Depression had struck several years earlier. People were out of work, and to give meant to really hurt. But as a family, we joined in what our pastor would call "Prove Me Month," based on Malachi 3:10. We were urged to prove the Lord by not only tithing, but also by doubling our tithe for one month to see whether or not God would bless us even more than before. It was quite a step for us all, but we proved Him, again and again.

Now, if it happened in 400 B.C. (to the Malachi three), and in 1935 (among the Wagner four), can it happen again today? Don't rationalize your "non-give position" and cover your doubt with a convenient doctrine. Claim God's promise! Don't wait until you can afford it—there's no faith involved in that. Besides, you'll never be able to "afford it." Decide, act, and watch the windows of Heaven. Blessings are on the way.

Winning Words for Daily Living

FAMILIAR WORDS FROM CERTAIN GIVERS
(Which kind are you?)

I'll give, but the percent I can't afford,
  I'm pressed these days, I know the Lord
Will understand my plight; I'll give,
  But then, you know, I've got to live.

"Not under the law," that I believe,
  "No law" about what I receive,
That all has passed, that's how I feel,
  Except of course, "Thou shalt not steal."

"What's yours is yours, what's mine is mine,"
  A thief I hate, of every kind,
"Thou shalt not steal" believe it all,
  But giving, no! That's "under Law."

Now, here's one thing, I just can't stand,
  A meddling minister making demands.
I know they're after my pocket book;
  They'll get my "wad" by hook or crook.

The Lord has blessed, I plan to share
  What, after all, is His; I care
About His church; I want to give
  That others through my gift may live.
                              —Charles U. Wagner

 Training for Running: "Bring ye all the tithes into the storehouse, that there may be meat in mine house, and prove me now herewith, saith the LORD of hosts, if I will not open you the windows of heaven, and pour out for you a blessing, that there shall not be room enough to receive it" (Malachi 3:10).

Someone has written, "Do your giving while you're living—so you're knowing where it's going." Each of us needs to reflect on the quantity of our giving. Do we realize that everything we have is God's, and that we are but stewards? Let's be sure we have really given all to Him, not just "the best of what we possess." What kind of a giver are you?

Ostracize

Nobody likes to be ostracized. There is something about being ignored or left out that is terribly uncomfortable. Our word *ostracized* comes directly from the Greek. It goes way back to Greek democracy. The Athenians of old would sometimes decide that someone had too much influence or that he was dangerous. The citizens would assemble, say the experts, in the marketplace and vote. They were to decide if the person should be banished. It was as simple as that. They took a tile called an *ostrakon* and wrote the name of the man or woman in question. There was no special trial, there was no redress; no appeal could be made. There was only the counting of the vote. If 6,000 *ostrakons* were cast, the person was banished from 5 to 10 years.

So *ostrakon* came into the English as to *ostracize*. While the banishment wasn't as cruel and tough, the idea was the same. You were placed on the outside. You were gently and politely banished from your peers—-you were ostracized.

Another word you might use would be the word *alienated*. That's the word that describes our past condition before we met Christ. We were alienated from the commonwealth of Israel (see Ephesians 2:12). We were once on the outside. Did you know that? We were "not a people" as the Bible puts it, in 1 Peter. We were "afar off." But we have been brought to a place of reconciliation, a place of acceptance, a place of fellowship as a result of Christ's work for us at Calvary. It wasn't a matter of God not loving us when we were afar off. It was rather a matter of a Holy God seeing us as we really were: enemies, lost people, ungodly. But the Bible says, "But now in Christ Jesus ye who were sometimes were afar off are made nigh by the blood of Christ" (Ephesians 2:13). What a wonderful position is this! There is no vote against us, no *ostrakon*, no banishment. We are as near and dear to God as Christ Himself is. We are "accepted in the beloved" (Ephesians 1:6).

We must not forget that we will be ostracized by the world when we take our stand as Christians. But that kind of *ostrakon* is not that hard to bear. It might even be a sign that we are where we should be as Christians. Christ once said, "If the world hate you, ye know that it hateth me before it hateth you. If ye were of the world, the world would love its own; but because ye are not of the world, but I have chosen you out of the world, therefore the world hateth you" (John 15:18, 19).

So however the world casts its vote, one thing is sure, there is no fear of an *ostrakon* when it comes to our coveted relationship with our Lord. We are reconciled; we are accepted. And that's enough to make us thankful.

 Training for Running: "Having predestinated us unto the adoption of children by Jesus Christ to himself, according to the good pleasure of his will, to the praise of the glory of his grace, through which he hath made us accepted in the beloved" (Ephesians 1:5-6).

Someone has written:

> Near, so very near to God
> Nearer I cannot be,
> For in the Person of His Dear Son
> I am as near as He.
> —Author unknown

Accepted in the beloved! Thank God for it!

The Ideal Pastor

I would like to address one of my favorite subjects: The Pastor. I know a little about this subject, having pastored for over 30 years in five different churches. And, if I may be so bold to mention it, I have written two books on the pastor and have taught pastoral theology for 15 years. So I know something about pastors, and I have a special place in my heart for them. Now I am the president of a college and seminary, and I *have* a pastor—a good one too!

Yet I don't know of a job where a person gets so much criticism as the pastor. Someone has written: "When the church seeks a pastor they often want the strength of an eagle, the grace of a swan, the gentleness of a dove, the friendliness of a sparrow, and when they catch that bird they expect him to live on the food of a canary."

In my book, *The Pastor: His Life and Work*, I quoted a clipping I found years ago. It goes like this:

"After hundreds of years, a model preacher has been found to suit everyone. He preaches exactly 20 minutes and then sits down. He condemns sin, but never hurts anyone's feelings. He works from 8 A.M. to 10 P.M. in every type of work, from preaching to custodial service. He makes $60 dollars a week, wears good clothes, buys good books regularly, has a nice family, drives a good car, and gives $30 a week to the church. He also stands ready to contribute to every good work that comes along. He is 25 years old and has been in the ministry for 30 years. He is tall and short, thick and heavyset in addition to being handsome. He has one brown eye and one blue, hair is parted in the middle, left side dark and straight, right side brown and wavy. He has a burning desire to work with teenagers, and spends all his time with older folks. He smiles all the time with a straight face, because he has a sense of humor that keeps him seriously dedicated to his work. He makes 15 calls a day on church members, spends all his time evangelizing the unchurched, and is never out of the office."

Oh, my! Silly, I'll agree. But so true, so very true.

How about your pastor? Do you pray for him? Do you make an effort to help him? After all, God gave your church a pastor to equip the saints (including you) for the ministry. The ministry is ours—not just his. We are trained by him to assist him in this great work of the ministry. So be gentle, be considerate, and when there is a need, be sure to let him know. Don't just expect him to know.

 Training for Running: "And he gave some, apostles; and some, prophets; and some, evangelists; and some, pastors and teachers; for the perfecting of the saints for the work of the ministry for the edifying of the body of

Winning Words for Daily Living

Christ, till we all come in the unity of the faith, and of the knowledge of the Son of God, unto a perfect man, unto the measure of the stature of the fullness of Christ" (Ephesians 4:11-13).

> Mrs. Huff is up a miff tree;
>   On a seat fixed good and firm.
> And she'd like to tell the pastor
>   A few things to make him squirm.
>
> Mrs. Huff was sick abated, sir,
>   Yes, sir, sick abated a week;
> And the pastor didn't call, sir,
>   Not even took a peek.
>
> Wasn't that enough, enough sir
>   To provoke a saint to wrath?
> And to make a Christian pilgrim
>   Wander from the churchly path?
>
> When I asked her if the doctor
>   Called to see her, she said, "Sure"
> And she looked as if she thought I
>   Needed some good strong mind cure.
>
> Then I asked her how the doctor knew
>   That sickness laid her low,
> And she said that she had called him
>   On the phone and told him so.
>
> So the doctor called to see her,
>   But the pastor didn't go,
> For the doctor knew that she was ill
>   And the pastor didn't know.
>
> Now the doctor gets his bill paid
>   With a nicely written check,
> But the pastor—for not knowing,
>   Simply "gets it in the neck."
>   —Author unknown

Planned Neglect

What makes the difference between a radiant Christian and the mediocre one? Is there some particular secret for the success of one and the failure of the other? Why is it that some younger Christians seem so bogged down with care while others are vivacious and "on top" most of the time? And why is it that some older Christians seem bitter and cynical with seldom a good word for anyone, while others are filled with cheerful sunshine and a kind word about almost everybody?

There may be similar circumstances in life, similar environments, and similar family situations; yet there is a world of difference between the two. Both have only 24 hours a day, but one is always rushed and frustrated; the other, while busy, seems to have time for even the little things. The similarities are quite apparent, but one is down under the burdens and the other is happy and lifted up.

Without oversimplifying, we would suggest that one secret for the difference between the two is the matter of priorities; that is, what really matters in life, what gets first place, what is really important. Who gets the greatest attention and receives absolute authority in your life? Priorities, that's the answer. It is the difference between the spiritual and the carnal, the success and the failure, the unusual and the common.

One young violin artist was asked the secret of her success. She said it was planned neglect. She explained that this may not sound too good, but still it was true. She continued, "When I went to my room, I made my bed, dusted the floor, and did whatever came to my attention. When it was done, I practiced my violin. That system failed to accomplish the result I wanted, so I reversed things. I deliberately planned to neglect everything else until my practice was done. Planned neglect accounts for my success."

Clearly then, the difference was one of priority—what came first in her life. She planned to neglect something until the most important things were cared for. This is one vital secret in victorious Christian living.

"But seek ye first the kingdom of God, and his righteousness, and all these things shall be added unto you" (Matthew 6:33). Put Christ first. Give Him the finest hours of your day, the freshest thoughts of your mind, the uppermost consideration in your plans, and make Him the object of your deepest affections. Then everything else will fall into its natural place and will find meaning in your rather complex life. Many of your problems and difficulties are not a matter of the rightness of certain things; rather, they are the order of their importance.

Think of any period of carnality in your life, present or past. Wasn't it because other things, however legitimate they might have been, took precedence over Christ and spiritual things? You have only 24 hours just like the rest of us. But if you are determined that Christ is going to be absolutely first, you will find the hours, the minutes, and the seconds taking on new meaning.

What and who has priority in your life? Maybe it's time you tried the system of planned neglect. It can make a great difference in your life. Try it and see.

Training for Running: "Let all those who seek thee rejoice and be glad in thee; and let such as love thy salvation say continually, Let God be magnified" (Psalm 70:4).

When one is reaching for the prize in an athletic contest, his success is often not based on whether or not he was involved in legitimate enterprises, but whether he gave priority to his training. This is so necessary to win the prize. Planned neglect will help you run the race with patience (Hebrews 12:1).

Poor Mr. Pessimism

Every once in a while you meet a person who lives off the fret of the land. (No, that's not a typographical error—I mean *fret*, not *fat*). Give this person an inch and he will measure it. He is Mr. Pessimism. His whole outlook is wrong. Every church has one or two (if they are fortunate enough not to have two or three times that many). They see life through morose-colored glasses. Philip had a little of that spirit. When he saw the hungry 5,000 plus, he said, "Two hundred pennyworth of bread is not sufficient for them, that every one of them may take a little" (John 6:7).

The children of Israel were like this when they said, "Wherefore hast thou dealt thus with us, to carry us forth out of Egypt? Is not this the word that we did tell thee in Egypt, saying, Let us alone, that we may serve the Egyptians? For it had been better for us to serve the Egyptians, than that we should die in the wilderness" (Exodus 14:11, 12). They had forgotten the sunshine in life and were complaining because they were temporarily in the shade. The children of Israel were always confirmed in their pessimism.

It isn't a valid rationalization to say that some people are just born with a "fretwork of wrinkles"—seeing the dark side of life. It is closer to the truth to say that such persons are carnal and have their eyes on situations instead of the Lord. They suffer from "skeptic poisoning" because they have been disappointed in life. The trouble is, they were looking in the wrong place. What should have been a glorious uplook was a gruesome outlook.

When we come to this place in life, we become like doubting Thomas. In John 11 we read, "Master, the Jews of late sought to stone thee; and goest thou there again? . . . Then said Thomas unto his fellow disciples, Let us also go, that we may die with him" (vv. 8, 16). Thomas isn't to be admired for his bravery, but pitied for his despondent pessimism. Such is the fruit of doubt and despair. It is far from commendable in the life of a believer. Of course Thomas was called Didymus, which means "twin," and you might not have to look over your shoulder to find out who the other twin was! If you had met Thomas that morning and said, "Good morning," to him, you might very well have heard a typical Thomas reply: "Well, probably." Before the day was over he would have been pulling tomorrow's cloud over today's sunshine.

There are many reasons why you should not be a pessimist. One is that pessimists aren't very pleasant to be around. If you are pessimistic about the scarcity of your friends, it could be that it's because people don't like to be around people who are mountain climbers—over molehills. Not that you should put on a false smile (a false lip and a pessimistic look—who wants to choose between them?).

Also, pessimism reflects upon the Lord. There is every reason to be optimistic. The answer is to change your outlook to an uplook—To see Christ instead of man, to be "looking unto Jesus, the author and finisher of our faith" (Hebrews 12:2). Paul had every reason, humanly speaking, to be pessimistic when jailed in Rome. Yet, his most joyful epistle was written during that time. He said "Rejoice in the Lord always; and again I say, Rejoice" (Philippians 4:4). Anyone who has read Paul's epistles to the Corinthians will agree that the Corinthians were carnal, carping, and critical. Yet, it was while Paul was there that he wrote to the Thessalonians, "Rejoice evermore. Pray without ceasing. In everything give thanks; for this is the will of God in Christ Jesus concerning you" (1 Thessalonians 5:16-18). By the way, the very next verse says, "Quench not the Spirit," and I think that one way to quench and grieve Him is by our attitude.

Don't let external things get you down—Christ is within you, rejoice! Don't let people discourage you, Christ is your constant friend; rejoice! Turn your eyes on Him. "And the things of the earth will grow strangely dim, in the light of His glory and grace" (Helen H. Lemmel).

 Training for Running: "And Simon, answering, said unto him, Master, we have toiled all the night, and have taken nothing; nevertheless, at the word I will let down the net" (Luke 5:5).

Peter was pessimistic and doubtful, but let's give him the benefit of the doubt. "Nevertheless . . ." in spite of his doubt, he obeyed the Lord! It is easy enough to become a pessimist in this difficult world. But the Lord is with us. Obey Him—you'll not be disappointed.

Praise Changes Things

"I will bless the Lord at all times; his praise shall continually be in my mouth" Psalm 34:1.

Every Christian has had occasion to praise the Lord! But this verse does not suggest that we praise the Lord occasionally when things go well. Rather it speaks of praising the Lord continually and blessing Him at all times. Someone has insightfully said that when you find it hard to pray, begin to give thanks and praise the Lord for His goodness. Then you'll have an ocean to swim in. Praise is the blossom of prayer. I came across an item from *The Missionary Worker* which speaks of value of praise:

> Mrs. Charles E. Cowman tells of a missionary in dark China who was living a defeated life. Everything seemed to be touched with sadness and although he prayed and prayed for months for victory over depression and discouragement, his life remained the same. He determined to leave his work and go to an interior station and pray till victory came. He reached the place and was entertained in the home of a fellow missionary. On the wall hung a motto with these words, "Try Thanksgiving." The words gripped his heart and he thought within himself, "Have I been praying all this time and not praising?" He stopped and began to praise and was so uplifted that instead of hiding away to pray and agonize for days, he immediately returned to his waiting flock to tell them that praise changes things. Wonderful blessing attended this simple testimony and the bands that had bound others were loosened through praise.

If we put our thanksgiving in the present tense, it will cure us from grumbling. Not only will praise help your own soul, but it will also do something for others around you. It is "catchy." Praising the Lord for His goodness will rub off on those around you. After David said, "I will bless the Lord at all times; his praise shall continually be in my mouth" (v. 1), he said, "O, magnify the Lord with me, and let us exalt his name together" (v. 3). Then in the fifth verse of Psalm 34 we read, "They looked unto him, and were lightened; and their faces were not ashamed." The word *lightened* means "radiant." A praising Christian is a radiant Christian. You can't be in the presence of such a Christian without being aware that something is different.

Stop and think about all the things you have for which you can praise Him. Begin with your salvation. Follow through with praise for His keeping power and His presence every moment . Then, praise Him for the way He has supplied your every need. Later in Psalm 34

David said, "The young lions do lack, and suffer hunger; but they who seek the LORD shall not want any good thing" (v. 10).

Now, hem-in your blessings with praise for all these things before they unravel. No wonder the psalmist ends the chapter with these words: "The Lord redeemeth the soul of his servants; and none of them that trust in him shall be desolate" (v. 22).

 Training for Running: "Then will I go unto the altar of God, unto God, my exceeding joy; yea, upon the harp will I praise thee, O God, my God. Why art thou cast down, O my soul? And why art thou disquieted within me? Hope in God; for I shall yet praise him, who is the health of my countenance, and my God" (Psalm 43:4–5).

When one runs a race, he is encouraged by various landmarks along the way. They help prod him on toward the goal. Having come so far, the landmarks urge him to greater zeal and resolution. Someone has written:

> He would not have taught us to trust in His name
> And thus far have brought us to put us to shame.

So, praise the Lord that you have gotten this far as you have trusted Him. The best is yet ahead!

Remembering

The word *amnesty* is an interesting word. It literally means "loss of memory." Wilfred Funk writes, "When a lawyer begs amnesty for his client, he is actually asking the judge to have an attack of amnesia." The writer continues, "The first person in history to grant amnesty was reported to have been a Greek general who said that he would forgive his enemies and "not remember." There are two Greek words here: *mnasthia*, meaning "to remember," and the letter *a* which means "not." So the word means "to not remember." We get two English words from this one: *amnesia*, which means "loss of memory," and *amnesty*, which means "a pardon for offenses."

There are times when God does not remember. I know it sounds strange that an omniscient God can forget, but we can use that language appropriately. David prayed "remember not the sins of my youth, nor my transgressions" (Psalm 25:7). Think of it! How is it possible for God to have amnesia and exercise amnesty? Well, David has the answer. "Remember not the sins of my youth, nor my transgressions; according to thy mercy remember thou me for thy goodness' sake, O LORD" (Psalm 25:7). The basis of God "not remembering" is His mercy, and the basis of that mercy is Christ's redemptive work on the cross. Because of His death for us, and based on the fact that we have trusted that work and have been born again, we can say that God does not remember our sin. Instead, he sees and remembers the substitutionary work of Christ on that cross.

When we were children we sang these words:

> Gone, gone, gone, gone,
> Yes, my sins are gone.
> Now my soul is free
> And in my heart's a song
> Buried in the deepest sea—
> Yes, that's good enough for me,
> Now, I'll live eternally,
> Praise God, my sins are gone!

How wonderful is this: In the sea of God's forgetfulness our sins are gone, and gone forever. Praise God for divine amnesia, for biblical amnesty. Through the finished work of the cross, God can forget our sin and remember His mercy.

Training for Running: "Consider what I say, and the Lord give thee understanding in all things. Remember that Jesus Christ, of the seed of David, was raised from the dead according to my gospel" (2 Timothy 2:7-8).

Remember Jesus Christ. That's good advice. What a paradox—God forgets our sin, we remember His grace and mercy. It is because our sins are washed away and we are forgiven that we have this freedom in life's course. As we run we remember that He has forgotten, yet we never forget what he has remembered to do!

Rigmarole

Ever find yourself saying, "I wish we could eliminate all that rigmarole in the morning service"? Or, "I don't want to go through all that rigmarole, it is a bore and takes so much time"?

Ever wonder where we got that strange and funny word *rigmarole*? The word means "statements that are disjointed." It also means "nonsense" and sometimes just "meaningless talk." Sometimes it means "a complex and ritualistic procedure."

Rigmarole has a curious history. It seems that back in 1291 King Edward I of England had his eye on Scotland to be a vassal kingdom. The kings of Scotland, while not thrilled with the idea, could hardly object, so they agreed. They presented the good English King Edward with various documents of allegiance, which were called "ragman roll." Now with a little work, when you say, "ragman roll" fast enough and often enough, it is not hard to determine how we got our word *rigmarole*. The documents were apparently not that important, and they were mixed, including various signatures, to appease the king.

In that light, let's talk about our allegiance to our King—the Lord. He is King of your life, isn't he? He demands allegiance, and He deserves it. As our Lord and our master, He should be given first place in every aspect of life. But when He makes these demands, seeking the honor, praise, and adoration due Him, do we ever find ourselves going through a sort of rigmarole with Him? Do we have our little ritualistic motion, our "ragman roll" of passing phrases and meaningless prayers that defers to Him, but does not take Him seriously? Do we feel that, because we are in no position to argue with Him, we give Him His due—even if it is mechanical and perfunctory? Do we find ourselves just going through the rigmarole of motions, with little heart?

Dr. Carl Bates of Amarillo, Texas once made the statement, "If God called His Holy Spirit out of the world, about 95 percent of what we are doing would go on and we would brag about it." In other words, there would be a lot of rigmarole, with hand and head but no heart. He continued, "What are you doing that you can't get done unless the power of God falls on your ministry?" Good question!

Let's determine to get rid of rigmarole. Let's do everything possible to give him not just our motions, but our emotions. He deserves not just a passing gesture of recognition, but a heart fully dedicated to do His will and rely on His power.

Training for Running: "That ye may approve things that are excellent; that ye may be sincere and without offense till the day of Christ, being filled with the fruits of righteousness, which are by Jesus Christ, unto the glory and praise of God" (Philippians 1:10-11).

Our word *sincere* means literally "without wax." In its original sense, it referred to the practice of repairing a porcelain vase with wax. The vase would look good until held up to the light. If it had not been broken and then repaired, it was *sine cera* or "without wax." Are we sincere, or are we surface Christians—going through the rigmarole? Let's ask the Lord to help us be *sincere*, then when we are "held to the light," we will be found to be real.

Soul-winning Is Important

"And they that be wise shall shine like the brightness of the firmament; and they that turn many to righteousness, as the stars forever and ever" (Daniel 12:3).

It is interesting to note the emphasis placed on the personalities in the world today. In sports, in Hollywood, and in politics, prominent people are considered stars. What is impressive to man is often nothing to God. God's "stars" are those who are involved in turning men to righteousness and showing them how to prepare for heaven. Another verse makes this clear, "And let us not be weary in well doing; for in due season we shall reap, if we faint not" (Galatians 6:9). Indeed, we "shall doubtless come again with rejoicing, bringing [our] sheaves with" us (Psalm 126:6).

There have been several people in the world who could well have been stars in other fields, but who turned out to be spiritual luminaries because they gave their lives to the ministry of soul-winning. One such man was Dr. John R. Rice, known the world over for his soul-winning books and for his living example in reaching men for Christ. For years, he reached many in the soul-winning arena with his mighty pen through his weekly magazine, *The Sword of the Lord*.

Dr. Robert Sumner, in his biography *Man Sent From God*, gives the account of Rice's surrender to God for the ministry and his initial burden of soul winning:

> One night he took off from his studies to attend services at Chicago's famous Pacific Garden Mission where Billy Sunday, Mel Trotter, and thousands of others have found Christ. He heard a plain-speaking, Spirit-filled preacher, Rev. Holland Oates, address the men from the familiar text in Romans 12:1 and 2. Oates stressed heavily that night the call of Isaiah and how Isaiah volunteered his services to Jehovah, saying, "Lord, here am I, send me." He told how he, a drunken stone mason, had been converted, then with only a fifth-grade education had surrendered to preach the gospel or do anything God wanted him to do. That dear man butchered the king's English but the power of God was obviously upon him and John Rice felt led to cry to God in his own heart, "Lord, I am a college English teacher. If you can use him, why can't You use me?"

> That same night he went to the altar, knelt beside a poor drunken bum, put his arm around his shoulder, opened the Word of God and showed that lowly lost sinner how he could experience God's so great salvation. God moved John Rice's heart that night as never before as he saw the light dawn in that bum's soul, saw the changed expression on his face, saw the evidence of peace in the troubled sinner's breast, and beheld the new-creation-kind-of-transformation take place. In a single

moment all the glamor and glitter wrapped around his ambition to be a great educator or politician fled away.

Describing that experience in his sermon, "Outside the Gate with Jesus," he says, "I got up from my knees beside this poor, dirty, unshaven, but now converted bum and found that all my ambitions for college teaching were gone! I wanted nothing better than to win souls and to have welling up in my heart continually the glad joy I felt at that moment. . . . I gave up my graduate work, gave up my contract, started revival work, then entered the seminary for ministerial training. What I did then, I have since done a hundred times, a thousand times. I have said good-by to good friends for Jesus' sake. I have laid on the altar the dearest things a man can know in this world, save the love of God and the presence of the Holy Spirit, and eternal blessings."

 Training for Running: "Now as he walked by the Sea of Galilee, he saw Simon and Andrew, his brother, casting a net unto the sea; for they were fishers. And Jesus said unto them, Come ye after me, and I will make you to become fishers of men. And straightway they forsook their nets, and followed him" (Mark 1:16–18).

I YIELDED OH LORD, MY HEART

Oh, Lord, when I apart from Thee
   Attempt to serve, I find within
My heart increasing tendency
   To seek approval from all men.

Then, in my vain attempts to do
   His will, I strangely realize
That I've remembered my will too,
   While pressing toward the highest prize.

What shame then floods my heart;
   To think I'd dare attempt to share
His glory, and to then depart
   From His command—His cross to bear.

I yield, O Lord, my life to Thee
   With full rejection of the goals
My flesh has made, and pray to be
   Lost in Thy will of reaching souls.
            —Charles U. Wagner

Taking Time

This is the day of rush, hurry, get it done! Accelerate! On the double! Time is running out! Are you on schedule? Do you have everything done you expected to do? Don't you feel guilty that you haven't done more. Come on, get with it!

Frankly, there is more to life than that attitude. It was Virginia Brasier who wrote:

> This is the age
>   Of the half-read page,
> And the quick hash
>   And the mad dash,
> And the bright night
>   With the nerves tight,
> The plane hope
>   And the brief stop,
> The lamp tan
>   In a short span,
> The bog shot
>   And a good spot,
> And the brain strain
>   And the heart pain,
> And the cat naps
>   Till the spring snaps—
> And the fun's done
>   And then come taps.

We smile, but my, isn't it true! Remember the Lord saying, in the midst of chaos and confusion, "Be still and know that I am God." Be still. Be still. Be still. What good advice! Wait on the Lord—patiently. What ever happened to the art of meditation, reflection, and patient praying—leaning hard on the Lord and not being in a hurry when you did it. Taking time for God isn't a lickety-split "I love you, Lord . . . but I'm in a hurry" kind of thing.

I don't blame you for having a schedule—for redeeming the time—the Bible says we ought to do that. But have you noticed that the Lord never seemed in a hurry. We would say he had it all together.

I am reminded of a father who brought things home from work in this "gotta do more" world. His little boy asked, "Mother, why does Daddy bring all that stuff home every night?"

Mother answered, "Well, honey, Daddy is so busy he just can't get all his work done—so he brings it home."

Innocently the little child asked, "Why don't they put him in a slower class."

Spiritually, it wouldn't hurt if we were put in a slower class—if we slowed down and took time to "smell the roses." Would you agree? Schiller said, "He who neglects the present moment throws away all he has." The present moment, right now—should be contrasted with hurry to an unknown destination—better known as the end of the day.

THE CLOCK OF LIFE

The clock of life is wound but once,
And no man has the power
to say just when the hands will stop;
At late, or early hour.

Now is the only time we own
To do His precious will,
Do not wait until tomorrow;
For the clock may then be still.
—Author unknown

That's good, isn't it! But take that minute, and make time for the important things.

 Training for Running: "Be still, and know that I am God; I will be exalted among the heathen, I will be exalted in the earth. The LORD of hosts is with us; the God of Jacob is our refuge. Selah" (Psalm 46:10-11).

Don't forget to meditate on our Maker, to pause for prayer, and to linger with the Lord. Relax in the calm stillness it takes to know that He is God. Don't be a part of the age of the half-read page and the mad dash. Take time for God.

This Is the Way the Devil Thinks

"If I only knew how he thinks." Ever find yourself saying that about another person? Missionaries sometimes feel that way. They work to find out how a "national" thinks and how the gospel can be properly communicated to him. You can tell a lot about a person if you know something of his mindset. You can even anticipate his actions and attitude.

This is also true of Satan. Paul wrote, "To whom ye forgive anything, I forgive also; for if I forgave anything, to whom I forgave it, for your sakes forgave I it in the person of Christ, lest Satan should get an advantage of us; for we are not ignorant of his devices" (2 Corinthians 2:10, 11). The word translated *devices* refers to Satan's "thought life" or "the way he thinks." In the King James Version, it is translated *devices* one time. Four times it is translated *mind* (2 Corinthians 3:14). It is also translated *thought* (2 Corinthians 10:4,5). So, when Paul says, ". . . we are not ignorant of his devices," he is saying we can be on guard because we know Satan's mindset. We know how he thinks!

Satan's game plan: Generally, when we track the action of Satan, the god of this world, we find two basic ideas that pervade his thinking. They have worked well over the years, and we find him still thinking and acting consistent with his most successful game plan. Let's look at two illustrations of Satan's mindset. Then you be the judge as to whether or not he works this way today.

Most of us are aware of Satan's temptation of Eve and his success in beguiling her. Remember Satan telling Eve that she had it all wrong and that she would not be punished for taking the forbidden fruit? (Genesis 3:4, 5).

1. Device Number One: *Deify Man.* When Satan said, "Ye shall be as gods" (Genesis 3:5) he was stating that Eve didn't need God, and that she was self-sufficient. It is the first reference in the Bible to humanism. You find this tactic used frequently by Satan. It is rampant in the cults. It is also seen in what we know as liberalism and is a system of "works" apart from God's grace. It even crops up in modern philosophies today when man is urged to assert himself and see himself as the very center of life. The Christian, of course, puts Christ in the center and life revolves around Him, not self (Philippians 1:21).

2. Device Number Two: *The Degradation of God.* The next Satanic device turns to degrading God (Genesis 3:5). If you draw two arrows on a sheet of paper, one extending upward and the other ex-

tending downward, you would have an adequate symbol of Satan's mind: deifying man and degrading God.

In Exodus 32, we have a clear illustration of this pattern. Remember that Moses was on the mountain receiving the law from God. The people revealed their true selves when they told Aaron that they wanted a god that was more in keeping with their fleshly desires. Aaron responded by forming a golden calf. Israel was well aware of the calf—a symbol of the heathen deity of Egypt from which they had been delivered. What the people wanted is what is desired by many today—a God that will accommodate their own lifestyle.

What about today? Do we find a great deal going on today that resembles the "Golden Calf syndrome"? Take a look at what is being said and sung today in the guise of religious programming. When Stephen preached his last sermon before his martyrdom, he put his finger on Israel's problem. "To whom our fathers would not obey, but thrust him from them, and in their hearts turned back again into Egypt, saying unto Aaron, Make us gods to go before us . . ." (Acts 7:39, 40).

How can we handle Satan? The way to cope with this crafty power is to "reverse the arrows." That is, instead of raising man up in a declaration of personal sufficiency, you should "humble yourselves, therefore, under the mighty hand of God. . . . Be sober, be vigilant, because your adversary, the devil, like a roaring lion walketh about, seeking whom he may devour" (1 Peter 5:6, 8). When we find our sufficiency in Christ we wreck havoc on Satan's game plan.

Then too, instead of seeking to make God conform to what we want Him to be, we need to see Him as He really is. We need to "glorify God" and "put Him up." David said it this way: "Let the Lord be magnified" (Psalm 35:27). Paul said, "That Christ might be magnified in my body, whether it be by life or by death" (Philippians 1:20). This will do Satan in every time.

 Training for Running: "Put on the whole armour of God, that ye may be able to stand against the wiles of the devil" (Ephesians 6:11).

"A lot of things seem in the devil's hand, but there is no devil in the first two chapters of the Bible and there is no devil in the last two chapters either. He is out of business when the Book closes. Everything is in God's hand, including the future of the Devil" (Vance Havner).

This, too, Shall Pass Away

Lanta Wilson Smith wrote the poem, "This, too, Shall Pass Away." Let me share it with you:

> When some great sorrow, like a mighty river,
>   Flows through your life with peace-destroying power,
> And dearest things are swept from sight forever,
>   Say to your heart each trying hour:
> *"This, too, shall pass away."*
>
> When ceaseless toil has hushed your song of gladness,
>   And you have grown almost too tired to pray,
> Let this truth banish from your heart its sadness,
>   And ease the burdens of each trying day:
> *"This, too, shall pass away."*
>
> When fortune smiles, and full of mirth and pleasure,
>   The days are flitting by without a care,
> Lest you should rest with only earthly treasure,
>   Let these few words their fullest import bear:
> *"This, too, shall pass away."*
>
> When earnest labor brings you fame and glory,
>   And all earth's noblest ones upon you smile,
> Remember that life's longest, grandest story
>   Fills but a moment in earth's little while:
> *"This, too, shall pass away."*

When you think a little about that poem, you can see that it brings both comfort and warning. Comfort because sorrow and hard times will pass. But also warning because even with the smiling of fortune, and even with fame and glory, it fills "but a moment in earth's little while" and it soon passes.

The Bible says the same thing, of course. We read, "But the day of the Lord will come as a thief in the night, in which the heavens shall pass away with a great noise, and the elements shall melt with fervent heat; the earth also, and the works that are in it, shall be burned up" (2 Peter 3:10). The next verses say that this should have an effect on the way we live. In James 1 we read, "But the rich, in that he is made low, because as the flower of the grass he shall pass away" (v. 10). Yes, even the rich man, with all his accomplishments, will soon be gone.

But I remind you there are some things that will not pass away. They are eternal and forever. Christ said, "Heaven and earth shall pass away, but my words shall not pass away" (Matthew 24:35).

In New Testament times, a man would run a race for the glory of wearing a garland for a crown. It was what Lanta Wilson Smith, the writer of our poem, would call, "fame and glory, and all earth's noblest ones upon you smile."

About this garland, Paul wrote, "Know ye not that they who run in a race run all, but one receiveth the prize? So run, that ye may obtain. And every man that striveth for the mastery is temperate in all things. Now they do it to obtain a corruptible crown, but we, an incorruptible" (1 Corinthians 9:24, 25). There it is! Something that shall not pass away, something that is not temporary, something that is eternal, incorruptible—a crown received by those who have run the race and served the Lord in faithfulness.

 Training for Running: "And every man that striveth for the mastery is temperate in all things. Now they do it to obtain a corruptible crown, but we, an incorruptible" (1 Corinthians 9:25).

The word *incorruptible,* means "not liable to corruption or decay." Vine puts is succinctly, ". . . is used of a) God, Romans 1:23; 1 Timothy 1:7 (KJV, *immortal*); b) the raised dead, 1 Corinthians 15:52; c) rewards given to the saints hereafter, metaphorically described as a 'crown,' 1 Corinthians 9:25; d) the eternal inheritance of the saints, 1 Peter 1:4; e) the Word of God, as incorruptible seed, 1 Peter 1:23; f) a meek and quiet spirit, metaphorically spoken of as incorruptible apparel, 1 Peter 3:4" (W.E. Vine, *Expository Dictonary of New Testament's Words*).

To wear a corruptible crown "fills but a moment in earth's little while," but an incorruptible one "fills every moment in heaven's eternity."

Too Late! Too Late!

The gospel is so very simple. Some pervert the gospel by adding baptism to it; the liberal perverts it by denying it or by seeking to substitute his system of works for it; and other theologians complicate it in their bewildering theological verbiage. But in spite of some who pervert it and others who unwittingly complicate it, the gospel stands so plain that even a child can understand it. The person who believes is saved; the person who does not believe is under the wrath of God. Moreover, the person who believes is the present possessor of eternal life: It is his now—he has everlasting life.

What a precious promise this is! How every believer clings to it! I have believed, therefore I am saved. It should also be said that even the fact of man's punishment for not believing is, in a sense, precious, as it shows the preciousness of God's righteousness and justice, just as salvation show the preciousness of His grace. How important it is that we continue to preach such a simple gospel to a lost and dying world.

Every believer is proof of this verse, and every unbeliever is proof of it too. The proof that God's promise is sure is found in the countless hundreds of millions of people who have believed and trusted Him as Savior. However, I think of one in particular.

A young boy and his brother were attending an evangelistic service with their parents. It was an old-fashioned gospel meeting held in a tent; the evangelist was a converted cowboy. He spoke the message clearly every night, bringing out the truths of the third chapter of John. Both young boys were under deep conviction. Yet they hesitated to respond to the invitation because they were told by their parents that they were not old enough to understand. Then, one night, on Father's Day, God so dealt with their hearts that the oldest of the two ran down the aisle and in simple faith claimed this precious promise. Minutes later his brother responded also, and God saved both of them that evening.

The youngest of the two is presently the organist of a large Baptist Church in Tennessee. His name is Jack Wagner. His older brother is the writer of this book.

In a day when it seems to be vogue to downplay evangelists as being unscriptural and invitations as extra-biblical, I would boldly respond that both my brother and I met Jesus Christ in response to an old-fashioned invitation in an old-fashioned evangelistic service.

Winning Words for Daily Living

Several years ago while I was pastoring Temple Baptist Church in Tacoma, Washington, we had the privilege of sitting under the powerful ministry of Dr. Robert Sumner. He preached a message on soul-winning and the need to evangelize. It was at this time, when touched by the message of the evening, that I penned these words:

TOO LATE! TOO LATE!

A vision, Lord, to comprehend
   A world that's lost, and bound
For an eternal terminal
   From whence the wailing, gnashing sound.

Oh, awful plight, Oh, frightful fate,
   I heard, and now I see a mass
Of never-ending souls step off
   Into that deep and dark cravass.

A vision, Lord, to see that friend
   Who once appreciated my
Respect of his religious views.
   Now, Lord, I hear his haunting cry.

To think that I should rationalize
   My action then, in warm, polite
Congenial ways, so fully aware
   Of his sad plight—eternal night.

What foul, pretentious pride
   Did shut and seal these lips so quick
To speak of other trifling things,
   But ne'er a word to souls . . . sin-sick.

A vision, Lord, to comprehend
   The fixed and final fate
Of writhing, striving crowds of men
   Whose misery doth cry, "Too late, too late!"
                —Charles U. Wagner

Training for Running: "He that believeth on the Son hath everlasting life; and he that believeth not the Son shall not see life, but the wrath of God abideth on him" (John 3:36).

If we really believe that those who die without Christ are lost forever, it should have a genuine effect on the way we live. Let us ask for a vision, "to comprehend a world that's lost, and bound for an eternal terminal."

Tying Your Shoes in the Shower

I can't think of anything more unpleasant than tying one's shoes while standing under an icy cold shower. Not only does it sound unpleasant, but it seems downright foolish.

It is not quite as foolish as it sounds, however, when you know who is doing it and why. Such a procedure is practiced with real profit in a school specializing in training mountain climbers. I'm told that the purpose of the practice is to test the readiness of mountain climbers for bearing up under inclement weather. Yes, they actually instruct them to tie their shoes when the cold water is turned on. If a person can accomplish this feat under the icy cold shower, it indicates a hearty readiness to endure the freezing cold while scaling a mountain. When seen in this context, tying shoes in showers loses its absurdity.

Many things in life, while seeming absurd and irrational on the surface, turn out to be quite reasonable and sometimes very necessary. For example, God often prepares us for a mountain-climbing experience by putting us through a stiff training period. Many believers aspire to serve the Lord to the fullest and ascend to a spiritual mountain peak, knowing something of the splendor and glory of His person there. It is natural for a child of God to seek such lofty heights and heavenly atmosphere. However, mountain-peak experiences involve more than wishing they were so. A dedication and surrender to the work at hand and an unfailing determination is vital.

But proceeding to "higher ground" often necessitates a time of testing and training. Moreover, this time of testing—like tying one's shoes in the shower—often seems both unpleasant and foolish. A quick "why" of puzzlement often ensues. But the Lord knows that greater storms may come before the mountain-peak experience. Can He trust us to weather these storms? Will we have the patient endurance when the rough ascent begins, or will we find quick defeat, falling short of complete conquest and victory? Surely our Guide knows just what is needed to eliminate the frustration of failure and the discouragement of defeat!

Do not question times of testing He allows in your life. They are certainly not an indication of forgetfulness on His part. The Lord is fully aware of your need. Someday what seemed to be the absurdity of affliction will prove the most valuable in times of heavy storms. When the zenith experience of victory comes, your testing will surely be evaluated in a totally different light.

As the mountain climber inhales the invigorating air of lofty heights, he must smile with some satisfaction as he thinks of tying his shoes in the icy cold shower.

 Training for Running: "Therefore, I take pleasure in infirmities, in reproaches, in necessities, in persecutions, in distresses for Christ's sake; for when I am weak, then am I strong" (2 Corinthians 12:10).

It sounds incredible! How can a person actually "take pleasure" in infirmities? It is all linked up with the "Therefore" of the verse. The apostle had just explained that God would show his strength in Paul's weakness. The way up is down. The way to strength is weakness. God uses these exercises of strain and pain to bring blessing and strength.

The Total Eclipse

On March 7, 1970, people on the East Coast were excited about the total eclipse of the sun. Radio, television, and newspapers gave the subject full coverage.

Eclipses are fascinating! When a heavenly body is hidden by the shadow of another, it is eclipsed. It is as simple as that. There are two kinds: the solar eclipse and the lunar eclipse. Both have real spiritual applications.

Take the lunar eclipse, for example. When the earth comes between the moon and the sun, the moon is eclipsed. Because the moon derives its light from the sun and has no light of its own, it fails to reflect the sun's light when the earth casts its shadow over it.

Like the sun, Christ is the "Light of the world" (John 8:12). However, Christ insisted that we born-again Christians are the lights of the world (Matthew 5:14). Actually, we have no light of our own. Moonlike, we derive our light from Christ; we reflect His glory and beauty. Beholding Him, we are "changed into the same image from glory to glory . . ." (2 Corinthians 3:18). When others see us, they should see Christ reflected in our lives.

When you view a beautiful moon at night, to be technical you could say, "How beautiful the sun is tonight." You are witnessing the reflected glory of the sun. And when others see Christians who are daily exposed to the light of Christ, they could exclaim, "How beautiful the Lord is."

However, when the world comes between the Christian and the Lord—casting a shadow on our lives—there is a spiritual eclipse. Sometimes it is only partial; the shadows of the world overcast only a portion of our lives. But the outcome is still strikingly noticeable. The amount of the Christ-light that is concealed is in proportion to the shadow of the world.

No wonder the Lord said, "Love not the world, neither the things that are in the world . . ." (1 John 2:15). Any time the world moves in between Christ and us, we lose our effectiveness as lights of the world.

Then there is the solar eclipse. A solar eclipse is an eclipse of the sun. It takes place when the moon comes between the earth and the sun. Experts tell us that the moon's shadow sweeps across the earth 1,100 to 5,000 miles an hour.

Is it possible for us to eclipse the Lord? Yes, when we stand between the world and the Lord, we eclipse Him. When we fail to get out of the way, concealing His glory instead of reflecting it, we do the cause of Christ a disservice. We are solar hindrances concealing the Light of the world. It is a sobering thought that some might fail to come to Christ because we are standing in the way of the Light.

Like solar and lunar eclipses, spiritual eclipses can be predicted. When we begin to compromise with the world and rationalize our actions—letting the world system take us from the Word of God and the people of God—a "lunar eclipse" is predictable. The world is casting its shadow over us.

When we begin to be so occupied with self and think more highly of ourselves than we ought, putting more emphasis on our lives than Christ, a "solar eclipse" is predictable. We have gotten in the way and are casting our shadow over His sufficiency.

With Christians, spiritual eclipses can be tragedies. Let's guard against them.

 Training for Running: "Then spake Jesus again unto them, saying, I am the light of the world; he that followeth me shall not walk in darkness, but shall have the light of life" (John 8:12).

"Ye are the light of the world. A city that is set on an hill cannot be hidden" (Matthew 5:14).

Our source of strength is from the Lord. That's why it is so important that we are not eclipsed by the world. It is like a weight, a hindrance. Paul, using the analogy of running, had this in view when he wrote, "Wherefore, seeing we also are compasses about with so great a cloud of witnessess, let us lay aside every weight, and the sin which doth so easily beset us, and let us run with patience the race that is set before us" (Hebrews 12:1).

In our running, everything will be either a weight or a wing.

Uncomplimentary Caper

When someone calls you "capricious," it isn't usually complimentary. A capricious person is "one who turns from one thing to another." He might not be very stable: there is a shifting of position, a careless moving from one area to another with the greatest of ease. A related word in our language is the word *caper*. A capricious person is one who is on a *caper*.

It all started many years ago with the goat. The old Latin word for goat is *capra*. People who watched the antics of goats in the pasture noticed that they would nibble a little and then jump around from one area to another, bounding and butting each other. Then they would be composed for a while, then nibble a little more, and then a sudden burst of excitement and exuberance would come. So the word expert Charles E. Funk says, "From the unaccountable leaps upward, forward, or sideward of these animals has come our word *caper*." He continues, "And when, through a quirk of the mind, one indulges in something unexpected, we call such an action a *caprice*, and one is *capricious* when, through whim, he turns from one thing to another."

Well now, nobody wants to be compared to an old goat (or even a young one). But the fact of the matter is, there are many goat-like capricious exuberants in our day in Christendom. A little whim here and a little whim there—here a whim there a whim, every where a whim whim! They nibble a little on the Word of God but are caught away with "every wind of doctrine," as Paul puts it (Ephesians 4:14). These believers have unpredictable bursts of speed followed by an intermittent butting of other believers who are not in step with their latest caper.

There is something refreshing about a steady, predictable, faithful servant of the Lord who can be counted on in even the most difficult and changing circumstances. Instead of a "fly-by-night" or "bursts-by-day" inconsistency, there is a constancy that is becoming to the Christian. It is being faithful "in season and out of season" while the world continues to march by whatever drumbeat is pounded out (2 Timothy 4:2).

Of course, this kind of consistency is Spirit-oriented, not flesh-oriented. It is walking in the Spirit rather than slipping into the mode of the most recent and popular whim.

Faithfulness—this is the key to a life that is pleasantly predictable. And it is unlike the on-again, off-again carnal caper.

Training for Running: "Moreover, it is required in stewards, that a man be found faithful" (1 Corinthians 4:2).

"And I thank Christ Jesus, our Lord, who hath enabled me, in that he counted me faithful, putting me into the ministry" (1 Timothy 1:12).

"And the things that thou hast heard of me among many witnesses, the same commit thou to faithful men, who shall be able to teach others also" (2 Timothy 2:2).

A young woman went to Africa as a missionary. There she met a young man and married him. They were blessed with a child and everything seemed to be going well. But the woman's husband died and she was left alone. The months that followed demanded that a decision be made as to what she would do. One day a servant boy came home singing:

> "Hold the fort, for I am coming,
> Jesus signals still!"

That was it! God's answer to her prayer. She answered back,

> "Wave the answer back to heaven:
> By Thy grace we will."
> —P. P. Bliss

The Wages of Wisdom

Wisdom. What is involved in what the Bible calls wisdom? It is not just head knowledge; it is not craftiness or knowledge developed by experience.

There are several words in the Bible that give clear ideas as to what pure wisdom is. One word carries with it the idea of character building through instruction. It is the discipline and training we receive from the Lord in life. A second idea is that of insight and discernment, not only to know what is acceptable, but what is best for us. The third word carries the idea of sharpness, to be subtle and aware of how the devil works. The fourth idea is a deep intimate knowledge of the Lord. It is knowing the truth personified in Christ and the truth inspired in God's Word.

Now let's think in terms of the benefits of wisdom. We could even say the wages of wisdom. They are good wages, good reaping:

1. *Long life*. Lots of people talk about extending life. To be aware of the Lord's commandments carries with it "length of days, and long life" (Proverbs 3:2). Experts tell us that a right mental attitude has a bearing on our health. To know the Lord and His Word is to be prepared when stressful situations come our way. Both mental health and physical health are involved here, and they are often related.

2. *Peace*. In Proverbs 3:2, we read, "For length of days, and long life, and peace, shall they add to thee." First, long life; second, peace. To know the Lord is to have peace *with* God and then the peace *of* God. Mankind is looking for peace. It is found in those who have learned to walk with God and obey Him.

3. *Doctrine*. "So shalt thou find favor and good understanding in the sight of God and man" (Proverbs 3:4). What you believe should have an impact on the people around you. Don't buy the idea that your doctrine doesn't matter.

4. *Divine guidance*. A wise man, living obediently, is one who receives divine guidance."Trust in the Lord with all thine heart, and lean not unto thine own understanding. In all thy ways acknowledge him, and he shall direct thy paths" (Proverbs 3:5, 6). To fear the Lord and acknowledge Him is to know His divine direction. What a great truth!

5. *Happiness*. "Happy is the man that findeth wisdom, and the man that getteth understanding" (Proverbs 3:13). Everybody wants to be happy. The happiness spoken of in the Bible is not a fleeting amusement. It is not a happiness that depends on happenings. Hap-

piness is being right with the Lord and having His wisdom. In a real sense the other benefits will lead to this one. To have peace and favor and divine guidance is certainly to be happy.

To tell a person to wise up is not enough. That can't result in wisdom. To know Christ and to grow in Him—this is to be wise. This results in the many fruits, or wages, of wisdom.

 Training for Running: "A wise man will hear, and will increase learning; and a man of understanding shall attain unto wise counsels, to understand a proverb and the interpretation, the words of the wise and their dark sayings. The fear of the LORD is the beginning of knowledge, but fools despise wisdom and instruction" (Proverbs 1:5-7).

In the course of life, running well is running wisely. To the Galatians Paul said, "Stand fast, therefore, in the liberty with which Christ hath made us free, and be not entangled again with the yoke of bondage" (Galatians 5:1). He urged the Galatians to be aware and be wise about the nature of the law and the yoke of bondage. Then he said, "For in Jesus Christ neither circumcision availeth any thing, nor uncircumcision, but faith which worketh by love. Ye did run well; who did hinder you that ye should not obey the truth?" (Galatians 5:6-7).

Running wisely means not getting "tripped up" along the way.

You and Your Attitude

Attitude means a lot. It affects the way you approach life every day. Take running, for example. In his fine book *Peak Performers*, Charles Garfield talks about Roger Bannister of England. He writes, "Until 1954, no one had ever run the mile in less than 4 minutes. During the year before Bannister, a young premed student, did it in 3:59.4, a number of scholarly papers were published arguing that the four-minute mile was physiologically impossible. The lungs, circulation, muscle fibers, autonomic nervous system of a human being were not designed to function at that level. That should have been environment enough to slow him down. Would any rational person feel he could do something that all of history said was not within human capability?"

Garfield continues, "But Bannister had internal resources that kept him from tripping over the so-called evidence; he was determined to see for himself. . . . Bannister broke more than a world record. He broke through a self-limiting attitude. . . . The barrier had been more mental than physical, more internal than external, more self-set than biologically set."

Sometimes there are limitations that others set for us: "You can't teach a Sunday school class; you can't sing; you can't be a Bible student—you can't." And we often believe it.

This does not mean to say that you can do everything you think you can. Not at all. But the fact is, we frequently don't attempt great things because we have a defeatist attitude, and we put ourselves down—or allow others to do it for us.

Paul said, "I can." "I can." Read it again, "I can." "I can do all things." What is delightful for the Christian is that we have a special, helping power, a source to put that "I can" into a reality. Of course, you know what it is: "I can do all things through Christ which strengtheneth me" (Philippians 4:13). Do you believe that?

Guy King puts it magnificently: "When things are glad, or sad; when things are prosperous, or calamitous; when things are gracious, or anxious—'I can', says Paul. I can stand up to life, whatever it brings, even if that means the imprisonment with all its deprivations and restrictions, and the daily, even hourly, irksomeness of the chain and soldier. He 'can'; and we can—for his secret is available to us."

Make up your mind as a Christian that you are going to let the Lord use you in any way He deems best. And remember, He will never ask anything of you without giving you strength to get it done. You can do it. Yes, you can—in the strength and power of the Lord.

Training for Running: "I can do all things through Christ, which strengtheneth me" (Philippians 4:13).

Attitude is one of the most important aspects in running the race. Roger Bannister proved that. No one had ever run the mile in less than 4 minutes. But he did it. Don't let the world (or even believers) speak for you. Their "I can't" should be your "I can" when you are drawing from the strength given to you by God. So run! Remember—you can! Go for it!

You and Your Bible

How many Bibles have you worn out by reading them and carrying them to church? Many, I hope. From the time I was a small boy, I have read and worn out Bibles. I have a Bible I call my study Bible that is written in, marked, and underlined. I have a Bible for marking verses I have memorized, plus a Bible to be used in preaching and teaching. How do I feel about the Bible? It is the Book of books. Someone has written about the Bible as being the Seven Wonders of the Word:

1. The wonder of its *formation*: the way in which it grew is one of the mysteries of time.
2. The wonder of its *unification*: a library of 66 books, yet one book.
3. The wonder of its *age*: most ancient of all books.
4. The wonder of its *sale*: best-seller of any book.
5. The wonder of its *interest*: only book in the world read by all classes.
6. The wonder of its *language*: written largely by uneducated men yet the best from a literary standpoint.
7. The wonder of its *preservation*: the most hated of all books, yet it continues to exist. "The Word of our God shall stand forever" (Isaiah 40:8).

> The New Testament is in the Old Contained,
> The Old is in the New Explained.
> The New is in the Old Concealed,
> The Old is in the New Revealed.
> The New is in the Old Enfolded,
> The Old is in the New Unfolded.
> —*Speakers Sourcebook*

God's Word will never fail:

Generation follows generation—yet it lives.

Nations rise and fall—yet it lives.

Kings, dictators, presidents come and go—yet it lives.

Hated, despised, cursed—yet it lives.

Doubted, suspected, criticized—yet it lives.

Condemned by atheists—yet it lives.

Scoffed at by scorners—yet it lives.

Exaggerated by fanatics—yet it lives.

Misconstrued and misstated—yet it lives.

Ranted and raved about—yet it lives.

Yet it lives—as a lamp to our feet.

Yet it lives—as a light to our path

Yet it lives—as the gate to heaven.

Yet it lives—as a standard for childhood.

Yet it lives—as a guide for youth.

Yet it lives—as an inspiration for maturity.

Yet it lives—as a comfort for the aged.

Yet it lives—as food for the hungry.

Yet it lives—as water for the thirsty.

Yet it lives—as rest for the weary.

Yet it lives—as light for the heathen.

Yet it lives—as salvation for the sinner.

Yet it lives—as grace for the Christian.

To know it is to love it

To love it is to accept it.

To accept it means life eternal.

—*Religious Digest*

Training for Running: "Open thou mine eyes, that I may behold wondrous things out of thy law" (Psalm 119:18).

The Bible is our training manual. Long distance races have been lost by people who didn't obey the rules and got off course. Not only are we told how to prepare for the run, but we are given the answers for strength in the running and the secrets for winning. So if you want to run the race successfully, keep referring to the manual and obey it. It will certainly give you the needed edge as you reach for the prize!

You Are What You Eat

It's amazing what some people will put into their mouths and swallow. The *Journal of the American Medical Association* reported that a patient checked into a hospital for a swollen ankle, but the real problem wasn't the ankle. The person had swallowed 258 objects, including a 3-pound piece of metal, 26 keys, 39 nail files, and 88 assorted coins. Sounds almost unbelievable.

Almost as bad are some of the records people have tried to set in "gastronomic competition." For example, the record for consuming raw eggs is 56 in 2 minutes. Someone ate 30 bags of potato chips in 29 minutes. If that's hard to believe, how about 480 oysters in 60 minutes or 100 prunes in 12 minutes! Whether it's 26 keys or 17 sausages in 90 seconds, these eaters seem to be way out in their appetites. We might say they are bizarre.

But before you judge, consider this: There are many Christians who are just as wild when it comes to what they put into their hearts and minds. For example, one-third of the nation's adults admit they spend too much time watching television. Are you one of them? Young people spend four times as much time watching television as they do reading and twice as much time in front of the TV as they spend doing homework.

Equally as disturbing is what is watched. Today, television is worse than ever. It's frightening to see what is allowed on the television and how many Christians willingly open their minds to all kinds of evil influence. Examples are too numerous to mention, but they include sexual situations in both daytime and prime-time TV. (The same accusations can be made against many of the books and magazines available today.)

Peter said, "Gird up the loins of your mind" (1 Peter 1:13). Back in Bible times a person who intended to walk, run, or serve, would gather up his long flowing garments and gird them up; that is, tie them under his belt. Peter was saying we ought to bring our minds into control. Paul spoke of "bringing into captivity every thought to the obedience of Christ" (2 Corinthians 10:5). And in Romans 12:2 he said we are to have a renewed mind. Be careful what you put into your mind!

Sure, it's silly to think of 56 raw eggs or 88 assorted coins in your stomach—only to complain that your ankle hurts. It is more ridiculous to open your mind to anything and everything and then complain that it's difficult to walk in the Spirit. Yes, physically you are what you eat, and spiritually you are what you allow to dwell in your mind. So "set your affection [mind] on things above, not on things on the earth" (Colossians 3:2).

 Training for Running: "And be not conformed to this world, but be ye transformed by the renewing of your mind, that ye may prove what is that good, and acceptable, and perfect, will of God" (Romans 12:2).

In a recent issue of *TV Guide,* concern was expressed by many people in the secular world about the direction of television. Many of us remember the day when movies made in Hollywood were branded of the world. (As indeed they were.) But what is taking place on TV today makes the earlier movies seem rather innocent. Are you vulnerable to this tool of the god of this world? It's time to make some resolutions about how we use our minds.

The Winds Came

It was called the most disastrous structure of this century, and it was located in Tacoma, Washington, a place where I ministered for 13 years. Everyone knew about "galloping girdy," as she was called. It was the Tacoma Narrows Bridge, a 2,800-foot bridge that was the third longest suspension bridge in the world. Built in 1940 it was a monument to architectural genius.

The Golden Gate and the George Washington bridges had been in use for years, so the principles of suspension-bridge construction were fully understood—or so the engineers thought. What they didn't account for was the winds: the howling winds that pushed against that super-suspension bridge, causing it to buckle. The winds caused undulating hills and valleys to form in the concrete roadway. Traffic decreased, and the work of the engineers increased as they went back to the drawing boards. Just 4 months after its completion, the roadway blew apart and the bridge tumbled into the waters below. What a terrible disaster! And it would have been worse had the bridge been spanned with cars and people.

What is interesting about this disaster is that all theories of suspension-bridge construction were thrown out of the window. The theory—the way it was supposed to be, the way they said it would hold—it was all tossed out when the winds came and buckled the bridge, causing its collapse. That made other, almost identical, bridges suspect. When the engineers discovered the problem—that the experts hadn't taken into account the effects of high winds—adjustments were made in several other bridges.

There is quite a lesson here. There are many spiritual theories about what really works and what doesn't. There are people who can put on paper some well-thought-out answers to spiritual dilemmas. It looks so good on paper too—all outlined and verbalized in attractive, alternative articulation. But when the crushing pressure of the winds of adversity and persecution arrive, when the unexpected blows against the theories and book-solutions buffet us, the theories often crumble. What is needed is a system that is storm-tested and sure to hold strong and steady against unexpected stress.

And that is exactly what we have as believers. Christ is our fortress; He is our rock; He is our "very present help in trouble" (Psalm 46:1); and He is our safety and security. He *is* storm-tested, and our confidence in Him is based on more than fanciful theories—however sincerely they were constructed.

Recently some dear friends of mine have had some rather hard and pressing stresses—some winds that hit hard; some staggering blows that would fell the average person. But in the midst of the storm, in the face of the winds, they stand secure in more than theory. They rest with utmost confidence in a never-wavering stronghold. He is greater than the storms and the winds of adversity.

 Training for Running: "Therefore, whosoever heareth these sayings of mine, and doeth them, I will liken him unto a wise man, who built his house upon a rock. And the rain descended, and the floods came, and the winds blew and beat upon that house, and it fell not; for it was founded upon a rock" (Matthew 7:24-25).

The word *wind* is often used biblically to mean "false doctrine." Paul says: "That we henceforth be no more children, tossed to and fro, and carried about with every wind of doctrine, by the sleight of men, and cunning craftiness, by which they lie in wait to deceive" (Ephesians 4:14). Every runner knows the difficulty of running against the wind. Opposition is never easy. But the Lord gives grace and strength; He is indeed wind-tested, and we are strong in Him.

Light for Walking

"...they shall walk, and not faint."
Isaiah 40:31

Hiking

Hiking is fun, especially if a challenge is involved. However, it will be anything but fun if you are not familiar with some simple rules and principles in hiking. As a matter of fact, there are some interesting similarities between the challenge of a good hike up a steep hill and the vigorous challenge of the Christian life.

Be in Shape. In hiking you can end up with sore muscles and a discouraged spirit if you haven't had some preliminary training. To become involved in more than a pleasant stroll, it would pay to get some preliminary exercise. Leg lifts, sit ups, and pushups are all good. Better yet, if you live near a stadium, going up and down the stairs a few minutes a day will be helpful. This will strengthen your leg muscles and help your endurance.

Spiritually too, you need to be in good condition if you are going to accept a challenge in going to "higher ground" with the Lord. A few knee bends in prayer is a good place to start. A conditioning diet of the Word of God, taken at regular intervals, will give you stamina and endurance.

Pace, Don't Race. One mistake some hikers make is to press hard at the outset of the climb. Without any warm-up, they start off at a pace that is almost impossible to maintain all day. It is much better to establish a steady pace that can be maintained for the day. Hiking then becomes a pleasure rather than a chore.

The application here is simple. How many times have you started off at a fast spurt in the Lord's service only to find yourself dragging behind a few days later? It is much better to be a steady, hard-at-it servant of the Lord than to demonstrate a quick flurry of energy that soon changes into a slow creep. It's consistent faithfulness that counts.

Pause, Don't Sit. I have learned that when you get tired while hiking, a short pause is advisable, giving you time to catch your breath. However, some climbers press hard, climb fast, and then find themselves taking long, extended rests. This is a mistake. Prolonged rests often result in muscles getting cold and stiff, making starting that much harder. Then the remaining miles are really rough. For this reason it is better to lean against a tree or pause for a few minutes, and then get at it again.

In Christian service, it's good to pause occasionally. The *Selah* at the end of many Psalms indicated that a pause for reflection was in order. However, long periods of rest—especially in the sedentary position—could well cause the spiritual and moral muscles to get stiff, discouraging attempts at higher ground. So whether we are talking about the physical or the spiritual climb —pause, but don't sit. This eliminates the groans and grumbles. Also, the steady growth and progress that you desire will be realized.

Know Where You Are. You will be more confident in hiking if you know your exact position. In some well-marked hikes, especially in our national parks, the way is plainly marked to help you reach your destination. With a little study, you can usually look at the sun to tell the direction you are going. And if you are traveling at night, remember that like the sun, the moon and stars rise in the east and set in the west. The two outer stars that form the bowl in the Big Dipper point to the North Star. Of course, you are better off with a compass, for then the weather will not be a factor in determining your direction.

This is a good illustration of spiritual truth. To know where you are spiritually is even more vital. And what better compass is there than the Word of God, the Bible. Of course, when we use this compass, we will always be following the *Son* of God.

In your quest for "higher ground," whether physically or spiritually, remember to shape up. Pace, don't race. Pause, don't sit. And always know where you are. Happy hiking!

 Light for Walking: "And they that are Christ's have crucified the flesh with the affections and lusts. If we live in the Spirit, let us also walk in the Spirit" (Galatians 5:24-25).

Walking in the Spirit is walking in full dependence on the Spirit. It is walking *by* the Spirit. He helps us to pray, to be consistent, and to use the Word He wrote to guide us day-by-day.

Companions

The word *companion* is an interesting word. Actually the word *company* corresponds with *companion*. They come from the Latin words *cum*, which means "with" and *panis*, which means "bread." Put them together and you have "with bread," or one who eats bread with you. You might call him a "messmate." When you have company in your home, you share a snack, a lunch, or maybe a full meal. At any rate, you break bread together; you are "with bread." You are companions. It's really a lovely word. It speaks of hospitality and fellowship, and has a most friendly association.

The word *companion* is found frequently in the Bible. In the Old Testament, the psalmist wrote, "I am a companion of all those who fear thee, and of those who keep thy precepts" (Psalm 119:63). Quite a good standard, I would think, when it comes to fellowship. How profound the companionship is between those who fear the Lord. Nothing is strained. There is a flow and a sweetness in their "bread-breaking."

Daniel, alone in Babylon, cherished his companions (Daniel 2:17). Remember how he prayed with his three friends as he was about to interpret the dream of the king. They prayed with him; their lives were on the line. Companionship in prayer is a wonderful thing as you face the enemy.

Paul spoke of a companion named Epaphroditus who had jeopardized his life for him. He wrote, "Yet I supposed it necessary to send to you Epaphroditus, my brother and companion in labor, and fellow soldier, but your messenger, and he that ministered to my wants" (Philippians 2:25). He was a "companion in labor." What a delightful relationship!

Daniel had companions in prayer. Paul had companions in labor.

In Revelation, John writes to the seven churches in Asia saying, "I, John, who also am your brother, and companion in tribulation" (1:9). This was not just a "company relationship" or some light-hearted, casual commitment. He wrote to people who were genuine Christians in those churches. They were believers who knew what it meant to stand together in a world that hated the name of Jesus Christ. This company of bread-breakers was a special spiritual group. It has always been so.

A companion in prayer, like that which existed between Daniel and his friends; a companion in labor like Epaphroditus, while Paul was in a Roman prison with almost no friends; and a companion in tribulation. All were tense circumstances; all pressure times; all precious times. That's what true companionship is all about.

 Light for Walking: "I am a companion of all those who fear thee, and of those who keep thy precepts" (Psalm 119:63).

Sometimes we are guilty of drawing lines between ourselves and other believers that are not pleasing to God. Certainly there is a place for genuine separation. Scripture asks, "Can two walk together, except they be agreed?" (Amos 3:3). The answer is obvious. But this verse shows that those who are walking in the same direction should be companions in walking. Here is a biblical standard: Those that fear Him and obey Him are our friends. It is a pleasure to walk with them and with God.

Creeps and Litters

"Now, there is an unusual creep if I ever saw one!"
"Yes, but you'll find it's what you need for your litter."

What picture flashes through your mind when you read the above conversation? Chances are, unless you live on a farm, you've got it all wrong.

A *creep* is a fenced-in eating place for baby pigs, allowing them to eat undisturbed. A *litter* is a group of pigs to which a sow gives birth. It is proper, then, to refer to a "litter in a creep."

If you missed that simple quiz, don't be alarmed. Most of us know surprisingly little about farm litters, to say nothing of distinguishing between a Berkshire and a Poland China, or between a Hampshire and a Tamworth. (An experienced farmer would assure you that a Berkshire ranks high as a meat hog, has little extra fat, and originated in England, while a Poland China was developed in Ohio and is a quick gainer. Lest we show partially, a Hampshire originated in England in the early 1800s and is black with white around the shoulders and front legs. The Tamworth is red with ears that stand up, and it has a long lean body.) As interesting as they are, I just can't get too excited about the peculiarities of a Chester White (whose delicate skin is subject to sunburn) and its drooping ears.

But there are lessons to be learned from the "Hog Household" in "Barnyard Village." As a child, I attended a meeting where the evangelist brought in a pig (a hog less than 10 weeks old) and scrubbed it with soap. When he was finished, the pig was as white as a lamb. Then he tied a ribbon around its neck, and one would almost think it was ready to go from the sty to the fold. But the evangelist pointed out that it was still a pig and had a pig's nature and propensities.

Imagination or not, the difference between a pig and a sheep can be easily noted without being an expert farmhand or an experienced shepherd. A pig can be miserably clean; a sheep can be miserably dirty—both are quick to make it quite obvious.

How true this is of professing Christians! What makes you miserable or uncomfortable tells on you and your true nature. Your appearance, habits, and reactions to certain situations add to the picture. Fresh applications of "religious soap"—sure to make you temporarily clean, fail to change any inward repulsion you might have to spiritual cleanliness.

Many professing Christians are quite similar to that pig scrubbed pink and shiny. After the initial profession, it is often clear that their natural liking for worldly things hasn't changed. Like the squeaking pig, they are happy only when they are back in their old environment, and they seem almost resentful that one would expect them to change. Their very nature demands the life they live. They are satisfied only when they can revert to their old haunts. Somehow, a litter gets accustomed to its own creep.

The only hope for such professing Christians is to possess a new nature. This is exactly what God gives to those who turn from their sin and put their trust in Him. We become sons of God and are born into a new family (John 1:12). We become "partakers of the divine nature, having escaped the corruption that is in the world thought lust" (2 Peter 1:4). The cleansing is more than a good outward religious scrubbing—it is a divine change and a transfer from one family to another.

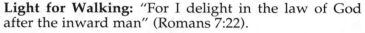

Light for Walking: "For I delight in the law of God after the inward man" (Romans 7:22).

Clearly, Romans 7 speaks of a man with a new nature who is still coping with the temptations of the world. But remember, there is a new nature. There is hope. There is potential. And there is a way to victory!

Lessons From a Stretched Canvas

The canvas was stretched drum-tight over the specially prepared wood frame. It had taken me only a few minutes, and now I was ready to splash brightly colored oils on the canvas and enjoy a gratifying and relaxing hobby.

Ever since I first began to dabble in oil painting, I have been stretching my own canvas. It's true, inexpensive, ready-made canvas board can be bought, eliminating the fuss and bother of stretching the canvas. And, of course, to do it yourself means not only purchasing your own linen canvas and cutting it into the desired sizes, but also getting wooden frames made. And then there are the tools needed to do a good job. But artists will tell you (both dabbling amateurs and skilled professionals) that there is nothing quite like painting on specially prepared stretched canvas. And I think the finished product is better.

Few people, viewing the nuances of color and shade as they admire the scene in a finished painting stop to consider what work goes into mixing the paints, much less preparing of the canvas. But those activities are all necessary steps leading to the finished product.

The canvas is cut to a specific size and stapled at one end of the wooden frame. Then a special tool is used to stretch it. Pressure is applied from all sides: first, in the middle of each side of the frame, and then gradually working toward the ends. Two people are generally needed to do a good job—one to pull and stretch and the other to staple the canvas. Slight wrinkles often appear in the process, but when the pressure is applied equally over the frame and the last staple is in place, the canvas is drum-tight and ready to use.

It is consoling to the believer to know that in God's preparation of the believer He always has the finished product in mind. Indeed, He sees the finished product before He begins. Sometimes, in the preparation of a prospective work He must prepare the canvas of our lives. And, much to our consternation, His divine hand begins to stretch and apply pressure, causing both discomfort and dissatisfaction. Often, such trial comes from all sides and affects every area of our lives.

Unexpected wrinkles sometimes appear, and the Lord intervenes. Insignificant as they may seem to be, if left unattended, they will surely be noticed when the finished product is displayed. Again pressure is applied by His skilled hand.

The Lord is not interested in quick ready-made materials upon which to do His work. Assembly-line canvas is unacceptable. Particular specifications are needed in order for Him to conform us to the image of His Son (Romans 8:29). Each canvas demands just the right amount of preparation to satisfy His discerning eye. How important it is for us to yield to His hand and remember that when the going is difficult He is often preparing us for something unique and special: To bring glory to His Name. Only when the product is finished and we are in full display in that coming day will we completely realize the importance of such painful preparation of pressure from His divine hand.

 Light for Walking: "Therefore, I take pleasure in infirmities, in reproaches, in necessities, in persecutions, in distresses for Christ's sake; for when I am weak, then am I strong" (2 Corinthians 12:10).

Although we don't always understand the reasons for testing, we will someday comprehend it. The Lord is working in our lives to make us more like His Son. He wants to use us to His glory, and He knows what is needed for this to be done. Let's trust Him!

Free Indeed

To illustrate the absolute blindness of man, one needs only to read John 8. The Lord had just said, "Ye shall know the truth, and the truth shall make you free" (v. 32). Then His Jewish listeners said, "We are Abraham's seed, and were never in bondage to any man. How sayest thou, Ye shall be made free?" (v. 33).

Their question is really quite astounding! The very hour they uttered that claim, they were in bondage to Rome. And prior to that, it was bondage to Greece—preceded by Medo-Persia and Babylon. For centuries they were in bondage as a nation, yet they were so blind to it that they confidently claimed to be really free.

Later in the chapter the Lord talked about another bondage, one that surpassed their national-political bondage. He said, "Ye are of your father the devil, and the lusts of your father ye will do" (v. 44). They were under the grip of their father, Satan. If they had only turned to the Lord! He promised that they would be "free indeed."

How true this is today! Man insists that he is free. All inhibitions are thrown off, all of the "old-fashioned, puritanical" standards are cast to the winds with the attending claim that man is liberated and free to exercise all the rights available to him. The truth is, mankind is in the grips of the "lust of the flesh, the lust of the eyes, and the pride of life" (1 John 2:16). Born with an Adamic nature, he is prone to do wrong. His only freedom is to yield to the Satanic powers of night and do his bidding. True liberation comes in knowing the Lord.

Over 25 years ago, when I was just beginning my ministry, I met Bill Kelly, a fellow worker in downtown Detroit. I had been hired by the Detroit City Rescue Mission as a part-time employee. Bill was the assistant superintendent of the mission. He was a young married man and the proud father of a little baby girl. He was clean-cut, forthright in his message, and respected by everyone on the Avenue (Michigan Avenue, which was known all over the world for its sin and degradation). But Bill had not always been a stalwart soldier of the cross. He had been a chronic alcoholic, given up by society.

The Navy's finest doctors had given up on Bill, and he had received a dishonorable discharge. An embarrassment to his parents, they asked him to leave and not disgrace them. Everyone had written this young Irishman off as being a hopeless, unfortunate derelict who would be better off dead. Even Billy Kelly agreed. Bound by sin, he was on his way to the river to commit suicide. But on the way he heard voices from a mission church and decided to go. At that point he figured he had nothing to lose.

There he heard that Christ loved him and would give him a new life, if he would turn from his sin and trust Him. Bill did just that! God performed a miracle in Bill's life, and he was completely and miraculously changed. When I met him, he was the finest example of the "truly liberated man" I had ever seen. Night after night I would see him put his arm around men who were his former cronies and tell them what God had done for him. I have seen thousands of similar miracles, but this first one taught me the full meaning of Christ's words, "Ye shall be free indeed."

 Light for Walking: "If the Son, therefore, shall make you free, ye shall be free indeed" (John 8:36).

MY RIGHTS—OR HIS

Yes, I know Him, the Lord of Whom you speak,
   For as a restless youth, that stubborn streak
Of the Adamic nature showed it's strong
   Compelling power, it's proneness to do wrong.

He spake to me, this Lord; revealed my heart
   For what it was, pressed on my soul to part
With all my cherished sin; promised to free
   Me from the chains of bondage gripping me.

MY rights! MY will! MY way! Could I afford
   To now relinquish all, and own Him Lord?
But, was this restless heart now satisfied
   With dying hopes—vainly living the lies?

What rights were mine, but propensity
   To sin; What did I know of being free?
My sin! My endless guilt! My only right
   Was yielding to Satanic powers of night.

I TURNED TO HIM, I trusted Him that hour,
   And claimed by simple faith HIS matchless power
To save me from my sin, my self, and give
   New life, new rights, a will to serve and live.

The years have passes; a retrospective view
   Brings joyful thanks, for He has seen me through
My every way; His easy yoke, His burden light
   Have brought this grateful soul endless delight.
                —Charles U. Wagner

Driving on the Wrong Side of the Street

We were riding a German train when we met a couple from Australia who were also touring Europe. As we talked, the topic of conversation turned to transportation. I suggested it might be to their advantage to rent a car. Then the husband said something that startled me: "I don't drive in Europe because here they drive on the wrong side of the street."

What he meant, of course, was that in Australia, like England, they drive on the left side of the street, different from the rest of Europe and America. While I knew what he was saying, the words were just not consistent with the way I drove. To me, he was driving on the wrong side. When we were in England, we marveled at how they drove absolutely contrary to what "everybody knows" as the right way.

After a little investigation, however, I have had to revise my "expert" opinion. Here's a little history about how we started driving on the "right" side of the road.

It seems that, originally, everybody who walked or rode in past generations did so in the "strange English" way. That is, it was the expected and proper thing to do. The rationale for it is as follows: When a man was walking with a woman, he saw to it that she was on the inside, for the sake of protection; but the inside had to be the left side, leaving the man's right hand free to draw his sword if needed.

When Napoleon was marching through Europe with an iron heel in his quest to rule the world, he changed the practice. All people traveling on the roads were to keep to the right, leaving the left and proper side of the road for the marching of his troops. History shows, however, that in Napoleon's quest for power, he was stopped short at Waterloo by Wellington. Therefore, unlike the rest of Europe, England never changed the original procedure. Europe retained its "right side of the road" procedure and it was ultimately brought from Europe to the United States.

A little thought on this subject reveals a spiritual application. How many times are we completely sold on our way of doing things? Often it is based on the way everyone around us is doing it, and anything different is obviously the wrong way.

For example, we often have our life all planned out. Sometimes the Lord has to tap us on the shoulder and tell us that we are walking on "the wrong side of the street." He steers us to the other

329

side and makes it clear that this is the true way for us. Involved is not only the right direction, but also the right side of the street in that particular direction. We can find a hundred and one witnesses who would agree with us that we are right and that anything else is strange and just doesn't seem right. But the Lord insists that, contrary to what we think, His way is the right way. What we need to do is not look around us at what others are doing, but get back to the original course of authority—the Bible. What seems right to us is not always in compliance with His will.

To carry the illustration further, not only is His way the right one—it is the way of protection and safety.

We may even occasionally bump into some people who are walking on our side of the road going the opposite direction, and they might consider our objective ludicrous. But God tells us, "For my thoughts are not your thoughts, neither are your ways my ways" (Isaiah 55:8).

Light for Walking: "There is a way which seemeth right unto a man, but the end thereof are the ways of death" (Proverbs 14:12).

There is a way that seems right and there is a way that is right. Christ said, "I am the way . . ." (John 14:6). What is important is that we know His will, that we know His way, and that we are pointed in His direction and on His side of the street.

Is Alto High or Low?

I've always had trouble understanding why altos in the choir sing low. I play an alto saxophone (some would question this) and my alto is pitched much higher than the tenor sax. When you take the word itself and analyze it, even its root meaning is on the saxophone side. *Alto* comes from the Latin word *altus,* which means "higher." It's the same word as the initial part of our English word *altitude,* which means "height." Then, of course, when we refer to the alto-stratus, we refer to the very high, veil-like clouds so familiar to us. On the other hand, when a lady is told she has a resonant alto voice, she is considered a female bass.

Well, the answer gives us a spiritual lesson. Alto does mean high, but when it was first used in music, it was the highest male voice. So, when a man was said to sing alto it was high considering the gender. When it came to be used of woman in the same general range, it was, for a woman, low.

So, when you speak of high and low you must determine what the gender is, whether you're talking about the highest male voice or the lowest female voice. This has many applications in the spiritual dimension. What is high for the world in their evaluating taste and standards, could well be low for the Christian. This is another way of saying you should consider the source of the voice before you judge its true character.

In this secular society, we must always be careful that our standards of low or high are not judged by the labels the world puts on them. Words like *morality, conscience, permissible, acceptable,* and *high calibre* are all to be judged and considered by the "spiritual gender." (Considering that "gender" means birth, descent, race and kind, it seems quite appropriate to use it in this sense. The difference is between those who are born again and those who are not.)

Now, let's be specific. God's standards are always "soprano." God wants us to "approve things that are excellent" (Philippians 1:10). This excellence is out of the range of the unbeliever. The Amplified translation of this verse is interesting: "So that you may surely learn to sense what is vital, and approve and prize what is excellent and of real value—recognizing the highest and the best, and distinguishing the moral differences . . ." (Philippians 1:10).

Light for Walking: "I therefore, the prisoner of the Lord, beseech you that ye walk worthy of the vocation wherewith ye are called, with all lowliness and meekness, with longsuffering, forbearing one another in love; endeavoring to keep the unity of the Spirit in the bond of peace" (Ephesians 4:1-3).

It is so important that we live in the "range" of our birth and descent and walk worthy of our high calling. How vital that we recognize we are a heavenly people with standards beyond that of the world. What the world calls "alto," to the believer may be really low; judged by another score, another gender.

Click . . . What a Disappointment!

There were four of us. We were stomping through the brush in eastern Washington—pheasant hunting. There is no hunting thrill quite like being out in the open and watching hunting dogs working an area for pheasants. My hunting companions (three other preachers) had agreed that the next bird was mine. They had all gotten one, and I was getting anxious for an opportunity at a good shot.

I was prepared for this moment. The field was one of the choice areas, the clump of brush was just right for pheasants, and we had it surrounded. If they were in there—we would get them! I held in my hands one of the finest shotguns money could buy. The equipment was loaned to me by the pastor of the church where I was participating in a Bible conference. He saw to it that we had the right *field*, the right *equipment* and even gave some advice on *how it was to be done*; he was an expert. I had rehearsed for this moment and was prepared to make a quick observation when I saw the bird ascend to the sky. If I saw a ringed, colorful neck I would know it was a rooster. Then I would draw a bead—careful now—don't get too anxious—and pull the trigger.

Tension mounted. I was getting excited. My fellow pastor shouted for me to get ready. All four dogs began to point—what a beautiful sight!

"There he goes," one of the men shouted. "A rooster!" I pulled the gun to my shoulder, lined up the pheasant with my gun sights, clicked off the safety, took a deep breath, and pulled the trigger.

"Click!" There was no loud fire from the gun. No hard kick against the shoulder from the action—just a faint, sickening click. The others fired, but it was too late. What a disappointment!

One of the men, almost as disappointed as I was, turned to me and said, "Throw that shell away; it's a dud."

But in my disappointment I learned a lesson. How typical of much of our Christian service. It was the right season; I was surrounded with game; there was a good field; and all the best equipment was at hand. The one thing that was most important was missing—POWER, fire power!

This is the right season for reaching the lost. Never has the field been more promising that it is now. And we have the good equipment, the "know how" in Christian service. But we need the power of the Lord in our lives.

This is the power the Lord promised just before the formation of the church. "But ye shall receive *power*, after the Holy Ghost is come upon you . . ." (Acts 1:8). Again, "For God hath not given us the spirit of fear, but of *power* . . ." (2 Timothy 1:7).

Only when we are not grieving the Spirit (Ephesians 4:30) or quenching the Spirit (1 Thessalonians 5:19), and instead walking in the Spirit (Galatians 5:16), can we expect to know the power of the Spirit. To be sure, the field, the equipment, the ability, and the opportunity are all important, but disappointment and frustration will certainly follow if we fail to have the necessary power.

 Light for Walking: "But ye shall receive power, after that the Holy Ghost is come upon you; and ye shall be witnesses unto me both in Jerusalem, and in all Judea, and in Samaria, and unto the uttermost part of the earth" (Acts 1:8).

The filling of the Spirit is not something mystical. It simply means the control of the Spirit. To be fully controlled by the Spirit means that the Spirit's power to produce is unhindered in our lives. This power is available to every surrendered Christian. We are told to be filled. It is a command—not a suggestion. To obey it is to know God's power.

Feathers

There are some English words that are rather simple and have just one meaning when they stand alone. But when they are coupled with others words, they take on new ideas. The word *feather* is one example. When you speak of one who has "a broken feather in one wing" you are speaking of a scandal. If someone has a "feather in his cap," he received an honor. Among the American Indians, a feather was added for every enemy slain.

Now, help me in this one; let's make it a quiz: What does it mean "to cut a feather." If you have a boat, or should I say a ship, and you go rather fast, you might be "cutting a feather." The allusion is to the ripple the ship throws off as she "cuts a dash."

Here's another one. "Fine feathers make fine birds." This is one that is not heard too often, but the phrase is used sarcastically of one who is overdressed and does not live up to the clothes he or she is wearing.

Here's one you know, and I hope you practice. "To smooth someone's ruffled feathers." It means to recover, or help someone else to do so, after they have been insulted. To say it like the phrase book does, it is "to recover one's equanimity after an insult."

There are several others too: "In full feather" means "flush of money." "Tickled with a feather" is one who laughs easily, and to "feather one's nest well" is to think of your own interests to secure financial stability. This, in a sense, is not a bad thing. But when the phrase is used, it has a negative implication and is said in a disapproving way.

"Birds of a feather flock together" is one we have heard since we were children. It is true. Simply put, it means that those of similar taste and station like to be together. This too can be right and proper. It was Shakespeare, who in *Timon of Athens* wrote:

> I am not of that feather to shake off
> My friend, when he must need me.

But, having said that, let me suggest that there is a biblical principle here that we should not forget. It is illustrated in Psalm 1. "Blessed is the man who walketh not in the counsel of the ungodly, nor standeth in the way of sinners, nor sitteth in the seat of the scornful" (v. 1). The word *blessed* means "happy," and he is a spiritual man who is not "walking," then "standing," and then being a part of "sitting" with the scornful. First comes just a walk—rather casual, then a stand, and finally you end up part of the flock. While we are not to be proud and "holier that thou" in our attitude, it is important that we watch our company.

To some, "separation" is a bad word. But let me remind you it is a biblical word. We are affected by the places we go, by the company we keep, by the gang we are in, by the group with which we associate. There is a happy balance here, isn't there? We are in the world, but we are not of it. We are to be friendly but not be friends with the world system (James 4:4). This is a principle to teach our children, and it is one to apply in our own lives. We are the salt and light of the world, and we cannot be isolated from them if we are going to help them. But we need Christian companionship, Christian friends, and to be a part of a Christlike assembly.

 Light for Walking: "Blessed is the man who walketh not in the counsel of the ungodly, nor standeth in the way of sinners, not sitteth in the seat of the scornful. But his delight is in the law of the LORD; and in his law doth he meditate day and night. And he shall be like a tree planted by the rivers of water, that bringeth forth its fruit in its season; its leaf also shall not wither; and whatsoever he doeth shall prosper" (Psalm 1:1-3).

The world seems to subtly pull us into a gradual compromise. There is a walking, then a standing, and then a sitting. But it all begins with a walk that is less than careful.

Follow That Mouse!

Who in the world would turn to a mouse for direction—any kind of direction? Well, a group of frustrated generals did just that back in 1796.

The war between Austria and France was going badly for Austria. Napoleon was gaining ground, and the Austrian generals were puzzled as to their next move. What strategy was the best one? Their intelligence was exceeded by their superstition. They daubed the feet of a mouse with ink, placed it on a map, and watched the movement of the mouse across the map to get "advice" in military maneuvering. They were applying an ancient method to decide a serious military confrontation. The mouse's tracks were clear, and the generals agreed to follow the tracks. The outcome of the battle? You guessed it! Napoleon annihilated the forces of Austria and won a decisive victory.

The action of the Austrian generals would be humorous—except thousands died in the battle. They were very sincere in what they were doing, but the mouse on the map would have been better in a trap.

As Christians, we are interested in the course of our lives. Do you ask questions like, What will I do with my life? What will tomorrow bring and how should I prepare for it? These are all sensible questions. But how will you find answers for them? There is so much at stake, and you are warring against a knowledgeable enemy.

The Bible says, "The weapons of our warfare are not carnal, but mighty through God" (2 Corinthians 10:4). Writing to the church at Ephesus, Paul said, "We wrestle not against flesh and blood, but against principalities, against powers, against the rulers of the darkness of this world, against spiritual wickedness in high places" (Ephesians 6:12).

You need divine direction from the Lord. To guess your way or to speculate on what the future might bring is almost as bad as to fall into the mousetrap of superstition. You need personal direction for your individual needs!

The answer? The Bible says it plainly, "Trust in the Lord with all thine heart, and lean not unto thine own understanding" (Proverbs 3:5). Include in "your own understanding" any planning you do or your intuition apart from the Lord.

You probably wouldn't be so foolish as to consult mouse tracks across a map—or a good-luck rabbit's foot or superstitions charts of astrology or the daily newspaper horoscope. But it is just as dangerous spiritually for you to try to choose your own life's course. The writer of Proverbs continued, "In all thy ways acknowledge him, and he shall direct thy paths" (3:6). How refreshing it is to know that "the steps of a good man are ordered by the LORD, and he delighteth in his way" (Psalm 37:23).

There are two ways the Lord directs your steps across the map of your life, and they blend wonderfully together:

1. *By His Word.* "Wherewithal shall a young man cleanse his way? By taking heed thereto according to thy word" (Psalm 119:9).

2. *By the indwelling Holy Spirit.* "For as many as are led by the Spirit of God, they are the sons of God" (Romans 8:14).

Search God's Word. The Holy Spirit will direct and lead you into the ways of His will. Only then will you know real victory against your enemy, Satan. It seems pretty silly to imagine a few otherwise intelligent generals watching an ink-footed mouse hop across a war map. It is almost as ridiculous—and certainly more dangerous for you—to lean on your own understanding when seeking God's will for your life. Acknowledge Him. Have the assurance that He will direct your paths.

 Light for Walking: "Trust in the LORD with all thine heart, and lean not unto thine own understanding. In all thy ways acknowledge him, and he shall direct thy paths" (Proverbs 3:5-6).

We live in a world that looks to many sources for direction, as indicated by the growth of the Eastern cults and the renewed interest in astrology. While the Bible is not a magical book, it is a miracle book. We cannot learn God's will by just "stabbing" at verses with our fingers. We can learn His will by walking by His principles and allowing the Spirit to use His Word to direct us.

For Such a Worm as I

I don't know of anything more uncomplimentary than to be called a worm. Yet, when the Lord wanted Israel to rely on Him, and Him alone, He said, "For I, the LORD Thy God, will hold Thy right hand, saying unto thee, Fear not; I will help thee. Fear not, thou worm, Jacob, and ye men of Israel; I will help thee" (Isaiah 41:13, 14).

The absolute nothingness of mankind is impressed upon us in this whole section of Isaiah. Here are some examples:

"All flesh is grass" (Isaiah 40:6).

"Behold, the nations are as a drop of a bucket, and are counted as the small dust of the balance" (Isaiah 40:15).

"It is he that sitteth upon the circle of the earth, and the inhabitants thereof are as grasshoppers . . ." (Isaiah 40:22).

"Behold, ye are of nothing, and your work of nought" (Isaiah 41:24).

How vividly the Lord describes the absolute nothingness of man! But the most descriptive of all the words is, "Fear not, thou worm Jacob . . . I will help thee."

Thirteen times in ten verses (Isaiah 41:10-19) we read the words, "I will, the Lord thy God will" or their equivalent. The Lord impresses on Israel that it is His power and strength that is needed. "He giveth power to the faint; and to those who have no might He increased strength" (Isaiah 40:29).

The verses that follow show that God takes us into partnership with Himself. "I will make thee a new sharp threshing instrument . . . I will open rivers . . . I will make the wilderness a pool of water . . . I will plan in the wilderness of cedar . . . I will set in the desert the fir tree. . . ." What a blessing! God and the worm in partnership!

Here is what one commentator said on this passage: "What a partnership! God and the worm. And how much we lose because we do not recognize what we really are. When men form a partnership, one man puts up money and another man puts up experience, or some similar division of various assets. But when we form a partnership with God, He demands that we do it on His terms. We put in weakness and he puts in His strength; we put up sin and He furnishes pardoning grace; we cast in our nothingness and He answers with His all-ness. God and the worm! Let not anyone dare attack that partnership. Yet how loathe men are to accept their own bankruptcy to have His fullness."

Dear friend, it is only when we realize that "in our flesh dwelleth no good thing" (Romans 7:18) that we are in the position to lay hold of God's power and do great exploits for Him.

Think of it like this. If a worm is offensive to you, remember that this is the very word Christ used of Himself. "But I am a worm, and no man; a reproach of men, and despised of the people" (Psalm 22:6). He humbled Himself to such great depths so He could lift us up to the glories of heaven.

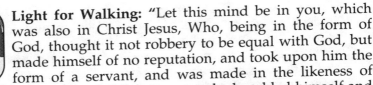 **Light for Walking:** "Let this mind be in you, which was also in Christ Jesus, Who, being in the form of God, thought it not robbery to be equal with God, but made himself of no reputation, and took upon him the form of a servant, and was made in the likeness of men; and, being found in fashion as a man, he humbled himself and became obedient unto death, even the death of the cross" (Philippians 2:5-8).

The example of Jesus' humility is before each of us. We read, "He that saith he abideth in him ought himself also so to walk, even as he walked" (1 John 2:6). His life was a pattern for ours.

> Alas, and did my Savior bleed? And did my Sovereign die?
> Would He devote that sacred head for such a worm as I?
> But drops of grief can ne'er repay, the debt of love I owe;
> Here, Lord, I give myself away, 'Tis all that I can do.
> —Isaac Watts

Gloves

Gloves are a very useful part of clothing during a cold Michigan winter. It's absolutely essential to have a warm pair of them on when you are exposed to the cold air.

Gloves have a long and interesting history. They were once worn as an emblem of royalty. It has been suggested that Richard the Lion-hearted tried to disguise himself on his way home from the Crusades but was recognized because his gloves gave him away. Many hundreds of years ago, displaying gloves was considered a sign of protection. One source says that in medieval Germany, the king's glove was displayed on market days to ward off robbers.

In the days of chivalry, knights wore a lady's glove in their helmets and were determined to defend it with their lives. One knight, it is said, was tested when his lady friend dropped her glove into a pit of lions. According to Robert Browning's version of the story, the knight jumped in after it, plucked the glove out, and heaved it in the lady's face. So much for knights.

I am told that until 1820, throwing down a glove or gauntlet was part of the coronation ceremony of English monarchs. It was a ceremonial invitation to anyone who dared dispute the king's right to rule. The phrase, "Here I throw down my glove," means "I challenge you." It is an allusion to this ancient custom of a challenger throwing down his glove or gauntlet.

It is my feeling that we need to be careful not to be forever throwing down the gauntlet. We shouldn't be forever looking for a challenge or a fight. On the other hand (no pun intended), we live in a rather passive society. Christians should dare to be different. They need to challenge injustice. They should "put on the whole armor of God, that ye may be able to stand against the wiles of the evil one" (Ephesians 6:11). "Stand, therefore," said Paul, "having your loins girt about with truth, and having on the breastplate of righteousness" (v. 14). When men dispute the King's right to rule or dispute their allegiance to their King, the Lord Jesus, throwing down the gauntlet is the proper thing to do. Do you agree?

"Be strong in the Lord, and in the power of his might" (Ephesians 6:10). I have great respect for people who stand for something and have the courage of their convictions. Nobody has respect for someone with Indian rubber convictions in invertebrate theology.

Yes, we have long since passed the days of knights in shining armor, but we should dare to defy the enemy and give a loyal allegiance to the King of Kings and Lord of Lords. The symbolism of the glove may be long passed, but the pledge of obedience to our King abides. Thankfully, there are still faithful warriors who dare to throw down the gauntlet.

 Light for Walking: "Stand, therefore, having your loins girt about with truth, and having on the breastplate of righteousness, and your feet shod with the preparation of the gospel of peace; above all, taking the shield of faith, with which ye shall be able to quench all the fiery darts of the wicked" (Ephesians 6:14-16).

> At the sign of the triumph Satan's host doth flee;
> On, then, Christian soldiers, on to victory!
> Hell's foundations quiver at the sound of praise;
> Brothers, lift your voices, loud your anthems raise!
> —Sabine Baring-Gould

Dipping Your Feet in Oil

Is it possible to live a life holy unto the Lord in such a day as this? Are we willing to admit that times are changing and that these are unusual days that make living a victorious life nearly impossible? Indeed not! When Moses was directed of the Lord to bless the tribes of Israel before he died, he gave something very special to each of them according to their needs.

"And of Asher he said, Let Asher be blessed with children; let him be acceptable to his brethren, and let him dip his foot in oil. Thy shoes shall be iron and brass; and as thy days, so shall thy strength be" (Deuteronomy 33:24-25).

We learn some secrets of a holy walk from this passage:

Dipping Your Feet in Oil. Oil is used symbolically in the Bible of the Holy Spirit. We are told to "walk in the Spirit" (Galatians 5:22). This means there is to be a daily trust, and abandoning of self to the Holy Spirit, a turning over of our affairs to Him, a trusting Him to lead and direct our paths (Proverbs 3:5, 6). It means walking "by faith, not by sight" (2 Corinthians 5:7). In the margin of Harry Ironside's Bible alongside the phrase, "let him dip his foot in oil" he has written, "He who dips his foot in oil leaves a mark behind." What a testimony one bears, when he lives in the Spirit and walks in the Spirit day-by-day. If we walk this way, we, like Asher, will be blessed with children—others will be brought to Christ through us in our witness.

Iron Souls for Rough Terrain. If you will look at the map section in the back of your Bible, you will see the divisions of the tribes. You will also find the part of the land designated to the tribe of Asher in the coastal area from Mount Carmel to Sidon. It was rocky and rough; it was also one of the most dangerous parts of the land. It was close to the enemy. If Asher were like most of us, he might have complained that he was not given an area like Benjamin or Judah in the heart of the land. Asher must have known from this passage in Deuteronomy that the Lord would give help and strength commensurate to its need. We read, "Thy shoes shall be iron and brass."

Remember that the Lord does not put us in a rough place without providing an adequate supply of strength. If the way is soft and easy, be sure that he will shod your feet accordingly. Never does He direct paths without supplying the needs to walk in those paths. "Thy shoes will be iron and brass; and as thy days, so shall thy strength be." They would have strength to endure, to explore virgin territory—by faith! Yes, strength to follow His steps, to climb mountains or to move through deep valleys of despair would be theirs.

 Light for Walking: "That he would grant you, according to the riches of his glory, to be strengthened with might by his Spirit in the inner man; that Christ may dwell in your hearts by faith; that ye, being rooted and grounded in love" (Ephesians 3:16-17).

But let us be careful that we connect the "dipping our feet with oil" with "shodding our feet in iron." That daily strength comes from the Holy Spirit.

Good Advice, in Case You Get "Lost in the Woods"

Did you ever feel lost in the woods? Perhaps not literally, but figuratively. All of us have had times when we were uncertain of our direction and needed special help. I have a book in my library titled *How to Stay Alive in the Woods,* by Bradford Angier. It is a complete guide to food, shelter, and self-preservation "that makes starvation in the wilderness next to impossible." In one chapter, "Keeping Out of Trouble," he deals with such subjects as fording a stream, how to make a torch, and how to deal with exhaustion. But in reading the chapter, one particular paragraph caught my eye and an illustration came to mind instantly. Suppose I quote the paragraph and see whether or not you can make the application. It is under the paragraph title, "Figure to Fall."

"A reasonable precautionary attitude is to expect to fall at any moment, for so realizing the possibility, we will be more likely to be prepared for it:

1. by avoidance of an area,
2. by extreme care when to bypass is not practical,
3. and most commonly by continually gauging beforehand where and in what manner, if we do fall, we will be able to let ourselves go most safely.

"Deadfalls project a special hazard, and one that is greatly multiplied when the ground is all wet. Dew can make a fallen log so slippery that the feet will fly out from beneath one so unexpectedly that any control is at once gone. Frost imposes grave danger. Especially tricky is dead bark that all of a sudden turns on the trunk itself. . . ."

Have you made the personal application? First, none of us likes the prospect of becoming uncertain of our spiritual bearings. To be sure, if we are "lost in the woods," it is because we made a wrong calculation somewhere along the line. We are never lost in the sense of the word that we are out of the Lord's care or concern. Rather, it is the uncertainty of our circumstances that makes us contemplate what we ought to do next.

Impulsive acts now could make a situation worse. As we walk, we should "figure to fall." We are not suggesting that this negative attitude is the normal one in all situations. What is meant here is that when our step is unsure, we ought to walk with extra-special accuracy and care. One good old English word, used in the King

James Version, is *circumspectly*. It means "to walk looking around with extreme accuracy." Another way of saying it is "figure to fall." It is this precautionary attitude that Paul had in mind when he said, "See, that ye walk *circumspectly*, not as fools [witless] but as wise" (Ephesians 5:15). He expressed the same idea when he said, "Let him that thinketh he standeth take heed lest he fall" (1 Corinthians 10:12). Sometimes it means that we should avoid certain places. That is, we ought to avoid the "counsel of the ungodly" and even their company (Psalm 1).

Angier's second bit of advice was to take "extreme care when to bypass is not practical." Spiritually, this could mean that we are not to act out of frustrated impulse. Such momentary excitement could do us in. We ought to watch certain hazards. Satan has his "slippery logs" and "dead bark" that could cause us to lose our spiritual equilibrium. About Satan, Paul said, "we are not ignorant of his devices (2 Corinthians 2:11). On another occasion he said, ". . . Satan hindered us" (1 Thessalonians 2:18).

In another part of his book Mr. Angier has a chapter titled: "Knowing Where You Are." He writes of the necessity of a compass. If one is not available, one should be made. Also, direction can be determined by the sun and the stars. Again the application isn't difficult to make. Our compass is the Word of God. Our spiritual direction can be determined by a right relationship with the compass and a right relation to the "Son."

 Light for Walking: "Nevertheless, whereto we have already attained, let us walk by the same rule, let us mind the same thing. Brethren, be followers together of me, and mark them which walk so as ye have us for an ensample" (Philippians 3:16-17).

Even in an extreme emergency it isn't that difficult to stay alive spiritually. A *circumspect* walk—using extreme care with every step—will bring us out of our dilemma. Don't panic. Keep looking up, get your spiritual bearings, and before long Satan will be defeated. You will be out of the woods, and you'll be better off as a result of your experience.

The Hallmark of Christianity

The official mark stamped on gold and silver articles after they have been assayed is called the hallmark. Experts say it is because this practice was first done at Goldsmith's Hall in England. Included in the hallmark was the standard mark, the assay office or "hall" mark, the date letter, and sometimes the duty mark, as well as the maker's mark. Take the standard mark, for example. It was a leopard's head if it was from London; an anchor, from Brimingham; and a castle, from Edinburgh.

Of the marks listed, the maker's mark is of special interest. It was a device or set of initials that the maker registered with the assay office, and it was the mark he stamped on any product he would set aside for "hall marking."

Today, we often use the word in a figurative sense, such as "Courtesy is the hallmark of a gentlemen." What do you suppose would be the hallmark of a Christian? What is the Christian's test of worth and genuiness? The Lord states it clearly in John's gospel: "By this shall all men know that ye are my disciples, if ye have love one to another" (John 13:35).

Certainly this is the maker's mark as well. Christ said, "A new commandment I give unto you, That ye love one another; as I have loved you, that ye also love one another" (John 13:34). This love shows ownership by the Holy Spirit. This is the essence of the truth that ". . . the love of God is shed abroad in our hearts by the Holy Spirit who is given unto us" (Romans 5:5).

Of course, this love is something that will go on forever. Scripture says, "And now abideth faith, hope, charity, these three; but the greatest of these is charity" (1 Corinthians 13:13).

From the *Sunday School Chronicle* comes this story. "As an aged Christian lay dying in Edinburgh, a friend called to say farewell. 'I have just had three other visitors,' said the dying man, 'and with two of them I parted; but the third I shall keep with me forever.' 'Who are they?' 'The first was Faith, and I said, Goodby, faith! I thank God for your company ever since I first trusted Christ; but now I am going where faith is lost in sight. Then came hope. Farewell Hope! I cried. You have helped me in many an hour of battle and distress, but now I shall not need you, for I am going where hope passes into fruition. Last of all came Love. Love, I said, you have indeed been my friend; you have linked me with God and with my fellow men; you have comforted and gladdened all my pilgrimage. But I cannot leave you behind; you must come with me through the gates, into the city of God, for *love is perfected in heaven.*"

Scripture makes it clear that, even if we had the gift of prophecy, understood mysteries and knowledge, and had the faith to remove mountains, the real test is the hallmark of love. This is the mark of the believer; it shows the difference between the counterfeit and the genuine. The hallmark of genuine Christianity is the owner's mark indeed. It speaks loudly and clearly that we are His disciples.

Light for Walking: "And walk in love, as Christ also hath loved us, and hath given himself for us an offering and a sacrifice to God for a sweetsmelling savor" (Ephesians 5:2).

Vance Havner said, "What we love usually manages to get into our conversation. What is down in the well of the heart will come up in the bucket of the speech."

If you love your wife or husband, it won't take long for others to discover it. If you love your church, you will show it in many ways. Also, if you love the Lord it will become very obvious by the way you live. Christ's love manifested itself in a "sacrifice to God for a savor." Our love should too!

If You Have a Friend

When I was a young college student working at the Detroit City Rescue Mission (a place that really helped me see others' needs), one of the favorite songs people would request was "What a Friend We Have in Jesus." Some of those men had just met that "special Friend" and they sang it with zest. Others perhaps wanted Jesus as their Friend but had not found Him, yet there was hope in their voices. "There is a friend that sticketh closer than a brother" (Proverbs 18:24). Jesus is our Friend!

There is nothing like true friendship, whether it is *the* Friend (the Lord Jesus) or a friend in church, at work, or maybe your best friend (your spouse). Sometimes we take friendship for granted and we don't tell our friends how much we appreciate them until it is too late. Let me share a poem with you from an anonymous writer. It says it well:

> If you have a friend worth loving,
>   Love him! Yes, and let him know
> That you love him, ere life's evening
>   Tinge his brow with sunset glow.
> Why should good words ne'er be said
>   Of a friend— till he is dead?
>
> If you hear a song that thrills you,
>   Sung by any child of song,
> Praise it! Do not let the singer
>   Wait deserved praises long.
> Why should one who thrills your heart
>   lack the joy you may impart?
>
> If you hear a prayer that moves you
>   By its humble, pleading tine,
> Join it! Do not let the seeker
>   Bow before its God alone.
> Why should not your brother share
>   The strength of "two or three" in prayer?
>
> If you see the hot tears falling
>   From a brother's weeping eyes,
> Share them! And by kindly sharing
>   Own our kinship in the skies.
> Why should anyone be glad
>   When a brother's heart is sad?

Winning Words for Daily Living

If a silvery laugh goes rippling
   Through the sunshine on his face,
Share it! Tis the wise man's saying
   For both grief and joy a place.
There's health and goodness in the mirth
   In which an honest laugh has birth

If your work is made more easy
   By a friendly, helping hand,
Say so! Speak out brave and truly
   Ere the darkness veil the land.
Should a brother workman dear
   Falter for a word of cheer?

Scatter thus your seeds of kindness
   All enriching as you go—
Leave them! Trust the Harvest-Giver;
   He will make each seed to grow.
So until the happy end,
   Your life shall never lack a friend.

 Light for Walking: "Ye are my friends, if ye do whatever I command you. Henceforth I call you not servants; for the servant knoweth not what his lord doeth: but I have called you friends; for all things that I have heard of my Father I have made known unto you" (John 15:14, 15).

To be a friend of the Lord is an honor. He wants to see us not only as a servant (although that is an honor too) but a friend. He wants to share with us as we share with Him. This is done through Scripture and prayer. This friendship is enhanced and blessed when we obey Him. Obedience is followed by spiritual insight and blessing. What a Friend we have in Jesus!

His Faithfulness

Have you ever wondered just how you were going to get through the day? Burdens seemed to get heavier and your whole world seemed to be caving in. All of us have felt this way at times and sensed we needed supernatural strength to carry on! Yet of one thing we can be sure: He will not "suffer us to be tempted above that which we are able, but will with the temptation, make a way of escape, that we may be able to bear it" (1 Corinthians 10:13). But what is that provision? The answer is really simple: It is the indwelling Christ! Christ lives within you and wants to take over in your life and do what you can't do. That which is an impossibility with us is not difficult at all for this indwelling Lord.

One of the most precious verses in the Bible is Galatians 2:20. It says, "I am crucified with Christ: nevertheless I live; yet not I, but Christ liveth in me; and the life which I now live in the flesh I live by the faith of the Son of God, who loved me and gave himself for me." The part of the verse that relates to the point I am making is Paul's use of the words, "Christ liveth in me." This should be more to us than a mere doctrine. It is a living reality. Right now He indwells you—whether you are in your living room or confined to your bed. You are not alone; you can say with Paul, if you know the Lord as Savior, "Christ liveth in me."

But there is something more in this verse that drives home this truth. It is in the word translated *faith* in the verse. "I live by the faith of the Son of God." What does this mean? The Greek word is *pistis* and can mean either "faith" or "faithfulness." The context of the passage would be a determining factor as to which of the two translations is best. Personally, I feel that the word would be better translated *faithfulness*. Read it that way and see what it says. ". . . and the life which I now live in the flesh I live by the faithfulness of the Son of God, who loved me, and gave Himself for me."

Do you see it? He lives in us, and He wants to live His life of faithfulness in us. Now apply the verse to your own situation. You might say, "Even though I might be handicapped or seriously ill, Christ lives in me and wants me to live a life of His faithfulness in me." Or, "although I can't be as physically involved as some, He is just as faithful living in me here as He is in others who are actively engaged in Christian service. My burden is His burden, my tasks are His tasks."

Norman Harrison said, ". . . when I see that it is His faithfulness—not mine—His faithfulness in me, how the light breaks. My, what a resource! Just what I need: All within my own person, for the re-making of my personality."

The problems and difficulties that are yours are really no problems to Him. He has been indwelling His own for almost 2,000 years and is fully experienced in handling difficulties. Again Harrison says, ". . . What a relief! I've learned how to live! There's not a department of my life, not a habit of carelessness, or undependableness, not a tendency to tardiness, nor anything unbecoming a Christian, but Christ's faithfulness corrects and covers it all. I have found the sought-for secret of living; it is just counting on Him Who lives in me. I have something to 'tell the world'!"

 Light for Walking: "They are new every morning; great is thy faithfulness" (Lamentations 3:23).

"Great is Thy faithfulness, O God my Father,
There is no shadow of turning with Thee,
Thou changest not, Thy compassions, they fail not;
As Thou hast been, Thou forever wilt be.

Pardon for sin and a peace that endureth,
Thy own dear presence to cheer and to guide;
Strength for today and bright hope for tomorrow,
Blessings all mine, with ten thousand beside!

Great is Thy faithfulness! Great is Thy faithfulness!
Morning by morning new mercies I see;
All I have needed Thy hand hath provided—
Great is Thy faithfulness, Lord unto me!"
—Thomas O. Chisholm

The Horse and the Nod

There is an old saying that "A nod is as good as a wink to a blind horse." The meaning is obvious: However obvious a hint or a suggestion may be, it is useless if the other person is unable to see it. So, whether it is a nod or a wink or any other obvious motion, don't expect a blind horse to get it.

There is a great spiritual truth to this principle. If a person is blind spiritually, you can preach and teach, or you can warn of impending doom, but it won't do any good. As intelligent as a person may be, his blindness makes the gospel as difficult to understand as a wink is to a blind horse.

It is no wonder that keeping men blind to the truth is a major tool of Satan. Scripture says, "If our gospel be hidden, it is hidden to them that are lost, in whom the god of this world [the devil] hath blinded the minds of them which believe not, lest the light of the glorious gospel of Christ, who is the image of God, should shine unto them" (2 Corinthians 4:3, 4).

Does it sometimes surprise you that intelligent people—those who may even be well-educated—cannot comprehend the gospel? Let's face it, the gospel is, in reality, quite simple. It is spelled out simply and clearly in the Word of God: Christ died for our sins, He was buried, and He arose the third day. Accepting this truth personally by trusting Christ as the one who died for the sinner will result in personal transformation by the power of the gospel. Yet, many do not understand.

We need to pray that God will open their eyes that they may see. Remember, divine intervention—this divine miracle of enlightenment on the part of the Spirit—is so very important.

Yes, a nod is as good as a wink to a blind horse—and if one is unable to see the gospel for what it is—it is just as useless. But the God who gave the gospel also gives the power for its application. He takes the initiative. So let's be faithful in telling the good word. And let's pray that Satan will be defeated and that blind eyes will be opened to receive it.

 Light for Walking: "For God, who commanded the light to shine out of darkness, hath shined in our hearts, to give the light of the knowledge of the glory of God in the face of Jesus Christ" (2 Corinthians 4:6).

Before we can walk and live the Christian life we must be born! Spiritual walk follows a spiritual birth. Are you born again? To trust Christ as Savior means that the "light is turned on," and you have "light for walking." The Spirit of God opens your eyes to the truth. There's *life*—we are regenerated. And there's *light*—a Spirit-directed walk as a Christian!

How Broad Is Your World?

Many Christians live in a very small and confined world. It is the world of "self" and it never broadens out to greater and finer dimensions.

Did you know that many small rodents live out their entire lives without straying more than 20 feet from the point of their birth. There are a lot of spiritual "rodents" in the world today. Now, don't misunderstand me, I am not condemning you if you have not been able to travel. I'm talking about a "narrowness" that is quite different from a geographical one.

Let me put it this way, if we are limited in our vision for God, it is because we have chosen to be. If our concern for others is confined to our immediate family, and we have no thought or care about anything outside of "us four and no more," we are like that rodent that knows only his few feet—and who is unaware of a larger world. How different is the humpback whale, which travels 4,000 miles a year. Think of it, a creature that makes it 20 feet for life, and a creature that makes it 4,000 miles a year.

But how, you may ask, can we venture out of our confined domain to explore other areas and all the excitement they promise? Good question.

First, you can do it in your prayer life. Think of it, you can add a new dimension to your life by touching the hand of God. Through prayer you can touch the neediest person in the far corners of the world. Prayer extends beyond our narrow, cloistered living places into the expanse of the world.

Second, you can reach beyond your limited circle into a wider dimension through missions. Take an interest in missionary work. Volunteer to help in the ladies' missionary fellowship or in a men's work group. Give to missions; dare to consider a short-term mission venture for God. Reach out and touch the world —and extend *your* world.

Think broadly; think beyond your own experiences to others around you. Read about the world; pray for the world; give to world missions; develop a vision that is all encompassing. In other words, don't be content to be a limited spiritual rodent. Be a whale. Launch out into the deep with a vision and a venture that brings spiritual adventure and challenge.

Light for Walking: "Go ye therefore, and teach all nations, baptizing them in the name of the Father, and of
the Son, and of the Holy Ghost: teaching them to observe all things whatsoever I have commanded you:
and, lo, I am with you alway, even unto the end of the
world. Amen" (Matthew 28:19, 20).

How broad is your world? Ask the Lord to expand your vision to
His glory and praise. Determine that you are not going to live in a
"boxed-in" environment of your own when the Lord has clearly
given the commandment to go into all the world. Ask Him to make
your ministry global for His glory.

How Old Are You?

Does getting older bother you? Now really, before you say no, think about it. Why are we so youth conscious these days? Why do we do everything possible to make ourselves look younger?

When I was a young preacher, I tried to look as old as I could. After all, who wants to take advice from a 22-year-old pastor! Now that I am more than twice that, I find myself cringing when someone asks me if I want a senior citizen discount. Are you that way too?

I once heard a woman say that when she was younger she was involved in all kinds of health foods—you know, yogurt, bran, black strap molasses, and all kinds of natural foods—without preservatives of course. Then she said, "Now, that I'm getting older, I feel I need all the preservatives I can get." Yes, it is a little humorous, but about a serious matter: age.

I must share with you a story about a young girl who was sitting on grandma's lap looking at her arms. She ran her little hand over the wrinkles and asked, "Grandma, what are these?" Her grandmother told her they were wrinkles and explained to her that they come with age. Then the little girl said, "Grandma, did God make your face before he made your arms?" Grandma probably thought: "Quite a kid!"

Let me suggest that you act your age—and not be ashamed of it. Thank God for the years of God's faithfulness and goodness to you. Thank Him for the experience you have gained and the blessings you've enjoyed. Thank Him for the little "nicks of time" on your face, and enjoy being older and wiser and even closer to the Lord. Thank Him for life and health and the prospect of many more years in which you can model the character of Christ before younger ones. Remember, the Bible says, "The hoary head is a crown of glory, if it be found in the way of righteousness" (Proverbs 16:31). When David prayed, "Cast me not off in the time of old age; forsake me not when my strength faileth" His prayer was answered (Psalm 71:9). God's promise is, "Even to your old age I am he; and even to hoar hairs will carry you; I have made, and I will bear; even I will carry, and will deliver you" (Isaiah 46:4).

There is nothing worse than a harsh, cynical old man or woman who has become hard and bitter in old age. God can take that harshness and change it into happiness. He can take bitterness and exchange it for blessing. He can take an ingrate and make him grateful. Yes, God can make us feel good about ourselves, our age, our destiny, and our opportunities in life. Young or old, it's nice to know that God has a plan for our lives and that it is being realized in us day-by-day.

I'm not that unhappy about my age, and I'm proud to be a grand-father five times. How about you?

Light for Walking: "But the path of the just is as the shining light, that shineth more and more unto the perfect day" (Proverbs 4:18).

Regardless of your age, you are aging. It is a fact of life. But those who know the Lord can walk in the light more and more until the final day when faith will be sight. The be-liever walks with God here on this earth, and just keeps on walking into glory, continuing that great communion and fellowship.

Just Like the Picture

One favorite pastime of many is working jigsaw puzzles. There's no doubt about it, they are fun and interesting. I must confess, however, that I never enjoyed them as much as my children did. They always worked on them with great zeal.

When the children were barely old enough to push pieces of colorful cardboard around on a table, we bought them some simple beginner sets. They were simple because the pieces were shaped like animals, making it easy to identify each piece and get it in its right place. When our first child, Mark, was young, we enjoyed seeing how fast he could get everything in place after a time or two.

Soon the children graduated to more difficult sets. It was quite a challenge to them, to say nothing of their father. The pieces were smaller, there were more of them, and they were all quite similar in shape. It was almost tempting to force a piece and make it fit; but one of the children would quickly insist that when you found its place, the piece would fit in easily. Once you got started and were over the hump, puzzle-making was a delight. However, the greatest thrill came when you began to see the landscape develop. That stubby little piece that nobody could find a place for turned out to be a very important part of the picture and blended in so well. You almost forgot that it had been such a problem. Then with a little justifiable excitement the final pieces were put in place and the completed puzzle was just like the picture on the box.

How similar is the puzzle of our lives. There are so many pieces, and they are sometimes so complicated with different shapes and sizes of situations that just don't seem to fit. How much more simple it would be if we could recognize every piece (like the animal-shaped pieces of the elementary set) and know ahead of time where it was going to fit. And, how tempting also to force some piece into areas where they weren't really meant to go, in attempting to solve the puzzle.

Yes, those awkward pieces of life almost make you wonder if something has gotten tangled up and some of the stubby little problems belong to someone else's set. If doesn't take long to learn that this particular circumstance was precisioned for an exact spot in our lives, and in the Lord's own time He would make it all fit perfectly.

How exciting it is to see the Lord working in us to make the difficult portions of our lives blend in to the important landscape of life's puzzles.

After a few years, what seemed to be a puzzle turned out to be a delight. When the job was done and all things were "worked together" (Romans 8:28), we turned out to be just like the picture. Or, to be more specific, just like the image of God's Son. This is the desired result of putting together the pieces of life's circumstances and vicissitudes.

Dear friend, whatever your lot (or puzzle), don't concern yourself with each individual piece of life and wonder why it exists. Just believe that no mistake is made, and be content to allow the pieces to be disconnected for a while, remembering that they all fit into the larger picture. Some day in time or eternity you will look back at the finished product and see just how important today's puzzling piece is to the finished product in God's tomorrow.

 Light for Walking: "And said, Naked came I out of my mother's womb, and naked shall I return thither. The LORD gave, and the LORD hath taken away; blessed be the name of the LORD. In all this Job sinned not, nor charged God foolishly" (Job 1:21-22).

Certainly Job's life was what we would call an "advanced puzzle." After all, he had lost almost everything. What a delight to know that Job did not sin in the midst of the "puzzle" by blaming God. And, as we know, in the end of the book the puzzle is complete and all things "worked together" to the glory of God and the growth of Job. "So the LORD blessed the latter end of Job more than his beginning" (Job 42:12).

The Last Boy Off

"Ye have not chosen me, but I have chosen you, and ordained you, that ye should go and bring forth fruit, and that your fruit should remain; that whatsoever ye shall ask the Father in my name, he may give it you" (John 15:16).

"Go and bring." In three words, Christ gave a simple order to His disciples regarding an important method in evangelism. GO— is visitation; BRING—is transportation. Connected to this vital statement is the promise of the Lord that whatever we ask of the Father in Christ's name He will give to us. It is not surprising to find a promise connected with marching orders. God gives a vital precept and follows it with a precious promise.

The same principle is seen in the Great Commission. After telling the disciples to go and teach all nations, baptizing and teaching, Jesus said, "Lo, I am with you always" (Matthew 28:19, 20). In John 15, He seems to be telling us to go and bring in a spirit of prayerful asking, with the promise that He will give us our request and that our fruit would remain.

Several years ago I was involved in door-to-door evangelism in our community. We were trying to build up our Sunday school bus route and witness to those on whom we called. This is interesting work, although there are some uncertain moments. For example, there was the sign I saw on one door. It said, "We shoot every third salesman—the second one just left."

One particular home on which we called was the Winder family. Mr. Winder had been an elder in the Mormon church. His wife had gone along with him, although she had attended a Salvation Army meeting when she was a girl. As a direct answer to prayer, Mr. Winder consented to let his children come to our church. We saturated this family in prayer, and before long both Mother and Father were coming. Then, praise the Lord, they were saved! It didn't take the Winders long to get busy "going and bringing" also. They were responsible for getting the Bouvier family's children to start coming. In a few months both Mr. and Mrs. Bouvier were saved and baptized.

Some time later I related this story during a Sunday evening service. I told them how "remaining fruit" was a reality through much work and prayer. When I gave the invitation, a Mrs. Boatner came forward to publicly confess Christ as Savior. You can guess who she was with! Yes, she had been coming every Sunday morning with the Bouviers. "Go and bring" produced results. From the Winders, to the Bouviers, to the Boatners—and we have yet to hear the final story!

Winning Words for Daily Living

God is good to His Word. He answers prayers and His promises are sure.

THE LAST BOY OFF

We waited as the bus pulled up,
  Such life, and such variety,
The teeming tiny tots who squirm,
  The young adults' propriety.

Some smiled, they'd been to
  Sunday school
Before; the young enthusiasts
Now felt the place belonged to
  them
  And hustled off to class.

Still others, quite reluctant yet,
  The maiden voyage on the bus,
The buildings new, the faces
  strange,
  All seemed still quiet
  mysterious.

Off jumps a happy little girl
  Holding a Bible in her hand;
Mischievous John follows behind
  Dressed like a little gentleman.

Then, pushing, teasing little Paul,

And prim and proper Jane,
Some dressed in fancy clothes,
  Others, still sweet, just clean and
  plain.

The last boy off, a little guy,
  Came to the door, expressed
  alarm,
The steps were long, his legs were
  short
  He closed his eyes—jumped in
  my arms.

The little fellow touched my heart,
  So young, so sweet, so free
From the distrusting world
  Had leaped and trusted me.

Reflecting on that incident
  I realized that my Lord, too,
Had now, this hour, entrusted me
  To give the child the message
  true.

So very little new, so ready to
  Receive the Word, I knew that
  he
Would face a day, a month, a life
  And then, through death—
  eternity.

"Dear Lord, the value of this soul
  Make each of us keenly aware;
Our bus brings him to Sunday
  school,
  Now, may he find salvation
  there."

—Charles U. Wagner

 Light for Walking: "But Jesus said, Suffer little children, and forbid them not, to come unto me; for of such is the kingdom of heaven" (Matthew 19:14).

When an evangelist remarked that he had two and a half converts, someone said, "Oh, two adults and a child?" "No," the evangelist answered, "Two children and an adult—for the children have whole lives to live for the Lord and the adult fewer years." Let's be concerned about children and their spiritual needs. Remember, "forbid them not."

Kaumas and Siestas

Originally the word *calm* meant "burning heat." The Greeks arranged their schedule so that they could have their siestas at midday. They called it *kauma,* which means the "heat of the sun." It was the time when the winds were still and everything was serene and calm. It is interesting that the Greeks still take their "calm" at midday.

Kauma came into the Latin and finally into the Old French as *calme.* The idea of "the heat of the day" was dropped, and it simply meant "the time when the flocks are at rest." Of course, the Spanish have a pleasant word for the calm of rest. They call it a *siesta,* taken from the Latin *sexta,* which means "sixth hour." Apparently the sixth hour to the monks was noon; again it was nap time.

There is an inner calm that is needed in today's world, even for Christians. Often the pressure and difficulties of the day cause us to seek relief. When the "heat is on" and pressures are mounting, the believer has a resource of peace and calm that he can enjoy wherever he is.

David spoke of the calm that follows the storm. He wrote, "They mount up to the heavens; they go down again to the depths; their soul is melted because of trouble. They reel to and fro, and stagger like a drunken man, and are at their wits' end. Then they cry unto the Lord in their trouble, and he bringeth them out of their distresses. He maketh the storm a calm, so that the waves thereof are still. Then are they glad because they are quiet; so he bringeth them unto their desired haven" (Psalm 107:26-30). How precious! He makes the storm a calm and brings us into the haven of rest. How many of us have been "at wit's end corner" only to find a serene calmness flood our soul as a blessed sense of His presence envelops us.

When we think of the storms of life, we remember of that day when the Lord stilled the troubled sea. For experienced fishermen to be upset about the condition of the sea indicates that it was no little storm. "There arose a great tempest in the sea, insomuch that the ship was covered with the waves; but he was asleep" (Matthew 8:24). The disciples panicked! In their desperation they cried to Jesus. First, He rebuked them for their little faith, "then He arose, and rebuked the winds and the sea; and there was a great calm" (Matthew 8:26).

So whether we are talking about the heat of the day or the storm of the night—the burning heat *(kauma)* or the heaving waves—as we look to Him, He brings quietness and calms the soul. How unlike the unsaved, "The wicked are like the troubled sea, when it cannot rest, whose waters cast up mire and dirt. There is no peace, saith my God, to the wicked" (Isaiah 57:20, 21). As one writer said:

> How calm, how beautiful, comes on
> The still hour, when storms are gone!

Yes, that is beautiful. But more beautiful than the calm that comes when the storm ceases is the calm within the storm.

Whether we are in the noonday heat or the eye of the storm, Christ is there with us. Let us believe it and rest in it.

 Light for Walking: "God is our refuge and strength, a very present help in trouble. Therefore will not we fear, though the earth be removed, and though the mountains be carried into the midst of the sea; though the waters thereof roar and be troubled, though the mountains shake with the swelling thereof, Selah. There is a river, the streams whereof shall make glad the city of God, the holy place of the tabernacles of the Most High" (Psalm 46:1-4).

Anyone who has experienced an earthquake knows how frightening it is. And there are many "earthquake situations" in this present day. The world is rocking and reeling with its "wars and rumors of wars" (Matthew 24:6) and with its changing moral climate. But God is with us and will sustain us as we trust Him.

Lessons From the Life of an Agnostic

One of the most prominent agnostics who ever lived was Robert G. Ingersoll (1833–1899). He was an American lawyer, a politician, and an outstanding orator. He is known for his strong opposition to the Bible and doctrines of Christianity. Some of his books include, *Some Mistakes of Moses, About the Bible,* and *Why I am an Agnostic.* Sometimes we assume that agnostics are simply intellectuals who try to figure everything out on their own and are therefore hard to reach. Such may sometimes be the case. But this doesn't seem to be true with Ingersoll, as impressive as he seemed to be.

Ingersoll was probably more influenced by what was happening around him than he was by his power to reason and think. For example, his father was a Congregational minister. (We would call Ingersoll a P.K.). But according to reliable sources, his home life wasn't warm and helpful. His mother was kind and indulgent, but his father was dictatorial and unsympathetic. Apparently he neglected his two boys, Robert and Ebon. They left home as young men with an explicit dislike for anything identified with the church.

Evidently what Ingersoll observed was not consistent with some of the religious claims he had heard from professing Christians. But there was at least one exception. Ingersoll had a relative, known to him as Aunt Sarah, who was a devout Christian and a lover of the Word of God. One of Ingersoll's books attacking the Bible was sent to her with these words on the flyleaf, written by Ingersoll: "If all Christians had lived like Aunt Sara, perhaps this book would never have been written."

Is this an indictment against all Christians? Certainly not. But most of the professing Christians known to this agnostic were apparently bigger on profession than possession.

Despite Ingersoll's defiance of God, the Lord was merciful to him. H.A. Ironside tells the following story.

"Robert Ingersoll, after delivering one of his addresses, pulled his watch from his pocket and said, 'According to the Bible, God has struck men to death for blasphemy. I will blaspheme Him and give Him five minutes to strike me dead and damn my soul.' There was a period of perfect silence while one minute went by; two minutes passed, and people began to get nervous; three minutes, and a woman fainted; four minutes and Ingersoll curled his lip. At five minutes, he snapped shut his watch, put it in his pocket, and said, 'You see, there is no God, or He would have taken me at my word.' The story was told later to Joseph Parker, who said, 'And did the American gentleman think he could exhaust the patience of God in 5 minutes?'"

Did Ingersoll recant on his deathbed, as is often reported? Apparently not. Several members of his own family later signed a sworn statement that he did not turn to God in his final hours. (What a pity that this was so important to them.)

Eight days before he died, he wrote to a friend: "I still deny the existence of the supernatural, and I still say that real religion is useless."

Less than eight seconds after he died, he became a "believer," but it was too late. God's patience had finally run out. Certainly, "It is a fearful thing to fall into the hands of the living God" (Hebrews 10:31). What a clear message to the unbeliever!

Light for Walking: "For ye were sometimes darkness, but now are ye light in the Lord; walk as children of light" (Ephesians 5:8).

There is a lesson here for every believer. We need to be faithful and consistent in our Christian living. The most powerful argument against unbelief is a holy, consistent, Christian life!

Little Gentleman in Velvet

When we think of velvet, we usually think of something smooth and soft. Back in the days of Queen Anne and William III, there was a phrase that was ripe with meaning. When a person talked about the "Little Gentleman in Velvet," it indicated more than a nice-looking man who was a gentleman dressed in velvet cloth. It actually referred to a mole. If you are confused how a mole could be called a gentleman, much less a gentleman in velvet, a very interesting story in England's history will explain.

It seems that an enterprising mole created a molehill. On this molehill, so the story goes, William III stumbled at Hampton Court. The accident caused the king to break his collarbone. This led to a fatal illness, and he died early in 1702. So William's enemies had a special place in their hearts for the mole—which came to be called "The Little Gentleman in Velvet."

When you think about it, there are several such "Little Gentlemen" in the world today. The "first drink" can lead to drunkenness, which can lead to a disastrous demise. It seemed so innocent, this "Gentleman in Velvet," but it was the first in a series of unfortunate steps. What can be said of drink can be said of promiscuous sex, which might have begun with a lustful look. An "innocent" drug, about which some might say, "Don't make a mountain out of a mole hill," could result in a great fall.

It is interesting that in Psalm 1 we read, "Blessed is the man who walketh not in the counsel of the ungodly, nor standeth in the way of sinners, nor sitteth in the seat of the scornful." (v. 1). Note the order. It is walking, then standing, then sitting. One thing leads to another, and what seems quite innocent at first turns out to be the beginning of the end.

Spurgeon observes on this passage: "When men are living in sin they go from bad to worse. At first they merely *walk* in the counsel of the careless and ungodly who forget God—the evil is rather practical than habitual—but after that, they become habituated to evil, and they *stand* in the way of open sinners who wilfully violate God's commandments; and if let alone, they go one step further, and become themselves pestilent teachers and tempters of others, and thus they *sit* in the seat of the scornful" (*Treasury of David*).

Satan is so subtle and so deceptive. He has his "Little Gentlemen in Velvet" that can cause the stumble resulting in heartache and disappointment. Let's be on the watch for his moles and avoid his ploy.

Light for Walking: "And have no fellowship with the unfruitful works of darkness but, rather, reprove them" (Ephesians 5:11).

Frequently we think of the idea of "fellowship" as a friendly get-together. Indeed, it can be that. But it is a broader word. The word literally means "joint participation." Any area in which we are jointly serving is, in that sense, a fellowship. While we may think, "a little fellowship with the enemy won't hurt," it is unwise. It is not only harmful to our testimony and our Christian life but it is also in direct disobedience to God. We must learn that the "Little Gentleman in Velvet" represents both demise and disobedience.

The Master Painter

Did you ever see an artist working with oils? Before him is a canvas set on an easel. By his side is a palette with multi-colored daubs of fresh oil squeezed from this tubes. In his hand is a specially selected brush with just the right size bristle. In the distance is a winter scene that caught his eye. His main colors include a bit of blue-green, a smudge of yellow ochre, with a mixture of blues and alizarin. He begins to mix other supplementary colors of burnt sienna and deep reds and yellows. Boldly he splashes the colors on the clean, white canvas. What seems to be a reckless hand is really the skilled movements of a master bringing together the reality of the image before him. He may even take the pallet knife and splash, with what seems to be a reckless abandon, broad strokes of oil on the canvas.

With interest you watch him paint the dark colors in the foreground and then apply faint brushstrokes of light, pale greys that begin to give the picture depth and perspective. What seem to be accidental upward strokes of brown and greens now takes-on the shapes of distant trees blending into the background of towering mountains. The streaky whites now develop into gentle reflections of the mountains in the placid lake. Suddenly, out of the bold and chaotic strokes of the artist's hand comes the development of a beautiful picture. The unique nuances and the discriminating blends of colors are now more than shining dabs of fresh oil on the palette. They are blendings that are forming the image which has long resided in the mind of the master painter.

Many of us are like the canvas upon which the Lord begins to work. The color combinations He selects for our lives seem to be less glamorous than what we would have chosen. The broad strokes of difficulties through a long illness or a financial reverse, the nuances of pressure and perplexity, the mixtures of joy and pain; the sweetness and the bitter seem too incongruous to us. With His sovereign pallet knife He applies bold and heavy oils, making what seem to be crude ridges and ugly patches and blotches on the smooth canvas of our lives.

But we dare not question the Master Painter. We must realize that He is conforming us to Jesus' image (Romans 8:29). How we would have preferred a simulated "paint-by-number" portrait available in discount variety stores. It is so simple and uncomplicated and the colors seem so easy to apply. But God is not interested in our becoming the result of a do-it-yourself kit. This product, in its end result, is not to be such a plain and synthetic image. What is created here on the canvas of our lives will in many ways be a masterpiece bringing glory to the Lord through the eons of eternity. The Master Artist is ". . . working all things together for good" in His time and His way (Romans 8:28). His divine technique will prove to be right, and what seems to be reckless strokes without rhythm or reason will prove to be part of a carefully developed plan for our particular canvas. Life will be seen taking on new dimensions and perspectives.

In eternity, as we step back and get a fresh evaluation of the life we lived, we will see the purpose of the burnt siennas and blacks along with the brighter shades of white and blue.

Light for Walking: "And we know that all things work together for good to them that love God, to them who are the called according to his purpose" (Romans 8:28).

So, dear Christian, leave the end result with the Lord. It is His prerogative to select the bristle, color, and design. Let us be content that He knows what He is doing and will never make a foolish brush mark. The final product will prove that His blends, however hard to understand at first, are always the best.

More Precious Than Gold

"That the trial of your faith, being much more precious than of gold that perisheth, though it be tried with fire, might be found unto praise and honor and glory at the appearing of Jesus Christ" (1 Peter 1:7).

Years ago, when a goldsmith prepared to purify his gold, he would subject it to extreme heat. After some time, any foreign elements would come to the top of that liquid mass, and he would dip them from the surface. This process would be repeated again and again until the goldsmith could see his face in the sea of gold. He would then know that the gold was pure and free from all undesired substance.

How true this is also in our lives! We are so precious to Him! He never subjects us to testings without a purpose, nor does He ever lose sight of our condition. Often he allows strange vicissitudes to come our way to try our faith. And He frequently lets the process of the trial continue until we are all that He wants us to be. When He looks into our lives and sees His face, His beauty, His glorious reflection, what a delight it must be to Him. As the divine goldsmith, He has His eyes on both the fire of trial and the gold of faith. Never does it get out of control. He is always in command of the situation and knows just when the trial must cease and the gold has reached its desired state.

Here are three guidlines for confronting a trial and being purified by it:

1. *Rejoice in the face of it.* Only the believer can do this. "In this ye greatly rejoice, though now for a season, if need be, ye are in heaviness through manifold temptations" (v. 6). We can do so because there is a:

2. *Reason for a taste of it.* To be like Him, conformed to His image, reflecting His glory and beauty—this is our goal. Some of the sweetest people I have ever met are those who have been subjected to such trials. Fire can have two effects. If the gold is not genuine—if it is counterfeit—the fire of testing will make it very evident. But if the gold is the real thing, the hotter the fire of testing, the brighter the glow and reflection. It doesn't surprise us to find some people bitter about experiences in their lives and weak under testing. Nor does it surprise us to find the sweet spirit of the Lord shining through the lives of others. The genuine quality of the material is truly seen when circumstances, however difficult, come our way. Finally, there is a:

3. *Reward in the place of it*. Some day our faith will be sight, and our trial and testing will be turned to glory. This can be our portion today. We can today live like Christ, endure affliction, and know His approving smile. But the final reward will come at the appearing of Jesus Christ. What honor and praise there will be in that day for those who came through the fire of testing for His name's sake.

Light for Walking: "But he knoweth the way that I take; when he hath tried me, I shall come forth as gold" (Job 23:10).

HE MAKES NO MISTAKES

He makes no mistakes, He knows
    Life's future plans, and then bestows
Sufficient grace to meet the need
    With waters still and pasture feed.

He makes no mistakes, for when
    The storm seems greatest, then
The peace be still is clearly heard
    Or the tempestuous waves which stirred.

He makes no mistakes. Delay
    Ordered by His command today
Is a development of plans
    He has for us in life's brief span.

He makes no mistakes. What thrill
    In knowing that His smile is still
Upon our lives, and that each hour
    Depends on His infusing power.
                —Charles U. Wagner

The Most Beautiful Words in the World

What are the most beautiful words in our English vocabulary? It would be interesting to know. Over 50 years ago, such a survey was taken. The researchers came up with these words: *melody, adoration, virtue, splendor, joy, honor, love, divine, hope, innocence, faith, modesty, harmony, happiness, eloquence, liberty, purity, nobility, sympathy,* and *heaven.*

Wouldn't you agree that 50 years later, they are still beautiful words? It is interesting that several of them deal with the theme of joy or rejoicing *(melody, harmony, happiness, joy).* Some of them deal with attitudes *(hope, faith, purity, sympathy).*

Three of them deal with the future *(hope, faith, heaven).* Certainly some seem to be what might be called old-fashioned ideas *(virtue, splendor, honor, innocence, purity, nobility).* I truly hope they are not old-fashioned concepts to you, because these words denote biblical attitudes and principles. Some of the words might be outlawed in the secular school system as being religious *(adoration, divine, faith, heaven).* If so, we have abandoned very beautiful words that ought to be the sum and substance of our lives. Then, there are some words that need to be emphasized and renewed in our usage—words that pertain to our attitude to God, like *adoration.* Which word is the most beautiful to you: *innocent* or *sophisticated*? What would be your choice: *stylish* or *modesty*?

If we did take a survey today, would the list include the words *rights* or *payday* or *fun*? Would the word *heaven* be replaced with something that is more relevant in a "have-it-now" society? I certainly don't want to be too hard on our present generation. But an examination of the most beautiful words 50 years ago, and our understanding and attitude toward them today, could well tell us a lot about our direction.

Three of these words were also popular and meaningful in Paul's day. He once wrote, "And now abideth faith, hope, love, these three; but the greatest of these is love" (1 Corinthians 13:13). Three beautiful words, in his day or ours, and *love* is the most beautiful.

 Light for Walking: "It is the spirit that quickeneth; the flesh profiteth nothing. The words that I speak unto you, they are spirit, and they are life" (John 6:63).

"Then Simon Peter answered him, Lord, to whom shall we go? Thou hast the words of eternal life. And we believe and are sure that thou art that Christ, the Son of the living God" (John 6:68-69).

> Sing them over again to me,
>   Wonderful words of life
> Let me more of their beauty see,
>   Wonderful words of life.
> Beautiful words, wonderful words,
>   Wonderful words of life.
> —Philip P. Bliss

Numbering Our Days (and Hours)

The Lord keeps good books. Because He is the God of the universe, we would expect Him to number the stars (Psalm 147:4). But He also numbers our steps (Job 14:16), and even our very hairs (Luke 12:7). Nothing passes His attention.

It is important that we do some numbering too! It is no wonder that God inspired Moses to pray, "So teach us to number our days, that we may apply our hearts unto wisdom" (Psalm 90:12). The reason we ought to number them is that compared to eternity, they are so few. In the same psalm He wrote, "For all our days are passed away in thy wrath; we spend our years as a tale that is told" (v. 9).

How many years do we have left to serve the Lord? Of course, none of us know the answer. There are so many imponderables. Christ may come at any moment, and our hearts cry, "Even so, come, Lord Jesus." None of us can be sure of tomorrow. "Boast not thyself of tomorrow; for thou knowest not what a day may bring forth" (Proverbs 27:1). However young a person might be, with all the vigor and vim of a healthy body, he has no assurance of tomorrow. James said, "Whereas ye know not what shall be on the morrow. For what is your life? It is even a vapor that appeareth for a little time, and then vanisheth away" (James 4:14).

Let's examine those words, "little time." Let's explore the years ahead and consider them in the light of what man calls "life expectancy." Granted that we have no assurance we will live the average length of time, we should be aware that even then life is really short.

For example, scientists have come up with this table of averages telling how many years we can expect to live, depending on our age:

Age Now	Years Left
20	52.8
25	48.1
30	43.4
35	38.7
40	34.1
45	29.7
50	25.5
55	21.6
60	17.9

Winning Words for Daily Living

Age Now	Years Left
65	14.6
70	11.6
75	8.9
80	6.6
85	4.8

Should you take the "years left" and deduct time you will spend sleeping, which would be about one-third, the results could be quite sobering. What should concern us all is how we will spend the years and hours left to us.

Will we be watching television? Will we be making life more comfortable for our family? How many of those hours will be spent in prayer? How many in reaching people for Christ? In the time allotted to us by a God who is sovereign over time, can we afford to be out of His will? Can we afford not to be involved in His church and in His service? Most of us live as though we are going to live forever. We need to be taught to number our days—and hours. We need to "walk circumspectly, redeeming the time" (Ephesians 5:15, 16).

What is important is not the quantity of time, but the quality of life. Not how long we lived but how we lived, and for whom. We have one life . . . and this is it. It will soon be past—only what's done for Christ will last.

 Light for Walking: "So teach us to number our days, that we may apply our hearts unto wisdom" (Psalm 90:12).

> I have only just a minute
>   Just sixty seconds in it.
> Forced upon me, and can't refuse it,
>   Didn't seek it, didn't choose it.
> I must suffer if I lose it,
>   Give account if I abuse it.
> Just a tiny little minute
>   But eternity is in it.
>   —Author unknown

Only God Can Make a Tree

In his book on trees, Rutherford Platt begins the first chapter by stating: "Take any tree. Hang a sign on it announcing, 'Something marvelous is going on here!' Everybody who has the least sense of wonder will stop to find out what is going on."

Such a sign does hang on trees—the flaming maples, the white form of dogwood, or the roar of trees in the storm. Through our eyes and our ears, trees speak to us. They talk through the eye-catching effect of the huge sequoia, the knees of the bold cypress, and the bizarreness of the Joshua tree.

The Bible has over 300 references to trees, often as illustrations of God's care for His own. Let's look at a few of them.

The tabernacles of Israel are described as being like the "trees of lign aloes which the LORD hath planted, and as cedar trees beside the waters" (Numbers 24:6).

David referred to the godly man as being like a tree "planted by the rivers of water, that bringeth forth his fruit in his season" (Psalm 1:3).

Jeremiah said that the man who trusts the Lord "shall be as a tree planted by the waters, and that spreadeth out her roots by the river" (Jeremiah 17:8).

Christ used the figure of fruit trees when He said of false prophets: "Ye shall know them by their fruits. Do men gather grapes of thorns, or figs of thistles? Even so, every good tree bringeth forth good fruit, but a corrupt tree bringeth forth evil fruit" (Matthew 7:16, 17).

The Lord identified two kinds of trees when illustrating divine truth about people: good and bad. He continued, "A good tree cannot bring forth evil fruit, neither can a corrupt tree bring forth good fruit" (v. 18).

The believer is known by his fruit. If there is no good fruit, there is reason to question whether or not the tree is correctly labeled. Certainly there will be variety in fruit. No two believers produce exactly the same fruit. As there are different varieties of apples (Baldwin, McIntosh, Delicious, Northern Spy), there will be different fruit produced by the Holy Spirit through our individual personalities. But the Baldwin or McIntosh or Delicious are still apples, whatever the variety. So every Christian will have the major traits and marks of a Christian. He can be identified as a Christian by his fruit.

On the other hand, there are some fruit trees whose appearance isn't impressive, yet they are most valuable. The black cherry tree is a prize example. It has little outward distinction. Its leaves are stereotyped and the surface of the bark is unappealing, but its fruit is sweet and succulent, and its wood rivals black walnut in beauty. Trees, like believers, are more than "bark deep."

Yes, the sign hanging on a true Christian is his fruit. It announces, "Something marvelous is going on here!" Everybody who has the least sense of wonder will stop to find out what is going on. When they do, they will discover that Christ is the source of this miracle of new life!

Light for Walking: "I am the vine ye are the branches. He that abideth in me, and I in him, the same bringeth forth much fruit: for without me ye can do nothing" (John 15:5).

Walking as the Lord walked is walking in the Spirit. It reflects both a union with Christ—by virtue of the New Birth—and a communion with Christ. It reflects an abiding relationship that produces much fruit.

The Other Fellow

Generally we give ourselves the benefit of the doubt. Would you agree? Recently I read a little piece in *The Speaker's Sourcebook* that says it well. Let me share it with you:

"Have you ever noticed? When the other fellow acts a certain way, he is 'ill tempered;' when you do it, it's 'nerves.' When the other fellow is set in his ways, he's 'obstinate'; when you are, it is just 'firmness.'

"When the other fellow doesn't like your friends, he's 'prejudiced'; when you don't like his, you are 'simply showing that you are a good judge of human nature.'

"When the other fellow tries to treat someone especially well, he is a 'flatterer;' when you try the same thing, you are using 'tact.'

"When the other fellow takes time to do things, he is 'dead slow;' when you do it, you are 'deliberate.'

"When the other fellow spends a lot, he is a 'spendthrift;' when you do, you are 'generous.'

"When the other fellow holds too tight to his money, he is 'close;' when you do it, you are 'prudent.'

"When the other fellow dresses extra well, he's a 'dude;' when you do it, it is simply 'a duty one owes to society.'

"When the other fellow runs great risks in business, he is 'foolhardy;' when you do, you are a 'great financier.'

"When the other fellow says what he thinks, he is 'spiteful;' when you do, you are 'frank.'"

That's the end of the quote. It's quite accurate isn't it? It just says that we don't look at what others do with the same sympathy, patience, and understanding we reserve for ourselves.

Didn't the Lord say that we were to love our neighbor as ourselves (Mark 12:31)?

> When you're criticizing others,
>   And are finding here and there
> A fault or two to speak of,
>   Or a weakness you can tear;
> When you're blaming someone's meanness
>   Or accusing some of self,
> It's time that you went out
>   To take a walk around yourself.

There's a lot of human failures
  In the average of us all,
And lots of grave shortcomings
  In the short ones and the tall;
But when we think of evils
  Men should lay upon the shelves
It's time that we all went out
  To take a walk a round ourselves.

We need so oft in this life
  This balancing set of scales
Thus seeing how much in us wins
  And how much in us fails;
But before you judge another,
  Just to lay him on the shelf,
It would be a splendid plan
  To take a walk around yourself.
                    —*Cincinnati Bulletin*

Light for Walking: "Look not every man on his own things, but every man also on the things of others. Let this mind be in you, which was also in Christ Jesus" (Philippians 2:4, 5)

The supreme example of "not looking at our own things" is the Lord Jesus Christ Himself. To have His mind is to have a different attitude toward others and to look upon others with a new and fresh perspective. We need to ". . . walk as he walked" (1 John 2:6). His was a walk of humility and self-sacrifice.

The Pastor Gets a Security Check

When you are traveling by air, it is important to allow ample time for the regular security check. Because of increasing terrorism in the past few years, every person flying is thoroughly checked for weapons, bombs, and other dangerous devices. Generally, you walk through a booth-like "tunnel" where a loud buzzer goes off if you are carrying something metal.

One time when I had just a few minutes before my plane was scheduled to depart for Los Angeles, I walked routinely through the booth. The shrill buzz sounded. The security attendant approached me and asked me if I had anything on my person that was metal. I reached into my pocket and pulled out a purse full of coins. I'm sure my smile didn't hide my impatience. She asked me to walk through the security booth again. I did, and the buzz sounded again. "Do you have an electric watch?" she asked. I wasn't sure whether my Accutron was considered electric or not, but I slipped it off and moved through the booth again. The buzz sounded again. This was becoming increasingly aggravating because it meant that something was still suspected. I felt that any moment now I would be frisked! The problem was baffling. What did I have on that would "sound the alarm"? Then I saw it. Could it be that my little tie bar would send the alarm screaming? Off came the bar, and I made my way through the detector again. I waited for the pestering buzz, but instead I heard a silence that was both surprising and pleasing. The attendant smiled, and I took some comfort in knowing that she was now convinced I wasn't a hijacker.

Stuffing my coins into my pocket, I put on my watch and tie bar and made my way to the departure gate. I still had time for a quick cup of coffee.

It's amazing how little things can change our immediate plans. One little tie bar had almost interfered with an important flight to Los Angeles, delaying a vital meeting I had scheduled. How true this is of spiritual things as well.

In Ephesians 4:30 we read, "And grieve not the Holy Spirit of God." Someone has suggested that when you grieve the Holy Spirit through sin in your life (however insignificant it may seem), the Spirit of God ceases to work *through* you because He is busy working *on* you.

Often we are in a hurry to get some important task done in our lives. The schedule is arranged in minute detail, yet we are stopped short with an awareness that something is not right. What is it that is grieving Him? Why don't I have a "go sign" and feel full freedom in my desire for service? We then begin giving ourselves some tough self-examination. More often than not it is some unnoticed inconsistency, some "minor" wrong that has to be righted. The sensitive monitor of the indwelling Holy Spirit knows that whether we are in a hurry or not, the job cannot be done until every sin has been dealt with. After the most obvious areas have been covered, He often reveals the specific problem.

The context of this passage in Ephesians is interesting: "And grieve not the Holy Spirit of God, by whom ye are sealed unto the day of redemption. Let all bitterness, and wrath, and anger, and clamor, and evil speaking be put away from you, with all malice; and be ye kind one to another, tenderhearted, forgiving one another, even as God, for Christ's sake, hath forgiven you" (4:30-32).

Even an unforgiving spirit or a little innocent gossip could be the "tie bar" that hinders us in our desired destination. Of course, the answer is to be sensitive to the Spirit's speaking, to right any wrong, and to deal with any secret sin in our lives. Only then can we reach the gate of our departure in a new day of blessed service for our Lord.

 Light for Walking: "But when I saw that they walked not uprightly according to the truth of the gospel, I said unto Peter before them all, If thou, being a Jew, livest after the manner of Gentiles, and not as do the Jews, why compellest thou the Gentiles to live as do the Jews? We who are Jews by nature, and not sinners of the Gentiles, knowing that a man is not justified by the works of the law, but by the faith of Jesus Christ, even we have believed in Jesus Christ, that we might be justified by the faith of Christ, and not by the works of the law; for by the works of the law shall no flesh be justified" (Galatians 2:14-16).

It must have been tough for Paul to speak up to Peter this way and confront him about his inconsistency. However, when one does not walk uprightly, it grieves the Spirit and He cannot work as He wants to. While Peter's sin was not a "little thing," apparently it was an overlooked sin. We need to be sensitive to any inconsistency in our own lives and deal with it. Also, we need to be open enough to a brother's help in getting us back on track.

Peculiar People

"He's psychoceramic," exclaimed one person about another. You won't find that word in a dictionary on psychology. It is the slang way of saying, "He's a cracked pot." Another way of saying it is to state that "he has a one cracked mind." Pardon the puns!

I suppose it is better to suggest that someone is "just different." I'm sure it doesn't surprise you when I say there is nothing really spiritual about being different if that difference means you look and act like an oddball.

I cringe when a person misinterprets the Bible passage that states we are "a chosen generation, a royal priesthood, a holy nation, a peculiar people" (1 Peter 2:9). Actually, the word *peculiar* is better translated, "A people for God's own possession," as it is rendered in the New American Standard Bible. The Amplified renders it, "God's own purchased, special people." But in defense of the good old King James Version, the word *peculiar* is a good translation when we see it in its 1611 setting. It is even interesting.

Back in King James' day it didn't mean to be "gone as a goose" or "nuttier than a fruitcake" as we use the word today. The English word comes to us from a Latin word. In much earlier Roman days, they had no minted coins as we do today. They used other things instead of money—things like cattle. So in Latin, cattle were called *pecus*. From that word we get *peculium*, which came to mean "one's own private property." In the Old French, the word became *peculier*; the English word was *peculiar*. It spoke of something that was exclusively one's own. So the King James translators were quite accurate when they decided that the word that best conveyed the original meaning in 1 Peter 2:9 was *peculiar*.

In this new light, the word has the exact opposite meaning from the way it is often used today. We belong to Him, we are owned by Him, we are greatly prized and a people of His possession.

This verse also says we are a peculiar people who "should shew forth the praises of him who hath called you out of darkness into his marvelous light." Surely this means there should be an attractive balance in our lives. Instead of being strange, we should be well-adjusted, normal Christians who reflect the character of Christ. While it is true that we ought to be detached from the world system, this can be done without looking and acting like an innovation from outer space.

Wuest, in his book *First Peter in the Greek New Testament*, states that the words *show forth* refer to "a spoken message." And *praises* is not the word generally used to indicate praise, but it means "excellencies, gracious dealings, glorious attributes."

When people see as they should, they will be impressed with the excellencies and attributes of Christ. Indeed, they should be impressed with the uniqueness of this wonderful relationship. Remember, you are Christ's own special person, saved to show forth His praise and not your own "peculiarities."

 Light for Walking: "But ye are a chosen generation, a royal priesthood, an holy nation, a peculiar people, that ye should shew forth the praises of him who hath called you out of darkness into his marvelous light; who in time past were not a people but are now the people of God; who had not obtained mercy but now have obtained mercy" (1 Peter 2:9-10).

We are a "people for God's own possession" (N.A.S.B.). "Love yearns for proprietorship; nor can the heart of God be satisfied unless it can speak of some as its own. Oh, happy they who have obeyed his summons, and have made a complete surrender of themselves to Him! He has already taken them for His own possession" (F. B. Meyer, in *Tried by Fire*).

Saved By a Spider

In 1306 Robert Bruce was crowned king of Scotland. His stay in his beloved country was a short one. After being driven out by the English, he found refuge on a small island between Scotland and Ireland. There he was concealed from the enemy in a castle, later to be known as Bruce's Castle.

Saddened and discouraged, the Scottish king was lying on his pallet when he observed a spider busily engaged in trying to attach its web to a ceiling beam. It worked persistently, but failed. The spider tried again and failed. A third attempt was made, yet he failed. This continued six times. "Now shall this spider teach me what I am to do," Bruce told himself, "for I also have failed six times."

On his seventh try, the spider succeeded. Bruce emerged from the castle, gathered his followers, and set out for Scotland. A series of successful campaigns followed. The Battle of Bannockburn in 1314 won for Scotland complete independence from England.

Some people treat this story as legend, but to most Scottish historians, it is fact. Legend or fact, we can learn a lesson from both the spider and the king.

The Lord who said we should forgive 70 times 7 did so Himself. Jonah disobeyed God when he was told to go to Nineveh. Yet we read, "And the word of the LORD came unto Jonah the second time" (Jonah 3:1).

Have you failed God? Hear what He said, "Behold, as the clay is in the potter's hand, so are ye in mine hand, O house of Israel" (Jeremiah 18:6).

This same truth is found in Psalm 72:6: "He shall come down like rain upon the mown grass, as showers that water the earth." This refers not simply to cut grass, but rather to the stubble left after hay has been taken. Nothing remains but the dry, parched ground. Then the rain comes the second time from heaven, and the dry, hopeless situation turns into a flourishing, productive field.

The Bible is filled with instances of a second and third, and even a seventh opportunity, to prosper after a time of failure. Who could forget bumbling, fumbling Peter with so many failing attempts? Add John Mark to the list as well. Our God wants to give you a new start, another chance. While failure has followed failure, and like Robert Bruce, you are incarcerated in your own castle of despondency, feeling discouraged and alone, you need not look for a spider on the wall to know that in the power and strength of God you can begin again and know real success in Him.

God wants you first to realize your own weakness. Then He wants you to yield to Him and His will for your life. Third, undiscouraged by your failure, you should believe that He is with you and will, out of your past failures, bring you to the place of real victory and success.

 Light for Walking: "Then I went down to the potter's house, and, behold, he wrought a work on the wheels. And the vessel that he made of clay was marred in the hand of the potter; so he made it again anther vessel, as seemed good to the potter to make it" (Jeremiah 18:3-4).

"In the potter's house he beheld the potter working his work on the wheels. He saw a vessel suddenly crushed and marred in the hands of the potter; and then he saw that selfsame vessel molded, and fashioned again, until it was finished and perfected. Having looked at the man at his work, God spoke to his soul, and He said, 'As the clay in the potter's hand, so are you in mine hand, O house of Israel.' . . . First, I watch the potter, and I learn God's interest, God's attention, God's power. What a help it would be to have a potter at work before our eyes at this moment! We should see him watching his work. If we watched his work closely, we should detect in his eyes a light of keen interest in this work. As we watch him, we should see power first restrained to the gentleness of an infinite delicacy, then crushing everything out of shape, and yet again molding it back into exquisite beauty. That would be a portrait of God" (G. Campbell Morgan, in *Studies in the Prophecy of Jeremiah*).

The Gentleman Among Snakes

The rattlesnake is sometimes called the gentleman among snakes. This is because it gives a warning before it strikes. After all, as deadly as the rattler is, you must give credit where credit is due. He does let you know that your life is in jeopardy. Or does he?

Is he really that considerate? According to experts, the answer is a definite NO! The rattles on a rattlesnake's tail are rings of dried and hardened skin. Because of the button on the end of the tail, they do not come off when the snake sloughs its skin.

When the snake is excited and gets ready to strike out of sheer nervousness, it moves its tail. This makes the rings of old skin rattle. Sometimes there is a warning, but not because of the gentlemanly nature of the snake. It's because of his nervous nature. What makes it more deceptive, however, is that you can't count on the snake to rattle. Sometimes it doesn't "sound off" at all. It just strikes. To sum it all up, the rattler is no gentleman.

It does not surprise us to learn that Satan appears as a serpent. Interestingly enough, the first time he appears as such, he sounds like a gentleman. There is nothing impolite about his approach. Indeed, he even sounds a little academic and rather easy to listen to. We read, "Now the serpent was more subtle than any beast of the field which the Lord God had made. And he said unto the woman, Yea, hath God said, Ye shall not eat of every tree of the garden?" (Genesis 3:1).

One of Satan's chief tools is doubt. This doubt takes many forms. Sometimes, as in this Genesis passage, he seeks (and always in a gentleman-like fashion) to get us to doubt what God says. He knows that our turning to the Book and believing it is his sure defeat. Other times he approaches us via our thought life and suggests that our salvation is less than genuine. Again, our only recourse is the Word of God which says, "He that hath the Son hath life" (1 John 5:12). As gentlemanly as he is, he is bold in his subtlety. He even approached the Lord and said, "If thou be the Son of God, cast thyself down; for it is written, He shall give His angels charge concerning thee" (Matthew 4:6). If you read the passage that Satan quoted, you will also read two verses in Psalm 91:13 (of course omitted by him): "Thou shalt tread upon the lion and adder. . . ." It is interesting that the two symbols used for Satan, the lion and the serpent, are mentioned.

We must remember that as far as God is concerned, Satan has been put out of business and we need not yield to his subtleties

(Hebrews 2:14). While he accuses us night and day before God in heaven (Revelation 12:10), we have an Advocate there who pleads our cause (Hebrews 7:25; 1 John 2:1). In reality, this serpent is anything but a gentleman. He takes advantage of any weakness, strikes where we are most vulnerable, and gets the thin end of the wedge into our lives when we are not suspecting it. We need to be on guard; no, this serpent doesn't always give a warning.

It is interesting that snakes are deaf to sound carried by air. They can only hear by sensing the vibrations from the ground. There seems to be a lesson in this too. Not only can we defeat Satan and deter his inculcations of doubts by the Word of God, but also by our prayers. He is deaf to such prayerful sounds. We can do him in with the twofold communication with the Lord: through the Word (His speaking to us) and prayer (our speaking to Him).

Discouragement, doubt, despair. These are all chief tools of the god of this world. But "greater is he that is within you, than he that is in the world" (1 John 4:4). Satan is no gentleman. By being aware of his existence and how he works, and by dealing with him through prayer and the Word, we can be assured of his defeat.

 Light for Walking: "Lest Satan should get an advantage of us; for we are not ignorant of his devices" (2 Corinthians 2:11).

The little girl couldn't quite remember the correct words of the memory verse, "Resist the devil, and he will flee from you" (James 4:4), but she got the idea. Her version: "Tell the devil to get out and he's got to go!" If we want to handle discouragement, doubt, and despair, the devil's got to go!

Today . . . Tomorrow

It's easy to get so involved in other parts of the work of the Lord that we neglect the most important thing; namely, winning souls. We are often involved in the perfunctory, routine matters, rather than the divine, urgent matters. Yet it is the will of God that we all be witnesses for Him. And He doesn't give us the command without promising enabling power: "Ye shall receive power" (Acts 1:8).

When we make up our minds to do the right thing and to put first things first, we can depend on the divine intervention of God. Sometimes it is in our Jerusalem (the local area). Other times He takes us out into Judaea or Samaria (highways and hedges) and even to the uttermost. But what is most important is that we are willing to be used every day, and in the most unlikely places, to bear a witness for Him. He will open the door. Count on it! He will give you the needed strength and power.

I was in an old-fashioned country store looking at the convicts' pictures, which were nailed to the wall. Two fine-looking, well-dressed gentlemen were sharing the "convict gallery" with me. I had never seen them before, but the Lord laid them on my heart.

"If it weren't for the grace of God, you might well have your picture on that wall," I said. I suppose it wasn't the most tactful thing to say, but it certainly got their attention.

"Just what do you mean?" they answered. Then I told them that all of us are capable of sinning the very sins that brought these men to the place of notoriety. After establishing the fact that we were all sinners and potential criminals, I asked them if they cared to discuss it further, assuring them that the Bible had the answers to man's problem of sin. They both insisted that I continue. Then I told them, as simply as I knew how, what Christ had done for me, and how they too, if they would recognize that they were sinners and trust Christ as their Savior, could know this newfound joy. They were quick to tell me that they were both religious. One was a Methodist and the other a Catholic. But they also added that never in their lives had they ever heard anything like this. I could sense the evidence of genuine conviction in their attitude.

After quickly breathing a silent prayer to the Lord, I asked, "Wouldn't you two men like to trust the Lord as Savior right now? You see," I continued, "I know the owner of this store and, should you desire, we could go into the back room and settle this matter this very hour." They looked at each other, as if to say, "I'm sure interested, aren't you?"

Yes, they were interested with an interest that reached beyond the intellectual. God was working in their hearts. The three of us kneeled down in the sawdust of the back room and each of the men poured out his heart to the Lord asking Him to save him. Praise the Lord for the simplicity and availability of this so great salvation (Hebrews 2:3). I learned that both were insurance salesmen in the area just for the day. Almost the first words they spoke after our time of prayer were, "Will you come and talk with our wives? We've been going to church all these years, yet no one ever told us of this wonderful plan of God for our salvation." The next week I went to their homes, again presenting the plan of salvation.

What makes the story so wonderful to me is this. That morning I had prayed that the Lord would lead me to one soul that day. I had gotten so bogged down with church business I had not recently talked to a soul about Christ. The Lord honored my prayer of faith and gave me two insurance salesman out in the highways and hedges of a country store.

 Light for Walking: "But ye shall receive power, after that the Holy Ghost is come upon you; and ye shall be witnesses unto me both in Jerusalem, and in all Judea, and in Samaria, and unto the uttermost part of the earth" (Acts 1:8).

TODAY . . . TOMORROW

The day is over and a retrospective look
  Follows with deeper thought of the day's span.
The thoughts, the deeds, the motives placed in
  Heaven's books
  Will be accounted for when we before Him stand.

The wasted minutes, yea, the hours of selfish service;
  The opportunities passed by to reach lost men,
The casual living without thought of plan or purpose
  The life so full of self, but small in dividends.

Should He be pleased to give this soul another day,
  A new fresh page I'll fill, surrendered then to yield
A heart, a soul, a mind—to serve and watch and pray
  Then lifting eyes again to ripening harvest fields.
                                        —Charles U. Wagner

Walk in the Spirit

"This I say then, Walk in the Spirit, and ye shall not fulfill the lust of the flesh" (Galatians 5:16).

Actually, you must look at this verse twice to realize that it is a promise. The condition is, "Walk in the Spirit." The promise part is, "Ye shall not fulfil the lust of the flesh." One of the major obstacles in the believer's life is the flesh. ("Flesh" spelled backward, after dropping the "h," spells "self.") "For the flesh lusteth against the Spirit, and the Spirit against the flesh; and these are contrary the one to the other, so that ye cannot do the things that ye would" (Galatians 5:17). "Walking in the Spirit" is one of three clear injunctions in the Bible that tell us how to be filled with the Spirit. The other two are negative.

To the Ephesians, Paul said, "Grieve not the holy Spirit of God" (4:30). To grieve Him is to allow unconfessed sin to be in our lives. The second prerequisite to the filling of the Spirit is found in 1 Thessalonians, where Paul enjoined the believers to "quench not the Spirit" (5:19). To quench Him is to say "No" to Him.

The positive note in the three prerequisites is in our promise: "Walk in the Spirit." This means we should have an absolute yieldedness to the Spirit in faith.

Sometimes preachers have a way of making truth vague. It may sound polished and impressive—but it is still nebulous. To tell people to "walk in the Spirit" obviously makes good sense because the Bible says it, but what does it really mean?

Many years ago the truth of this promise was made clear to me through an incident with my son, Mark, who was then just a year old. We were living in Highland Park, Michigan, in an apartment. We were proud of our son. Like most parents, we thought that for a 1-year-old he was very advanced for his age. (Parents long to have others tell them this about their offspring—it gives them a feeling that they must have been geniuses to have such a precocious child.) The only problem was that in the same apartment house lived my cousin, who also had a child about Mark's age, and she (though not nearly as brilliant) was walking! So we decided that it was time for Mark to walk. Already we had been somewhat successful in his crawling training (Mrs. Wagner took the arms and I took the legs).

Now it was walking time.

I put the little guy up against the wall and held one of his arms while Ruth stood in front of him just a few feet. She said, "All right,

Mark. Walk!" There was one problem, as Mark saw it. He was sure that he would fall on his face. Instinctively, he realized that the first step could either please his parents or bruise his head.

We don't often stop to analyze the art of walking. But if you think about it for a moment, you will agree that every step is an incipient fall. One's whole body must lose its natural equilibrium in order to take a step. But suddenly, what was an incipient fall results in a bonafide step. This is why it was difficult for Mark to take that first step. Once it was taken, however wobbly, another was almost natural. So, he took it, and then another, and another. He was walking! Soon he was doing it easily and naturally.

How like the Christian walk! Every step is an incipient fall. It is a step-by-step, faith proposition. After it is done for awhile, the unsure step results in a certain walk and spiritual progress. What was once quite a project becomes natural. So, walking in the Spirit is a step-by-step abandonment of self and a step-by-step trusting in Him.

The real proof of this promise is found in the last part of Galatians 5. Walking in the Spirit not only means that we will not fulfill the lusts of the flesh, but it also means that we will be producing the fruit of the Spirit. "But the fruit of the Spirit is love, joy, peace, longsuffering, gentleness, goodness, faith, meekness, temperance: against such there is no law" (Galatians 5:22, 23).

The lesson is clear: Stop grieving Him, stop quenching Him, stop demanding your rights, and walk in the Spirit. The relinquishment of our rights and the willingness to "walk in the Spirit" will result in a grand and glorious spiritual adventure.

 Light for Walking: "He that saith he abideth in him ought himself also so to walk, even as he walked" (1 John 2:6).

"As ye have therefore received Christ Jesus the Lord, so walk ye in him" (Colossians 2:6).

Christ, of course, is the supreme example of the spiritual walk. A yieldedness to the Holy Spirit will result in a walk like our Lord's.

Walking With God

"And Enoch walked with God, and he was not; for God took him" (Genesis 5:24).

A little girl once explained this verse. "One way Enoch went for a long walk with God. They walked so long and so far that they discovered it was getting late. Then God said to Enoch, 'We've walked so far together, why don't you just come home with Me."

"And he was not; for God took him."

Scripture says, "Enoch walked with God after he begat Methuselah three hundred years" (Genesis 5:22). Apparently, this was a time of crisis in Enoch's life. When his son was born, he woke up to his responsibility to the Lord and the importance of a right relationship with Him. It was a staggering, striking experience for Enoch. We are not told the details. We know only that after the birth of his son, he walked with God. Could it be that there was some special promise given to him when Methuselah was born?

Scholars tell us that the name *Methuselah* means, "When he is gone, it will come." On the day Methuselah died, God sent the flood! Enoch lived in a time of lawlessness much like our own. He knew from divine revelation that the Lord would come and bring an end to the ungodliness. He saw beyond the conditions to that day, and he looked up to the coming of the Lord. This is the significance of walking with the Lord: seeing beyond today's shadows and watching for tomorrow's glory.

"And Enoch also, the seventh from Adam, prophesied of these, saying, Behold, the Lord cometh with ten thousands of his saints, to execute judgment upon all, and to convince all that are ungodly among them of all their ungodly deeds which they have ungodly committed, and of all their hard speeches which ungodly sinners have spoken against him" (Jude 14, 15).

To walk with God is to see the world through the eyes of the Lord and to see ungodliness as it really is. It means we don't look pessimistically at the ungodliness, but optimistically to the Lord.

There are times when the sunshine of our lives seems overcast with the cloud of man's awful sin. "How can I be happy," you may ask, "when there is so much sin in the world?" When such questions come to your mind, remember Enoch. He lived in a day when "the wickedness of man was great in the earth, and . . . every imagination of the thoughts of his heart was only evil continually" (Genesis 6:5).

The testimony of God was that "the earth is filled with violence . . . behold, I will destroy them with the earth" (Genesis 6:13). In all the antediluvian civilization, after Enoch was translated and Methuselah died, there were only eight people on earth who were righteous in God's eyes. This was indeed a morally depraved and unholy civilization. Yet Enoch, after 65 rather uneventful years, experienced a crisis in his life that caused him to walk with God.

While the world lurked beneath the shadow of God's judgment, he knew the sunshine of the Lord's presence. "By faith Enoch was translated that he should not see death; and was not found, because God had translated him; for before his translation he had this testimony, that he pleased God" (Hebrews 11:5). Yes, walking with God is to walk in faith in the midst of a faltering, faithless generation.

Could it be that crisis has come to your life? It has caused you, like Enoch, to do some solemn reflecting. Suddenly the world and its values have changed; you are now forced to see beyond the circumstances of the present and look into the face of the Lord. It has become even more necessary to "walk by faith." Yes, this crisis, this confrontation with destiny, this unexpected problem or sorrow could be the beginning of a new and precious walk with God.

It is possible that, in some distant day, when an unsaved friend notices your sudden absence, you—like Enoch—will have moved into another stage. For we believe that, as we see the signs of the times, the coming of our Lord is very near.

 Light for Walking: "If ye then be risen with Christ, seek those things which are above, where Christ sitteth on the right hand of God. Set your affection on things above, not on things on the earth. For ye are dead, and your life is hid with Christ in God. When Christ, who is our life, shall appear, then shall ye also appear with him in glory" (Colossians 3:1-4).

We need to so "set our affection on things above" so that when we "appear with Him in glory" it might be said of us, "He walked with God, he belonged to God, and . . . God took him."

Will the Valiant Men Please Stand Up?

For years I have been intrigued with the comic strip *Prince Valiant*. I can remember standing with this prince in the heat of the battle in my childhood imagination. Indeed, a victory for him was a victory for me. I lived his life and shared his adventures vicariously week after week. He was my childhood hero.

The Bible has a great deal to say about the need of valiant men. The word is used repeatedly in the Old Testament. The word in the Hebrew is *hayil* and means "power" or "might." It is used when reference is made to mighty men of valor (1 Samuel 4:52; 31:12). If ever we needed men and women to stand up and be valiant, it is today. However, this is not the day of dreaming childishly about our valiant stand. This is a time for spiritual realism. Men of valor, valiant soldiers are needed today, men who will take their place in the ranks of soldiers of the cross. Vision is needed for service and so is bold venture, but neither vision nor venture can come without a valiant heart that dares to see the potential and seize the power of God.

In the long list of men who took up arms to fight the battle for the Lord, the tribes of Reuben, Gad, and half the tribe of Manasseh are listed. Scripture says they were "valiant men, men able to bear buckler and sword, and to shoot with bow, and skillful in war" (1 Chronicles 5:18). But their valor was the result of their equipment, not their natural acumen in battle. We read, "And they were helped against them, [the enemy] . . . and the Hagarites were delivered into their hand, and all who were with them; for they cried to God in the battle, and he was entreated by them, because they put their trust in him" (1 Chronicles 5:20). The minority became mighty because they were operating in God's power, not their own.

The same Hebrew word *(hayil)* is used in other places, showing that the road to valiant service is a road of reliance on a strength greater than ours. "Give us help from trouble; for vain is the help of man. Through God we shall do valiantly; for He it is who shall tread down our enemies" (Psalm 60:11, 12). This truth is strengthened even to a greater extent in another psalm: "The LORD is my strength and song, and is become my salvation. The voice of rejoicing and salvation is in the tabernacles of the righteous; the right hand of the LORD doeth valiantly. The right hand of the LORD is exalted; the right hand of the LORD doeth valiantly" (118:14-16). When Scripture mentions the hand of the Lord, it speaks of His power and help; but when it speaks of His right hand, it denotes a special power and intervention. A boldness that comes from a sense of His presence and power will result in great exploits.

A number of other English words used in our language find the same root as the word *valiant*. For example, our word *avail* is a kindred one and means to have strength and courage to accomplish. We cannot do this without divine strength. Also, the word *invalid* finds its root in the same Latin *valere*. It means "not strong, without force or weight." How characteristic of Christians who work in their own strength. No wonder their testimonies can become invalid; they know little of the day-by-day strength of the Lord. Our English word *prevail* is another kindred of *valiant*. It means "to be strong and able, to triumph, to succeed." In Him we prevail. Satan knows nothing of this in his war. Christ said, "Upon this rock [Christ, the Son of the Living God] I will build my church, and the gates of hell shall not prevail against it" (Matthew 16:18).

 Light for Walking: "For I rejoice greatly, when the brethren came and testified of the truth that is in thee, even as thou walkest in the truth. I have no greater joy than to hear that my children walk in truth" (3 John 1:3-4).

To stand for the truth against error is to be a valiant Christian. Will the valiant Christian please stand up?

One Hundred Percent Wool

"Good afternoon, sir. What can I do for you today?"

"Well, I'm in the market for a warm coat; something for winter use."

"I see, sir. Well, I have just the coat for you. Here is a little number that is composed of five substances: carbon, nitrogen, hydrogen, sulphur, and oxygen. I think it will meet your needs."

"Oh, really? Is this something new on the market? Let me try it on. Yes, it fits me well, just my size. And, more important, it's warm. We're going to have another hard winter. I'll take it. By the way, what did you say this coat was made of?"

Smiling, he says, "Carbon, nitrogen, hydrogen, sulphur, and oxygen. Pardon me, sir, I guess I was just being a little facetious. You see those are the basic elements in the rather old-fashioned material we call wool."

The buyer smiles, a little embarrassed, pays the total amount, and makes his way home. "Now, how about that," he says to himself. "I've been wearing wool shirts, wool socks, and wool coats all my life and I didn't know that."

Of course, the story is fictitious. But a question is in order here. Was the buyer any less warmed by the wool products for the many years for not having known the scientific composition of the material? He could have gone all his life wearing wool products and never be any less helped by them.

There is a special truth for us in this. Many Christians know little or nothing of the original languages of Hebrew and Greek. Others are a little puzzled by some things in the Bible they do not understand. This could be the reason why many regard the Bible as a book that only the pastor or teacher can study. How foolish! You don't need to understand all the Bible to be saved by the message it proclaims. Furthermore, you don't need to understand all about the Bible to be instructed by its message.

The Lord has something very special for you every day from this blessed Book. It will warm your soul and thrill your heart. To neglect it would be as foolish as a man who might reject the warmth of a coat because he was not fully aware of the carbon-nitrogen-hydrogen-sulphur-oxygen content of his garment.

It was Robert Lee who said, "I don't have to know there are seven colors in every ray of light to recognize my mother's face."

Helpful as it may prove for a man to know the technical aspects of theology and to be able to read fluently from the original languages, don't let another's "superior knowledge" keep you from getting the Bible down off the shelf and exploring it for your own personal benefit. A cold winter has set-in in this world in which we live. Good protection is needed from the dangers of the winter storms. Some of the synthetic garments make rash promises but fail to give you the same warmth and protection. There is nothing that takes the place of God's "all wool" provision—THE BIBLE.

 Light for Walking: "Furthermore, then, we beseech you, brethren, and exhort you by the Lord Jesus, that as ye have received of us how ye ought to walk and to please God, so ye would abound more and more" (1 Thessalonians 4:1).

While it is never smart to be dumb, and while God does not put a premium on ignorance, there are many smart people who do not please God. Conversely, there are many people who are not in the genius class, but who are content to know English (and are thankful for that) and are pleasing God in their walk.

Be An Optimist

I am a confirmed optimist! How about you? Many people would hardly admit it because there has been so much kidding about the kind of man who always looks on the brighter side of life. One definition of an optimist is a man who looks at things through an optic mist. That is, he doesn't really see things as they are. An optimist is often considered to be someone who hopes for the best when the worst is inevitable—like the man who looks for eggs in a cuckoo clock. Then, there is the feeling that the optimist just doesn't know any better and is sure to come against disappointment similar to the man who starts working on a crossword puzzle with a fountain pen.

More often than not, the optimist is told to wise up—that life is not just one big bowl full of cherries. Well, even if the optimist is a little blind to the way things might turn out, I would prefer him to a man who greets you with a "Good morning, probably!" I take issue with the pessimistic look on optimism. There are reasons, good Bible reasons, for the Christian to be optimistic. We are right when we say that things are getting worse, but the believer should be looking over the top of the worse to the better. Here are some reasons why you, as a Christian, should be optimistic.

The Assurance of Christ's Comforter. Before Christ left the earth He said, "Nevertheless, I tell you the truth: it is expedient for you that I go away; for if I go not away, the Comforter will not come unto you; but if I depart, I will send him unto you" (John 16:7). The Comforter is the Holy Spirit, who lives within us. Not only is God *with* us, God is *in* us in the Person of the Holy Spirit. Do you realize that? He speaks to us of Christ and shows us things to come. The Christian remembers that Christ said, "I will not leave you comfortless." He said that He would come and abide with us forever (John 14:16, 18). Someone has said that optimism is "the cheerful frame of mind that enables a teapot to sing though it is in hot water up to its nose." Of course, we should expect difficulties and trials, but we can sing in the midst of them because Christ is in the midst of us in the presence of the Holy Spirit.

The Assurance of His Control. God is sovereign! He controls every situation and we are assured by Him that "all things work together for good to them that love God" (Romans 8:28). He knows our lot, He knows our burdens and needs, and He knows just how much we can take in such burdens. We are assured, "There hath no temptation taken you but such as is common to man; but God is faithful, who will not suffer you to be tempted above that ye are able, but will, with the temptation, also make a way to escape, that ye may be able to bear it" (1 Corinthians 10:13). Yes, all things are under His control; He holds the reins in every situation. Let us be glad in this. I heard it said about one woman, "She broadcasts over such a fretwork of wrinkles, she needs to get her faith lifted." Yes, a lifted faith in One who is in full control and knows our limitations will help prevent the "nicks of time" on our brow.

The Assurance of His Return. This should really make you optimistic. Jesus Christ is coming back: bodily, literally! When? We do not know, but perhaps soon. Are you tired in body and aggravated with your limitations? Remember that He is coming, and He will "change our vile body [body of limitation]—like unto His glorious body" (Philippians 3:21).

Have you looked around recently to find a pessimistic world? Try the up-look, "looking for that blessed hope, and the glorious appearing of the great God and our Savior, Jesus Christ" (Titus 2:13). Discouraged by the recent loss of a loved one? "For the Lord Himself shall descend from heaven with a shout . . . the dead in Christ shall rise first; then we who are alive and remain shall be caught up together with them in the clouds" (1 Thessalonians 4:16, 17).

Oh, believer friend, there are so many reasons for being an optimist. And this optimism is not a false optimism. It is as good and real as the indwelling Spirit—the assuring Word of His full control and His certain return.

Light for Walking: "Fear not; for they who are with us are more than they who are with them" (2 Kings 6:16).

"What shall we then say to these things? If God be for us, who can be against us?" (Romans 8:31).

"We need to get our eyes cleared up. You can't be optismistic with a misty optic. Get your eyes open, and when you do, you'll see that 'there are more with us than they that be with them,' as Elisha told his servant" (Vance Havner).

Things Are Developing in the Dark

There are a number of lessons we can learn in the dark; in the darkroom, that is. I speak of the process of developing film and prints. Most of us are familiar with the glossy finish of a photograph—the result of our photographic prowess. But there is a great deal that goes on in the photo lab—before the finished product comes to us.

In total darkness the film is taken from the cassette or roll and placed in a development tank. A developing solution, specially prepared both in quality and temperature, is poured into the tank and left there about 6 minutes. Then, strictly according to the book, the solution is poured out and a stop solution is poured into the tank. This stops the developing process. After the photograph spends 30 seconds in the stop bath, this solution is also emptied, and another solution, called the fixer, is poured in. After 3 or 4 minutes, this is poured out and the film is washed. The film is then dried, and the negative is ready to be used.

We are now halfway through the process. The negative then goes into the enlarger, which contains specially prepared light sensitive paper. After the lens setting is selected, the light is turned on for a few seconds. Once again the process begins. This time the print goes into the developing tray for a minute and a half, into the stop bath for 5 seconds, and then into the fixer again. The print is rinsed and dried and, at last, you have the finished product. It's quite a process!

What a picture this is of God's dealing with us! Often when we see a greatly used man of God—pastor or layman—we fail to see what God has done in "developing" him. Indeed, He spends a great deal of time preparing that saint in His own way and time. Yes, sometimes there is a carefully timed "stop bath" that is planned. While we may think the developing has stopped, in the final analysis it hasn't because it all is planned with the finished picture in mind. There is the "fixer," which gives the saint a permanence in his testimony (otherwise the life would be effective for only a short time). Indeed, if we are not in the "fixer" long enough, the testimony will appear thin and gray and the image will be hardly discernible. Of course, the washing that the Lord does through the Word of God is the most important of all (Ephesians 5:26; John 15:3).

There is another step in developing pictures that is often vital. It is called agitation. When the film is in the tank, there must be a regular, periodic turning of the tank to keep the solution freshly applied on the film. This agitation in both the developer and the fixer is important. How true in the life of the believer! God not only moves us from one "solution" to another, but there are periodic times of agitation that seem so unnecessary to us. We must remember they are vital, planned steps in the divine laboratory.

When the final print is complete, the Lord will then see us as "without spot or wrinkle" and clearly reflecting the image of the original—the Person of Jesus Christ. Each step from beginning to end in the developing was done with this in mind, that we might be conformed to His image and be a credit to His name.

Developing solutions, stop baths, and fixers (with plenty of agitation) was all worthwhile. The finished product speaks for itself.

 Light for Walking: "But we all, with open face beholding as in a glass the glory of the Lord, are changed into the same image from glory to glory, even as by the Spirit of the Lord" (2 Corinthians 3:18).

It is easy enough to apply this verse to the developing process in our lives. When the negative is put in the enlarger, the light shines down through the negative and puts the image on the print. So it is with us, the Spirit of God shines down through the Word of God (the negative) and puts the image of the Son of God on the child of God (the print), and we are changed.

Circumlocutions

Have you noticed that there are some words people do not like to use? They will do anything they can to avoid them. Take the word *death* for example. When a person dies, we often avoid saying, "He died." Instead, we say, "He isn't with us anymore." Or, "He passed away." Death is one of our top conversational fears. The ancient Greeks called the cemetery "a sleeping place." A soldier isn't "killed," he is "lost in battle." A sailor isn't drowned, he is "lost at sea." When was the last time you heard a person say, "When I am dead do so and so." It is, "When I am gone."

The Christian has no reason to fear death. Christ took the sting out of death when He died (Hebrews 2:14). On second reflection, it isn't that bad to say, "When I am gone" when we refer to death, because, for the believer, we just change locations, from earth to heaven. But it is understandable that people would avoid certain words because they have fearful connotations.

The Malays have no word for *tiger* lest the sound of it offends. Peasants in Madagascar never mention the word *lightning*. They think to say it would be to cause it. Russian peasants have no name for *bear*. He is called the *honey-eater*. This is what we call circumlocution, which comes from two Latin words which means "to speak around."

The great thing about being in the family of God is that we can take straight talk because fear has been cast out. There is a lion that we can face up to. He is called the devil. We can dare to defy him in the name of our Savior who broke his power over us. There is no reason for hidden fears and silly superstitions. Death is no longer a mystery, but a path that leads to the Father's house.

When Daniel Webster was dying, his physician suggested that a favorite hymn might be read to him. The physician knew Webster was a Christian. So, taking the hymnal he read one of Webster's favorites, a hymn by Cowper.

> There is a fountain filled with blood
> Drawn from Immanuel's veins.

He continued reading until he finished the last stanza:

> Then in a nobler, sweeter song,
> I'll sing thy power to save,
> When this poor lisping, stammering
> tongue
> Lies silent in the grave.

Webster, in a clear, strong voice replied, "Amen! Amen! Amen!" No wonder! The fear of death was gone, for evil had long been defeated "at the fountain filled with blood!"

 Light for Walking: "Forasmuch, then, as the children are partakers of flesh and blood, he also himself likewise took part of the same, that through death he might destroy him that the power of death, that is, the devil, And deliver them who, through fear of death, were all their lifetime subject to bondage" (Hebrews 2:14, 15).

When we think of the incarnation, we must remember that the purpose of Christ's coming in the flesh, "partaking" of flesh and blood, was to put the devil out of business. While he is still active, his power over us is broken and we need not respond to his commands and wishes. The fear of death need no longer be a reality. The power of death is snatched from Satan's hands. Christ is the resurrection and the life, and death is but a gateway into God's blessed presence.

God's Et Ceteras

The word *et cetera* looks rather strange when it is spelled out as a full word. More often than not, when you see it you just get the first three letters; *etc.* Every school child knows its meaning. The dictionary tells us that it comes from Latin and means "and others; and the rest; and so forth."

When talking about material things you might say: For lunch this afternoon we had a roast beef sandwich; for supper last night we had roast beef, a salad, potatoes, carrots, etc., etc., etc." Or, when discussing spiritual benefits or blessings we might be heard to say: "The Lord blessed us this past Sunday. Every department was up in attendance, with a number of decisions. The Beginners Department was up 14, the Primary Department increased 20, the Junior Department was up 15, etc., etc., etc." Now, there's nothing necessarily wrong with the use of this little verbal helper.

However, it is important for us to realize that the general "and so on and so forth," and the all-encompassing "and the rest," is from the hand of the Lord. We often take for granted some of the Lord's "and so forths." His *et ceteras* often include sustaining *et ceteras* of grace in the hour of need; continued *et ceteras* of strength, physically and spiritually. Often He comes through with *et ceteras* of "very present help, in times of trouble" (Psalm 46:1). It's only when some of these things from His hand are taken from us that they move out of the *et cetera* category and become exceedingly important. From the *et ceteras* of our physical breath, to the breath of God on our lives spiritually, we are only aware of its preciousness when it seems to be waning.

Paul talks about the *et ceteras* of God's grace when he says, "Moreover, the law entered, that the offense might abound. But where sin abounded, grace did much more abound" (Romans 5:20). God matches the *et ceteras* of man's sin abounding in all its evil forms and noxious nuances with a plenitude of sufficient grace. If you were to list the sins of the evil heart of mankind and the grace that is greater than all our sins, you would probably end up with the use of the familiar "etc., etc."

When Paul prayed for deliverance from his physical infirmity the Lord said,"My grace is sufficient for thee; for my strength is made perfect in weakness" (2 Corinthians 12:9). To say that His grace is sufficient for the Christian's trial, sickness, bereavement, disappointment, heartache, etc., etc., etc., is not wrong. It simply tells us that this "et cetera grace" is limitless and cannot be measured.

When Paul said, "I can do all things through Christ which strengtheneth me" (Philippians 4:13), he could have enumerated some of the things and used the Greek equivalent of our handy "etc., etc." He also said, "My God shall supply all your need according to His riches in glory by Jesus Christ . . ." (v. 19). To begin to name some of the "all your needs" and the "all sufficient supply," the word's tiny abbreviation would come in handy.

So the next time you begin to be a little down and discouraged, count your blessings. Begin to enumerate the benefits of His grace to you. Start surveying your life and the way the Lord has revealed His hand. Note the multiplying of His grace on your behalf. Then stop and thank the Lord for the blessings of His precious *et ceteras*.

 Light for Walking: "He that spared not his own Son, but delivered him up for us all, how shall he not with him also freely give us all things?" (Romans 8:32).

When upon life's billows you are tempest tossed,
When you are discouraged, thinking all is lost
Count your many blessings, name them one by one
And it will surprise you what the Lord hath done
—Johnson Oatman, Jr.

"Casting All Your Care"

"Casting all your care upon him; for he careth for you" (1 Peter 5:7).

When Peter wrote these words, the Spirit of God speaking through Him must have had in mind a similar passage in the Old Testament. "Cast thy burden upon the Lord, and he shall sustain thee" (Psalm 55:22). On the cross, the Lord carried our sin (1 Peter 2:24). Today, as our living Lord, he wants to carry our burdens and cares. He delights in our casting them on Him. One translator has it, "Let all your anxieties fall upon Him." Another translates it, "Throw back on Him the burden of all your anxiety." The Amplified translation renders the passage: "Casting the whole of your care— all your anxieties, all your worries, all your concerns, once and for all on Him." That says it well, doesn't it?

J. Nieboer tells the story of a man who was carrying a heavy burden as he walked along a road. "A man riding along in a wagon invited him to ride. He climbed into the wagon and sat down, but kept the load on his back. The driver said, 'Put your bundle down in the box.' 'Oh, no, sir,' he said, 'It is very nice of you to give me a ride, but to make the horse carry the bundle also is just too much.'"

How this fits us! We are aware that the Lord is carrying us, but somehow we will not let Him carry our burdens too. It would be humorous if it weren't so pitifully true. We must come to realize that all our cares are His; our concerns are His concerns. That's the meaning of those words, "He careth for you." It means that "you are His personal concern, His great interest." To cite the Amplified translation again, ". . . He cares for you affectionately, and cares about you watchfully."

Now, what concerns you most today? Don't you realize that the Lord will bear that burden for you? It is only because of this Lord to whom we can turn and upon whom we can cast our burden that Paul was able to say, "Be careful for nothing" (Philippians 4:6). He said, "Take no thought [care, anxiety] for your life, what ye shall eat, or what ye shall drink; nor yet for your body, what ye shall put on . . . " (Matthew 6:25).

The word *casting* in 1 Peter 5:7 means "casting once for all." It means, "Take your burdens to the Lord and leave them there." A little reflection on the subject of cares and worries brings me to the conclusion that there usually isn't a great deal of variety in our cares and worries. That is, we usually worry and fret about the same things. We have our little pet concerns which wear us down (our health, our financial situation, our children). This might mean that we have failed to really cast them—once for all—on the Lord.

To leave them in His lap brings a twofold delight. First, it delights our hearts because it proves that He will not fail us. Second, it delights the Lord, who loves to have us trust Him and rely on Him.

Dear friend, roll your burden on the Lord. Cast it upon Him. He who holds you will hold your burdens too!

 Light for Walking: "Humble yourselves, therefore, under the mighty hand of God, that he may exalt you in due time, casting all your care upon him; for he careth for you. Be sober, be vigilant, because your adversary, the devil, as a roaring lion walketh about, seeking whom he may devour" (1 Peter 5:6-8).

CASTING ALL YOUR CARES UPON HIM

When from a world of tumult we retreat,
　To commune with the Lord in secret prayer,
We often bring our burdens to His feet
　Who bids us cast on Him our every care.

We do, but find that we have failed to leave them there;
　So when again the busy world we meet,
We lack that peace of God so truly sweet,
　Which comes of telling God our wants in prayer.

Oh, let us "roll our burdens on the Lord"
　And leave them there, although our way be dim,
His peace our lot, our care consign'd to Him
　His grace accepts and now sustains our load.

—Selected

Changing Your Tune

They tell me that the mockingbird is unusual in many ways. For one thing it has different tunes. For sheer variety you can't beat this little bird, which has almost a hundred different tunes. It is said by the experts that a mockingbird can change his tune 87 times in 7 minutes.

I suppose all that variety is good. But remember, it isn't always a meritorious thing to be constantly changing your tune. Few people have respect for those who adjust their tune according to the person with whom they are talking. Nobody has respect for a person who talks out of both sides of his mouth. Shakespeare had one of his characters say (in *Richard III*), ". . . and thus I clothe my naked villainy with old ends stolen out of holy writ; and seem a saint, when most I play the devil." In other words, there is terrible hypocrisy involved. It is singing "out of holy writ" with the "song of a saint" while the heart was not holy at all.

There is something very special about a person whose life is even, constant, and consistent. What a blessing to know that one's tune is the same, year in and year out, consistently uniform. This person is very steady in his commitment and lifestyle.

One of the best testimonies parents can give to their children is to be the same person at home that they are in church. Such consistency speaks volumes and will leave lasting effects on their lives in the years to come. Conversely, if "different tunes" are sung in different places it will have injurious consequences in the future. There is nothing so blessed and precious as a consistent life. Such a sweet, unchanging song will multiply itself a hundred-fold in the next generation.

There is a real danger in changing one's tune. It is hypocritical to live an impressive life in church on Sunday, but sing a different song when one is with his peers. The saintly smile, displayed in our Sunday best, might hardly be recognized when someone has offended us during the week. Sometimes we change our tune when misfortune comes our way. Shouldn't it be a characteristic of Christians to rejoice, even in times of persecution and difficulty? Doesn't that make us different from the world around us?

A variety of "tune changing" might well be commendable for the mockingbird, but it is hardly a good testimony for Christians. Let's determine that we are going to be sweetly consistent in our song and constant in our Christianity.

Light for Walking: "That ye might walk worthy of the Lord unto all pleasing, being fruitful in every good work, and increasing in the knowledge of God" (Colossians 1:10).

Hypocrisy is certainly not becoming to the believer. Someone has suggested that what we sing and what we do is often different. Listen to these "tune changes."

> We sing "Sweet Hour of Prayer" and are content with 5-10 minutes a day.
>
> We sing "O for a Thousand Tongues to Sing" and we don't use the one we have.
>
> We sing "There Shall Be Showers of Blessing" but do not come when it rains.
>
> We sing "Blest Be the Tie That Binds" and let the least little offense sever it.
> —Author unknown

Christian Quirks

Christians have quirks, just like the rest of the world. However, those two words, *Christian* and *quirks* don't seem to go together.

Let's consider a few examples of those who were prone to quirks. Rudyord Kipling had to have pure black ink before he could write a word. He had a quirk. Beethoven poured cold water over his head to animate his brain. Schiller, the poet, was stimulated by the smell of rotting apples, which he always kept on his desk. Charles Dickens, believing that magnetic forces helped him to create, kept his bed pointed toward the North Pole. And Sam Johnson, it is said, needed a purring cat, an orange peel, and a cup of tea in order to write. Are you beginning to understand what a quirk is? You may have noticed that all those mentioned were geniuses, which could be of some comfort if you are prone that way as well.

Let's talk about some modern day Christian quirks. Some of us have health quirks. Christians are often different that way. Sometimes those who are very conservative in spiritual matters have a different propensity when it comes to health foods. I often facetiously suggest that if you eat brewer's yeast, black strap molasses, and "bird seed," you may not live longer, but you sure will feel like it.

Some of us have quirks when it comes to our relationship with others. While we are certainly justified in our stand of separation, we should not be guilty of going off in cloistered seclusion from the world. While we are not of the world, we are still in the world. It is insulation from the world system rather than isolation from the world of people that is important. We can't be the salt of the earth if we are content to be in cloistered "salt shakers."

Sure, maintain your purity and take your stand. I'll do the same, but let's rub elbows with those who need to be exposed to our lives and the good news of the gospel. Let's bear a witness to those who need our help. Let's determine to be Christ-like, remembering that He ate with publicans and sinners without condoning their sin. We need to ask the Lord to deliver us from bizarre and eccentric behavior, knowing that such quirks are not a credit to true Christianity.

Light for Walking: "In which in times past ye walked according to the course of this world, according to the prince of the power of the air, the spirit that now worketh in the children of disobedience; among whom also we all had our conversation in times past in the lusts of our flesh, fulfilling the desires of the flesh and of the mind, and were by nature the children of wrath, even as others. But God, who is rich in mercy, for his great love with which he loved us, even when we were dead in sins, hath quickened us together with Christ, (by grace ye are saved)" (Ephesians 2:2-5).

Do you agree, based on this passage and others, that God expects us to remember who we *were*, then remember who we *are* and the changes that He has made? The difference ought to be a credit to the name of the Lord. Others are to see our good works and glorify the Lord. The big difference is not some odd quirk, but that we were dead, now we are alive, and our lives reflect our new life in Christ.

Costly Commas

Commas can be costly. For example, in 1872, a tariff act was passed by Congress listing various nontaxable items that included "fruit-plants, tropical and semi-tropical, for the purpose of propagation and cultivation." Well, that's what the lawmakers thought they had passed. Apparently a comma had been mistakenly placed between fruit and plants instead of a hyphen, making the bill read ". . . fruit, plants, tropical, and semi-tropical . . ." This, of course, elated fruit importers. They sued the government for tariff refunds and won over $3 million as a settlement. The money was used to finance the Culver Line Railroad in Brooklyn, later to become a part of New York City's rapid transit system. Quite an undertaking—from one small comma!

But there is a punctuation mark that was more costly yet. It was November, 1962, when the omission of a simple little hyphen from directions transmitted to a Venus space probe rocket resulted in its destruction.

Now, are you ready for an even more costly comma? It is so costly it could cost your church a great deal in the area of Christian service. Actually, it makes the $3 million "fruit comma" and the Venus space probe mistake seem like simple errors. And, believe it or not, the comma is in your Bible. Now, before you get unduly upset, remember that punctuation marks are not inspired! There is one little comma in the King James Version that, if taken the way it reads, can spell devastation in our churches. Let me give you the passage the way it appears in my old Scofield King James Bible.

"And he gave some, apostles; and some, prophets; and some, evangelists; and some, pastors and teachers; for the perfecting of the saints, for the work of the ministry, for the edifying of the body of Christ" (Ephesians 4:11, 12). Now, we are going to give the verse again, but this time omit one comma. See if you recognize the difference at the first reading.

"And he gave some, apostles; and some, prophets; and some, evangelists; and some, pastors and teachers; for the perfecting of the saints for the work of the ministry, for the edifying of the body of Christ."

Did you catch the omission? It was the comma after the word *saints.* Now what difference does it make, and why is it costly? The first quotation, with the comma after the word *saints,* seems to be saying that there are several jobs for the pastor. They are the perfecting of the saints and the work of the ministry.

However, the real meaning is that the pastor perfects, or equips, the saints for the work of this ministry! Well! Do you see the difference one comma makes? Incidentally, if you have a New Scofield Bible, you will note that the comma has been properly dropped and the true sense of the passage is given. This is important. While we facetiously claim that this is a "carnal comma" or a "pernicious punctuation mark," it is true that the difference between the comma in and the comma out is the difference between one man serving and the whole congregation seeing their responsibility to serve with the pastor.

Now, to state that we are all doing the work of the ministry doesn't mean we should do away with pastors. We can't all be pastors; this was never the intent of the Lord. But the pastor is to equip us so that we can be involved with him in fulfilling the Great Commission.

To expect the pastor to do it all is costly indeed. Think of the people who can be reached, for example, in a visitation program if one hundred people are calling for 1 hour a week. One hundred hours a week! That is almost 6 months' visitation for a pastor who calls 4 hours a week on his congregation.

Your church needs *you* to do your share in serving Christ. Right now, think of five ways you can help out in the work of your church. Now write them down. Before the day is over, do at least one thing to help in the ministry of your church.

 Light for Walking: "And His gifts were [varied; He Himself appointed and gave men to us,] some to be apostles [special messengers], some prophets [inspired preachers and expounders], some evangelists [preachers of the gospel, traveling missionaries], some pastors [shepherds of His flock] and teachers. His intention was the perfecting and the full equipping of the saints [His consecrated people], [that they should do] the work of ministering toward building up Christ's body (the church)" (Ephesians 4:11, 12, Amplified version).

If you know the Lord as Savior, you are a part of the body of Christ and are in the work of the ministry. We are in this together! Let's accept the challenge and get busy!

You Are Not Alone

Ever feel like you are absolutely alone in the world? Quite a few years ago, I ran across the following item which might illustrate this loneliness. Although the population figures are outdated, the point is still clear.

"Population of the United States—160,000,000. People 65 years or older—49,000,000. Balance left to do the work—111,000,000. People 21 years or younger—56,000,000. Balance left to do the work—55,000,000. People working for the government—29,000,000. Balance left to do the work—26,000,000. People in armed forces—11,000,000. Balance left to do the work—2,200,000. Bums and others who don't work—2,000,000. Balance left to do the work—200,000. People in hospitals and asylums—126,000. Balance left to do the work—74,000. Persons in jail—73,998. Balance left to the work—2. Two? Why that's you and me! Then you'd better get to work because I'm getting tired of running this country alone."

This reminds me of the man who said to another, "Most everyone is crazy these days but you and me, and sometimes I wonder about you!"

There is no doubt about it, you can do almost anything with statistics. They are used every day by people who are looking for convincing proof to buttress their bias.

On the other hand, sometimes you just can't help but think that you are alone and that no one really takes a stand like you or understands your particular problems. You may also feel that there are few with whom to share your burden or help you with your work.

Cheer up! There are more people than you think who care, who stand where you do, and who want to help you.

First, of course, there is the Lord! Paul said, "Let your conversation be without covetousness, and be content with such things as ye have; for He hath said, I will never leave thee, nor forsake thee!" We may boldly say, "The Lord is my helper, and I will not fear what man shall do unto me" (Hebrews 13:5, 6). Christ also said, "Come unto me, all ye that labor and are heavy laden, and I will give you rest" (Matthew 11:28). And listen to this from our Lord, "Lo, I am with you always, even unto the end of the world" (Matthew 28:20). Praise God, you can count on Christ to understand, to help, and to intervene when you need Him most. The saying is right: "One with Christ is a majority."

Who else cares? Your church. The church is standing with you. While they may not be on your doorstep every week, and they may not understand all your needs and problems (as the Lord would), a great many people are praying for you—more than you could possibly imagine. People do care and are willing to help you in your need. You are not alone.

One sign of poor spiritual health is to feel that you are standing alone and that the only one doing the job or taking a right position is you. You need to ask the Lord to help you not to take yourself so seriously and to see things as they really are, rather than so subjectively.

Of course, you are not the first to have the problem. Some of the finest and godliest men have revealed a weakness in this area. Elijah, for example, when alone on Mount Horeb thought of himself as very godly, but standing alone in that godliness. He said, "I have been very jealous for the LORD God of hosts. For the children of Israel have forsaken thy covenant, thrown down thine altars, and slain thy prophets with the sword; and I, even I only, am left, and they seek my life, to take it away."

Patiently the Lord answered, "Yet I have left me seven thousand in Israel, all the knees which have not bowed unto Baal, and every mouth which hath not kissed him" (1 Kings 19:10, 18).

I thank God for your stand, for your desire to honor the Lord in everything. There are others who care about you and who love the Lord. You are not alone. Thank God for your Savior, your church, and your friends.

 Light for Walking: "If we say that we have fellowship with him, and walk in darkness, we lie, and do not the truth; but if we walk in the light, as he is in the light, we have fellowship one with another, and the blood of Jesus Christ, his Son, cleanseth us from all sin" (1 John 1:6-7).

I thank God for believers with a passion to walk in the light and know the fellowship that comes in that walk. Let's press on together to accomplish the work of God in the world today!

Yowzitch

I once read a story about a young schoolboy who made 13 mistakes in spelling the five-letter word *usage*. The amazing thing about it is that he used eight letters and not one of them was correct. The word he was trying to spell was *usage*, but he spelled it *yowzitch*. You might say that for him everything went wrong in his sincere attempt to spell.

Our lives are often filled with days when everything goes wrong. Or, as the salt company puts it, "When it rains it pours." But there is little comfort in being told that to have trouble means you are liable to have more. It is not an uncommon thing to find that when you are not feeling well and your spirits are low, the roof will leak, an unexpected bill will come in the mail, or a letter will arrive to inform you that unexpected company is coming from out-of-town to stay with you for a few weeks. You shake your head in disbelief and wonder why the Lord has allowed such trials to be yours. You might even ask, "What have I done to be placed in such circumstances as these?"

Now is the time to think again about the statement that everything has gone wrong. It hasn't, really. As a matter of fact, the most important things in the world are still going right. Heaven is still alert and aware of your need. The Lord is still pleading your cause in glory (Hebrews 7:25). Christ is carefully allowing certain things to take place in your life, often for purposes known only to Him, but He "will not suffer you to be tempted [tested] above that which ye are able" (1 Corinthians 10:13). Day-by-day the divine Sculptor is conforming you to the image of His dear Son (Romans 8:29). To be sure, everything may seem to be going wrong as you see your life—but there is no such thing as "things going wrong" with the Lord.

On the other hand, as the world sings, "Everything's going my way," they are often guilty of the same reasoning that brings you to wrong conclusions. That is, they judge by today's circumstances without evaluating what today's circumstances might mean when evaluated in the distant tomorrow.

For the believer, this is where faith comes in. Faith to believe that all things are really "working together for good" (Romans 8:28). Faith to believe that the Lord is too good and loving to allow anything in our lives that is not truly necessary. Faith to claim His promises that He never forgets and always understands our needs. Faith to thank Him for difficult experiences that draw us closer to Him.

When the young man in school spelled *yowzitch*, you might say he was just spelling it by ear. He wrote it the way he heard it and not the way it really was. We must be careful in our spiritual vocabulary that we aren't guilty of putting down words as they sound to us with our limited knowledge, rather than the way they really are—as God sees them.

 Light for Walking: "For we walk by faith, not by sight" (2 Corinthians 5:7).

Sometimes I said, I know not why
    My heart is sore distressed;
It seems the burdens of the world
    Have settled on my heart.
And yet I know . . . I know that God
    Who doeth all things right
Will lead me thus to understand
    To walk by FAITH . . . not by SIGHT.
                    —Author unknown